Critical Infrastructure Security

WITPRESS

WIT Press publishes leading books in Science and Technology.
Visit our website for the current list of titles.
www.witpress.com

WITeLibrary

Home of the Transactions of the Wessex Institute, the WIT electronic-library
provides the international scientific community with immediate and permanent
access to individual papers presented at WIT conferences.
Visit the WIT eLibrary athttp://library.witpress.com

Critical Infrastructure Security

Assessment, Prevention, Detection, Response

Edited by

Francesco Flammini

WITPRESS Southampton, Boston

Editor:

Francesco Flammini

Published by

WIT Press
Ashurst Lodge, Ashurst, Southampton, SO40 7AA, UK
Tel: 44 (0) 238 029 3223; Fax: 44 (0) 238 029 2853
E-Mail: witpress@witpress.com
http://www.witpress.com

For USA, Canada and Mexico

WIT Press
25 Bridge Street, Billerica, MA 01821, USA
Tel: 978 667 5841; Fax: 978 667 7582
E-Mail: infousa@witpress.com
http://www.witpress.com

British Library Cataloguing-in-Publication Data
A Catalogue record for this book is available
from the British Library

ISBN: 978-1-84564-562-5
eISBN: 978-1-84564-563-2

Library of Congress Catalog Card Number: 2010943114

*The texts of the papers in this volume were set
individually by the authors or under their supervision.*

To Liana

Contents

Part IV Monitoring and Surveillance Technologies

Part V Security Systems Integration and Alarm Management

Preface

The security of critical infrastructures is a paramount issue in modern society. In fact, infrastructures like those for transportation, energy, telecommunication, banking, etc. whose operability is essential for the well-being of a large number of individuals are nowadays exposed to severe threats, both natural (earthquakes, landslides, flooding, etc.) and intentional (thefts, vandalism, terrorism, etc.). In recent years, the scientific community has addressed the issue of Critical Infrastructure Security (CIS) through conferences, journals and other publications. However, in most cases, the published material fails to address the CIS issue as a multi-faceted and multi-disciplinary problem which needs to be analysed in an integrated manner both at the organizational and technological levels, and looking at digital ("cyber") as well as physical security.

The purpose of this book is to provide a comprehensive picture of the state-of-the-art and trends in methods and tools for infrastructure protection, focusing on the following topics:

- *Assessment*, that is the understanding of risks and vulnerabilities as well as expected results of possible mitigations. This can be achieved by analysis, modelling and simulation.

- *Prevention*, that is the reduction of risk by predicting threat effects. This can be achieved by means of deterrence and other "passive" countermeasures (e.g. security by design).

- *Detection*, that is the capability of real-time recognition of abnormal conditions or behaviours. This can be achieved by means of "active" sensors and other technological tools.

- *Response*, that is the quick reaction to threats. This can be achieved by adopting early warning, situational awareness and decision support systems.

Most of the current best practices are based on intrusion detection / access control, people scanning and video surveillance designs which are often weak and poorly effective since they are not rigorous enough and frequently not systematically guided by risk analysis principles. This book provides the necessary balance between the analysis aspects, which involve people (personnel, operators, adversaries, etc.) taking into account organizational and interdependency effects, and the technological tools (smart-detectors, information networks, control software, etc.), which are required to implement modern integrated surveillance and security management systems. Therefore, the topics presented in the volume progress smoothly from security evaluation methods and tools to security enhancement approaches and technologies.

It is the Editor's belief that the book provides the most up to date compendium of Critical Infrastructure Security and he is grateful to all authors for their excellent contributions.

The Editor, 2012

Part I
Fundamentals of Security Risk and Vulnerability Assessment

Model-based risk analysis for critical infrastructures

Ted G. Lewis[1], Rudolph P. Darken[1], Thomas Mackin[2] & Donald Dudenhoeffer[3]

[1]*Center for Homeland Defense and Security, Naval Postgraduate School, Monterey, CA 93943*
[2]*Mechanical Engineering Department, CalPoly University, San Luis Obispo, CA 93402*
[3]*Priority 5 Holdings, Inc., 31 State Street, 3rd Floor, Boston, MA 02109*

Abstract

This chapter describes a risk-informed decision-making process for analysing and protecting large-scale critical infrastructure and key resource (CI/KR) systems, and a Model-Based Risk Analysis (MBRA) tool for modelling risk, quantifying it and optimally allocating fixed resources to reduce system vulnerability. MBRA is one of the first tools to adopt a systems approach to risk-informed decision-making. It applies network science metrics, height, degree, betweeness and contagiousness to a network of interdependent infrastructure assets across multiple sectors. Resource allocation is applied across entire networks to reduce risk and to determine threat, vulnerability and consequence values using Stackelberg game theory. MBRA is compared with non-network assessment tools: CARVER, Maritime Security Risk Analysis Model (MSRAM) and Knowledge Display and Aggregation System (KDAS) – three leading infrastructure analysis tools currently in use by practitioners. MBRA has been used successfully to model a variety of sectors, ranging from water, power, energy and telecommunications to transportation.

Keywords: Critical Infrastructure, Risk, Probabilistic Risk Assessment, Network Science, Optimal Risk Reduction, System Risk, Risk Minimization, Attacker–Defender Model, Stackelberg Game

1 Introduction

One of the most important and difficult tasks of national defence is the protection of a nation's critical infrastructures (CI) and key resources (KR). These assets are typically divided into sectors. For example, the United States' National Infrastructure Protection Plan of 2006 [1] divides infrastructure into 18 sectors: agriculture/food production, energy/power, drinking water treatment, information technology/telecommunications, transportation systems, defence industrial base (DIB), public health, banking/finance, postal/shipping, critical manufacturing and key resources, which include national monuments/icons, government facilities, chemical facilities, commercial facilities, hydroelectric dams, emergency services and commercial nuclear reactors, materials and waste. Each of these sectors is extremely large, complex and open to attack by natural or human actors. The first challenge, then, is one of size: the vastness of critical infrastructure means some sort of prioritization scheme is needed to decide how to get the most out of limited resources.

For example, the U.S. telecommunications sector contains 2 billion miles of cable; there are 2,800 power plants in the electric power grid, 300,000 gas and oil production sites, 120,000 miles of railroads, 590,000 highway bridges, 2 million miles of pipelines, 66,000 chemical plants and 137 million postal delivery sites [1]. The complexity of CI/KR security is compounded by the reality that sectors are interdependent – gas and oil transmission pipelines, airports, telecommunications networks, energy/power supplies and most other critical infrastructure systems depend on one another. Therefore, it is essential that sectors be considered as systems, as opposed to stand-alone individual refinery plants, power plants, bridges, telecommunication switches or isolated buildings.

The U.S. National Strategy for the Physical Protection of Critical Infrastructure and Key Assets [2] recognized the challenge posed by the size and complexity of these systems. It recommends,

> The first objective of this Strategy is to identify and assure the protection of those assets, systems, and functions that we deem most 'critical' in terms of national-level public health and safety, governance, economic and national security, and public confidence. We must develop a comprehensive, prioritized assessment of facilities, systems, and functions of national-level criticality and monitor their preparedness across infrastructure sectors.

But little progress has been made towards a unified approach to critical infrastructure protection even though more than 250 tools and methods currently exist for evaluating criticality in infrastructure [3]. Identification and prioritization of the most critical components of a critical infrastructure remains a challenging intellectual problem. This has left the field of critical infrastructure protection without a widely accepted standard approach to vulnerability and risk assessment.

More recently the U.S. Department of Homeland Security (DHS) has evolved from a position of 'no-policy' to a 'risk-informed decision-making' policy [1]. According to this policy, decisions regarding risk and resiliency are based on risk assessment followed by risk management. The first step in this process is to evaluate the massive CI/KR systems to identify risk, and then apply a rank ordering on the assets in these vast systems [4]. Risk management applies risk reduction investments over a period of time to reduce asset risk, which is thought to also reduce system risk.

Unfortunately, this approach still falls short of the goal of securing entire systems, largely because risk metrics, modelling and tools have not been standardized. Therefore, DHS is currently unable to compare risk across different regions, sectors, industries or governmental divisions. Instead, a plethora of methods, tools and metrics have blossomed, each targeting a different aspect of risk-informed decision-making. In short, the critical infrastructure problem remains unsolved.

2   The critical infrastructure problem

The 'critical infrastructure problem' is as follows: nearly all critical infrastructure sectors pose enormous protection challenges because of their sheer size and complexity. They are so large that it is economically impossible to fully protect every component of even one sector, let alone all sectors. Quite simply, there is too much to protect, which begs the question, 'What do we protect?'

In addition to sheer size, many sectors are so complex that it is technologically and economically impossible to anticipate all unintended consequences of an incident, whether that incident is perpetrated by humans or caused by a natural disaster. Consider the following examples: Internet service in South Africa was disabled by the fall of the Twin Towers on 9/11 [5]; the relatively minor fault at electrical power utility FirstEnergy in Ohio precipitated the Blackout of August 2003 affecting 50 million people thousands of miles from the origin of the outage [6]. Generally, it is extremely difficult to predict the consequences of small perturbations in one part of a critical infrastructure sector on other parts. It seems our infrastructure is vulnerable simply because it contains so many components, and their interdependencies are too intricate for most technical advisors and policy makers to fully comprehend.

This kind of complexity is well known and the subject of numerous articles but rarely confronted as a fundamental challenge of critical infrastructure protection [4,7]. A little fault in one minor component of a system can propagate and magnify as it spreads to other parts, thereby leading to a massive collapse of the entire system. Major portions of the global telecommunications and Internet infrastructure can be disabled, either partially or fully, by damaging a small number of components. For example, asymmetric cyber attacks have rendered portions of the Internet inoperable for short periods of time, including Bank of America's network of 16,000 ATM machines and the Davis–Besse nuclear power plant in Ohio [8]. Such attacks are inexpensive and rather 'easy' to perform but precipitate major consequences.

And yet security analysts continue to address the cyber-security problems of ATM networks and nuclear power plants at the component level rather than as a chronic symptom of an entire system. Operators install antivirus software, firewalls and employ cyber-security policies at a local level rather than at a global level. The Davis–Besse problem was patched by increasing security at the Davis–Besse plant, not at the global Internet level.

While incremental progress is being realized in cyber security, the problem is largely unchecked and continues to be a major challenge to the security of the telecommunications/information sector [5]. Thus, operators are still left without an effective answer to the question, 'What is the best strategy to prevent such asymmetric attacks?' Will an increase in spending solve this problem, or is there a more effective strategy for reducing, or perhaps eliminating, all malicious software from the Internet? Or is this an unreasonable expectation?

Protection of all components of the telecommunications and Internet system would be enormously expensive. In addition, the complexity of the Internet is such that it is not known for sure what impact protection of all telecommunications components would have on overall system security. We are led to believe that an all-components protection policy would have an enormously beneficial impact, but we do not know if the cost of such a policy might financially damage the telecommunications and Internet sector. What we do know is that more and more of our infrastructure is becoming dependent on the Internet because it offers greater interoperability and control at lower unit cost.

The complexity problem is not restricted to telecommunications. In fact, complexity is characteristic of most infrastructure systems. The electrical power grid is not only large but also so complex that it often suffers from massive outages, even though it has been improved continuously for more than 100 years [9]. For example, the massive power outage of 2003 that spread across the upper Midwest and north-eastern United States was considered a 'once in a 1,000 years' event because of its impact. But the previous outage of this size occurred only 40 years after the 1962 blackout! There have been other complete blackouts to other regions of the country with consequences far out of proportion to normal expectations.

The examples cited here are representative of the intellectual and financial challenges we face in critical infrastructure protection. Accordingly, our approach focuses on systems rather than components: (1) Infrastructure policy must address entire systems, not merely individual assets of each system; (2) successful policies must attack root architectural issues of these systems in order to 'make a difference'; and (3) network science provides us with the tools to model entire systems, study their architectural foundations and suggest solutions to the critical infrastructure problem that other approaches cannot. This means combining theory and practical application of network science to inform homeland security policy [10–12,13].

3   Tools

To begin, we need an operational definition of risk. By operational, we mean a simple, quantifiable definition with an associated repeatable method that non-specialists can apply with the assistance of a software tool for crunching the numbers. Dudenhoeffer et al. [3] surveyed 30 software tools and methods of quantifying threats, vulnerabilities, recovery effort and cross-sector dependencies.

Generally, these can be categorized according to a core metric, such as consequence (damage), vulnerability and susceptibility.

For example, AIMS is an Agent-Based Infrastructure Modelling and Simulation tool that uses agent-based simulation to analyse national and cross-border interdependencies and survivability of Canada's critical infrastructures. CI3 (Critical Infrastructures Interdependencies Integrator) is a Monte Carlo simulation software for estimating the amount of time and cost to restore a given infrastructure component, a specific infrastructure system or an interdependent set of infrastructures to an operational state. FAIT (Fast Analysis Infrastructure Tool) is an economic analysis tool for conducting economic impact assessment across multiple sectors. Generally, tools and methods of analysis fall into two broad categories: (1) multi-criteria analysis and (2) quantifiable risk analysis.

True risk analysis tools fall into two subclasses: (1) single asset and (2) system analysis. Single-asset tools evaluate the vulnerability or risk of a single asset such as a building, bridge or water treatment plant. System analysis tools take a very different approach: they attempt to evaluate system risk as a function of single or cascade failures across multiple assets. Knowledge Display and Aggregation System (KDAS) is a tool that uses network modelling of multi-sector systems to evaluate interdependencies of cross-sector systems. While it does not calculate risk, it is able to determine potential cascade effects in cross-sector systems.

Risk analysis tools attempt to quantify risk in a variety of ways. It is the author's belief that simple definitions are the best because they are easy to put into practice. Therefore, for the remainder of this chapter, the following definitions will apply, except where otherwise noted. Let an event with the potential to cause damage to an asset or system be defined as an *attack* if perpetrated by a human and as an *incident* if caused by nature. Let T, V, C and R be defined as follows:

T: $0 \leq$ threat ≤ 1: the probability that an attack or incident is attempted, where $0 =$ no threat and $1 =$ certain threat.

V: $0 \leq$ vulnerability ≤ 1: the (conditional) probability that if an attack or incident occurs, it also damages the asset, where $0 =$ completely hardened asset and $1 =$ completely vulnerable asset.

C: $0 \leq$ consequence: the damage caused by a successful attack or incident, usually in terms of financial cost.

$R = TVC$: $0 \leq$ risk: the risk associated with a successful event.

The next section illustrates a multi-criteria tool called CARVER, which ranks single assets according to several criteria – not risk. However, Maritime Security Risk Analysis Model (MSRAM) applies the $R = TVC$ metric to single assets evaluated by the U.S. Coast Guard. In the final section, Model-Based Risk Analysis (MBRA) illustrates how $R = TVC$ is applied to an entire system, modelled as a network. MBRA and KDAS are the only known tools that combine network science metrics with infrastructure modelling and simulation to evaluate potential system cascading. KDAS is briefly described and contrasted with MBRA in the remainder of this chapter.

4   Multi-criterion tools (CARVER and MSRAM)

Multi-criteria analysis typically employs a number of criteria (dimensions) along with a ranking system to rank vulnerability, consequence, costs and so forth on a scale of, for example, one to ten. Rankings are tallied to obtain an overall score. The higher the tally, the more vulnerable or subject to damage is the asset. Multi-criteria tools typically focus on single assets and are unable to quantify cascade effects such as experienced during the 2003 Blackout.

4.1   CARVER

CARVER is marketed as a risk and vulnerability assessment tool that has seen widespread use across a large number of sectors. Although CARVER originated in the Vietnam era as a target selection tool for the U.S. Special Forces, it has been repurposed to meet the needs of homeland security and adapted as a tool that could support resource allocation to prevent damage to critical components of the infrastructure.

CARVER's success is largely due to its simple user interface. The tool employs drop-down menus in each of six different categories, allowing the user to analyse an asset and produce a report in a matter of minutes. It is important to note that, given the original intent, CARVER is an asset-level tool: that is, CARVER allows the user to score individual targets for their relative ease of elimination. As an asset-level tool, CARVER does not account for the interconnected nature of an infrastructure or how that interconnectedness can lead to cascade failures. The score arising from a CARVER analysis IS NOT based on risk! It is a weighted sum of rankings in each of six key categories, as described below, and cannot be directly related to scores or rankings that arise from other tools.

Originally, as a target selection tool, CARVER was an acronym that stood for Criticality, Accessibility, Recuperability, Vulnerability, Effect on population and Recognizability. As it evolved into a homeland security tool, the acronym shifted as follows:

- *Criticality*: How important is the asset to the locality, and how many people would be affected by removal of that asset? Users are asked to score the facility using drop-down windows in three separate ways: What would be the economic impact if the asset was lost, how many people would be affected by the loss of the asset and how many deaths would occur if the asset was destroyed?
- *Accessibility*: How easy is it to gain access to the facility. Users use a drop-down window to select the level of security at the asset.
- *Recoverability*: A measure of how long it would take to rebuild the asset or to return it to service.

- *Vulnerability*: A measure of how easy it would be to access and destroy or disable the asset.
- *Espyability*: How well known is the asset. Is the asset an icon or landmark?
- *Redundancy*: Are there other assets that could replace the function of the particular asset under consideration?

It is easy to see that CARVER is not a risk tool. Instead, CARVER asks the user to decide what is critical and assigns scores based upon the users' understanding of criticality. These scores are assigned using look-up tables that are hidden behind the user interface. Although convenient, it is not clear to the user how these scores are assigned or what the scores actually represent. CARVER is quick and easy to apply but lacks a rigorous quantifiable basis for ranking. It is perhaps best used to obtain a first-order estimate of single-asset vulnerability.

4.2 MSRAM

The MSRAM was developed by the U.S. Coast Guard to provide a uniform and comprehensive approach to assessing risks and allocating resources throughout all areas of responsibility of the U.S. Coast Guard. It replaces PSRAT (Port Security Risk Analysis Tool) and provides a comprehensive, risk-based approach to assessing the nation's ports and waterways. MSRAM defines risk as the product of Threat, Vulnerability and Consequence, $R = TVC$. It includes software-guided input tools for estimating each element of risk: T, V and C. Although the Coast Guard reports their risk using a Risk Index Number (RIN), that number can be directly associated with a dollar cost of consequences.

The MSRAM process uses a single tool, a single set of definitions and a cadre of trained risk analysts. In addition, all data from their analyses are rolled up to a single national database and checked for consistency and reasonableness at four levels of review: (1) the Captain of the Port, (2) the District, (3) Areas and (4) Headquarters. Furthermore, historical data for consequences, for a range of asset classes, are used to create reasonable ranges for user input. This level of quality control is unprecedented in a risk tool and offers a best practice for other risk analysts.

At present, MSRAM is the ONLY tool used on a nationwide basis to inform resource allocation decisions. The advantages of this approach are obvious: it provides a single methodology, applied to all assets under the jurisdiction of the Coast Guard. The disadvantage of the MSRAM approach is the time and expertise required to populate the MSRAM database. Unfortunately, MSRAM is not available outside of the U.S. Coast Guard.

Quality assurance is provided by comparing new data to averages computed from the national database for each attack scenario. This is accompanied by an alert, informing the user whenever the new data are outside of recommended ranges. If a user insists on entering data outside of recommended ranges, the software requires the user to enter a detailed explanation and flags any such entries for further review at the local, district, area and headquarters levels.

MSRAM defines 23 attack modes (methods used by terrorists to cause harm) and 62 target classes (based on specific functionality), which are provided by the tool through selectable drop-down windows. Each target class/attack-mode pair is called a *scenario*. The possible pairings of target class with attack modes represent a reasonable sampling of plausible event scenarios. However, scenarios are 'hard-wired' into the tool and cannot be changed by users.

Threat numbers for each scenario are determined by subject matter experts at an Intelligence Coordination Centre (ICC) and provided through the MSRAM tool. It is important to note that users DO NOT calculate threat probabilities. Instead, they use threat probabilities provided by the MSRAM tool. This is an important feature of the tool because it provides a level of consistency lacking in other tools. Because of this, MSRAM comes closer than any other tool to standardizing risk analysis. Such careful data control is essential for establishing risk numbers that inform investment/resource allocation decisions.

5   CI/KR as a Network

Networks have been used to model infrastructure since the inception of graph theory. Leonhard Euler modelled the Bridges of Königsberg transportation infrastructure as a graph in 1735 and showed that it was impossible to cross every bridge one time only and return to the starting point without crossing at least one bridge twice [14]. Euler's critical infrastructure problem created the mathematical field of graph theory and established the foundation of modern network analysis.

Let $G = \{N, L, f\}$ be a graph consisting of set N of n nodes, set L of m links and mapping function $f: N \times N$ that defines how nodes are linked together. Mapping function f is often encoded as an adjacency matrix, A, containing zeros everywhere except for $a_{i,j} = 1$, if node i is connected to node j. The connectivity of G may be succinctly expressed, with loss of uniqueness, by the degree sequence distribution, $g = \{g_0, g_1, \ldots, g_k\}$, where g_i is the number of nodes with degree i divided by n and k is the degree of the most connected node, called the *hub*.

For example, the simple network of Figure 1 contains $n = 2$ nodes, $m = 3$ links and is characterized by the degree sequence distribution, $g = \{0, 1/2, 0, 1/2\}$. Nodes are abstract representations of any asset of interest, such as a telecommunications carrier hotel, bridge, Internet server or water treatment plant, and links are abstractions of any connection of interest, such as a communication line, road segment, peer relationship or pipeline segment. Links do not need to be directional. In fact, most network models incorporate bidirectional links to model bidirectional flow such as transportation traffic, flow of data in communication systems and electric power lines.

Barabasi [11], Barabasi and Bonabeau [12], Strogatz [13], Watts [15,16] and others stimulated interest in modelling critical infrastructure systems as networks by showing how network science informs the analysis of robustness of

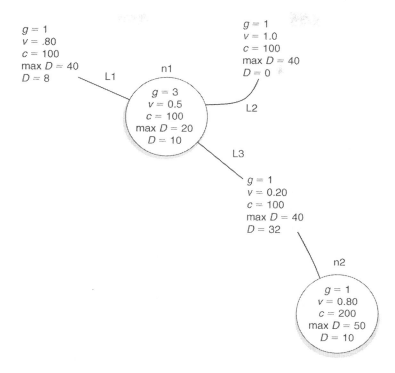

Figure 1: Simple network model of a critical infrastructure sector.

the electric power grid, Internet and other complex systems. They observed that networks with hubs – such as power grids, telecommunications and transportation systems – are more vulnerable to attacks than randomly chosen nodes [17]. Albert *et al.* [10] termed this the 'Achilles Heel' of networks because removal of a hub has a dramatic impact on the connectivity of a network. Conversely, it is wiser to heavily protect these highly connected hubs at the expense of less-connected nodes because hubs are more 'critical'.

Network science properties have been exploited in two major tools to date: MBRA and KDAS. MBRA evaluates risk and KDAS evaluates dependencies among assets. MBRA is a risk analysis tool, while KDAS is largely used as a situational awareness tool.

5.1 MBRA

Barabasi's revelation led Lewis to combine the 'Achilles Heel' theory of networks with the basic risk equation $R = TVC$ to define network risk as the degree-sequence weighted sum of individual asset risks [14]. This definition forms the basis of MBRA:

$$\text{Network risk, } R = \Sigma g_i t_i v_i c_i, \tag{1}$$

where summation is across all nodes and links and

g_i = normalized network property of node or link i
t_i = probability of attack
v_i = vulnerability or probability of success, if attacked
c_i = consequence of successful attack

The property 'weight' $0 \leqslant g_i \leqslant 1$ is a normalized fraction selected by the user. If g is node degree (number of links connected to the node), g_i is the node's degree divided by the hub's degree; if g is the *betweeness* of a node or link, g_i is the betweeness divided by the largest betweeness value in the network. Betweeness is the number of paths passing through a node or link, from and to all other nodes in the network. It is a measure of node and link criticality in models of flow – water, pipelines and so on.

MBRA implements other metrics: *height* is equal to the maximum number of hops from each source node to sink nodes, and *contagiousness* is defined as $g_i t_i v_i$.

For example, a water network might simulate flow from reservoir to treatment plant to consumer. Therefore, the reservoir is 'higher' than the treatment plant because damage to the reservoir has a downstream impact that the analyst may want to analyse. Similarly, the hub is more contagious than other nodes because it spreads cascade failures proportional to its probability of failing, $t_i v_i$, times number of links, g_i. Contagiousness is particularly useful for analysing interdependencies and domino effects in power grids, Internet viruses and so on.

As it turns out, ranking nodes and links according to $g_i t_i v_i c_i$ also determine the order of optimal risk-reducing allocation of resources.

Vulnerability is a probability indicating the likelihood of a successful attack on a node or link. When vulnerability is greater than zero, this means an asset is partially protected and partially vulnerable.

Consequence is a measure of damage due to an attack and can be measured in a number of ways: as loss of life, loss of capital asset, economic value or loss of utility. For example, loss of a power line in the electric power grid may be measured in repair cost, loss of customer power, loss of a life or loss of time. We only require that consequences be in like units, for example, all asset consequences must be in lives, dollars or hours.

When threat is unknown, we assume it is 1.0 – a worst-case assumption. However, MBRA implements a Stackelberg game whereby threat may be calculated by iteratively maximizing attacker risk by allocating resources to an attacker and minimizing defender risk by allocating resources to a defender. MBRA implements an iterative attacker–defender optimization algorithm which halts after 100 iterations or when additional attacker/defender allocations cease to change the max–min value of risk.

Given five numbers for each node and link – threat, vulnerability, consequence, prevention cost and response cost – and three budgets – prevention, response and attacker – MBRA calculates optimal objectives risk, consequence and contagiousness, and allocates the three budgets such that vulnerability and consequence are minimized and threat is maximized.

5.2 KDAS

MBRA models risk, while KDAS uses network science to model interdependency. If node A depends on B and node B depends on C, then KDAS analyses the effect of a failure due to C on nodes A and B. KDAS's primary use is in situational awareness. In fact, KDAS is the real-time situational awareness/common operating picture tool installed in the Global Situational Awareness Facility (GSAF) at the U.S. Pentagon. KDAS supports the Office of the Assistant Secretary of Defence for Homeland Defence and Americas' Security Affairs (OASD (HD & ASA)). OASD (HD & ASA) is responsible for policy and resource allocation decisions regarding defence continuity, military support to civil authorities and critical infrastructure.

One key area of focus of OASD (HD & ASA) is the use of KDAS to model the critical infrastructure assets and key resources associated with the DIB and real-time events that could impact DIB sector operations. KDAS assists decision-makers and analyst in determining the impact of natural and man-made events on critical assets and key resources associated with the DIB. Network nodes represent these assets while links represent dependencies. Thus, failure of one asset may propagate to dependent assets along links.

KDAS nodes behave like finite state machines that are connected in a networked node–link configuration to represent relationships and dependencies between assets. Assets (nodes) are actionable in that the user can update the state of an asset on the screen which initiates two key actions: (1) it provides a visual cue as to asset (node) state, and (2) it initiates simulated system dynamic behaviours related to the internal asset behaviour which may drive dependent behaviour of other assets (Figure 2). In this fashion, the user can see the causal chain of events that might occur because of a state change. The system's dynamic model is always persistent to reflect the operational state of assets, but the user can shift to a 'what-if' mode for projected analysis and course-of-action development. Multiple distributed workgroups within KDAS platforms can collaborate and interact within one shared environment for joint analytics and course-of-action planning.

KDAS possesses an underlying discrete time-stepped simulation framework such that third-party simulations can be integrated as active components in the systems model and therefore can directly interact with the asset objects. One example is the integration of the Naval Research Laboratory's CT-Analyst® dispersion and plume model (http://lcp.nrl.navy.mil/ct-analyst/Home.html). An operator can initiate an event representing the release of a hazardous gas such as chlorine, thus activating the CT-Analyst® simulation. As the plume propagates over time, it actually interacts with the infrastructure asset models and

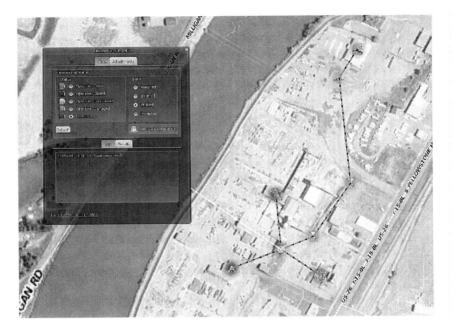

Figure 2: Illustration of KDAS infrastructure components and the systems dynamic model based on network dependencies. This illustrates the loss of power to a distribution substation and the downstream effect.

may cause state changes due to the underlying behaviour and vulnerabilities. This type of interaction allows the analyst to see the time-stepped propagation of the plume and the resultant impact.

KDAS technology is employed in situation assessment and infrastructure analysis tools at Federal Emergency Management Agency (FEMA) – National Capital Region, Port Fourchon Port Commission – Louisiana, the Arizona Counter Terrorism Information Center (ACTIC), and Amtrak. In addition, it was used during the 2009 U.S. Presidential Inauguration and for situation awareness and coordination during the Horizon Oil Spill in the Gulf of Mexico.

6   Resource allocation

One of the additional benefits of network modelling as it applies to infrastructure is the ability to calculate system-wide risk. MBRA illustrates how risk minimization can be applied to entire systems modelled as a network. MBRA reduces risk (and other objective functions) by allocating resources to nodes and links according to some optimal strategy. Risk is reduced by 'buying down' vulnerability, consequence or both. Vulnerability is reduced by investing in prevention, and consequence is reduced by investing in response. If the asset is a building, then construction of a fence buys down vulnerability. Similarly, buying more fire engines or hiring more firefighters buys down consequence.

As more resources are applied, vulnerability and/or consequence, and hence risk, decreases. Both kinds of buy down – prevention and response – are modelled as decreasing returns exponentials.

More formally, let an investment of D_i dollars reduce vulnerability for asset i according to an exponential vulnerability reduction relationship:

$$v_i(D_i) = V_i(0)\exp(-\alpha_i D_i/\max D_i), \tag{2}$$

where $V_i(0)$ is initial vulnerability before any reduction, max D_i is a *maximum vulnerability elimination* cost that drives vulnerability to its minimum value and α_i is a constant determined by the minimum vulnerability buy down determined by max D_i. Typically, α_i is determined by assuming a minimum vulnerability of 5% after maximum buy down of max D_i. Thus, $\alpha_i = -\ln(0.05/V_i(0))$.

The more operators invest in asset i, the lower its vulnerability, which in turn reduces risk according to the relation $gTVC$. If resources are plentiful, allocate $D_i = \max D_i$, and risk is minimized! However, in most cases, there are insufficient resources to eliminate all risk. Instead, operators are forced to choose which nodes and links to completely or partially protect. This begs the question, 'What is the best way to allocate a budget of B dollars to minimize network risk?'

It can be easily shown that rank ordering of nodes and links according to the product $gTVC/\max D$ also leads to an optimal allocation of a fixed budget to nodes and links. Note that this is an *efficient* rank ordering rather than a *critical* node/link ranking because investment in high-return-on-investment nodes or links reduces risk more than low-return investments. The elimination cost max D_i plays a key role in determining return-on-investment. In practical terms, high-risk but expensive assets are poor investments, while high-return-on-investment allocations are good investments.

Similar arguments apply to response – reduction in consequence. MBRA assumes exponential vulnerability and consequence reduction and applies them sequentially: first, vulnerability is reduced followed by consequence.

6.1 Network science

MBRA models critical infrastructure sectors as networks of assets where the assets are nodes and the connections between them are links. Nodes most often represent physical assets and facilities. In many cases, the links represent physical infrastructure that connects nodes together such as power lines, oil pipelines or water pipes. However, links can also represent symbolic relationships such as relationships between people in a command structure or the flow of a contagion through a population. Links can have direction indicating flow, but if direction is not specified, we assume bidirectional connectivity.

It is important to note that MBRA does not attempt to model the physical workings or state of an infrastructure. Instead its generic network model approximates any type of infrastructure network and then uses network science metrics in concert with the risk equations (1) and (2) to compute risk contributions from every asset weighted by the selected network science metric.

Because MBRA is risk based, using the $R = gTVC$ equation, the analyst must provide threat, vulnerability, consequence and elimination cost estimates for each node or link. In addition, if the analyst selects an appropriate network metric, g, MBRA allocates a fixed budget to nodes and links by reducing V or C. If an attacker budget is supplied, MBRA maximizes risk by optimally allocating an attacker's resources to threat, T. This is done by simulating a Stackelberg game.

MBRA assumes T varies according to an exponential function that ranges from 0% (no chance of attack) to 100% (certainty of attack) and then implements a Stackelberg game to determine threat values by max–min iteration. First, a defender tries to reduce risk by reducing vulnerability (or consequence or both). Next, an attacker tries to maximize risk by increasing threat. This process of risk minimization followed by risk maximization is repeated until a stalemate is reached. When equilibrium is reached, MBRA outputs the calculated values of T, V and C, along with the corresponding value of risk.

$$t_i(A_i) = 1-\exp(-\gamma_i A_i/\max A_i), \qquad (3)$$

where max A_i is a *maximum threat* cost that drives threat close to 1.0 and γ_i is a constant determined by the maximum threat buy down determined by max A_i. Typically, γ_i is determined by assuming a maximum threat of 95% after maximum buy down of max A_i. Thus, $\gamma_i = -\ln(0.05)$.

Prevention, response and *threat costs*, max D, max C and max A, are estimates of countermeasure, and attack costs must be provided by the analyst. The model assumes that vulnerability (consequence) can never be zero and allows the user to specify a minimum value as a system-wide preference. Threat is assumed to be the value input by the user, unless calculated by the Stackelberg simulation.

Because reduction per dollar invested decreases with increased investment, according to an exponential rule, MBRA will not fund a single asset all the way to its minimum before switching to the next asset. It is more likely that investment will be spread across a number of assets optimizing the reduction of risk across the entire network.

MBRA implements several network science metrics as weights: height, degree, betweeness and contagiousness. These metrics serve as weights on each node or link. Typically, height is used to give greater importance to upstream nodes and links; degree is used to emphasize cascade effects, betweeness to determine flow effects and contagiousness to emphasize probabilistic cascade failures.

Lastly, the analyst specifies an objective function for MBRA to optimize on. Most often, we use risk. However, there are cases where the analyst might want to study the effects of optimizing threat, vulnerability, consequence or a combination of these.

6.2   An illustration

As an illustration, consider a small piece of the Western power grid shown in Figure 3. Nodes are ranked according to risk after risk optimization – using

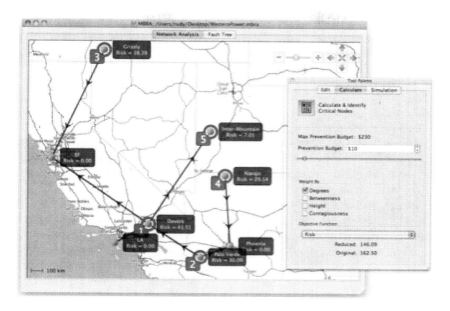

Figure 3: A simple electric power grid network connecting the Palo Verde power
plant to consumers in Arizona, Nevada and California.

degree weighting in this case. This means that a node with more links connected
to it is considered more important than a node with fewer links. All asset risk
values are multiplied by their weight, which in this case is a normalized value
of degree (a number from 0 to 1). Node Devers is more important because it
has a degree of four while all other nodes have only one or two links. The product *gTVC* establishes the ranking shown in Figure 3 after allocating a budget of
$10 million. Even though Devers has a lower consequence value than the very
large Palo Verde facility, it is more critical because of its connectivity. Note
that power from Palo Verde to San Francisco and Los Angeles must go through
Devers.

Using this technique, MBRA is able to analyse complex networks with hidden structure. Many large infrastructures have the appearance of randomness;
yet hidden structure can be exploited towards catastrophic ends. Using this
network science approach, MBRA is able to reveal the structure to help guide
investment intended to reduce risk, not at any single asset but of the infrastructure as a whole.

MBRA is unaware of regional boundaries or the political implications of any
funding strategy. MBRA is able to identify when a critical asset to one region actually resides in another region. The approach at the individual asset level as shown
here is relatively simplistic when compared to an operational single-asset tool such
as MSRAM or KDAS. We believe the best solutions lie in the confluence of these

two approaches where a single-asset model can be applied at the asset level with appropriate weighting, as indicated by a network model such as shown here.

7   Conclusion

Risk analysis through modelling and simulation of critical infrastructure systems is in its infancy. Though a great many tools have been developed and utilized to support risk-informed decision-making, very few tools use the same risk metrics. Worse, the lack of a standard approach creates a great deal of confusion, waste and misrepresentation. Operator/owners will never be able to protect our critical infrastructure if they do not agree on what is critical.

Several different tools were presented in this chapter, including CARVER, MSRAM, MBRA and KDAS. The CARVER tool is an asset-level tool that generates a relative ranking of assets. Though CARVER is not a risk-based tool, it has found widespread use and offers a quick way to assist in target-level prioritization. Even so, the output is not well suited to inform asset protection decisions and does not allow comparison with other methods. MSRAM is a comprehensive asset-level tool that uses a transparent, probabilistic risk assessment approach. It breaks new ground by providing a rigorous approach to risk analysis with extensive quality control, setting a new standard for such tools.

Both MBRA and KDAS are successful implementations of system-level risk and situational analysis techniques, but they still lack some important features:

1. There remains no standardized operational definition of network risk, although MBRA employs the equation, $R = gTVC$, where TVC is generally accepted by other disciplines. Network risk, however, is not universally accepted as the weighted sum of TVC.
2. Dependency analysis as defined by MBRA and KDAS is in its infancy. Although KDAS implements a simple state-machine model, it is not clear what analysts mean by 'dependency' beyond simple cascading. There is currently no standard definition of the risk due to cascading in infrastructure systems.
3. MBRA implements a handful of network science metrics: hub, betweeness, height and contagiousness. Are these complete and meaningful? Additional research is needed to determine the correlation between these metrics and actual risk.
4. Network models are theoretically scalable to large systems, but it remains to be shown that such large networks are manageable. It may be that additional methods are needed to handle networks containing hundreds, thousands or even millions of nodes. Scalability may be a limiting factor to realistic application of this approach.

MBRA and KDAS have shown that it is possible to combine theory and practice in tools that users can apply to real problems in critical infrastructure analysis. Hopefully, additional research and development will follow in these footsteps.

References

[1] National Infrastructure Protection Plan, U.S. Department of Homeland Security, 100 pp. (2009), available at www.DHS.gov.

[2] National Strategy for the Physical Protection of Critical Infrastructure and Key Assets, U.S. Department of Homeland Security (2003), available at www.DHS.gov.

[3] Dudenhoeffer, D.D., Permann, M.R. & Manic, M., 'CIMS: A Framework for Infrastructure Interdependency Modeling and Analysis'. In L.F. Perrone, F.P. Wieland, J. Liu, B.G. Lawson, D.M. Nicol & R.M. Fujimoto (Eds), *Proceedings of the 2006 Winter Simulation Conference.* Institute of Electrical and Electronics Engineers, Piscataway, NJ, pp. 478–485 (2006).

[4] Perrow, C., *Normal Accidents.* Princeton University Press, Princeton, NJ, 450 pp. (1999).

[5] National Research Council, *The Internet Under Crisis Conditions: Learning from September 11.* National Academies Press, Washington, DC (2003), available at www.nap.edu.

[6] 'Final Report on the August 14, 2003 Blackout in the United States and Canada: Causes and Recommendations', April 2004, U.S.–Canada Power System Outage Task Force, pp. 12 (January 12, 2004), available at https://reports.energy.gov

[7] Ramo, J.C., *The Age of the Unthinkable.* Little, Brown & Company, New York, NY, 280 pp. (2009).

[8] Paller, A., Testimony Before the House Committee on Homeland Security: Subcommittee on Economic Security, Infrastructure Protection, and Cybersecurity, Hearings on SCADA and the Terrorist Threat: Protecting the Nation's Critical Control Systems, October 18, 2005, available at http://www.gpoaccess.gov/congress/index.html.

[9] Dobson, I., Carreras, B.A., Lynch, V.E. & Newman, D.E., 'Complex Systems Analysis of Series of Blackouts: Cascading Failure, Critical Points, and Self-Organization', *Chaos*, 17, 026103. 2007.

[10] Albert, R., Barabasi, A-L., & Jeong, H. 'The Internet's Achilles' Heel: Error and Attack Tolerance of Complex Networks', *Nature*, 406, 378–382. 2000.

[11] Barabasi, A-L., *Linked: How Everything Is Connected to Everything Else and What It Means for Business, Science, and Everyday Life.* Perseus Publishing, Cambridge, MA, 280 pp. (2002). ISBN 0-7382-0667-9.

[12] Barabasi, A-L., & Bonabeau, E., 'Scale-Free Networks', *Scientific American*, 288, 60–69. 2003.

[13] Strogatz, S.H., 'Exploring Complex Networks', *Nature*, 410, 268–276. 2001. available at www.nature.com. doi:10.1038/35065725.

[14] Lewis, T.G., *Critical Infrastructure Protection in Homeland Security: Defending a Networked Nation.* John Wiley & Sons, Hoboken, NJ, 500 pp. (2006).

[15] Watts, D.J., 'Networks, Dynamics, and the Small-World Phenomenon', *American Journal of Sociology*, 105(2), 493–527. 1999.

[16] Watts, D.J., *Six Degrees: The Science of a Connected Age.* W.W. Norton, New York, NY, 374 pp. (2003). ISBN 0-393-32542-3.

[17] National Security Telecommunications Advisory Committee, NSTAC Task Force on Concentration of Assets: Telecom Hotels (2003), available at www.ncs.gov/nstac/nstac.html nstac1@dhs.gov.

Physical vulnerability assessment

Roger G. Johnston[1]

[1]*Vulnerability Assessment Team, Nuclear Engineering Division, Argonne National Laboratory, Argonne, IL*

Abstract

Effective infrastructure (security) Vulnerability Assessments require creative and resourceful personnel, whichever methods are employed. It is essential for vulnerability assessors to try to assume the mind-set of the adversaries and to look at vulnerabilities, attacks, and possible countermeasures from their perspective. Unfortunately, a lot of what passes for Vulnerability Assessments is actually Threat Assessment or relatively mundane checking of compliance with formal security regulations and guidelines. It is often highly unimaginative. Brainstorming is a powerful tool for helping, and there are a number of tips for enhancing its effectiveness. Vulnerability assessors also need to be alert to common security mistakes found in many organizations. They must try to avoid the widespread myths about security vulnerabilities and the common Vulnerability Assessment mistakes that hamper analysis.

Keywords: Vulnerability Assessment, Threat Assessment, Security Maxims, Physical Security, Security Myths

1 Introduction

A (security) Vulnerability Assessment (VA) is potentially one of the most powerful tools for improving infrastructure security. It is important, however, to use effective VA techniques, to employ creative/resourceful personnel with the proper mind-set, and to avoid common VA myths and mistakes. It is also crucial to understand what a VA is and is not, especially because this issue is a common source of confusion.

1.1 Terminology

For purposes of this discussion, we will define *vulnerabilities* as security weaknesses that could potentially be exploited by adversaries (the "bad guys") for nefarious purposes. A (security) Vulnerability Assessment is an analysis meant to discover (and perhaps demonstrate) these security vulnerabilities and possible *attacks*; it may also include suggesting and demonstrating possible counter-measures to the "good guys," that is, the people who own the infrastructure and provide for its security.

A Threat Assessment (TA) is different from a VA in that the focus is on ana-lyzing *threats*, that is, who might attack, where and when, using what resources, and with what ultimate goals and probabilities.

(Security) Risk Management involves trying to deal prudently with potential security hazards and to provide as much prevention and mitigation of attacks (and recovery afterwards) as practical. Risk Management relies on both VAs and TAs, but it is also concerned with understanding the valuable *assets* at risk of being harmed, the *consequences* should adversaries succeed in harming them, and what security resources to deploy and how to deploy them in order to pre-vent or limit harm, or provide resiliency after an attack.

An infrastructure's valuable assets can include (among other things) people, equipment, products, services, money, facilities, buildings, networks, logistics, communications, intellectual property, trade secrets, personally identifiable information, and an organization's reputation. The harm that might befall these assets includes theft, damage, sabotage, vandalism, adulteration, tampering, terrorism, or espionage.

1.2   What a VA is not

The purpose of a VA is to improve security and to provide important informa-tion that can be used for effective Risk Management. Though it is unfortunately common, we should not view a VA as some kind of test to pass. It is not even clear what it means to "pass" a VA; it certainly cannot mean there are no vul-nerabilities, as will be discussed below. Indeed, an infrastructure, security pro-gram, or organization can no more pass a VA than a person can pass an IQ test.

Similarly, a VA is not some kind of certification. It should also not be used to justify the status quo; claim there are no vulnerabilities; apply a mindless and bureaucratic stamp of approval on the existing security infrastructure, hard-ware, and strategies; or praise or criticize security managers, vendors, contrac-tors, or frontline security personnel. The results of a VA should never be used in employee performance appraisals. Doing this simply encourages a culture of denying and covering up security problems and will lead to a hostile or paranoid environment that makes VAs difficult to perform effectively.

It is not uncommon for security managers to confuse a TA with a VA. Effec-tive Risk Management requires a good understanding of both threats and vul-nerabilities. Both TAs and VAs require looking at the security problem from the standpoint of the bad guys. Both require some attempt to gauge likelihoods. VAs tend to require more creativity, whereas TAs require a good understand-ing of real-world conditions and how the adversaries think. Generally speak-ing, VAs give you more "bang for the buck" than TAs. The reason is that if you understand and mitigate your vulnerabilities, your security may be in good shape even if you get the threats all wrong, which is easy to do because judging threats often involves a lot of speculation about unseen (and maybe nonexistent) adversaries and their agendas. Conversely, if you thoroughly understand your threats, but have no clue at all about your vulnerabilities, you are probably in trouble because you will not know how to prevent and mitigate the attacks you foresee coming.

2   Common techniques for finding vulnerabilities

This section briefly discusses some of the methods commonly used to conduct infrastructure VAs. Many of these techniques are not particularly good at finding vulnerabilities. Indeed, some are not VA techniques at all.

2.1   Security Survey

A Security Survey involves walking through the infrastructure, facility, or building of interest, typically with a checklist in hand [1]. Sometimes this checklist is prepared primarily by the security manager(s) responsible for the infrastructure security. Unfortunately, however, the Security Survey checklist is often composed primarily of boilerplate items taken from generic Security Survey checklists (which is less effective).

The typical goal of a Security Survey is to see if the security measures planned for the infrastructure are actually being implemented and if they are being implemented effectively. For example, are the doors that are supposed to be locked really locked? Is the security guard at his/her station and fully alert?

Security Surveys can be very important tools for improving the implementation of security measures. As such, they are very much worth doing and worth doing often. They can turn up important surprises. The problem with Security Surveys in the context of a VA is that they do not usually uncover previously unrecognized vulnerabilities or suggest new countermeasures. With their binary, checklist mentality, Security Surveys do not encourage fresh, independent, profound, or creative thinking about security vulnerabilities and attack scenarios. They force the security manager conducting the Security Survey to think like a good guy, not view the situation from the perspective of a bad guy. The existing security strategy, hardware, and personnel come to define the security problem in the mind of the security manager. This is undesirable because the unfortunate reality about security is that the bad guys are the only ones who truly get to define the problem.

2.2   Security Audit

A Security Audit involves checking to see if the infrastructure security is in compliance with (usually high-level) security rules, regulations, laws, policies, and guidelines. Sometimes it also involves reviewing the merits or language of the local or low-level security rules and policies.

Like Security Surveys, Security Audits do not usually turn up new vulnerabilities, provide substantial insights into security issues, or encourage independent, creative thinking about security. Security Audits similarly do not encourage thinking like the bad guys.

Another problem is that compliance-based security is frequently not good security. Unfortunately, adherence to security rules, policies, and regulations—while often necessary—is no guarantee of good security. In fact, rigid compliance and good security can be wholly incompatible. Especially when the security rules, regulations, laws, policies, and guidelines are imposed by high-level bureaucrats in a one-size-fits-all manner, with few (if any) sanity checks at the local level, security can suffer. If nothing else, ill-conceived or ill-fitting security rules can draw valuable time, energy, and attention away from real security efforts. They may also create cynicism about security among security and nonsecurity employees. This almost always negatively impacts security.

2.3   Design Basis Threat (DBT)

Despite the gibberish-sounding name, Design Basis Threat is based on a very commonsense idea. DBT means designing security to deal with the current real-world threats [2]. Though this ought to be self-evident, it is surprising how many security programs are operated without much thought as to the nature of the threats, including the adversaries and their goals and resources.

As its name might suggest, DBT is really more of a TA technique than a VA technique. It is also typically more attuned to helping to decide how to allocate security resources than to discovering vulnerabilities. The technique itself does not have much in the way of practical suggestions for how to find vulnerabilities. The whole process of how to recognize vulnerabilities is often glossed over in discussions about the DBT technique.

There are other serious problems with DBT commonly found in practice that are not necessarily fundamental, theoretical weaknesses with the technique. They include tending to focus too much on protecting physical assets (at the cost of ignoring more valuable assets like people, information, and organizational reputation); letting the existing hardware, personnel, and security strategies define the security problem; and being overly reactive instead of proactive. DBT is frequently obsessed with force-on-force attacks and often ignores more subtle attacks, including those based on the use of disloyal or compromised insiders. DBT frequently ignores simple and cheap countermeasures when the attack probabilities are judged (rightly or wrongly) to be low or zero. Moreover, DBT is often done unimaginatively by committee or using bureaucrats and relatively uncreative personnel. It is frequently used to justify the status quo.

DBT can suffer from the Fallacy of Precision—thinking that because we assign a somewhat arbitrary numeric ranking or value to the probability of a threat or attack that we actually understand it. Though it often involves the use of rankings and estimated probabilities, DBT ironically sometimes engenders a kind of binary thinking about security—that a potential attack or type of adversary is either blocked or not blocked. Tellingly, DBT is often used to "test" security effectiveness, something that makes no sense for a VA technique.

As with Security Surveys and Security Audits, DBT can be a useful tool for assisting with Risk Management despite its shortcomings in practice. It is just not typically a very effective VA tool.

2.4 CARVER Method

The CARVER Method [3,4] is popular among security managers who work for government agencies, especially police departments and the United States Department of Defense. CARVER is an acronym that stands for Criticality, Accessibility, Recuperability, Vulnerability, Effect, and Recognizability. It was developed by U.S. Special Forces during the Vietnam War to help decide which targets had the highest priority for attacking.

The CARVER Method provides a logical, semiquantitative way to judge how to allocate security resources by considering the value of a given target and the ease of successfully attacking the target given the resources available for the attack and for its defense. Basically, targets (i.e., assets) are assigned estimated scores for the five attributes of Criticality, Accessibility, Recuperability, Vulnerability, Effect, and Recognizability. These relative rankings are placed in a table or matrix. The assets that score highest get the most attention and resources devoted to protecting them [3,4].

Though it is often discussed as if it were a VA technique, the CARVER Method is actually a Risk Management tool for deciding how to allocate security resources. It has little to teach about how to discover vulnerabilities or design effective countermeasures.

2.5 Delphi Method

The Delphi Method [5,6] was developed in the 1950s and 1960s as a systematic way to make forecasts about complex issues. It involves procedures to iteratively poll various subject-matter experts in a way that preserves minority viewpoints, while trying to converge the whole group toward a single, optimal forecast or decision.

The Delphi Method has merit for making single decisions such as "where do we put the new bridge?" or in forecasting complicated future events. It can potentially be useful for deciding how to field security resources once the threats, vulnerabilities, consequences, and resources are fully analyzed. There is little evidence, however, that the Delphi Method is an effective way to find security vulnerabilities or devise practical countermeasures. Indeed, the focus is on the internal mental process of experts coming to some kind of consensus, not on creatively thinking like the bad guys, or on discovering a multitude of previously unknown vulnerabilities and countermeasures. If the subject-matter experts have not carefully studied the security issues specific to the infrastructure in question, their ignorance will prevent their expertise and consensus from being very useful.

2.6   Fault Tree Analysis

Fault Tree Analysis (FTA) is a safety tool used to predict industrial and technology failures [7,8]. It is based on the idea of using a model of logical AND and OR gates in conjunction with information or estimates of hardware failure rates, stochastic event probabilities, and cascading chains of occurrences to predict system failure. It is a useful technique for understanding the effect of individual faults of a complex system, but it is not particularly good at finding the causes for these faults or even in cataloging all the faults that are possible.

FTA is of dubious value for security VAs because adversaries tend to attack in a deliberate manner at the point of greatest weakness, not in some random manner akin to component failure.

2.7   Software tools

Many organizations use software tools for doing infrastructure VAs. These tools are often specific to certain industries, such as the chemical industry, transportation, utilities, education, energy, and so on [9].

The software tools typically consist of lists of infrastructure security issues that security managers should consider and questions they should ask (much like a Security Survey). The user of the software program may be asked to input relative rankings or estimates of probabilities for use in matrices along the lines of the CARVER Method. Sometimes generic security measures will be suggested.

These software tools are often a useful place to start in doing an infrastructure VA. They can provide some ideas about what issues the vulnerability assessors need to consider. They are not, however, particularly effective tools for finding vulnerabilities in specific infrastructures; they are simply too generic. Most vulnerabilities and most effective countermeasures depend critically on details of the specific infrastructure in question, its location, personnel, their training, and other factors. The "cookie cutter" approach to security that these programs encourage is not conducive to good security.

Another common problem with software VA tools is that the people who write or provide input to these generic software programs usually have some security expertise but typically lack a history of doing true VAs. They may be experienced with TAs and overall Risk Management, knowledgeable about common security practices, and/or familiar with choosing and integrating security products. They are often, however, not the creative, hacker types needed to find vulnerabilities and devise effective countermeasures. They often do not think intuitively like the bad guys. (See Section 3.1 on VA Personnel.) Sometimes they are not even all that familiar with the industrial sectors their software program is focused upon.

2.8   Adversarial Vulnerability Assessments

An Adversarial Vulnerability Assessment is based on the idea that finding security vulnerabilities and suggesting effective countermeasures is more of an art than a science. That VAs require creative, critical thinking. That the vulnerability assessors must take on the perspective and the mind-set of the adversaries. They need to look at an infrastructure with fresh eyes, no preconceived notions, and not let the existing security measures and security managers define the problem.

Adversarial Vulnerability Assessments attempt to mimic the creative reasoning process that the adversaries will go through in thinking about how to attack an infrastructure. Because adversaries are not usually inclined to use formal methods such as Security Surveys, DBT, software tools, or even the CARVER Method, vulnerability assessors should not rely solely on these tools either.

The typical steps in an Adversarial Vulnerability Assessment are as follows:

1. Assemble a team of creative, hacker types and knowledgeable security experts.
2. Try to REALLY understand the infrastructure, its operation, assets, and current security program. The official policies, what high-level managers think, and the way the infrastructure and its security are supposed to work are less important than the ground-level truth. Thus, it is essential to walk around and to closely observe and talk to frontline personnel to learn how things really operate. Ask a lot of questions.
3. Play around with the infrastructure, either through thought experiments or (to the extent safe and practical) with actual attempts to poke the infrastructure or test the security.
4. Brainstorm possible attacks and vulnerabilities. Anything goes! There is no editing or down selecting of ideas at this stage. The crazier, the better! (Section 3.2 discusses good brainstorming practice.)
5. Based on the ideas generated in the brainstorming session, poke and play with the infrastructure some more.
6. More brainstorming.
7. Begin editing and prioritizing potential attacks and vulnerabilities so that the most promising can receive the most careful analysis.
8. Carefully study the potential attacks and vulnerabilities on the list. Remain open, however, to new ideas that may appear at any time.
9. Partially develop some attacks and determine their feasibility.
10. Devise potential countermeasures.
11. Perfect and demonstrate certain attacks to the extent it is safe and practical. It may be necessary to do some or all of this in a test lab.
12. Perfect and demonstrate countermeasures to the extent it is safe and practical. It may be necessary to do some or all of this in a test lab.
13. Remain open for new attacks, vulnerabilities, and countermeasures that inevitably appear late in the VA process.
14. Prepare the final VA report.
15. Ideally the vulnerability assessors are invited back at some time in the future after security modifications are implemented to comment on the new security regime.

3   VA best practices

Whatever method or methods are chosen to conduct the infrastructure VA, there are certain critical attributes needed for an effective VA.

3.1   VA personnel

Choosing the right personnel is critical for an effective VA. Often outsiders are more psychologically predisposed to identifying security problems and solutions than insiders; plus they bring a fresh perspective to security analysis. Insiders, however, should also be part of the VA team, for they understand best how the infrastructure operates and what countermeasures might be practical to implement.

Whoever is involved, the vulnerability assessors must not have any conflicts of interest. They must genuinely want, consciously and subconsciously, to aggressively search for security problems and to find practical countermeasures (and ideally have a history of doing so). There are two major types of conflicts of interest. One is a *financial* conflict of interest, for example, if the vulnerability assessors are also the vendors or potential vendors for the infrastructure's security.

Another type of conflict of interest occurs if the vulnerability assessors fear retaliation for finding security vulnerabilities. Indeed, "shooting the messenger" is not an uncommon problem for vulnerability assessors and must be scrupulously avoided. (Thinking about the discovery of vulnerabilities as good news, not bad news, as discussed in Section 4, can also help.)

Fear of retaliation (in the form of damage to one's career) is often a problem if the security professionals who provide the infrastructure's security are also part of the VA team. This is why they should provide substantial input to the outsiders conducting the VA, but they should not be allowed to control the findings. Another example of fear of retaliation may occur if the outside consultants or contractors hired to do an independent VA are concerned about not being rehired in the future if they find security problems or not receiving positive references. This can be partially avoided by judging the efficacy of the VA (and the vulnerability assessors) by the number and importance of new vulnerabilities found and the number and quality of suggested countermeasures—not by how comfortable the sponsor of the VA is with the findings.

Avoiding conflicts of interest is a good start but is not sufficient to guarantee a good VA. Another common problem with infrastructure VAs is using unimaginative personnel. It is remarkable how often the people chosen to conduct a VA are not "outside the box" thinkers. Vulnerability assessors need to be highly creative in identifying vulnerabilities and thinking about how the bad guys might attack. This is not only because the bad guys may be highly imaginative themselves but also because the good guys need to be substantially *more* imaginative. Offense is usually easier than defense. The bad guys need only stumble upon and exploit one or a small number of vulnerabilities and can often attack at the time and location of their choosing. The good guys, on the other hand, have to deal with a very large number of vulnerabilities and potential attacks (including those they know nothing about) and usually must protect assets that are widely distributed in time and space.

The key attribute for effective vulnerability assessors can be called the "hacker's mentality." This is the ability to perform a mental "coordinate transformation" to think like a bad guy and to intrinsically see the weaknesses and contradictions in complex systems. It is surprising how difficult it can be for security professionals—having devoted their lives and careers to being the good guys and desperately wanting security to succeed—to think like bad guys and find security vulnerabilities. It is essential that the VA team include people who have this hacker's mentality. Because this is a trait not common among security managers, bureaucrats, foot soldiers, and party-line "company men," it may be necessary to involve unconventional personnel, even nonsecurity personnel, who possess the hacker mentality.

People with this hacker mentality tend to be independent, skeptical or cynical, intuitive, clever, hands-on types who routinely find loopholes in their jobs, outmaneuver bureaucrats, and question authority. Hacker-type people are often nonconformists, wise guys, troublemakers, smart alecks, schemers, organizational critics, outside-the-box thinkers, artists, tinkerers, problem solvers, attention grabbers, and "techno-nerds." They tend to have little respect for tradition or the chain of command.

Involving employees from the infrastructure being assessed who are not security professionals, but possess the hacker mentality, can pay big dividends. Vulnerabilities are often obvious to employees who understand the infrastructure but are not caught up in the day-to-day realities of providing security. Moreover, involving nonsecurity personnel in security issues can increase overall security awareness for the organization. The irony, of course, is that hacker types within an organization are often considered some of the organization's biggest security headaches. Nevertheless, they are precisely the individuals who should be part of a VA team. (Genuinely disloyal employees, of course, should be excluded.)

In the author's experience, engineers do not typically make good vulnerability assessors (though there are no doubt exceptions). It is basically a mindset problem. Engineers tend to work in solution space, not problem space. They often view Nature, stochastic failure, and economics as the enemy, and are not accustomed to dealing with a deliberate, intelligent, nefarious adversary who attacks at the time and location of his/her choosing. Engineers focus on order, logic, control, system reliability, user friendliness, and serving the customer— not thinking creatively evil like a bad guy.

3.2 Brainstorming

Many organizations attempt brainstorming, but few are good at it. Regardless of the VA techniques they use, vulnerability assessors need to be effective brainstormers in order to discover new vulnerabilities, attacks, and countermeasures.

Creativity has actually been well studied [10,11], and there are a number of practical tips for effective brainstorming [12,13]. These are not specific to security and VAs but presumably are nevertheless applicable.

Experts seem to agree that probably the biggest mistake is to place value judgments on ideas far too early in the brainstorming process. According to Eugene Raudsepp [14],

> Nothing can inhibit and stifle the creative process more—and on this there is unanimous agreement among all creative individuals and investigators of creativity—than critical judgment applied to the emerging idea at the beginning stages of the creative process. [. . .] More ideas have been prematurely rejected by a stringent evaluative attitude than would be warranted by any inherent weakness or absurdity in them. The longer one can linger with the idea with judgment held in abeyance, the better the chances all its details and ramifications [can emerge].

Thus, in early brainstorming exercises, every idea, no matter how wacky or stupid, gets written down and treated as a gem. Crazy ideas are strongly encouraged, not only because they encourage thinking outside the box but also because it is surprising how often zany ideas can be massaged into something useful. Generally, authority figures should not be involved in brainstorming sessions, or at least should not act like authority figures, because of the risk of suppressing crazy ideas.

Generally, individuals are creative, not groups. It is, however, difficult to get away from groups when infrastructure security is involved. Moreover, the right group dynamics can energize, egg-on, and fertilize individual creativity. The group needs to be diverse, high energy, humorous, and joyful, in an urgent but not stressful mood; cohesive but not too cohesive; competitive in a friendly and respectful way; and enthusiastic about individual differences and eccentricities. Individuals must be given ownership of their original ideas and should be personally recognized for their creativity. A good model seems to be comedy writing [15].

Other brainstorming tips based on the author's experience with VAs include the following:

- Pay close attention to explicit or unstated assumptions, and to security features that are widely praised or admired. These are often the source of serious vulnerabilities.
- Concentrate on the second and third best attacks or countermeasures. You are likely to be overlooking something that would make them the best solutions.
- If there is widespread agreement about the efficacy of an attack or countermeasure, reexamine. Something important was probably overlooked.
- Pursue what is interesting, controversial, contrarian, exciting, or silly.
- Quantity breeds quality.
- With all ideas: elaborate, expand, modify, subvert, exaggerate, and combine with other ideas.
- Pursue hunches and intuition.

- The best ideas come late and when you are not thinking about the problem.
- Think backwards: How can we make security completely ineffective? How can our attacks fail miserably? How do we as the bad guys escape from the facility after completing our attack?
- Solve the problem that is not here yet, for example, how are we going to provide effective security when there are smart robots or nanotechnology attack tools?
- Mentally remove some security devices, measures, or personnel. Then consider the implications.
- Draw lots of diagrams.
- Develop and explore models, metaphors, and analogies.
- Terminology constrains our thinking. Rename everything in your own (and/or silly) words and think about them in light of the new terminology.
- Consider different verbs for what the bad guys might want to accomplish: attack, steal, demolish, embarrass, tag, terminate, uncover, purify, discredit, poison, and so on.
- Picture attacks from the ceiling and the floor. How would attacks work if everything was underwater or if gravity stopped working?
- Ridicule existing security measures and strategies. This frees the mind to see their shortcomings.
- Explore extremes: best and worst case scenarios for both the good guys and the bad guys.
- How will the bad guys feel during the attack? Try to imagine their satisfaction if they succeed.
- How would the bad guys attack if they had infinite resources or had almost no resources?
- What would the security look like if it had infinite resources or had almost no resources?
- What questions would a 10-year-old ask about the existing security? What questions would your mother-in-law ask?

3.3   Common security mistakes

In conducting an infrastructure VA, it is useful to be on the lookout for common security mistakes. One of these is to be overly focused on prevention, while ignoring or underemphasizing mitigation, recovery, and resiliency. Prevention (especially for terrorism) is a very difficult challenge and may not be fully possible. Mitigation of vulnerabilities, and recovery and resiliency after an attack, are important security goals that deserve careful consideration by vulnerability assessors.

Many security programs are overly focused on protecting hardware, instead of more important assets such as people, continuity, facilities, buildings, networks, information, intellectual property, trade secrets, and the reputation of the organization. Often there is poor *physical* security (as opposed to cyber security) for computers, peripherals, computer media, and digital data.

Vulnerability assessors should also be on the lookout for security rules that only good guys follow. For example, banks often require customers to remove hats and sunglasses, but individuals there to rob the bank will not follow that rule. As another example, some organizations ban cameras in certain areas of their facility, even when disloyal employees would have little trouble smuggling them in and out. Rules that only good guys follow have a high probability of being Security Theater, that is, fake security mostly for show. There are other telltale signs of Security Theater [16].

Another common problem, especially in large organizations, is having overly complex, constantly changing, variably interpreted, and even stupid security rules. This engenders cynicism among employees about security, which is not conducive to good security. Cynicism also happens when VIPs are allowed to bypass security procedures, when security becomes the enemy of productivity, and when employees have no input on security regulations.

Security managers often underestimate the creativity and resourcefulness of adversaries, and frequently lack cradle-to-grave security for locks, access control, biometrics, and other types of security devices (which can typically be hijacked by an adversary with just 15–20 seconds of access, perhaps while the devices are sitting on a loading dock prior to shipment or installation). Tamper-indicating seals are often used very poorly by many organizations [17], and video surveillance cameras often have unnecessarily poor resolution. Other mistakes made by many organizations include failing to deal effectively with imposters and with the Insider Threat. The latter must include the use of effective measures to mitigate employee disgruntlement [18] and to deal with the serious risks of social engineering [19,20], espionage, and workplace violence [21].

Many organizations also greatly overestimate the effectiveness of layered security [22]. Layers of bad security do not automatically add up to good security. Often the layers do not really back each other up or may even interfere with one another. Layered security increases complexity, which is not helpful for good security. It is not uncommon for the existence of layered security to result in overconfidence, complacency, and an unwillingness to make security improvements. Many organizations also overestimate the effectiveness of high technology [23].

Finally, vulnerability assessors should bear in mind the following security maxims [24]. While these are not absolute truths, they are often true and worth keeping in the back of one's mind.

Shannon's (Kerckhoffs') Maxim: The adversaries know and understand the security systems, strategies, hardware, and software being used. Thus, "security by obscurity" is not a viable long-term security strategy.

Rohrbach's Maxim: No security device, system, or strategy will ever be used properly (the way it was designed) all the time. This must be factored into any security program.

Antique Maxim: A security device, system, or measure is most vulnerable near the end of its life.

Mission Creep Maxim: Any given device, system, or program that is designed
for inventory (counting and locating assets) will very quickly come to be
viewed—quite incorrectly—as a security device, system, or program capable
of dealing with deliberate spoofing.

Doctor Who Maxim: The more sophisticated the technology, the more vulnerable
it is to primitive attack. This is why vulnerability assessors should focus on
low-tech attacks, even against high-tech security devices, systems, and programs. High-tech attacks are usually unnecessary.

Schneier's Maxim No. 1: If you think technology can solve your security problems, then you don't understand the problems and you don't understand the
technology.

Schneier's Maxim No. 2: Control will usually get confused with security.

Mahbubani's Maxim: Organizations and security managers who cannot envision
security failures will not be able to avoid them.

3.3   The VA report: Delivering the "bad news"

The final report by the vulnerability assessors should begin by praising the positive aspects of the infrastructure's current security program. There are three reasons for doing this. First, the good practices need to be recognized so that they
will continue. They may merely be an accident or might be removed in the future
when new security managers take over. Second, praising the good aspects of
the current security regime gives the security department and security managers some cover from potential retaliation when new vulnerabilities are disclosed.
(In a healthy organization with a good security culture, this will not be a problem,
but the author has frequently experienced the situation where a security manager,
having been shown new vulnerabilities, pleads with the vulnerability assessors not
to disclose the vulnerabilities to his superiors.) The third reason for praising the
infrastructure's positive security practices at the start of a VA report is to make
the organization more psychologically willing to hear about security problems.
A litany of security flaws is easier to accept when preceded by sincere praise.

The VA report and briefing should be given to the highest appropriate level
without editing, interpretation, or censorship by middle managers.

If it is a good VA, the report will contain far more vulnerabilities than can be
eliminated or mitigated in a short period of time. Many will never be eliminated
or mitigated. There should also be suggestions and countermeasures for improving security. Security managers (not the vulnerability assessors) are the ones
who should ultimately decide which (if any) make sense to implement.

The report and briefing should include video to document and demonstrate
vulnerabilities, potential attacks, and possible countermeasures. An *in situ*, live dem-
onstration of vulnerabilities associated with locks, seals, and access control devices
may, however, more vividly demonstrate the vulnerabilities and attack scenario.

The VA report should include information on the identity and experience
of the vulnerability assessors, any possible conflict of interest, and any *a priori*

constraints on the time, resources, and scope of the VA. The time, resources, skill, expertise, practice, and level of effort required by the adversary for each envisioned attack should be provided, along with an estimate of the probability of the attack succeeding. Suggestions for improved security and potential countermeasures to security vulnerabilities should be discussed, but the report should emphasize that the organization's own security managers may be better qualified to decide on practical security modifications and countermeasures.

A sanitized, statistical summary of the VA findings should be prepared for public release, along with the identity of the vulnerability assessors, if the organization that owns the infrastructure wishes to take public credit for the VA.

4   Vulnerability myths and mistakes

There are a number of widespread myths about VAs and a lot of common mistakes in thinking about vulnerabilities and performing VAs. One myth is that there are usually only a small number of vulnerabilities. In fact, even a simple security device typically has dozens of vulnerabilities. The number of vulnerabilities in a complex infrastructure is virtually unlimited, and most will never be known by either the good guys or the bad guys. The wishful thinking involved in believing that most infrastructure vulnerabilities can be found and eliminated (or at least significantly mitigated) is also unhelpful.

A popular myth is that the ideal result for an infrastructure VA is finding zero vulnerabilities. In fact, such a VA is worthless and should be redone— this time by competent personnel. It is also a mistake to view the discovery of vulnerabilities as bad news. In fact, finding a vulnerability is excellent news because it means that something can potentially be done about it. (That particular viewpoint, however, is rare among organizations, security managers, and even some vulnerability assessors.) Viewing or presenting vulnerabilities as bad news makes it much more difficult to get an organization and security managers to implement needed security improvements. It also increases the odds that security managers and other security professionals will face retaliation when vulnerabilities are inevitably discovered.

Another common myth about infrastructure VAs is that once a thorough VA is completed, future VAs can be cursory efforts. In fact, rapid changes in technologies, threats, personnel, and assets—plus the ever present large pool of undiscovered vulnerabilities—make it essential to conduct thorough VAs whenever possible.

It is also a myth that VAs should be rigorous, consistent, and fully reproducible so that any vulnerability assessors find exactly the same thing. In fact, finding vulnerabilities is a creative endeavor (more art than science) that is difficult to quantify, reproduce, characterize, control, or predict. Demanding rigor, consistency, and reproducibility—at least at this stage of our understanding of security, vulnerabilities, and the creative thought process—is surely a recipe for the lowest common denominator, that is, poor VAs. Vulnerability assessors sometimes claim to use formal, rigorous approaches to VAs but in reality offer only sham rigor.

Some of the mistakes that vulnerability assessors sometimes make include (as discussed previously) confusing a TA with a VA. Also, vulnerability assessors sometimes rely too much on past security incidents to predict future vulnerabilities and attacks. The past is often a good place to begin one's analysis, but the world is a rapidly changing place. Moreover, rare, catastrophic attacks (e.g., 9/11) often have no obvious precedent. Security needs to be proactive, not just reactive.

Another common mistake when conducting an infrastructure VA is to consider infrastructure features as vulnerabilities. For example, a public road might run close to the facility of interest, and this might be thought of as a vulnerability. In fact, a feature independent of an envisioned attack scenario is not a vulnerability.

The road might, for example, be used to get a truck with explosives close to the facility. This might well be a vulnerability, which we will call Vulnerability 1. The road might also make it easier for an adversary to park along the side of the road and conduct visual or electronic surveillance without attracting attention (Vulnerability 2), or to get closer to the facility before launching an all-out frontal assault (Vulnerability 3). An adversary might also park along the side of the road to load up stolen items passed to him by nearby facility insiders (Vulnerability 4). Adding video surveillance cameras along the road might be an effective countermeasure for Vulnerabilities 2 and 4 but would probably be of limited use for Vulnerabilities 1 and 3 because of the response time. Thus, it is not the feature itself (the road) that represents a vulnerability in need of a countermeasure but rather the feature combined with a particular attack scenario. VAs are sometimes done on a sector-by-sector, module-by-module, or function-by-function basis. Cyber vulnerabilities are often analyzed separately from physical security vulnerabilities. These are mistakes because vulnerabilities and attacks often occur at interfaces or seams. Infrastructure VAs should be done holistically, not on a component, subsystem, function, sector, or layer basis.

Acknowledgments and disclaimer

This chapter was prepared under the auspices of the United States Department of Energy (DOE) under contract DE-AC02-06CH-11357. The views expressed here are those of the author and should not necessarily be ascribed to Argonne National Laboratory or DOE. Jon Warner provided useful suggestions.

References

[1] Broder, J.F., *Risk Analysis and the Security Survey*, Butterworth-Heinemann, 2006.
[2] Garcia, M.L., *The Design and Evaluation of Physical Protection Systems*, Butterworth-Heinemann, 2007.

[3] Bennett, B.T., *Understanding, Assessing, and Responding to Terrorism: Protecting Critical Infrastructure and Personnel*, Wiley, p. 244ff, 2007.

[4] Fay, J., *Encyclopedia of Security Management*, Butterworth-Heinemann, p. 500ff, 2007.

[5] Turoff, M. & Linston, H., *The Delphi Method: Techniques and Applications*, 2002, http://is.njit.edu/pubs/delphibook/.

[6] Rowe, G. & Wright, G., The Delphi Technique as a Forecasting Tool: Issues and Analysis, *International Journal of Forecasting*, 15(4), pp. 353–375, 1999.

[7] International Electrotechnical Commission, *Fault Tree Analysis. Edition 2.0*, (IEC 61025), 2006.

[8] Vesely, W.E., et al., *Fault Tree Handbook*. Nuclear Regulatory Commission. NUREG–0492, 1981, http://www.nrc.gov/reading-rm/doc-collections/nuregs/staff/sr0492/.

[9] IVA—Industrial Vulnerability Assessment, Gulf Publishing, 2011, http://www.gulfpub.com/product.asp?PositionID=campaign&ProductID=9641.

[10] Runco, M.A., *Creativity: Theories and Themes: Research, Development, and Practice*, Academic Press, 2006.

[11] Sternberg, R.J., *Handbook of Creativity*, Cambridge University Press, 1998.

[12] Michalko, M., *Cracking Creativity: The Secrets of Creative Genius*, Ten Speed Press, 2001.

[13] van Oech, R., *A Whack on the Side of the Head: How You Can Be More Creative*, Business Plus, 2008.

[14] Raudsepp, E., *Managing Creative Scientists and Engineers*, Collier-Mac, 1963.

[15] Caesar, S. & Friedfeld, E., *Caesar's Hours: My Life in Comedy, with Love and Laughter*, PublicAffairs, p. 121ff, 2003.

[16] Johnston, R.G. & Warner, J.S., Security Theater in Future Arms Control Regimes, *Proceedings of the 51st INMM Meeting*, Baltimore, MD, July 11–15, 2010.

[17] Johnston, R.G., Tamper-Indicating Seals, *American Scientist*, 94(6), pp. 515–523, 2005.

[18] Johnston, R.G. & Warner, J.S., Handbook of Security Blunders, *Proceedings of the 51st INMM Meeting*, Baltimore, MD, July 11–15, 2010.

[19] Long, J., et al., *No Tech Hacking: A Guide to Social Engineering, Dumpster Diving, and Shoulder Surfing*, Syngress, 2008.

[20] Mitnick, K.D., Simon, W.L., & Wozniak, S., *The Art of Deception: Controlling the Human Element of Security*, Wiley, 2003.

[21] Kerr, K., *Workplace Violence: Planning for Prevention and Response*, Butterworth-Heinemann, 2010.

[22] Johnston, R.G., Lessons for Layering, *Security Management*, 54(1), pp. 64–69, 2010.

[23] Johnston, R.G. & Warner, J.S., The Dr. Who Conundrum: Why Placing Too Much Faith in Technology Leads to Failure, *Security Management*, 49(9), pp. 112–121, 2005.

[24] Johnston, R.G., Editor's Comments, *Journal of Physical Security*, 3(1), pp. ii–xiii, 2009, http://jps.anl.gov/v3iss1.html.

Part II
Modeling and Simulation Tools for Critical Infrastructures

Modeling and simulation of critical infrastructures

Gabriele Oliva[1], Stefano Panzieri[1] & Roberto Setola[2]
[1]*University Roma Tre of Rome, Italy*
[2]*University Campus Bio-Medico of Rome, Italy*

Abstract

While the knowledge of human operators and stakeholders is becoming more and more sector specific, infrastructures are becoming more and more interoperable and interdependent. Hence representing the behavior and the characteristics of such a scenario is a mandatory task, in order to assess the risk of multiple disruptions and domino effects, and in order to provide adequate policies and countermeasures to react to structural vulnerabilities, failures, or even intentional attacks. In the literature many approaches have been proposed; *holistic* methods consider infrastructures with an high level of abstraction, while *topological* frameworks consider the interaction of multiple homogeneous subsystems. Nevertheless, *simulative* approaches are focused on a detailed representation of isolated subsystems or *agents*, evaluating their interaction by means of simulation platforms. Finally multilayer methodologies consider interconnected agents according to multiple levels of abstraction or perspectives.

Keywords: Critical Infrastructures, Interdependency Modeling, System of Systems

1 Introduction

The representation of *interdependency* is a fundamental task for the comprehension of the relations that exist between infrastructures and subsystems, in order to quantify threats, identify structural vulnerabilities, and define adequate countermeasures, policies, and strategies. This is the goal of the so-called *Critical Infrastructure Protection* (CIP) strategies developed by several governments and international organizations [1].

Indeed infrastructures are becoming so relevant to be *critical* for the welfare, economy, and security of any developed countries; in fact any disruption or failure in these complex systems "would have a serious impact on the health, safety, security or economic well-being of Citizens or the effective functioning of governments" [2]. However, while modeling and simulation techniques are well-established for the single infrastructure, the representation of highly coupled and interdependent infrastructures is still immature.

In recent years infrastructures have reached an high degree of interoperability, mainly due to the pervasiveness of Information and Communications Technologies (ICT) in fact cyber inter-dependency potentially couples an infrastructure with every other one, in spite of their nature, type, or geographical location [3]. Moreover, because of the huge growth of the complexity of each infrastructure, the skills of technicians, operators, and stakeholders are becoming more and more sector specific. Therefore, while it is often possible to retrieve exhaustive information about the behavior of any single infrastructure and its elements, cross-infrastructure inter-dependencies are often implicit, hidden or neither well understood by the same stakeholders.

In this chapter the state of the art in the representation, analysis, and simulation of interdependent critical infrastructures is reviewed. The chapter is organized as follows: After a preliminary overview of interdependency modeling and simulation (Section 2), *Holistic* modeling approaches are described in Section 3; Section 4 reviews *topological analysis*, both from the structural (Section 4.1) and functional (Section 4.2) points of view; *simulative* frameworks are depicted in Section 5, further describing *Agent-Based* (Section 5.1) and *Multilayer* (Section 5.2) methodologies; finally some conclusive remarks are collected in Section 6.

2   Interdependency modeling

In order to review the state of the art of interdependency modeling and simulation techniques, there is the need to provide some initial definitions.

The *inoperability* of an infrastructure or subsystem is the inability to perform its intended function. A *failure* is a negative event that influences the inoperability of infrastructures and subsystems; a failure can also be propagated or propagate its effects, according to specific concepts of proximity. An infrastructure or subsystem A is *dependent* on another infrastructure or subsystem B when a degradation of B, that is, an increment of its level of inoperability, induces a degradation into A [4]. Obviously, A and B are *interdependent* if they are mutually dependent.

These definitions are very general and, besides including evident and direct dependencies, embrace more complex behaviors, such as amplifications, domino effects, and loops.

Indeed, in highly interdependent scenarios, a degradation in one infrastructure or subsystem may generate consequences on the others, which are not easy to represent. For instance, a failure in a given infrastructure may induce degradations into another one; this may induce some further degradation into the first infrastructure, exacerbating the original problem, and so on. Another relevant example is *indirect* (inter)dependency; in this case two infrastructures or subsystems may be (inter)dependent even if they do not directly interact, that is, when their interaction is mediated by means of a chain of (inter)dependencies.

In the literature many approaches have been proposed to address the problem of interdependent critical infrastructures; these methods are, typically, adopted in order to perform "what if?" analyzes and ex-post simulations, with the aim to understand structural vulnerabilities, to asses and mitigate the risk of domino effects and multiple disruptions, and to provide a support to decision makers. In [3], the authors emphasize how dependency and interdependency should be analyzed with respect to different dimensions. In particular they catalog dependencies into four, not mutually exclusive, classes:

- *Physical dependency*: Two infrastructures are physically dependent if the operations of one infrastructure depend on the physical output of the other.
- *Cyber dependency*: An infrastructure presents a cyber dependency if its state depends on information transmitted by means of the information infrastructure.
- *Geographical dependency*: A geographic dependency occurs when elements of multiple infrastructures are in close spatial proximity. In this case, particular events, such as an explosion or a fire in an element of an infrastructure, may create a failure in one or more near infrastructures.
- *Logical dependency*: Two infrastructures are logically dependent if their dependency is generated via control, regulatory, or other mechanisms that cannot be considered physical, geographical, or cyber.

The above categories have been further enriched in [5] by explicitly considering also the following:

- *Sociological dependency*: An infrastructure shows a sociological dependency when its operativeness is affected by the spreading of "disorder" related to human activities, that is, the emerge and diffusion of collective behaviors that have some negative impact on the capability of the infrastructure to correctly work.

The representation of human behavior within models is a challenging yet mandatory task. In fact the ability to take into account malicious behaviors, lack of coordination and cooperation among human operators, and sociological interactions and dynamics (such as strikes or the spread of an epidemic) will tremendously enrich the predictive ability of models. In [6], it is emphasized that, to correctly understand the behavior of interdependent infrastructures, it is mandatory to adopt a three-layered perspective:

- *Physical layer*: the physical component of the infrastructure, for example, the grid for the electrical network;
- *Cyber layer*: hardware and software components of the system devoted to control and manage the infrastructure, for example, Supervisory Control and Data Acquisition (SCADA) and Distributed Control System (DCS);
- *Organizational layer*: procedures and functions used to define activities of human operators and to support cooperation among infrastructures.

Notice that a similar kind of decomposition was used also to analyze the 2003 blackout in the United States and Canada [7]. Most of existing methodologies can be referred as *Holistic*, since each infrastructure is represented as a unique, monolithic entity. Among the others, the *Input–Output Inoperability Model* (IIM) [8] gained large attention. Within this class of models, however, the interactions between different infrastructures are modeled with an high level of abstraction, while the behavior of subsystems is masked. Such an high level of abstraction (and simplification) does not take into account the structure and the geographical extension of the infrastructures. Considering each infrastructure as an atomic entity represents a very crude simplification that does not take into account its geographical extension and its structure. There is, therefore, the need to adopt bottom-up approaches, as largely done when dealing with scarce or ill-defined macro-scale information, like in the field of bio-complexity.

Following the bottom-up philosophy, each infrastructure can be decomposed into a set of elementary interconnected components, taking into account both intra-infrastructure and cross-infrastructure dependencies and interdependencies. In order to obtain more insight on the behavior of interdependent infrastructures, a first step is to represent them as complex networks composed of similar basic elements (i.e., a network of distributed and interconnected generators may represent an electrical infrastructure), inspecting emerging behaviors generated by the interconnection of such elements [9,10,11,12]. The assumption of homogeneity, however, limits the applicability of these methodologies, since in real cases infrastructures are composed of highly heterogeneous subsystems; moreover, topological methods typically limit their scope to the geographical interaction of subsystems.

A step further is done by adopting *Simulative* perspective, focusing on a sophisticated representation of the isolated behavior of subsystems and then considering their interaction by means of simulation platforms and tools. Within this latter category, the most diffused is the *Agent-Based* approach [13,14], where infrastructures are decomposed into a set of interacting *software agents*, each with a dynamic and with heterogeneous level of abstraction.

In order to enhance the comprehension of highly interdependent scenarios, in [15,16], the agent-based perspective was further enriched, considering, at the same time, multiple and partly overlapping representations of the scenario (i.e., physical, functional, and global representations).

3   Holistic approaches

Holistic approaches (See Figure 1) are, generally speaking, very abstract, simplified, and strategic oriented. These frameworks can be setup quite easily; even if several important aspects are neglected (e.g., the geographical dispersion that characterize several infrastructures), they have the merit to be compact and understandable; moreover, these methods allow to represent several interdependent infrastructures at the same time, even if all the interaction is generally reduced to an abstract parameter, the inoperability.

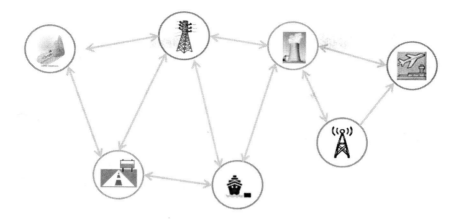

Figure 1: Holistic approaches. Within this framework infrastructures are considered as a whole, focusing on their high-level interaction.

Among the others the IIM model [8] and its further evolutions (for instance, the *Dynamic Input–Output Model* (D-IIM) [17], which considers the *dynamic* of the system, until an equilibrium is reached, or the *Multi-Regional IIM Model* (MR-IIM) [18], which allows to represent multi-sectoral and multiregional economic interdependencies) are widely diffused.

The main objective of the IIM model, introduced in [8,17] as an application of the economic theories of the Nobel Prize winner Wassily Leontief [19], is to represent within a simple framework the global effects of negative events in scenarios composed of highly interdependent infrastructures.

With a high level of approximation, the approach assumes that each infrastructure is modeled as an atomic entity, whose level of operability depends on the availability of *resources* supplied by the other infrastructures. Then, an event (e.g., a failure) that reduces the operational capability of the i-th infrastructure may induce degradation also in the other infrastructures that require goods or services produced by the i-th one. These degradations may be further propagated to other infrastructures (cascade effect) and even exacerbate the situation of the i-th one due to the presence of feedback loops.

The model, based on economic data, analyzes how the effects of natural outages or terroristic attacks in one infrastructure may affect the others, highlighting cascading effects and intrinsic vulnerabilities. The main assumption, for this approach, is that "two companies with a large amount of economic interaction will have a similarly large amount of physical interdependency" [17].

The estimation of such interaction has been addressed in many different ways; however, the most diffused and reliable data sources (for the United States) are the Bureau of Economic Analysis (BEA) database of national Input–Output (I-O) accounts and the Regional Input–Output Multiplier System (RIMS II).

The BEA database provides a series of tables depicting the production and consumption of *commodities* (goods and resources) by various sectors in the

U.S. economy. These data are then combined to calculate the *Leontief technical coefficients*, which are used within the IIM framework.

In the original Leontief model, each industry is assumed to produce a single commodity; since this assumption is not realistic, the BEA considers different commodities for each industry and provides two different data matrices: the *industry by commodity* and the *commodity by industry* matrices [20]. These matrices, often referred as *make* and *use*, have to be composed to derive the I-O matrix [17,21].

Mathematically, IIM describes these phenomena on the basis of the level of inoperability associated to each infrastructure. The inoperability of the *i*-th infrastructure, at each time instant k, is represented by the variable $x_i \in [0,1]$, where $x_i = 0$ means that the infrastructure is fully operative, while $x_i = 1$ stands for complete inoperability. In a very general formulation, IIM model can be written as follows:

$$x(k + 1) = Ax(k) + c, \tag{1}$$

where x and c are the vectors composed, respectively, by the level of inoperability and by the external failure and A is the influence matrix, that is, the matrix of the technical coefficient of Leontief. The element a_{ij} of this matrix represents the fraction of inoperability transmitted by the *j*-th infrastructure to the *i*-th one or, in other terms, how much the inoperability of the *j*-th infrastructure influences the *i*-th infrastructure.

Although the IIM framework is very compact and elegant, and is able to model cascading effects, its high degree of abstraction does not allow to perform accurate analyzes on the real nature of dependencies; in fact such an approach considers only relations that involve whole infrastructures, while it is impossible to understand and represent the contribution of each subsystem. This latter aspect is fundamental, in order to address the huge complexity of geographically dispersed systems.

Moreover, the economic origin of IIM model represents a structural limitation: In fact, even if use/make matrices are considered, taking into account the production and consumption of multiple commodities for each infrastructure, only the economic value of such commodities is typically available. Although some attempts have been proposed to decompose infrastructures with a finer grain perspective and relate the Leontief coefficients to components or subsystems [13], it is difficult to retrieve exact quantitative data required to setup the model. In fact, IIM models are typically based on macro-economic data, which cannot be easily decomposed. An alternative, then, is to represent interdependency according to the sector-specific knowledge of operators, technicians, and stakeholders.

Anyhow, since each stakeholder has a limited knowledge of the interaction phenomena that may cross the boundary of the single infrastructure, there is the need to involve the different stakeholders and interact with them in order to correlate, compare, and encode their sector-specific knowledge. An attempt in such a direction has been done in [22], where IIM coefficients have been assessed by means of specific questionnaires and technical interviews. Another effective approach, introduced in [14] is the *Agent-Based IIM Model* (AB-IIM), where the production, consumption, and transmission of resources at low level was considered, providing interdependency matrices with a physical meaning.

4   Critical Infrastructures as Complex Systems

In the past century, the scientific community has been more and more devoted to decompose and analyze reality, assuming that complexity would be easily reduced if every elementary subsystem was perfectly known. Unfortunately, this will never happen; in fact, according to Aristotle's *Metaphysics*, "The whole is more than the sum of its parts." Indeed in many fields complexity arises when the *interaction* between elementary parts is considered. A *Complex System*, then, is a system composed of interconnected parts that as a whole exhibit one or more properties not obvious from the properties of the individual parts [23]. This characteristic is called *emergence*. Consider, for instance, the human brain, which is composed of a huge set of heavily interconnected neurons, or the ecosystem, whose behavior cannot be fully explained by considering only the isolated behavior of animals and plants.

Indeed, critical infrastructures show a number of structural and "behavioral" features that cannot be explained by considering isolated infrastructures or subsystems; such properties have been widely investigated in the past years [24,25,26,27,28]. The promise of these efforts is to unveil relevant insights on growth mechanisms, causes of vulnerability, dynamic behavior under perturbation, onset of emerging phenomena, and so on, even neglecting some peculiar characteristics.

According to the recent developments there are two aspects that, if properly analyzed, may allow to gain relevant insights on critical infrastructures:

- the study of *topological* properties of the graph representing the infrastructure and
- the study of *functional*, emerging behaviors and properties that arise when the different subsystem are considered as dynamically coupled systems, (See Figure 2) relying on some functional model able to reproduce the dynamic process (mainly transport of some entity, like electricity, data, vehicles, etc.) taking place on them.

4.1   Topological analysis

Topological analysis of critical infrastructures received a renewed interest after the pioneering works of Strogartz and Barabasi [9,10]. In these studies, they emphasized that many technological, social, and biological networks may evolve without any central authority, nevertheless showing peculiar structural patterns like *small world* and *scale free*, with immediate consequences on many properties and characteristics of the corresponding infrastructures.

Specifically, it has been shown that scale-free models, with few hubs (i.e., nodes with a high number of connections) and a poorly connected peripheries, show good

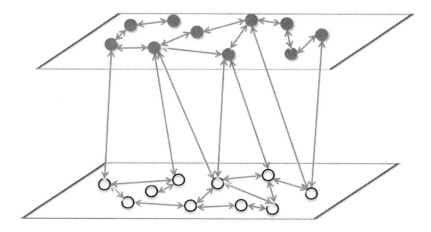

Figure 2: Topological approaches. Within this framework infrastructures are considered as networks composed of homogeneous elements, inspecting their topological properties (i.e., their resilience to node removal) or their functional behavior (i.e., the effect of node removal on the power flow).

resilience against accidental (or random) failures but are prone to deliberate attacks [29]. At the same time, the small-world property, which implies low average path lengths with respect to the number of nodes in the network, can lead to a very fast propagation of pandemic events, carried out by viruses, failures, or ill-services.

These approaches, in their most simple formulation, assume that each infrastructure is composed of a set of identical elements (generally represented as nodes on a graph) and infer dependencies analysis assuming some sort of relationship existing among nodes belonging to different networks [12,30,31].

Within this framework the degree of interdependency is generally assessed by taking into account structural properties of the overall graph (e.g., connectivity, betweennes, minimal path length, etc.), either in normal or critical conditions (i.e., after the disruption of some nodes or edges) [25]. These approaches, therefore, operate with an ON/OFF assumption, that is, each node either is fully working or it is completely out of work.

Topological analysis is quite easy to setup, since only the topologies of the different infrastructures considered are required.

However, although this approach is very effective in the case of two infrastructures characterized by a single predominant dependency mechanism (e.g., physical), the generalization to multiple infrastructures and dependency mechanisms is absolutely not straightforward.

Indeed these methods assume physical couplings as the primary source of interdependency while, especially for highly technological and automated infrastructures, cyber dependency is not considered.

Moreover, it is worth to notice that large technological infrastructures do not often show a clear "scale-free" structure, especially due to technological constraints that limit the growth of node's degrees [32]. As a consequence, results about robustness and resilience, based on the assumption of pure scale-freeness, cannot be directly applied in many technological contexts, leaving the issues related to structural vulnerability to be differently evaluated on each case [25].

Finally, in several cases, for example, for telecommunication network, topologic analyses are unsatisfactory because the static properties of the network do not have immediate consequences on its capability to provide the intended services (i.e., because of the presence of buffers, batteries, and multiple paths).

To overcome the above issues, it has been suggested to consider also network dynamics, and to this end they superimpose to the topological structure some form of flux dynamic models [33].

4.2 Functional analysis

Unlike the structural analysis, functional analysis of Critical Infrastructure is an hard task. Besides the intrinsic complexity of the topic, that is due to the lack of accurate and complete functional data of the infrastructures, often treated as confidential and classified by the stakeholders.

Even if in the literature there are several studies devoted to the functional analysis of a single infrastructure, only recently some studies about coupled infrastructures have appeared. The results reported in the literature emphasize how structural and functional vulnerability are substantially blandly correlated concepts that capture different properties, that is, two networks should be strongly coupled from the structural point of view, and in the same time lightly coupled when considering the functional properties and vice versa. Unfortunately, there are no final indications able to emphasize which one of these properties is the most relevant to explain those apparent incoherences.

In order to overcome such limitations, some simplifying hypothesis are generally assumed, enabling the development of "simpler" functional models, still able to capture the basic features of the networks but disregarding the most complex effects related to the exact technological implementations.

Then, the main aim of functional analysis is to evaluate the effects on the flows existing on the different networks and induced by simple topological perturbations. However, in order to perform a functional vulnerability assessment it is not sufficient to acquire information about the topological structure of the network, but there is also the need to model the characteristics of the fluxes and their specific parameters. This introduces several degrees of freedom into the model that may drive to erroneous conclusions.

Kurant and Thiran [34] have analyzed a system composed of several homogenous networks (i.e., of similar nature) interacting by exchanging loads, while in [35] there is an attempt in the direction of studying heterogeneous inter-dependent networks (i.e., formed by infrastructures of different nature), showing that the coupling makes the system more susceptible to large failure. A similar result has been reported in [30] where statistical mechanics and mean field theory are used to extrapolate steady state solutions in response to removal of a fraction of nodes. In [36] there is an attempt to formalize the interdependent dynamics among several heterogeneous infrastructures. In this framework, a metric for the level of functionality of an infrastructure is given by the sum of the functionality of the infrastructure components divided by the number of components. This approach has been used in [31] to analyze the interconnection of electric grid and telephony network: To investigate the effect, on the telephony network, of removing from the power distribution network one or two nodes, they introduce as metric the remaining fraction of functional telecommunication nodes. A similar formalism has been proposed in [37] where five types of infrastructure interdependencies are presented and incorporated into a network flow framework and tested with reference to the lower Manhattan region of New York. In [11,33] the interconnection properties of an electric grid and a Telecommunications (TLC) network that mimic the Italian situation are studied, relying on the *DC Power Flow Model* [38] to represent the electric power flow and considering also the packet routing in the TLC network. It has been shown that the cut of one or more links induces a change of the power flow distributions over the network. However, exploiting this simple model, it results that, for several different cuts, a solution is inhibited by the physical constraints imposed by the model itself. In other terms, due to overload conditions or unbalancing situations, the electric grid is no longer able to supply energy, implying the presence of possible blackouts if any corrective action is taken. Such a kind of dramatic consequences do not comply with the real data (and the common sense). Indeed, in order to prevent such catastrophic conditions, the operators of the electric networks continuously perform corrective and adjustment actions to limit the insurgence of blackouts. Hence, in order to take into account such mechanisms of self-tuning, there is the need to consider also some *re-dispatching* strategies that, miming the typical policies adopted by electrical operators, enable to modulate produced and dispatched powers [11].

The key aspect of such methods, therefore, is that complex behaviors in highly interdependent scenarios can be evaluated by focusing on the interaction among sets of simple and well-known elementary components; the true weak point, however, is that only homogeneous subsystems are typically considered while, in real scenarios, infrastructures are composed of highly heterogeneous subsystems, each characterized by a particular behavior. Moreover, it is not easy to extend such methodologies in order to consider the interaction among multiple and heterogeneous infrastructures.

5   Simulative approaches

In order to overcome the limitations of a mere topological framework, *simulative* approaches are introduced as methods focused on the analysis of the dynamic of each single component; then, the interdependency existing among the infrastructures is evaluated considering the interaction among such subsystems (See Figure 3).

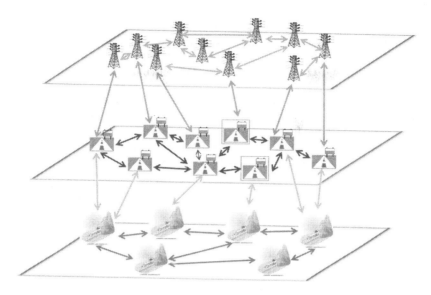

Figure 3: Simulative agent-based approaches. Infrastructures are decomposed into a set of software agents or entities, focusing on their behaviors; then the interconnection among these entities is considered, taking into account both intra-domain and inter-domain dependencies.

Generally, these approaches are quantitative in nature and operative oriented. In fact, it is possible to consider a continuous level of degradation in the component functionalities and the concurrent presence of several types of phenomena (like the absence of resources, external failures, and internal dynamics).

Simulative approaches, therefore, are mainly devoted to provide an answer to the following questions:

- What are the consequences of attacks, failures, incidents, and natural disasters on the different infrastructures existing in a given area in terms of national security, economic impact, public health, and conduct of government?
- The failure of which elements, once affected by failures, have the largest impact in the areas, taking into account both direct consequences and those induced by domino effects?

These methods, then, exploit the power of simulation platforms in order to estimate the impact of a given failure into a scenario composed by several heterogeneous and interdependent infrastructures (see, among the others [39,40,41]).

In order to deploy a simulation scenario, the researchers have to acquire/define:

- the internal model of each single component of the different infrastructures;
- the intra-dependency model, that is, how components interact inside each single infrastructure; and
- the interdependency model, that is, how components belonging to different infrastructures interact.

A variety of simulation have been developed in these years to analyze the operational aspects of individual infrastructures (e.g., load flow and stability programs for electric power networks, connectivity and hydraulic analyzes for pipeline systems, traffic management models for transportation networks). In addition, simulation frameworks that allow the coupling of multiple, interdependent infrastructures are beginning to emerge [39,40,41,42]. The Idaho National Lab conducts an interesting overview of the different approaches and tools used for the modeling and the simulation of interdependent infrastructures [39]. Another useful review about simulation tools is those performed inside the Design of an Interoperable European Federated Simulation Network (DIESIS) project [43].

Unfortunately, the set up of such simulators is a hard challenge; in fact a huge amount of detailed data is required to tune the models, and often, subjective hypothesis are introduced by the modelers, influencing the correctness of the solutions.

One of the most promising patterns for the analysis of the interdependencies between complex networks is the agent-based paradigm [44]. The fundamental idea that drives these models is that the complex behavior is the fruit of the interactions between autonomous and elementary individuals, which operate on the basis of simple rules, and that interacting together makes the collective behavior of the system emerge.

Nevertheless, in order to provide more insight on the overall System of Systems, *Multilayer* approaches have recently been introduced [15,16,45] as an extension of the agent-based paradigm able to consider, at the same time, multiple and partly overlapping representations of the same scenario, in order to capture the most important behaviors and dynamics from different perspectives.

5.1 Agent-based approaches

Within the agent-based framework, the behavior of an interdependent infrastructure is analyzable by resorting to a bottom-up approach, which models the whole system starting from the (local) behavioral knowledge of single components and then taking into account the interaction among these subsystems. Infrastructures, then, are decomposed into a set of interconnected *software agents* or *entities* [44].

A good example of such simulators is EPOCHS [40], which is designed to analyze interactions between the electric grid and telecommunications networks. Another example is SimCIP, which is being developed under the IRRIIS Project [42].

The most challenging issue is how to encode different, vague, and often contradictory information sources; a probabilistic approach seems not feasible, since here information is vague and linguistic, rather than stochastic.

In order to overcome these limitations, in [41] the Critical Infrastructure Simulation by Interdependent Agents (CISIA) simulator was introduced, as an

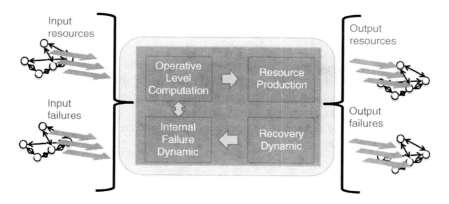

Figure 4:   Detail of an entity within CISIA framework. The whole model is composed of n entities belonging to N different infrastructures, which exchange m different types of resources and p different typologies of failures, belonging to M and P networks, respectively; each of these networks is used to take into account a specific concept of proximity.

agent-based framework where the behavior of entities and their interaction are modeled by means to fuzzy logic and fuzzy inference. Figure 4 represents the detail of an entity; within this framework the exchange of different classes of resources and failures is explicitly modeled. Besides computing the operative level, the behavior of each entity can be influenced by internal failures; moreover, the severity of failures can be influenced by the operational conditions of the entity and by the presence of recovery/restoration mechanisms.

Within such an approach, the exchange of resources and the spread of failures were represented, also taking into account the delays and dissipations due to the transportation of resources and failures and peculiar internal dynamics of the different agents. This approach has been successfully tested on a realistic scenario on a regional scale, composed of 233 entities belonging to 7 infrastructures and exchanging 43 quantities (of which 13 failures) by means of 13 networks for a total of about 844 links.

5.2   Multilayer approaches

As exposed above, limiting the scope to the interaction among subsystems may lead to crude approximations [6], in fact, besides being a set of interconnected components, an infrastructure is characterized by emerging functional behaviors and is greatly influenced by human behavior and sociological phenomena. When dealing with complex, highly interdependent scenarios, a single perspective may be reductive, as stressed in [46].

An effective approach, then, is to take into account multiple representations of the same reality, each devoted to highlight a particular class of phenomena.

In [15], critical infrastructures are represented according to three hierarchical layers:

- *Micro-level*: represents the physical components that constitute the functional elements of an infrastructures (i.e., electrical equipments, gas valves, etc.),
- *Meso-level*: represents an infrastructure network at the system level (i.e., network nodes and links, power generators and loads, etc.),
- *Macro-level*: represents the territory or zone that depend on the service provide by the infrastructure.

Within this framework, each level is considered as a nested subsystem, which can be analyzed independently. Moreover, the propagation of effects is assumed to spread from the micro- to the macro-level, neglecting downstream consequences and focusing on the effect of outages and failures on higher levels.

A more sophisticated approach is the *Mixed Holistic–Reductionistic* (MHR) framework, introduced in [45] and refined in [16], where three not mutually exclusive layers were considered:

- *Reductionistic layer*: Infrastructures are decomposed, following the agent-based perspective, into a set of interrelated subsystems. Physical behaviors and dynamics are encoded at this level. Moreover, it is possible to represent the spreading of failures with a physical meaning (i.e., a fire blast).
- *Service layer*: Infrastructures are decomposed according to a functional perspective, considering entities able to provide aggregate resources or services. At this level, it is possible to represent infrastructure functionalities provided to the final customers (i.e., [GSM], VoIp services) or consider intermediate services and behaviors required for the correct operativeness of the same or different infrastructures (i.e., power network reconfiguration, message dispatching, etc.). At this level, it is possible to represent higher level failures (i.e., computer viruses, sociological failures), which are not easy to represent at lower level.
- *Holistic layer*: Analogously to IIM model, at this level the global interaction among infrastructures is analyzed. At this level, it is possible to model complex phenomena, for example, a strike, which are difficult to represent at the other levels.

Starting from previous experience of CISIA simulator, the MHR–CISIA [16] tool was developed, in order to take into account the above three layers, considering both intra-layer and inter-layer interactions. Such an approach has been used within the MICIE European Project [47] as the modeling framework for the definition of a distributed online risk predictor.

6 Conclusions

In this chapter, the most diffused approaches for the modeling and simulation of interdependent critical infrastructures have been reviewed.

Starting from a pure holistic approach, where infrastructures are modeled with an high level of abstraction, and taking into account economic interaction, infrastructures are subsequently decomposed into networked sets of homogeneous subsystems, considering their topological properties or even the flow dynamic under critical conditions. However, topological approaches are not easily extensible to multiple, highly heterogeneous scenarios; in order to overcome these limitations, simulative approaches are introduced. Initially, infrastructures are decomposed into sets of software agents, focusing on their internal behavior; then the interaction among these subsystems are inspected. Finally, multilayered models try to capture interdependency phenomena by considering multiple agent-based layers, with a physical, functional, or systemic perspective.

Increasing the complexity of models may lead to more sophisticated and predictive representations; however, as the level of detail increases, it is hard to retrieve adequate quantitative data. Moreover, each stakeholder has a good knowledge of its infrastructure and subsystems, while the comprehension of cross-infrastructure dependencies is generally poor and unclear.

There is, therefore, the need to define adequate data-collection procedures, in order to cope with uncertain, incomplete, and often contradictory information.

References

[1] M. Suter & E. Brunner, *International CIIP Handbook 2008/2009*, Center for Security Studies, ETH Zurich, 2008.

[2] E.U. Commission, *Green Paper on a European Programme for Critical Infrastructure Protection COM(2005)576*, Commission of the European Communities, Brussels, 2005.

[3] S. Rinaldi, J. Peerenboom, & T. Kelly, "Identifying Understanding and Analyzing Critical Infrastructure Interdependencies," *IEEE Control System Magazine*, vol. 21, pp. 11–25, 2001.

[4] R. Setola, "How to Measure the Degree of Interdependencies among Critical Infrastructures," *International Journal of System of Systems Engineering*, vol. 2, no. 1, 2010.

[5] S. De Porcellinis, R. Setola, S. Panzieri & G. Ulivi, "Simulation of Heterogeneous and Interdependent Critical Infrastructures", *International Journal of Critical Infrastructures*, vol. 4, n 1/2, pp. 110–128, 2008.

[6] R. Macdonald & S. Bologna, "Advanced Modelling and Simulation Methods and Tools for Critical infrastructure Protection," *ACIP project report*, 2001.

[7] U.S. and Canada Power System Outage Task Force, "Final Report on the August 14, 2003 Blackout in the United States and Canada: Causes and Recommendations," 2004, http://reports.energy.gov.

[8] Y. Haimes & P. Jiang, "Leontief-Based Model of Risk in Complex Interconnected Infrastructures," *Journal of Infrastructure Systems*, vol. 7, no. 1, pp. 1–12, 2001.

[9] D. J. Watts & S. H. Strogartz, "Collective Dynamics of Small-World Networks," *Nature*, vol. 393, pp. 440–442, 1998.

[10] H. Jeong, S. P. Mason, A. L. Barabasi, & Z. N. Oltvai, "Lethality and Centrality in Protein Networks," *Nature*, vol. 411, pp. 41–42, 2001.

[11] S. De Porcellinis, L. Issacharoff, S. Meloni, V. Rosato, R. Setola, & F. Tiriticco, Modelling Interdependent Infrastructures Using Interacting Dynamical Models. *International Journal of Critical Infrastructures*, vol. 4, no. 1/2, pp. 63–79, 2008.

[12] L. Duenas-Osorio, J. I. Craig, B. J. Goodno, & A. Bostrom, "Interdependent Response of Networked Systems," *Journal of Infrastructure Systems*, vol. 13, no. 3, pp. 185–194, 2007.

[13] R. Setola, S. De Porcellinis, & M. Sforna, Critical Infrastructure Dependency Assessment Using the Input–Output Inoperability Model, *International Journal on Critical Infrastructure Protection*, vol. 2, no. 4, pp. 170–178, 2009.

[14] G. Oliva, S. Panzieri, & R. Setola, "Agent-Based Input–Output Interdependency Model," *International Journal on Critical Infrastructure Protection*, vol. 3, no. 2, pp. 76–82, 2010.

[15] C. Di Mauro, S. Bouchon, C. Logtmeijer, R. D. Pride, T. Hartung, & J. P. Nordvik, "A Structured Approach to Identifying European Critical Infrastructures," *International Journal of Critical Infrastructures*, vol. 6, no. 3, pp. 277–292, 2010.

[16] S. De Porcellinis, G. Oliva, S. Panzieri, & R. Setola, A Mixed Holistic–Reductionistic Approach to Model Interdependent Infrastructures, *Critical Infrastructure Protection IV*, M. Papa and S. Shenoi eds., vol. 311, pp. 215–227, Springer, Boston, 2009.

[17] Y. Haimes, B. Horowitz, J. Lambert, J. Santos, C. Lian, & K. Crowther, "Inoperability Input–Output Model for Interdependent Infrastructure Sectors I: Theory and Methodology," *Journal of Infrastructure Systems*, vol. 11, no. 2, pp. 67–79, 2005.

[18] K. G. Crowther & Y. Y. Haimes, "Development of the Multiregional Inoperability Input–Output Model (MRIIM) for Spatial Explicitness in Preparedness of Interdependent Regions," *Systems Engineering*, vol. 13, no 1, pp. 28–46, 2010.

[19] W. Leontief, *The Structure of the American Economy 1919–1939*. Oxford University Press, Oxford, 1951.

[20] J. Guo, A. M. Lawson, & M. A. Planting, "From Make-Use to Symmetric I-O Tables: An Assessment of Alternative Technology Assumptions," *Proceedings of the 14th International Conference on Input–Output Techniques*, Montreal, Canada, October 10–15, Bureau of Economic Affairs, U.S. Dept. of Commerce, Washington DC, 2002.

[21] E. Kujawski, "Multi-Period Model for Disruptive Events in Interdependent Systems," *Systems Engineering*, vol. 9, no. 4, pp. 281–295, 2006.

[22] R. Setola, S. De Porcellinis, & M. Sforna, "Critical Infrastructure Dependency Assessment Using the Input–Output Inoperability Model," *International Journal of Critical Infrastructure Protection*, vol. 2, no. 4, pp. 170–178, 2009.

[23] C. Joslyn & L. Rocha, "Towards Semiotic Agent-Based Models of Socio-Technical Organizations," *Proceedings of the Conference on AI, Simulation and Planning in High Autonomy Systems Conference*, Tucson, AZ, pp. 70–79, 2000.

[24] R. Albert, I. Albert, & G. L. Nakarado, "Structural Vulnerability of the North American Power Grid," *Physical Review E*, vol. 69, no. 2, pp. 025103(R), 2004.

[25] P. Crucitti, V. Latora, & M. Marchiori, "A Topological Analysis of the Italian Electric Power Grid," *Physica A*, vol. 338, no. 1–2, pp. 92–97, 2004.

[26] R. Pastor-Satorras, A. Vazquez, & A. Vespignani, "Dynamical and Correlation Properties of the Internet," *Physical Review Letters*, vol. 87, no. 25, pp. 276–282, 2001.

[27] L. Issacharoff, S. Bologna, V. Rosato, G. Dipoppa, R. Setola, & F. Tronci, "A Dynamical Model for the Study of Complex System's Interdependence," in *Proceedings of the International Workshop on Complex Network and Infrastructure Protection (CNIP'06)*, Rome, March 28–29, pp. 276–282, 2006.

[28] F. Tiriticco, S. Bologna, & V. Rosato, "Topological Properties of High-Voltage Electrical Transmission Networks," *Electric Power Systems Research*, vol. 77, no. 2, pp. 99–105, 2006.

[29] R. Albert & A. L. Barabasi, "Statistical Mechanics of Complex Networks," *Reviews of Modern Physics*, vol. 74, no. 1, pp. 47–97, 2002.

[30] B. A. Carreras, D. E. Newman, P. Gradney, V. E. Lynch, & I. Dobson, "Inter-dependent Risk in Interacting Infrastructure Systems," *Proceedings of the 40th Hawaii International Conference on System Sciences*, Hawaii, January 3–6, 2007.

[31] N. K. Svendsen & S. D. Wolthusen, "Multigraph Dependency Models for Heterogenous Critical Infrastructures," *Proceedings of the First Annual IFIP TC 11.10 International Conference on Critical Infrastructure Protection*, Hanover, NH, March, pp. 337–350, 2007.

[32] L. A. N. Amaral, A. Scala, M. Barthelemy, & H. E. Stanley, "Classes of Small-World Networks," *Proceedings of the National Academy of Sciences of the United States of America*, vol. 97, no. 21, October 10, pp. 11149–11152, 2000.

[33] V. Rosato, L. Issacharoff, S. Meloni, F. Tiriticco, S. De Porcellinis, & R. Setola, "Modelling Interdependent Infrastructures Using Interacting Dynamical Models," *International Journal of Critical Infrastructures*, vol. 4, no. 1/2, pp. 63–79, 2008.

[34] M. Kurant & P. Thiran, "Layered Complex Networks," *Physical Review Letters*, vol. 96, no. 13, 2006.

[35] D. E. Newman, B. Nkei, B. A. Carreras, I. Dobson, V. E. Lynch, & P. Gradney, "Risk Assessment in Complex Interacting Infrastructure Systems, HICSS 05," *Proceedings of the 38th Annual Hawaii International Conference on System Sciences*, IEEE Press, Big Island, HI, January 3–6, p. 63, 2005.

[36] N. K. Svendsen & S. D. Wolthusen, "Analysis and Statical Properties of Critical Infrastructure Interdependency Multiflow Models," *Proceedings from the Eighth Annual IEEE SMC Information Assurance Workshop, United States Military Academy*, West Point, NY, June, pp. 247–254, 2007.

[37] E. E. Lee, J. E. Mitchell, & W. A. Wallace, "Restoration of Services in Inter-dependent Infrastructure Systems: A Network Flow Approach," *IEEE Trasactions on Systems, Man and Cybernetics—Part C*, vol. 37, no. 6, pp. 1303–1317, 2007.

[38] P. A. J. Wood, & B. F. Wollenberg, *Power Generation, Operation and Control*, John Wiley, New York, 1984.

[39] P. Pederson, D. Dudenhoeffer, S. Hartley, & M. Permann, *Critical Infrastructure Interdependency Modeling: A Survey of U.S. and International Research*, Idahho National Laboratory, Idaho Falls, ID, 2006.

[40] K. Hopkinson, K. Birman, R. Giovanini, D. Coury, X. Wang, & J. Thorp, EPOCHS: Integrated Commercial Off-the-Shelf Software for Agent-Based Electric Power and Communication, *Proceedings of the Winter Simulation Conference*, New Orleans, LA, December 7–10, pp. 1158–1166, 2003.

[41] S. De Porcellinis, S. Panzieri, & R. Setola, "Modelling Critical Infrastructure via a Mixed Holistic Reductionistic Approach," *International Journal of Critical Infrastructures*, vol. 5, no. 1/2, pp. 86–99, 2009.

[42] IRRIIS Consortium, The IRRIIS European Integrated Project, Fraunhofer Institute for Intelligent Analysis and Information Systems, Sankt-Augustin, Germany (www .irriis.org).

[43] EU project DIESIS (Design of an Interoperable European Federated Simulation Network for Critical InfraStructures), http://www.diesis-project.eu/.

[44] T. Brown, W. Beyeler, & D. Barton, "Assessing Infrastructure Interdependencies: The Challenge of Risk Analysis for Complex Adaptive Systems," *International Journal of Critical Infrastructures*, vol. 1, no. 1, pp. 108–117, 2004.

[45] S. Panzieri, S. De Porcellinis, & R. Setola, "Model critical infrastructure via a mixed holistic–reductionistic approach," *International Journal on Critical Infrastructures*, vol. 5, pp. 86–99, 2009.

[46] F. Flammini, N. Mazzocca, C. Pragliola, & V. Vittorini, A Study on Multiformalism Modelling of Critical Infrastructures, *Proceedings of the 3rd International Workshop on Critical Information Infrastructures Security* (CRITIS 2008), LNCS 5508, Rome, Italy, October 13–15, 2008, pp. 336–343, 2009.

[47] MICIE European Project, http://www.micie.eu.

Graphical formalisms for modelling critical infrastructures

A. Bondavalli, P. Lollini & L. Montecchi
Department of Systems and Computer Science, Florence University, Florence, Italy

Abstract

Modelling and simulation are well-suited approaches to analyse critical infrastructures (CIs), providing useful insights into how components' failures might propagate along interconnected infrastructures, possibly leading to cascading or escalating failures, and to quantitatively assess the impact of these failures on the service delivered to users. This chapter focuses on the usage of graphical formalisms for modelling and simulation of CIs. It first identifies and motivates the main requirements that a modelling and simulation framework for CI analysis should have. Then, it provides an overview of the available graphical formalisms, discussing how they have been used in the literature for CI analysis and assessing the extent to which they actually meet the identified modelling and simulation requirements. The second part of the chapter investigates how a subset of the identified requirements are actually met adopting a specific graphical modelling formalism, the Stochastic Activity Networks formalism, which has been extensively used by the authors of this chapter in past European FP6 projects dealing with CI analysis.

Keywords: Critical Infrastructures, Modelling and Simulation, Graphical Formalisms, Modelling Requirements, Stochastic Activity Networks

1 Introduction

Critical infrastructures (CIs) are complex and highly interdependent systems, networks and assets that provide essential services in our daily life. They span a number of key sectors, including energy, finance, authorities, hazardous materials, telecommunications, information technology, supply services and many others. In view of this widely recognized criticality, it is paramount that they be reliable and resilient to continue providing their essential services. Hence, there is the need (i) to build such CIs following sound engineering design principles, (ii) to protect them against both accidental and malicious faults and (iii) to evaluate them to assess their degree of resilience/trustworthiness.

Modelling and simulation play a key role in CI protection, since experimenting on such critical systems is often costly or dangerous. Because of the complexity and interconnectedness of such systems, modelling and simulating CIs is a well-recognized challenge, especially if the interactions between different infrastructures are to be considered. Several approaches to master this complexity have been proposed in the past literature. In this chapter, we focus on modelling and simulation approaches that are supported by *graphical formalisms*. Besides surveying the available graphical formalisms, we will also inspect their capability to satisfy a set of basic requirements that a modelling and simulation framework for CI analysis should satisfy, both considering the works available in the literature and basing on the experiences gained by the authors of this chapter in recently ended European projects.

The rest of the chapter is organized as follows. Modelling and simulation requirements are identified and discussed in Section 2. Section 3 surveys the available graphical formalisms and discusses, from the authors' perspective, the extent to which they actually meet the basic requirements. In Section 4, we deeply investigate how a subset of the basic requirements provided in Section 2 are actually met by a specific modelling formalisms, the Stochastic Activity Networks (SAN) formalism, which has been extensively used by the authors of this chapter in past European FP6 projects. Finally, conclusions are drawn in Section 5.

2   Requirements for CI modelling and simulation

Requirements for CI modelling and simulation are strictly related to the objectives of the analysis. Among the approaches proposed in the past literature, some of them focus on the interdependencies among infrastructures, and they elaborate integrated approaches capable of capturing the specific characteristics of the different CIs as well as their relationships. Complexity and heterogeneity can be overcome by modularity and composition, using multiformalism approaches (e.g., see [1]). For what concerns model solutions, the concept of *federated simulation* (e.g., see [1]) has emerged as a viable solution to the simulation of large and interconnected systems. Such approach aims at creating a composable simulator, supporting interoperability among separately developed simulators through a unified programming interface. Following this 'system of systems' philosophy, IEEE has defined the High-Level Architecture (HLA) specification [3] with the aim to provide a standardized interface. Works exist in literature that define requirements for the construction of a 'universal' CI modelling environment following such approach (e.g., see [2] and [5]). The main requirements for integrated modelling and simulation of CIs are as follows:

R1: *The integrated simulation environment should be able to represent physical, cyber, geographical and logical interdependencies.*

Four kinds of interdependencies between CIs have been defined in literature [6]. Such a universal simulation environment should take into account all these interactions and their effects.

R2: *The integrated simulation environment should be able to represent and simulate cascading effects.*

A cascading failure occurs when a disruption in one infrastructure causes the failure of a component in a second infrastructure, which consequently causes a disruption in the second infrastructure. Such dynamics should be taken into account in an integrated simulation approach.

R3: *Modelling and simulation solutions for CI analysis should provide a method for accommodating different simulation methodologies.*

Different infrastructure models may leverage different simulation methodologies. This requirement highlights the necessity for an approach to mediate the differences among simulation methodologies, for example, between continuous and discrete simulation methodologies.

Besides defining the requirements for an integrated modelling and simulation approach dealing with 'system of systems', it is paramount to analyse the requirements for modelling single, isolated infrastructures in order to faithfully represent the specificity of each domain. To the best of our knowledge, two of the most detailed works in identifying and discussing these modelling requirements are [5], which aims at evaluating the elements to be included in a composable simulator, and [7], which is specifically tailored to the electric power domain. Based on these works and on the experiences gained by the authors in two past European projects addressing CIs (see Section 4), we identified the following basic modelling requirements:

R4: *The formalism should support the modelling of large and hierarchically structured CIs in a convenient way.*

Many systems in general, and CIs in particular, have a natural hierarchical structure with a large number of components belonging to different levels and arranged in a treelike structure. At a certain level of detail such systems are typically composed by many similar components having the same logical structure, which can be grouped on the basis of their similarities. From a modeller's perspective a key need is to have some modelling features that facilitate the model construction exploiting such similarities. This would also provide benefits in model maintainability, readability and reusability.

R5: *The formalism should support the representation of discrete, continuous and hybrid state, using a compact representation.*

Most CIs are hybrid state systems, in the sense that part of their state-space is continuous and another part is discrete. The continuous state-space is usually related to the physical aspects of the system, which are governed by complex mathematical relations; the discrete part is instead related to the control layer, which comprises a set of operational states and decision policies.

R6: *The formalism should support the interaction with external tools and functions, which may properly capture the details of specific parts of the system.*
This requirement is also related to the application of the federated simulation approach described above. In general, being able to interact with external tools and functions allows the model to have access to external data, for example, data collected by experiments on the real infrastructure.

R7: *The formalism should support the definition and evaluation of both dependability and performance-oriented metrics.*
CIs are often subject to market constraints and must therefore achieve some predefined levels of performance in addition to fulfil their dependability requirements. It is the case, for example, of the electricity market within the electric power system (EPS) or QoS levels in networking systems. Therefore, an overall evaluation of a (critical) infrastructure is likely to be based on both dependability and performance-oriented metrics. The formalism should allow the specification of many different measures of performance, dependability and performability in a unified manner.

In the following section, we give an overview of the graphical formalisms introduced in the literature, and we shortly discuss how they fulfil the identified set requirements both concerning the 'system of systems' approach (*requirements R1–R3*) and an individual infrastructure analysis (*requirements R4–R7*).

3   Graphical formalisms for CI modelling and simulation

Several approaches to CI modelling and simulation have been adopted in the literature, each having different levels of detail, modelling power, user-friendliness and computational efficiency. The works in [8] and [9] provide a general understanding of common methods for CI analysis, including visualization and data-presentation techniques, while a specific survey focused on modelling and simulation can be found in [10]. For what concerns existing tools for CI analysis, a large collection of them is reviewed in [11] and [12].

Depending on the formalism, graphical information plays a different role in model construction and evaluation. Essentially, the use of graphical information to aid CI analysis may be grouped in few main areas, which are detailed in the following.

3.1   Graph-based techniques

Many approaches to CI modelling are based on graph-analysis techniques. In such approaches, the physical topology and configuration of the infrastructure are mapped to some kind of graph, which can then be analysed to reveal useful information about the system. Through this representation, many of the already available graph-analysis techniques can be used to analyse the behaviour of the modelled infrastructure(s). For example, using this representation, resource allocation problems may be formulated in terms of graph colouring problems, while some reliability properties may be analysed through clique problems [9].

To perform assessments with respect to faults or external attacks, CIs are often modelled as networks, and then nodes are progressively removed to evaluate the possible cascading effects on the system. These kinds of analyses are used to compare infrastructure designs and topologies, for example, showing the maximum number of random attacks that a certain topology may handle before becoming disconnected (e.g., see [13]).

Although these analyses may provide useful insights on the infrastructure properties, it is often necessary to take into account also other aspects of the system. Network flow approaches are used to model resource requirements and utilization among different infrastructures. In such paradigm, interdependent infrastructures are viewed as networks, with movement of commodities (i.e., material, electric power etc.) corresponding to flows and with services corresponding to a desired level of these flows. Approaches based on network flow are easily modelled using supply–demand graph; in such kind of graphs, nodes are seen either as supply, transhipment or demand nodes, while arcs represent links through which commodities flow from producers (supply) to consumers (demand) nodes. Nodes may be both producers and consumers at the same time; for example, a gas alimented power generator supplies electric power, but it demands natural gas to perform its function. Supply–demand graphs have been used, for example, in [14] to identify the telecommunication components which are more vulnerable to failures of power components within a certain CI design.

Different mathematical formalisms may be associated to supply–demand graphs, leading to many variants of such approach. In [15], link capacities are taken into account, considering both deterministic and stochastic values; in [16], nodes may have buffers to hold storable resources, for example, water or gas.

3.2 Petri Nets (PNs)

PNs and their extensions are graphical modelling formalisms that are widely used in dependability analysis. Although they have a simple graphical representation, they provide a great modelling power and are therefore well suited for the modelling of complex systems like CIs. Many variants of PN formalisms exist, which may have different properties and modelling power.

In [17], a set of CIs are modelled at a very high level of abstraction, focusing on interdependencies between them; then it is shown how invariant analysis on the PN model can be used to identify vulnerable elements in the scenario. The authors of [18], using the Generalized Stochastic Petri Net (GSPN) formalism, define some useful primitives to model common mode faults and cascading effects in CIs, using an actual power blackout as motivating example. In [19], a GSPN model is developed to evaluate the impact of a potential intrusion due to a cyber attack on the Supervisory Control and Data Acquisition (SCADA) system, which is in charge of controlling and monitoring the EPS. There are two submodels in the PN model, a firewall model and a password model, which are instantiated based on the configuration of the internal SCADA network and its possible access points. A combined modelling approach in the evaluation of the interdependencies between the electric power infrastructure and its SCADA system has been developed in [20], where the quantification is achieved through the integration of two models. The first is a SAN model, which concentrates on the structure of the power grid and its physical quantities; the second is a Stochastic Well-Formed Net (SWN) model, which concentrates on the algorithms of the control system and on the behaviour of the attacker. The scenario modelled in such work considers a situation in which a load shedding activity is needed to re-establish the nominal working conditions upon an electrical failure, but the control system is not working properly due to a Denial of Service (DoS) attack. Finally, in [21], PNs have been employed in the evaluation of pricing issues related to congestion in deregulated power market systems.

3.3 General simulation environments

A large collection of simulation environments exists for CI analysis, which can essentially be categorized in single domain and multiple domain simulators. The electric power infrastructure, together with telecommunication networks and transportations, has been the focus of development of domain-specific simulators, featuring many simulation tools having different granularity [12].

Graphical facilities play a key role in simulation environment: first, they allow the user to focus on the high-level details of the model and simulation experiments; next, a graphical simulation tool provides by its very nature a graphical representation of the model, which may be of invaluable benefit for model maintainability. Finally, user-friendliness may make the success of simulation tools: a well-designed graphical environment can provide cost-effective, integrated and automated support of simulation model development throughout the entire modelling and simulation life cycle.

Visualization refers to the discipline that 'focuses on helping people explore or explain data, typically through software systems that provide static or interactive visual representations' [8]. Visualization techniques may focus on graphical representation of the model itself, for example, 3D representation of infrastructure entities [22], or map overlay of multiple layers, which may include other infrastructure models or even Geographic Information System (GIS) data [23]. Other visualization techniques focus on the presentation of simulation results, contributing to the identification of correlation between the parameters of a system or the detection of logical interdependencies. Just to cite a few, these techniques include function fitting, overlaying, shading, spectral planes, interactive (and continuous) rotation of 3D displays [9].

3.4 Agent-based modelling and simulation

The agent-based paradigm is a promising approach to software development, which has been proven particularly useful in modelling and simulation of CIs.

It consists of a bottom-up approach to manage system complexity, in which the simulator is built as a population of interacting, intelligent *agents*. An agent is 'an autonomous system (software and/or hardware) that is situated in an environment (possibly containing other agents) and acts on it in order to pursue its own goals, and is often able to learn from previous experiences' [10]. Each agent is an individual entity with location, capabilities and memory. Interaction between them produces an *emergent behaviour,* that is, a behaviour which is not predictable by the knowledge of any single agent [24]. Using such approach, a simulator is developed, where an agent may model physical components of infrastructures, decision policies or, possibly, the external environment [4,24].

As other modelling techniques, the agent-based paradigm can be applied at different levels of detail, which are sometimes referred to as micro- and macro-agent-based simulation [25]. The micro-agent-based approach uses a bottom-up approach modelling for every single component of an infrastructure, putting them successively together to simulate the whole infrastructure(s). The macro-agent-based simulation represents a whole infrastructure with a single agent, hiding the implementation details from the other agents. Using such approach, it is also possible to apply the federated simulation approach, leaving the physical, detailed simulation of each infrastructure to some specific sector tool controlled by an associated agent and expose only a predefined interface to other agents.

In addition to visualization techniques that are not specific to agent-based modelling, but may be employed in any simulation tool, this approach is often supported by graphical facilities to aid the definition and development of agent-based simulators. The authors of [26] define a graphical way to represent entities and interdependencies in complex systems composed of different infrastructures, using Unified Modelling Language (UML) as graphical formalism; such entities are then mapped to one or more agents in the simulation environment. The example scenario takes into account a Civic Emergency Management system and its dependence on power grid (for the information system functionality), on communication network (for communications) and on transportation network (for emergency operations). Moreover, some specialized agent-based frameworks have built-in graphical capabilities to define the interconnection between the agents or even their behaviour. For example, the Repast Toolkit [27] allows the graphical specification of agents' behaviour, using graphical primitives like *task, decision, join, loop.*

3.5   Discussion of requirements

In this section, we discuss how *requirements* R1–R7 are actually fulfilled by the available formalisms and analysis approaches that have been proposed in the literature. Such evaluation is based on the authors' perception of the average capabilities of the formalisms belonging to each category and on their usefulness with respect to the identified requirements. The overall results are summarized in Table 1, where we denote with '+' the requirements that can be more easily achieved within the different categories.

Table 1: Evaluation of formalisms with respect to requirements

	R1	R2	R3	R4	R5	R6	R7
Graphs	+	+		+			
Petri nets	+	+		+			+
Simulation	+	+			+	+	
Agents	+	+	+			+	

Graph-based approaches are generally good at defining the hierarchical structure of the system (R4) and the interdependencies that exist between infrastructures (R1), as graphs are a natural way to represent relations between elements.
For the same reason, cascading failures may be represented as well (R2). The
limitations of graph-based approaches consist in their reduced scalability and
their limited modelling power. Graphs may be used by other advanced formalisms to represent the structure of the system or the analysed scenario, but with
this exception they are practically unable of integration with other modelling
tools (R3 and R6). Graph-based formalisms are often tailored to a specific measure or analysis type and do not allow the definition of different measures (R7).

Formalisms belonging to PN category are usually also well suited to the definition of performance and performability measures (R7), but they have similar
limitations of generic graph-based approaches. PN models allow the modelling
of interdependencies and cascading effects at a very high level of detail, but
representing the hierarchical structure of the whole system, taking into account
of all the interdependencies, may be a difficult task and the scalability of the
model is often a limiting factor. The extent to which they are able to represent
both discrete and continuous states (R5) highly depends on each individual PN
formalism, but with some exceptions, they are usually tailored to model discrete
state systems. Integration with other tools and differing simulation methodologies (R3 and R6) is not possible, with the exception of few PN formalisms.

Simulation packages may easily represent non-discrete system states (R5),
and to some extent they allow the modelling of interdependencies and cascading
effects (R1 and R2). Integration with external tools (R6) is possible, although it
often requires a significant effort to be achieved. The HLA and other similar initiatives are supposed to facilitate this task in the long run. Simulation environments may allow the evaluation of very complex measures, but they are usually
able to evaluate a limited predefined set of them.

Agents perform particularly well in satisfying the requirements related to
the integrated modelling and simulation approach (R1–R3): by their nature,
they model the system as a population of interdependent autonomous subsystems (i.e., agents). External tools can be usually integrated quite easily in agent-
based frameworks (R6), thanks to the macro-agent and federation approach.
Agent-based simulation frameworks have the same limitations that arise in
other simulation frameworks for what concerns the available measures that can
be evaluated.

Although there is no formalism category that, as a whole, is capable to fulfil all the identified requirements, some specific formalisms belonging to specific categories feature more advanced capabilities that can be used to profitably model complex systems as CIs. An example belonging to the PN class is the SAN formalism, which provides the modeller with some primitives that can be profitably exploited to fulfil the identified requirements, thus overcoming the limitations of most of the other PN-based models. In the next section, we provide more details on such capabilities, also showing in particular how to exploit some particular SAN features to model the hierarchical system structure in a convenient way (R4) and to facilitate the integration of external tools and functions (R6).

4   Practical experiences in modelling CIs: meeting the requirements with SAN

SAN [28] formalism is a powerful and flexible extension of PNs, and for its characteristics it has been extensively applied to model and analyse complex CIs. As discussed in the following, the formalism meets the whole set of identified requirements. The SAN capabilities in representing the different kind of interdependencies (*requirement* R1) have been discussed in [7], focusing on the cyber and physical interdependencies in the electric power domain. The same work has also inspected their use for capturing cascading failures (*requirement* R2) from the information control system towards the controlled electric power grid, which can finally lead to blackout phenomena. The accommodation of different simulation methodologies (*requirement* R3) could be supported by specific SAN primitives (input and output gates), general functions written in languages like C that could trigger different simulation methodologies. The representation of both discrete and continuous states (*requirement* R5) is another SAN feature: the SAN formalism supports continuous valued tokens, thanks to a special primitive called 'extended place' that allows token of more complex data types to be included in the model. Each extended place is assigned a 'type' (much like in ordinary programming languages), and it is allowed to hold tokens of such type. The definition and evaluation of both dependability and performance-oriented metrics (*requirement* R7) is fully met resorting to the Performance Variable (PV) reward model, which can be used to represent either dependability or performability measures.

In the following we will further discuss the two remaining *requirements* R4 and R6, instantiating them in the CRUTIAL and HIDENETS contexts, respectively. For each requirement, we analyse the useful features of the SAN formalism, and we show how they have been exploited in the projects to fulfil each requirement. The research activities on the usage of SAN for modelling CIs, started within these two projects, are now carried on within the ongoing Italian project PRIN [29] DOTS-LCCI, which focused on the analysis and evaluation of Large-Scale Complex Critical Infrastructures (LCCI).

4.1 CRUTIAL and HIDENETS: a brief introduction

The European project CRUTIAL [30] addressed new networked systems based on information and communication technology for the management of the electric power grid. A major research line of the project focused on the development of a model-based methodology for the dependability and security analysis of the power grid information infrastructures. One of the approaches pursued in CRUTIAL was a model-based quantitative support for the analysis and evaluation of critical scenarios in EPS, as incrementally documented in [7,31,32].

The European project HIDENETS [33] addressed the provisioning of available and resilient distributed applications and mobile services in highly dynamic environments characterized by unreliable communications and components. A set of representative use-case scenarios were identified, each one composed by different applications (mostly selected from the field of car-to-car and car-to-infrastructure communications), different network domains, different actors and characterized by different failure modes and challenges. As incrementally documented in [34] and [35], the authors of this chapter focused on the QoS analysis of a dynamic, ubiquitous Universal Mobile Telecommunication System (UMTS) network scenario, which comprised different types of mobile users, applications, traffic conditions and outage events reducing the available network resources.

4.2 On the usage of SAN to match requirement R4

Let us consider the EPS analysed within CRUTIAL, which is composed of two cooperating infrastructures: the Electric Infrastructure (EI) for electricity generation and transportation, and its Information Technology Based Control System (ITCS) in charge of monitoring and controlling the EI physical parameters and of triggering appropriate reconfigurations in emergency situations. A complete view of the EPS logical structure at regional level can be found in [7] and is illustrated in Figure 1.

In the lower part of Figure 1, we have depicted the main logical components that constitute the EI: generators (N_G), loads (N_L), substations (N_S) and power lines (A_L). From a topological point of view, the power transmission grid can be considered like a network, or a graph, in which the nodes of the graph are the generators, substations and loads, while the arcs are the power lines. In the upper part of Figure 1, we have depicted the logical structure of a regional ITCS, that is, the part of the information control system controlling and operating on a region of the transmission grid. The components LCS (Local Control System) and RTS (Regional Tele-Control System) differ for their criticality and for the locality of their decisions, and they can exchange grid status information and control data over a (public or private) network (ComNet component). LCS guarantees the correct operation of a node (generator, substation or load) and reconfigures the node in case of breakdown of some apparatus. RTS monitors its assigned region in order to diagnose faults in the power lines. In case of breakdowns, it chooses the most suitable corrective actions to restore the functionality

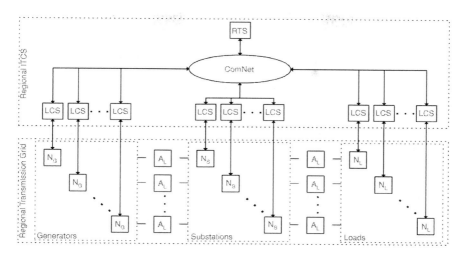

Figure 1: Logical structure of a regional transmission grid, with the associated information control system.

of the grid. When considering a large portion of the grid, we have to deal with a huge number of components that need to be modelled, replicated and composed to form the hierarchical structure of the whole EPS, as shown in Figure 1. A way to proceed could be to manually duplicate the template models representing the different basic components of EI (generators, loads, substations, power lines) and ITCS (LCS, RTS), to manually assign them a specific parameters setting and finally to compose them obtaining the model for the overall system. This modelling process can be very expensive in terms of time and very error prone, so we would like to have a modelling formalism that *facilitates the construction of the overall model allowing model composition and automatic model replication*. The hierarchical structure should be defined by automatically replicating the basic template models and composing them as needed. For example, the model that represents a generic power line needs to be replicated to obtain all the necessary A_L components of the grid. In the same way, the basic LCS model associated to a node of the grid needs to be replicated to obtain all the necessary LCS components. Finally, the model for the overall system should be obtained through composition of the different replicated submodels.

The *Replicate/Join* composed model formalism (see [36] and [37]) for SAN actually provides very useful supports for building hierarchical models, allowing the modeller to define a composed model as a tree in which the leaves are the submodels and each non-leaf node is a Join or a Replicate node. The root of the tree represents the complete composed model. A Join is a general state-sharing composition node used to compose two or more submodels, and it may have other Joins, Replicates or other submodels defined as its children. A Replicate is a special case of the Join node used to construct a model consisting of a number of *identical copies* of a submodel. Since all the copies are identical, the resulting model has the same behaviour of the model where all the copies of the same submodel are composed using a Join node. A Replicate node has one child, which may be another Replicate, a Join or a single atomic or composed model. The modeller may also specify a set of state variables to be held in common among all replicated instances of the submodel.

Although Replicate can be profitably used to automatically build replicas of the same model, it has the limitation that all the replicas generated in this way are *anonymous*, as they are all identical copies of the same submodel. Conversely, the replicas within the CRUTIAL model needed to be *non-anonymous* (i.e., distinguishable), as each of them had a specific role and position within the electric grid as well as a different setting of parameters. However, exploiting the Replicate compositional operator and the ability to define shared places, it is possible to create *non-anonymous* replicas as well. In detail, we defined a template SAN model that, once plugged (i.e., added) into a generic model that needs to be replicated, allows to distinguish between the different replicas assigning each replica a different index, represented by the number of token that the replica holds in a certain place.

The SAN model implementing this specific feature is shown in Figure 2. Let us consider the A_L components of Figure 1 (the power lines); if m is the total number of power lines in the system, the model corresponding to the A_L component needs to be anonymously replicated m times, using the Replicate compositional operator. The number of tokens in the local place ALindex represents the index of the replica. This place is set by the output gate setIndex when the immediate activity setupIndex completes, which is defined as follows: ALindex $\rightarrow$ Mark() = (m-ALcount $\rightarrow$ Mark()) $-$ 1. The place Start is initialized with one token.

The common place ALcount is shared with all the replicated instances, and it is initialized with m tokens. The immediate activities setupIndex of the replicated instances are all enabled in the same marking at time 0. Thus, the first instantaneous activity setupIndex that completes removes one token from places ALcount and Start, and then the code of setupIndex is executed, thus setting to 0 the place ALindex of the same instance. In the same way, the second activity setupIndex that completes will finally set 1 token in the associated place ALindex and so on. Therefore, at the end of this (instantaneous) 'initialization' process, a different index (ALindex $\rightarrow$ Mark()) will be associated to each instance of the model, thus obtaining non-anonymous replicas of the A_L component.

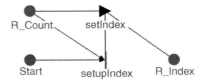

Figure 2: SAN plugin for the indexing of replicas.

4.3 On the usage of SAN to match requirement R6

As stated in Section 2, federated simulation is envisioned as the most promising approach, as CIs are highly dependent on each other, and a vast collection of domain-specific tools are available for CI modelling and simulation. A similar approach has been used also in the HIDENETS context, where the evaluation is performed using a composed simulator, namely, a simulated SAN model in which the mobility aspects are federated to an external vehicular mobility simulator. In fact, such dependency exists between transportation infrastructure and the analysed UMTS networking system, since terminals mobility may heavily affect the QoS metrics. Therefore, we felt within the project that a detailed modelling of the mobility aspects was paramount and would deserve the *integration of an ad hoc mobility simulator into the modelling process itself.* The output of this simulator was then exploited to refine the estimation of the cell load factor increment produced by each service request, thus obtaining a more detailed and faithful model of the UMTS network. Basically, a particular SAN atomic model, called TraceParser, was added to the UMTS network model, having the tasks of executing the external mobility simulator tool, progressively read the trace produced by it and keeping the SAN simulation in sync with the time steps specified in the trace file.

The SAN formalism allows the modeller to include C++ code inside input and output gates. Moreover, while building SAN models, we can define custom functions for the model using C++ header files and libraries. User-defined functions can be extremely useful when trying to make modular models, or if multiple elements within the model, such as SAN output gates, are performing similar operations. The ability to execute C++ code can also be used to call external applications, in this case to execute the mobility simulator, which will generate as output a trace in textual format. The basic TraceParser atomic model is shown in Figure 3.

Although the model developed in HIDENETS is more complex as it contains some features specific for that use case, we provide here a general parser model, which can be used to read a generic trace from the SAN model. In its simplest version, the TraceParser atomic model consists of four places and two activities. Nodes is an extended place which can hold an array of coordinates (i.e., an array

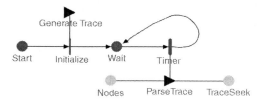

Figure 3: The TraceParser atomic model, which performs the parsing of an external trace.

of structured variables having two float fields, x and y), and it is used as interface with the replicated models representing the UMTS users; TraceSeek is an extended place which is used to remember the last position that was read in the trace file. Initially one token is held in place Start, thus enabling activity Initialize. Trace generation takes place in the output gate GenerateTrace, thanks to the following call which runs the mobility simulator: system("java -jar VanetMobiSim.jar scenario.xml"). The firing time of the activity Timer is deterministic, and it is set to the length of the time step used in the input trace. In this way, the trace is read incrementally, keeping the simulation time synchronized with the sampling time specified in the trace. The actual parsing of the trace is performed in the output gate ParseTrace, whose function is the following:

```
FILE *ptrFile; int iNode = 0; float fTime = 0, x = 0,
y = 0;
ptrFile = fopen("mobility.trace","r");
for(int i = 0; i , UserCount; i++) {
        fseek(ptrFile, TraceSeek→Mark(), SEEK_SET);
        fscanf(ptrFile," #%d %f %f %f",&iNode, &fTime,
        &x, &y);
        Nodes→Index(iNode) →x→Mark() 5 x;
        Nodes→Index(iNode) →y→Mark() 5 y;
        TraceSeek→Mark() = ftell(ptrFile); }
fclose(ptrFile);
```

The function opens the trace file in the traditional way; then for each user in the model (as specified by the global variable UserCount) the new position is parsed from the trace, using the fscanf function. Together with the new position, the node index is also parsed from the trace, and it is then used to map the new coordinates to a specific replica of the model representing each user. In this way, thanks to non-anonymous replicas, parameterization and the use of structured data types, the new coordinates are easily forwarded to each atomic model instance. The position (in bytes) in the trace file is then saved into the place TraceSeek, in order to resume the parsing on the next iteration.

5   Conclusions

This chapter has addressed the usage of graphical formalisms for the modelling and simulation of CIs. A list of basic modelling and simulation requirements for CI analysis has been provided and discussed. Then, the available graphical formalisms have been surveyed and inspected to understand the extent to which they actually meet the identified requirements. It has been shown that each graphical formalism category is particularly suited to fulfil a subset of the identified requirements. Finally, it has been shown how the SAN features can be profitably used to meet the modelling requirements, concretely discussing some of them in the context of past FP6 European projects.

Acknowledgements

The authors acknowledge the support given by the European Commission to the research projects CRUTIAL and HIDENETS. This work has been partially supported by the Italian Ministry for Education, University, and Research (MIUR) in the framework of the Project of National Research Interest (PRIN) 'DOTS-LCCI: Dependable off-the-shelf based middleware systems for Large-Scale Complex Critical Infrastructures' [29].

References

[1]   Flammini, F., Vittorini, V., Mazzocca N. & Pragliola, C., A study on multiformalism modeling of critical infrastructures, Lecture Notes in Computer Science, vol. 5508, pp. 336–343, 2009.

[2]   Casalicchio, E., Galli, E. & Tucci, S., Federated agent-based modelling and simulation approach to study interdependencies in IT critical infrastructures. *Proceedings of the 11th IEEE International Symposium on Distributed Simulation and Real-Time Applications*, Chania, Greece, October 22–24, 2007.

[3]   IEEE *Standard for Modelling and Simulation (M&S) High Level Architecture (HLA) – Framework and Rules*. IEEE Std. 1516, Institute of Electrical and Electronics Engineers, New York, 2000.

[4]   Tolone, W.J., *et al.*, Enabling system of systems analysis of critical infrastructure behaviors. *Proceedings of the Third International Workshop on Critical Infrastructure Security (CRITIS08)*, Frascati, Italy, October 24–35, 2008.

[5]   Flentge, F., *et al.*, *Catalogue of Requirements for SYNTEX*, Integrated Risk Reduction of Information-based Infrastructure Systems (IRRIIS) project, Deliverable available at the following url: http://www.irriis.org/File0475.pdf?lang=2&oiid=8996&pid=572.

[6]   Rinaldi, S.M., Peerenboom, J.P. & Kelly, T.K., Identifying, understanding, and analyzing critical infrastructure interdependencies. *IEEE Control Systems Magazine*, vol. 21, no. 6, pp. 11–25, 2001.

[7]   Chiaradonna, S., Lollini, P. & Di Giandomenico, F., On a modelling framework for the analysis of interdependencies in electric power systems. *Proceedings of the IEEE/IFIP 37th International Conference on Dependable Systems and Networks (DSN 2007)*, Edinburgh, UK, June 25–28, 2007.

[8]   Bloomfield, R., Chozos, N. & Nobles, P., *Infrastructure Interdependency Analysis: Introductory Research Review*. Produced for CPNI, TSB and EPSRC, under contract NSIP/001/0001, 2009, http://www.csr.city.ac.uk/projects/cetifs/d422v10_review.pdf.

[9]   Ghorbani, A.A. & Bagheri, E., The state of the art in critical infrastructure protection: A framework for convergence. *International Journal of Critical Infrastructures*, vol. 4, pp. 251–244, 2008.

[10] Rigole, T. & Deconinck, G., A survey on modelling and simulation of interdependent critical infrastructures. *3rd IEEE Benelux Young Researchers Symposium in Electrical Power Engineering*, Ghent, Belgium, April 27–28, 2006.

[11] Pederson, P., Dudenhoeffer, D., Hartley, S. & Permann, M., *Critical Infrastructure Interdependency Modelling: A Survey of U.S. and International Research*, Idaho National Laboratory (INL), Technical Report, 2006, http://cipbook.infracritical.com/book3/chapter2/ch2ref2a.pdf.

[12] Duflos, S., *et al.*, *List of Available and Suitable Simulation Components*, Integrated Risk Reduction of Information-Based Infrastructure Systems (IRRIIS) project, Deliverable D1.3.2, 2006, http://193.175.164.67/?lang=en&nav=241&object=110&item=8786.

[13] Dekker, A.H. & Colbert, B., Scale-free networks and robustness of critical infrastructure networks, *Proceedings of the 7th Asia-Pacific Conference on Complex Systems*, Complex 2004, Cairns, Australia, December 6–10, 2004.

[14] Lee, E.E., Mitchell J.E. & Wallace, W.A., Assessing vulnerability of proposed designs for interdependent infrastructure systems. *Proceedings of the 37th IEEE Annual Hawaii International Conference on System Sciences (HICSS '04)* – Track 2, Big Island, Hawaii, January 05–08, 2004.

[15] Nozick, L.K., Turnquist, M.A., Jones, D.A., Davis, J.R., & Lawton, C.R., Assessing the performance of interdependent infrastructures and optimizing investments. *Proceedings of the 37th IEEE Annual Hawaii international Conference on System Sciences (HICSS '04)* – Track 2, Big Island, Hawaii, January 05–08, vol. 2, 2004.

[16] Svendsen, N.K. & Wolthusen, S.D., Connectivity models of interdependency in mixed-type critical infrastructure networks. *Information Security Technical Report*, vol. 12, no. 1, pp. 44–55, 2007.

[17] Gursesli, O. & Desrochers, A.A., Modelling infrastructure interdependencies using Petri nets. *IEEE International Conference on Systems, Man and Cybernetics*, October 5–8, vol. 2, pp. 1506–1512, 2003.

[18] Krings, A. & Oman, P., A simple GSPN for modelling common mode failures in critical infrastructures. *Proceedings of the 36th IEEE Annual Hawaii International Conference on System Sciences (HICSS '03)* – Track 9, Big Island, Hawaii, January 6–9, vol. 9, 2003.

[19] Chen-Ching, L., Chee-Wooi, T. & Govindarasu, M., Cybersecurity of SCADA systems: Vulnerability assessment and mitigation. *Power Systems Conference and Exposition (PSCE '09)*, IEEE/PES, Seattle, Washington, USA, March 15–18, pp. 1–3, 2009.

[20] Beccuti, M., *et al.*, Quantification of dependencies in electrical and information infrastructures: The CRUTIAL approach. *4th International Conference on Critical Infrastructures (CRIS)*, Linköping, Sweden, April 28–30, pp. 1–8, 2009.

[21] Lu, N., Chow, J.H. & Desrochers, A.A., A multi-layer Petri net model for deregulated electric power systems. *Proceedings of the American Control Conference*, Anchorage, Alaska, USA, May 8–10, vol. 1, pp. 513–518, 2002.

[22] Dudenhoeffer, D.D., Permann, M.R. & Manic, M., CIMS: A framework for infrastructure interdependency modelling and analysis, *Proceedings of the 2006 Winter Simulation Conference*, Monterey, CA, December 3–6, pp. 478–485, 2006.

[23] Tolone, W.J., *et al.*, Critical infrastructure integration modelling and simulation. *Symposium on Intelligence and Security Informatics*, Tucson, AZ, June 10–11, vol. 3073, pp. 214–225, 2004.

[24] Panzieri, S., Setola, R. & Ulivi, G., An agent-based simulator for critical interdependent infrastructures, *Proceedings of the Conference on Securing Critical Infrastructures*, Grenoble, France, October 25–27, 2004.

[25] Casalicchio, E., Galli, E. & Tucci, S. Macro and micro agent-based modelling and simulation of critical infrastructures, *Complexity in Engineering*, Rome, Italy, February 22–24, pp. 79–81, 2010.

[26] Cardellini, V., Casalicchio, E. & Galli, E., Agent-based modelling of interdependencies in critical infrastructures through UML. *Proceedings of the 2007 Spring Simulation Multiconference – Volume 2.* Norfolk, VA, March 25–29, pp. 119–126, 2007.

[27] Repast Agent Simulation Toolkit (http://repast.sourceforge.net/).

[28] Sanders, W.H. & Meyer, J.F., Stochastic Activity Networks: Formal definitions and concepts. *Lectures on Formal Methods and Performance Analysis*, Brinksma, E., Hermanns, H. & Katoen, J.P. (eds), LNCS, Springer Verlag, New York, pp. 315–343, vol. 2090, 2001.

[29] PRIN, Programmi di ricerca scientifica di rilevante interesse nazionale – Progetto di ricerca DOTS-LCCI: Dependable off-the-shelf based middleware systems for Large-Scale Complex Critical Infrastructures, 2008, http://dots-lcci.prin.dis.unina.it/.

[30] IST-FP6-027513 CRUTIAL – CRitical UTility InfrastructurAL resilience (http://crutial.erse-web.it/default.asp).

[31] Chiaradonna, S., Di Giandomenico, F. & Lollini, P., Evaluation of critical infrastructures: Challenges and viable approaches. *Architecting Dependable Systems V*, Lemos, R., Di Giandomenico, F., Gacek, C., Muccini, H., Vieira, M. (eds), LNCS, Springer, Heidelberg, pp. 52–77, vol. 5135, 2008.

[32] Chiaradonna, S., Di Giandomenico, F. & Lollini, P., Interdependency analysis in electric power systems. *Proceedings of the 3rd International Workshop on Critical Information Infrastructures Security (CRITIS 2008)*, Setola, R. & Geretshuber, S. (eds), LNCS, Springer, Berlin/Heidelberg, vol. 5508, pp. 60–71, 2009.

[33] IST-FP6-26979 HIDENETS – HIghly DEpendable ip-based NETworks and Services (http://www.hidenets.aau.dk/).

[34] Bondavalli, A., Lollini, P. & Montecchi, L., Analysis of user perceived QoS in ubiquitous UMTS environments subject to faults. *Software Technologies for Embedded and Ubiquitous Systems*, LNCS, Springer, Berlin/Heidelberg, vol. 5287, pp. 186–197, 2008.

[35] Bondavalli, A., Lollini, P. & Montecchi, L., QoS perceived by users of ubiquitous UMTS: Compositional models and thorough analysis. *Journal of Software*, special issue on Selected Papers of the 6th IFIP Workshop on Software Technologies for Future Embedded and Ubiquitous Systems (SEUS 2008), vol. 4, no. 7, pp. 675–685, 2009.

[36] Sanders, W.H. & Meyer, J.F., Reduced base model construction methods for stochastic activity networks. *IEEE Journal on Selected Areas in Communications*, special issue on Computer-Aided Modelling, Analysis, and Design of Communication Networks, vol. 9, no. 1, pp. 25–36, 1991.

[37] Derisavi, S., Kemper, P. & Sanders, W.H., Symbolic state-space exploration and numerical analysis of state-sharing composed models. *Proceedings of the 4th International Conference on the Numerical Solution of Markov Chains (NSMC '03)*, Urbana, IL, September 3–5, pp. 167–189, 2003.

Semantic interoperability among federated simulators of critical infrastructures – DIESIS project

Vincenzo Masucci

CRIAI – Consorzio campano di Ricerca per l'Informatica e l'Automazione Industriale, Portici, Italy

Abstract

Growth, safety and quality of life in industrialised countries are more and more linked to continuous and coordinated functioning of a complex system of infrastructures which are referred to as critical infrastructures (CIs) for their importance. Nowadays infrastructures such as power and water supply networks, telecommunication networks and transport networks have become vital and are becoming more and more intermingled. The continuous increase of interconnections and interdependencies among them causes a consequent increase in the complexity of this 'system of systems'. Yet the full understanding of the CI system is still immature, and it is not possible to provide the needed protection against cascading failures that may affect several sectors. Therefore, research in the field of critical infrastructure protection (CIP) has to rely upon simulation systems. A modelling approach which involves heterogeneous infrastructures at the same time would show dependencies among different sectors, but a single simulator which can totally or partially simulate the system of interconnected infrastructures operating at the same time is not yet available. The EU funded project DIESIS aims at laying the foundations for a European modelling and simulation research facility based on open standards to foster and support research on all aspects of CIs, with a specific focus on their protection. Its main goal is the study and the design of a complex simulation model through the federated simulation of CI, analysing in detail its integration inside the interoperability framework for federated simulators from both the physical and logical/semantic perspectives.

Keywords: Critical Infrastructure Protection (CIP), European Infrastructures Simulation and Analysis Centre (EISAC), European Research Infrastructures, Modelling and Simulation for CIP, Federated Simulation, Distributed Simulation, Semantic Interoperability.

1 Introduction

In recent years Western countries have become aware that some infrastructures that are fundamental for safety, growth and quality of life are highly vulnerable because of human threats (i.e. terroristic attacks, cyber crime, long-running strikes by road hauliers) and because of natural catastrophes (i.e. volcanic eruptions, hurricanes, earthquakes, landslides). Such infrastructures are considered critical to grant the basic standards of security, growth and lifestyle of Western people, and for these reasons they need to be protected properly. Above all protection is needed against cascading failures, that is, failure effects of a certain critical infrastructure (CI) whose uncontrolled spread may affect several different infrastructures, even belonging to different sectors and to different countries.

Recently Europe has experienced air traffic problems due to a volcanic eruption in Iceland which had unexpected consequences on the European rail transport network – the eruption generated a huge quantity of ash which forced several airlines to hold nearly all their European flights. Travellers were compelled to use trains to reach their final destinations. This resulted in the disruption of railway networks, which were completely unprepared to face such a sudden increase of traffic (Figure 1).

The disruptions of German power grids on 4 November 2006, which involved 11 European nations and Morocco and affected 15 million people, are another case in point. The disruptions were due to a scheduled high-voltage power supply interruption of a grid which crosses the River Ems. A ferry had to sail along the river and for this reason a temporary interruption of power supply was scheduled. The German operator did not follow the safety procedures, and consequently the lack of information by the operators of other European

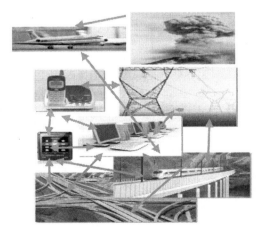

Figure 1: Complexity of interconnections and interdependencies among CI.

transmission systems created disruptions and these extended to all the European power supply transmission/distribution networks. France and Spain recorded the worst effects, with a million people experiencing the blackout.

A further serious disruption happened on 28 September 2003 and involved almost all of Italy and southern Switzerland. A short circuit in the Lucomagno grid caused a blackout. Lucomagno is a transit line from northern to southern Switzerland. The failure in reconnecting the Lucomagno line and an under-estimation of the problem caused disruptions to trains and flights, with serious delays which gave several problems to travellers.

On 2 January 2004 an accident occurred in the southern outskirts of Rome, Italy; it did not cause serious problems to the population, and yet it is another different example of interconnected CIs. A breakdown occurred in the air-conditioning system of the building where Telecom has one of its main junctions. It caused a short circuit and all telephone and satellite services were interrupted. As a consequence check-in operation systems were shut down at Fiumicino air-port, the main airport near Rome, because of the interruption in IT services. Many post offices and banks underwent the same experience. Furthermore, Acea (a company which runs power, water and gas supplies in Rome) had lost its remote control on its supply systems for more than 1 hour because it used services provided by the disconnected Telecom junction.

These examples are a confirmation of the fact that, on a global level, infra-structures are more and more interconnected and this gives several interdepend-encies, with the risk of a cascading effect: a failure or a service interruption may have serious internal or foreign consequences spreading also through hetero-geneous infrastructures.

Up to now there are two ways to foresee all the possible consequences in case of a failure of a certain infrastructure. The first and slightly easier way is to make a simulation on an infrastructure model which needs to be analysed; its failures are simulated and from the analysis of simulation results the critical infrastructure components are pointed out; hence if we try to simulate a more real model, we will obtain more realistic results.

And yet, at the moment, only vertical simulators are available, that is, current simulators operate only in a certain domain (power supply or Telecommunication network or road transport, etc.); therefore, one cannot consider effects among different domains and eventual dependencies among infrastructures belonging to different sectors; one can only focus on to the simulated infrastructure.

The second way is to use statistical models such as Leontief input/output economic models or the complex networks theory. Thanks to the latter, it is pos-sible to solve the problem of being restricted into a single domain, but it does not allow to reach realistic and detailed results that could show the dependences among several components belonging to different infrastructures. None of the two ways allows to foresee the consequences of a series of failures caused by a natural disaster or by a well-organised series of terroristic attacks involving several components of different infrastructures. The final aim to understand which components are more critical than others is still unachieved.

To overcome the lack of a system which helps to understand the nature of dependencies between different CIs, the European Union financed the DIESIS project (Design of an Interoperable European Federated Simulation Network for CI) [1]. It proposes to create a pan-European research facility called European Infrastructures Simulation and Analysis Centre (EISAC) and conduct a design study to protect CIs. The design study shall assess the technical, economic, organisational and legal feasibilities of the EISAC e-Infrastructure research. As its main feature, EISAC shall offer methods and technologies to achieve semantic interoperability of federated simulators, tools to support the various tasks in Modelling and Simulation (M&S) and a repository for data and for research and consultancy results on different aspects linked to M&S activities in critical infrastructure protection (CIP).

This chapter first gives a short description of structures and programmes dedicated to CIP modelling and simulation. Second, an overview on the work of DIESIS project will give a detailed description of its representation model and of its knowledge management. The proposed model is the project's main focus as it will solve the problem of semantic interoperability among federated simulators, and this will result in a simulation that involves several CIs at the same time, as described in the Proof of Concept (PoC) section.

2   Related works and initiatives

The idea of a research facility dedicated to CIP modelling and simulating is not an isolated or a unique one. There are a few similar facilities and initiatives in the world that address similar or related topics. This section will briefly describe them.

The National Infrastructure Simulation and Analysis Center (NISAC) of the United States [2] was founded in 2000 as a cooperation between the Sandia National Laboratory and the Los Alamos National Laboratory. Later, it became part of the US Department of Homeland Security. NISAC controls 17 CI sectors on national, regional and local levels. It provides strategic, multidisciplinary analyses of dependencies and the consequences of infrastructures disruptions. NISAC provides its services to several US departments and agencies.

In Canada, the Infrastructure Interdependencies Simulation Team (I2SIM) was founded in 2005 [3]. It aims to develop a better understanding of infrastructure dependencies and at the operational level coordination among multiple infrastructures. I2SIM deals mainly with checking dependencies through infrastructure dependency simulation for CI in the fields of power supply, telecommunications and airports. I2SIM is financed with public funds.

In the European Union, the Open Modelling Initiative (Open MI) was developed in 2005 and focused on the water supply sector [4]. Its current activities are funded by the LIFE Environment Programme. OpenMI addresses standards for federated modelling and simulation of a wide range of technical, organisational and economic aspects related to water (sea, dams, ground water, water management etc.).

The latest initiative is Australia's Critical Infrastructure Protection Modelling and Analysis (CIPMA) programme [5], started in 2007 as a cooperation between the Attorney General's Department, Commonwealth Scientific and Industrial Research Organisation (CSIRO) and Geoscience Australia. CIPMA aims to develop technologies to model and analyse relationships and dependencies among Australian CI systems and address specifically the power supply, telecommunication, banking and financial sectors. The proposed technology includes simulation models, databases, economic models and geographic information systems (GIS). CIPMA also supports the work of the Trusted Information Sharing Network (TISN), a shared platform for Australian CI operators [6], for CIP.

All these facilities, programmes and initiative are publicly funded, and all have different goals from EISAC (Figure 2). Moreover, most of them operate only on a national level. The European reality is more complex since a member state's internal CIs get more and more linked with CIs of other member states; hence it is essential that EISAC analyses transnational dependencies.

In this framework, the Italian project called CRESCO aims at strengthening the Italian potential to study complex systems. Preliminary activities have been implemented on three levels: modelling heterogeneous infrastructures in one framework, modelling several interdependent events belonging to heterogeneous

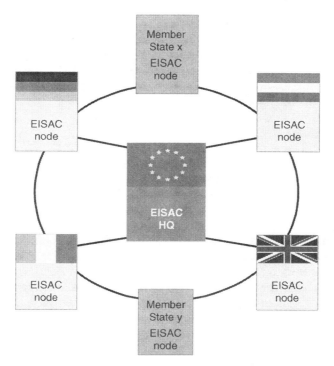

Figure 2: Scheme of an international organisation for CIP: European Infrastructures Simulation and Analysis Centre.

infrastructures and modelling interdependent events between heterogeneous infrastructures and the surrounding environment.

Researchers faced problems with a proposal of a simulation framework where several simulators of specific sectors are integrated into one environment to simulate interdependencies.

Finally, the simulator of interdependencies is used to model inter-domain connections and to merge heterogeneous information; meanwhile, specific simulators are used to provide a better model of intra-domain dynamics [7].

3   DIESIS project

DIESIS's goal is to perform a design study for an e-Infrastructure which accelerates and supports the research on CIP. The creation of an infrastructure such as this, which operates in several member states, needs a firm foundation.

Thus, DIESIS was to

- analyse the detailed requirements for the e-infrastructure research needed by researchers, industrial stakeholders, political decision makers and by governmental organisations;
- assess the scientific, technical, financial and legal feasibility and the potential scientific and technical impact of such an e-Infrastructure;
- develop a strategy and a road map for the e-Infrastructure deployment, including a business model and an organisational model for EISAC, a list of potential sponsors for the e-Infrastructure, a list of potential services that EISAC would offer and finally a list of its potential users and customers.

3.1   Managerial, legal and economic features

EISAC management features will partly depend on its legal structure. EISAC will have several sites in different member states so that it is able to provide local services such as specific know-how on CIP in every individual nation; it can attract national stakeholders, agencies and ministries whose cooperation would support most of the functional activities for the CIP.

From the legal aspect, in order to facilitate the foundation of a pan-European research body, the European Commission submitted a guideline proposal for a European research infrastructure (ERI) [8] according to the community legal framework. If it comes into force, it will be the ideal legal structure for EISAC.

Other legal aspects to be considered concern specific products, from an economic point of view, and also the legal aspects of the services that EISAC will provide, such as licensing issues, intellectual property rights and so on.

The economic assessment includes the identification of target users and customers; identification and description of a business model for EISAC, including a detailed description of products and services and customer benefits; and, last but not least, gaining support from member states.

A fundamental step towards EISAC realisation will be its insertion in the research infrastructure road map of the European Strategy Forum on Research Infrastructures (ESFRI) [9], a body which supports the European Committee policies.

3.2   Technical features

The need to obtain a federated simulation stems from the need to include several simulators in one simulation environment in order to observe the development of a series of failures which may occur in a larger and more complex system, including heterogeneous CIs. Interactions among different parts of this 'system of systems' show effects and behaviours that would not be clear if one considers only a specific behaviour in a specific system section.

In order to approach these problems from a technical perspective, the following activities will be undertaken: the detection of a set of interoperability requirements; the review and the assessment of CI federated simulation technologies, an activity which includes further analysis of available middleware and of available CI simulators; and the identification of a process or a workflow to set up federations of CIs of CI simulators. The general structure of the setup is displayed in Figure 3.

Each layer would need a detailed description, but this chapter aims at analysing the semantic interoperability among different CI simulators according to the study of DIESIS project, so we will only focus on ontologies. For a description of the other layer, please refer [10].

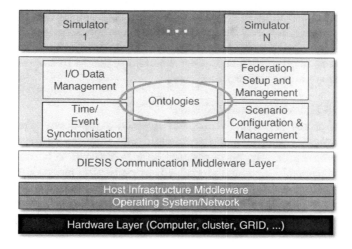

Figure 3: Relation between CI simulators, DIESIS middleware, host infrastructure and hardware layer.

Semantic interoperability

DIESIS federated simulation is made up of stand-alone simulators which are interdependent, thanks to a comprehensible and unambiguous information exchange. Two different problems arise at this point: a matter of physical interoperability and a matter of semantic interoperability. The following metaphor will help to better understand the difference: we may think of two faraway people who need to communicate ; the obvious solution is that they use a telephone. Similarly, if we want to obtain a realistic simulation of a complex system involving several simulators, we need all the simulators to be able to exchange pieces of information; thus we need to develop an instrument similar to a telephone, that is to say, a communication layer which would solve the problem of physical interoperability through a series of communication protocols. Now we may go on with our metaphor and include a further level of difficulty: we may consider that our people on the phone are able to hear each other's voice but they cannot understand each other because they use two different languages; moreover, each of them has very specific knowledge and very different skills. Let's consider a surgeon in New York who is trying to explain to a Polinesian builder how an emergency operating room has to be equipped. We need someone who translates information and transfers it to the receiver. Likewise, two federated simulators belonging to two different sectors are not able to exchange the necessary information; it could be related to the electrical energy sector on one side and to telecommunications on the other side. These pieces of information would not be comprehensible for the two federated simulators we are considering; a communication layer which translates information and transfers it from the sender to the receiver would be needed, and the second interoperability level, the semantic one, would also be a requirement for successful communication.

The solution proposed in DIESIS is a knowledge-based system (KBS) which uses ontologies and rules in a hybrid approach [11]. It stems from the idea that a simulators federation may be modelled like a system of systems where each simulator is initially conceived as independent for its functions and targets but is connected and interoperates with other simulators, thanks to a communication layer in a cooperative framework.

The DIESIS Knowledge-Based System

The design of the KBS in DIESIS has adopted a top-down approach. The domain ontologies are often too specialised and may represent concepts in a very heterogeneous way. So they could be very difficult to harmonise when semantic interoperability must be enabled. In particular, merging too specific and heterogeneous ontologies into a more general representation could be a very hard task for an ontology designer. For this reason, the following proposal starts from a very abstract ontology, the World ONTology (WONT) that provides a common definition of core terms for all CIs.

WONT represents the metaknowledge of the CI. It can be considered as a model or a template for modelling both the more specific CI domain ontologies (Infrastructure ONTology, IONT) and the semantic layer where the federation ontology can be realised (Federation ONTology, FONT). The FONT ensures the definition of semantically consistent *interconnections* among IONTs and *rules* in order to enable the discovery of the effects of CI dependences. Once the IONTs have been instantiated, the related *simulator models* (representing the IONT in the proprietary simulator language) must be realised and incorporated into the specific CI simulator. The bridge between the KBS and a particular simulator is represented and realised by a *gateway*. The gateway executes the task using an *associative table* that maps the IONT entities into model entities. The KBS represents one of the main components of the DIESIS middleware, where the semantic of CI dependencies can be addressed. Figure 4 shows the elements of the proposed KBS.

In the following paragraph, all the elements of the proposed KBS will be described, as will the rationale for their design.

WONT   The overall KBS framework relies on the WONT definition. It defines a general template ('initial ontology') for the conceptualisation of basic concepts and essential relationships of both CIs and their possible interconnections (Figure 5). The WONT is based upon the assumption that it is possible to model every CI as a set of connected system components. In this regard, the WONT constitutes a global model or template in the sense that it defines these highly abstracted

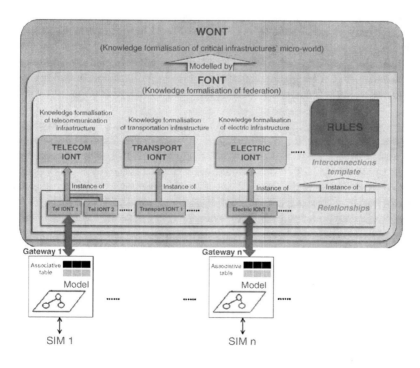

Figure 4: Knowledge-based system.

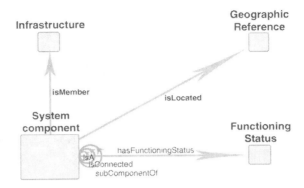

Figure 5: WONT representation.

concepts that will be shared and used by every CI definition (IONT). To summarise, every IONT can be defined in terms of WONT by the specialisation of its concepts and properties to the particular domain of interest. Moreover, the use of the WONT also enables the representation of CI cross-domain interconnections and the related semantics.

From the KBS implementation point of view, the general and abstract concepts of the WONT are represented as classes (super-classes or meta-classes) and relations (properties). The IONTs and FONT will be defined through specific WONT sub-classes and sub-properties.

Thus, the definition of a WONT allows an object-oriented approach for IONTs and FONT formalisation, providing the essential means to capture all the knowledge about different CI domains with their interconnections.

IONT   An IONT represents knowledge of a specific CI (i.e. telecommunication infrastructure (Figure 6), transportation infrastructure, electric infrastructure and so on). This ontology will be a specialisation of WONT concepts and properties. In particular, an IONT domain defines a set of concepts and properties able to model and formalise the conceptualisation of a particular domain. This ontology is simulator independent. It does not include any specific simulator-related concept, in order to decouple domain knowledge from simulator details. For this reason, IONT developers (IONT knowledge managers) are to be both knowledge representation and infrastructure domain experts. So starting from WONT concepts and properties, it is possible to create different IONTs and, consequently, to create the presupposition for a semantic interoperation among CIs belonging to the federated environment.

Once an IONT domain has been created, it must be instantiated by populating it with data. Then, the classes defined in IONT must be instantiated to represent an effective CI model. For example, an instance of an IONT could be the power electric grid of the city of Rome. This representation is simulator independent yet; it only represents the model to realise the simulator model (described in the

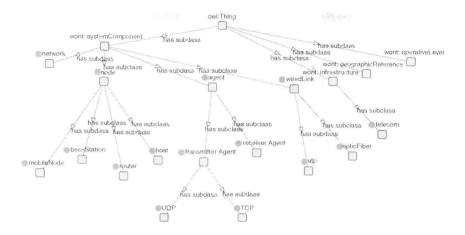

Figure 6: Telecommunication IONT representation.

following paragraphs). The bridge between an IONT instance and a specific simulator is realised through an associative table, that maps the objects defined in
the ontology instance (using the ontology language) with the objects defined in
the simulator model (using the simulator proprietary language).

Finally, it should be noted that different levels of granularity can exist for a
particular CI. In fact, a particular domain can be viewed under different levels
of detail characterised by different sizes of components. In the next section, the
way different granularities are managed by the proposed KBS is described.

FONT   The FONT realises the federation among CI. It represents the knowledge about how different domains are interconnected and how rules administrate
those interconnections. FONT has to include all objects and relationships that
are key elements for a federated simulation. For this reason, IONT's domains are
included into the FONT as they contain all the elements able to affect the federated simulation through their interconnection.

The FONT provides an interconnection template on which relationships
among IONT instance items can be stated. At this point, a distinction between
interconnections and dependencies must be made. Interconnection is an explicit
identification between items belonging to different domains of conceptualisation, whereas dependency is the interaction modality between two interconnected objects. For this reason, the definition of the interconnection topology is
not sufficient to represent and generate dependency phenomena; so the FONT
needs to define the interconnection semantic of interconnections. This semantic is provided by a set of rules that constitutes the FONT core, where interaction among IONTs becomes effective. In particular, a rule specifies the way two
interconnected objects interact, that is, how they depend on each other. In this
way, the propagation of effects from domain to domain is allowed.

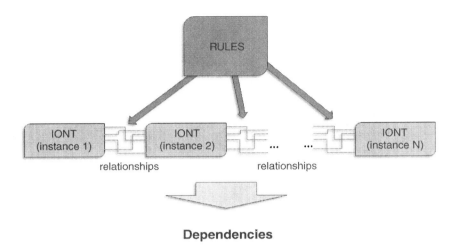

Dependencies

Figure 7: Enabling dependencies.

Once FONT has been realised, the interconnection template has to be instantiated. Instances of interconnection template are called relationships; they define connections between objects of different domains. The rule engine will run with FONT rules and FONT relationships in order to enable the cross-domain propagation of events.

Figure 7 illustrates how the rules, the IONT instances and relationships (that are instances of the interconnections) enable dependencies to be represented and managed. Knowledge experts and infrastructure experts develop a set of rules to represent knowledge about cross-domain objects' interactions. Then, these rules constitute the base to start an inferential process acting on both instances of IONTs and their relationship topology; in this way cross-domain dependencies can be included in a federated simulation environment and their effects can be analysed. Eventually, interdependencies could emerge too.

This approach allows federated simulation of different granularities of infrastructures. There are two ways to provide this feature. For example, it is possible to realise an Italian IONT level and then to detail the model by integration of Italian's IONTs region level. It will result in an IONT including the different granularities that will run on a single simulator. But this solution could result in something very difficult to implement. In fact, it does not consider separation of different granularities in different IONTs, and it is based on the assumption that the simulator allows simulations that involve different granularities of components simultaneously. For this reason, it is desirable to keep separate IONTs of different granularity. In this case, to run a federated simulation, it is necessary to provide FONT with appropriate intra-domain interconnections. In this way, IONTs of different granularities will be simulated by different simulators, and their interaction will be enabled by the FONT. This approach allows modular composition of the federation and the possibility to include different levels of detail for an infrastructure.

Gateway   The gateway constitutes the missing link between the KBS and simulators (each simulator involved in the federation has its specific gateway). Through the gateway, it is possible to exploit the functionalities of stand-alone simulators. In fact, the gateway manages the simulator input/output in order to realise the effective federation inside the framework, through the KBS. A gateway is constituted by

- a simulator model and
- an associative table

Each IONT instance represents and formalises knowledge about an existent CI belonging to a certain domain. This knowledge needs to be represented into specific domain simulator application software. For this reason, simulator experts have to carry out simulator models that are the equivalent of instances of IONT, formalised with the simulator-specific internal language.

Simulator experts have to define a simulator model for each IONT instance and, possibly, for each simulator able to simulate it. This means that each simulator will dispose of specific topologies for simulations, each one corresponding to an IONT instance. For example, if a telecommunication IONT has as instances the telecommunication networks of the cities of Rome, Naples and Milan, then, in a federated simulation framework, at least a telecommunication network simulator, with the simulator models of the networks of Rome, Naples and Milan, should exist.

The associative tables realise the isomorphism (correspondence) between IONT instances and simulator models. They map objects represented by the IONT instance to objects represented inside the simulator.

Table 1 shows an example of an associative table where the simulator experts have to include also the normal working range of the components. This information is useful for the *gateways*. In fact, *gateways* have to monitor the working status of simulator components to communicate eventual malfunctions to DIESIS middleware. Through the federation rules, these events can affect the federated simulation.

In addition, the *gateway* has to include functions for data conversion (to ensure data consistency during the simulation). For example, if a simulator output

Table 1: A kind of associative table

Iont language	Simulator language	Normal working range
Pc1	Primary cabin 1	$8.4\,kV < x < 20\,kV$
Sc55	Secondary cabin 55	$400\,V$
Lo12	Load 12	$60\% < x < 75\%$
Ba99	Battery 99	$70\% < x < 80\%$

is the measure of voltage in Volt (for instance for a battery in a power grid simulator), and IONT knowledge representation adopts the measure in mV, then the gateway is in charge of the appropriate conversion functions.

PoC

DIESIS plans a demonstrator for a subset of its technical concepts, including communication concepts for distributed simulation (Figure 9, left), ontologies for CI and the outlined ICT architecture approach for achieving interoperability of the federated simulators.

The demonstrator, as shown in Figure 8, include an electricity network simulator (SINCAL) [12], a telecommunication network simulator (NS2) [13], a railway simulator (OpenTrack) [14] and a simple flood simulator. The scenario simulated is the disruption of CI services in a large urban region in Rome due to local flooding.

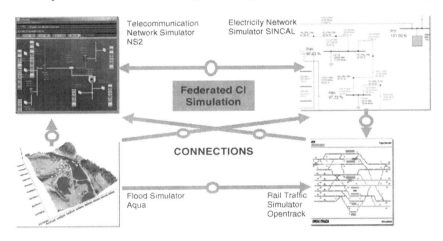

Figure 8: Evidence of CI simulator involved in the federated simulation.

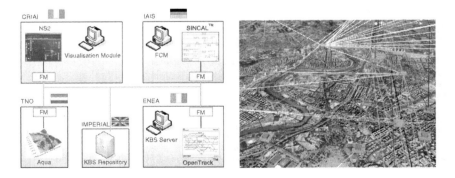

Figure 9: Federated CI simulation realised in the PoC: distributed simulation (left) and visualisation module (right).

The simulation results can be viewed thanks to an appropriate application mixed with Google Earth Maps (Figure 9, right). It shows the simulation temporal sequence; it highlights the failures caused by the flooding into different infrastructure parts and it also shows the failure cascading effect.

4 Conclusion

This chapter focuses on the semantic interoperability among federated simulators of CIs that work at the same time in a federated simulation. It aims at identifying interdependent effects among heterogeneous CIs so that it is possible to support and to lead preventive actions on areas which simulations show as weak and at risk. This chapter especially explains the solution proposed in the DIESIS project and implemented in its technical PoC. The demonstrator includes four CI simulators, SINCAL (electricity network), NS2 (telecommunication network), OpenTrack (railway traffic) and Aqua (a flood simulator), to simulate external events. A scenario service network has been defined. The demonstrator reuses data from the Integrated Risk Reduction of Information-Based Infrastructure Systems (IRRIIS) project, describing a part of the electricity and telecommunication networks of the city of Rome, Italy.

DIESIS can be considered as a feasibility study for the definition and realisation of EISAC. EISAC will consist of a geographically distributed research e-Infrastructure aimed at analysing the CI interdependencies.

Acknowledgments

The research leading to these results was funded by the European Community's Seventh Framework Programme FP7/2007-2013 under Grant Agreement No. 212830. The author also expresses his gratitude to his wife Elena and other DIESIS partners: Sandro Bologna, ENEA; Erol Gelenbe, Imperial College; Eric (H.A.M.) Luiijf, TNO; Erich Rome Fraunhofer, IAIS; Francesco Adinolfi and Paolo Servillo, CRIAI.

References

[1] DIESIS: website of the EU project DIESIS, http://www.diesis-project.eu.
[2] US Department of Homeland Security: NISAC – National Infrastructure Simulation and Analysis Center, USA, http://www.sandia.gov/nisac/.
[3] I2SIM: Infrastructure Interdependencies Simulation Team, http://www.ece.ubc.ca/~jiirp/.
[4] OpenMI Association: http://www.openmi.org/.
[5] CSIRO: CIPMA – Critical Infrastructure Protection Modelling and Analysis Program, Australia, http://www.csiro.au/partnerships/CIPMA.html.
[6] TISN: The Trusted Information Sharing Network for Critical Infrastructure Protection, Australia, http://www.tisn.gov.au/www/tisn/tisn.nsf/Page/Home.

[7] Setola, R., Bologna, S., Casalicchio, E., & Masucci, V., 'An Integrated Approach for Simulating Interdependencies', in Papa, M. and Shenoi, S. (Springer), *Critical Infrastructure Protection II*, IFIP Series, Vol. 290, pp. 229–241, 2009.

[8] European Commission: 'Proposal for a Council Regulation on the Community Legal Framework for a European Research Infrastructure', COM(2008) 467/2, Brussels, 2008.

[9] ESFRI: European Strategy Forum on Research Infrastructures, http://cordis.europa.eu/esfri/.

[10] Bologna, S., Rome, E., Gelenbe, E., Luiijf, E., & Masucci, V., 'DIESIS – An Interoperable European Federated Simulation Network for Critical Infrastructures', in Proceedings of EURO SIW, 2009.

[11] Masucci, V., Adinolfi, F., Servillo, P., Dipoppa, G., & Tofani, A., 'Critical Infrastructures Ontology Based Modelling and Simulation', in Proceedings of the Third Annual IFIP Working Group 11.10 International Conference on Critical Infrastructure Protection, Dartmouth College, Hanover, New Hampshire, USA, March 22–25, 2009.

[12] SIEMENS: SINCAL simulator, http://www.simtec-gmbh.at/sites_en/sincal.asp.

[13] NS2: The Network Simulator, http://www.isi.edu/nsnam/ns/.

[14] Open Track: Railway Traffic Simulator, http://www.opentrack.ch/.

Game theory in infrastructure security

V.M. Bier & S. Tas

Department of Industrial and Systems Engineering, University of Wisconsin–Madison, Madison, WI 53706, USA

Abstract

Game-theoretic security models have gained popularity in infrastructure security in recent years, due to the fact that game theory is suitable for dealing with intelligent threats. In this chapter, we briefly discuss some of the key concepts in game theory, categorize game-theoretic models in infrastructure security and give some examples, and finally discuss some of the limitations of game-theoretical models.

Keywords: Game Theory, Attacker–Defender Games, Sequential Games, Infrastructure Security.

1 Introduction

There has been increasing use of game-theoretic models in infrastructure security, especially after September 11, 2001. This is appropriate because game theory considers the intelligent and adaptive nature of an adversarial threat. Therefore, in this chapter we review the application of game-theoretic models to infrastructure security. We first explain some of the important concepts of game theory. Then, we discuss several categories of game-theoretic models in infrastructure security and present some examples. Finally, we discuss some of the limitations of game-theoretic models.

A *game* is a formal description of the strategic interactions of multiple agents (in infrastructure security, typically an attacker and a defender). These interactions can be between those defending a system and those attacking it or between multiple defenders. Game theory assumes that each agent or "player" in a game wishes to find its best strategy given the strategies adopted by the other player(s). This assumption makes it possible for an analyst to make predictions about which strategies players would be likely to choose (under the assumption of rationality); for example, in game theory, an agent would never choose a strategy if it is strictly dominated by another strategy, in the sense that the other strategy performs better for all possible strategies of other player(s) in the game.

In game theory, an *equilibrium* is any set of strategies where no player has an incentive to change its strategy, if all other players continue to play their equilibrium strategies. An equilibrium can be either *pure* (where each agent has a unique and deterministic equilibrium strategy) or *mixed* (where at least one agent is assumed to choose probabilistically from among multiple equilibrium strategies).

Games can be classified along multiple dimensions. With regard to payoffs, in a *constant-sum game*, the sum of the agents' payoffs is the same for all possible outcomes of the game. A special case of constant-sum games is *zero-sum games*, in which one agent's loss is equal to the other agent's gain, so the sum of the agents' payoffs is zero. For zero-sum games, there is ensured to be at least one equilibrium, although it may be a mixed rather than a pure equilibrium [1]. These games are relatively straightforward to analyze but will not always be realistic in practice. Therefore, *non-zero-sum games* may often be needed; however, some non-zero-sum games have no equilibrium.

With respect to the timing of play, in *simultaneous games*, agents choose their actions without knowing the actions of the other players. (Note that the moves of the agents do not necessarily have to be simultaneous, as long as no player can observe the actions of any other player.) By contrast, in *sequential games*, the agents act in a certain order, instead of simultaneously. In these games (also known as leader–follower games in economics and attacker–defender (AD) or defender–attacker (DA) games in security), the leader moves first and the follower moves second, generally after observing the action(s) of the leader. The leader generally has a first-mover advantage, since the choices made by the leader can limit the options available to the follower(s). In infrastructure security, decisions about observable capital investments are typically modeled as sequential games (since an attacker can often observe such defensive investments before choosing an attack strategy), while decisions that can be changed easily and rapidly (like allocation of police patrols) may be modeled as simultaneous games.

Games can also be classified with respect to how much players know. A game is one of *complete information* if the payoffs for each combination of actions chosen by the various players are *common knowledge* to all players. By contrast, when some information is not common knowledge (in other words, when the players do not share all information about one another's preferences or behavior), then the game is one of *incomplete information* (also known as a *Bayesian game*). In a Bayesian game, some players may have only probabilistic information about the preferences of other players (e.g., a probabilistic distribution over what "type" another player is). Likewise, in a game of *perfect information*, all players know all past moves in the game at any given point in time. By contrast, in a game of *imperfect information*, at least one player does not know all past moves of the other player(s).

2 Game-theoretic models

We can categorize as follows the game-theoretic security models that have been discussed in the literature:

1. Simultaneous AD games
2. Sequential DA games
3. Sequential AD games
4. Sequential defender–attacker–defender (DAD) games
5. Simultaneous defender–defender (DD) games

Each of these games is discussed in detail below. (One should note that players may be decentralized; for example, players may attack or defend only specific parts of an infrastructure system, instead of centralized attack and defense of the entire system.)

2.1 Simultaneous AD games

Simultaneous AD games are a special case of AD games where the attacker and the defender select their strategies independently, without knowing the strategy chosen by the other player. In other words, the attacker does not know the defender's decision when the attacker makes his own decision, and the same is true for the defender.

Bier *et al.* [2] used simultaneous AD games (where the attacker has no information about the defensive investments made by the defender) to identify optimal strategies for protecting the components of a simple series system. In this model, the attacker wants to maximize the expected loss experienced by the defender. The defender is assumed to minimize the expected loss (plus the cost of any defensive investments, in the unconstrained version of this model). Bier *et al.* found that the defender has greater flexibility in allocating defensive investments cost effectively when the attacker cannot observe those investments, compared to games in which the attacker can observe the defensive investments. This result shows the potential benefits of secrecy for the defender. Zhuang and Bier [3] also modeled secrecy as a simultaneous game.

Similarly, in Hausken *et al.* [4], the defender makes tradeoffs between protecting against terrorism only, natural hazards only, or both (all hazards). The authors considered a simultaneous version of this game (in which the adversary and the defender do not know each other's actions) and determined under what conditions the defender would prefer to play a simultaneous rather than a sequential AD game (and, likewise, when the attacker would prefer to play a simultaneous rather than a sequential DA game).

Simultaneous games have also been used to analyze intrusion detection for decentralized (i.e., peer-to-peer or *ad hoc*) networks. For example, Patcha and Park [5] considered a simultaneous game between a sender and a receiver. This is a Bayesian game because the sender can be of two types, either malicious or not. The objective of the attacker (the malicious type of sender) is to successfully send a malicious message without being detected by the defender's intrusion-detection system. The defender wants to intercept these attacks, while minimizing the rate of false alarms for regular messages.

Unfortunately, the simultaneous-move assumption (while simple) is often not realistic in infrastructure security since, for example, the defender may engage in costly infrastructure improvements over time and at least some of those defensive investments may be observable by the attacker. Therefore, in Section 2.2, we consider sequential DA games, which are able to overcome some of the aforementioned limitations of simultaneous AD games.

2.2 Sequential DA games

Sequential DA games determine how a defender should optimally protect a system if the attacker can observe its defensive actions. The sequence of play in such games is as follows: The defender moves first by implementing an optimal defense; the attacker than observes the defense and identifies the best possible attack strategy given that defense. See Figure 1 for a typical DA game.

Bier *et al.* [2] used a sequential DA game to determine how to protect both series and parallel systems (in addition to the simultaneous model for series systems discussed earlier). They found that for series systems, it is optimal in a sequential game to equalize the expected damage from attacks on all defended components, as opposed to the simultaneous game (in which the marginal reduction in expected damage from incremental investment in any component is the same). Thus, in contrast to the simultaneous case, the defender has less ability to choose the most cost-effective defensive investments in the sequential game.

Azaiez and Bier [6] extended this work to systems with more general structures (combined series/parallel systems). They also revised the defender's objective function from minimizing expected loss to maximizing the cost of an attack to the attacker; in this model, defensive investments are assumed to increase the cost of an attack but not to decrease the success probability of the attack. As in Bier *et al.* [2], the results suggest that defensive investment should equalize the attractiveness of all defended components in any series subsystem of the overall system; however, the definition of component attractiveness is somewhat different, due to the more complex structure of the systems being analyzed and the different nature of the objective function.

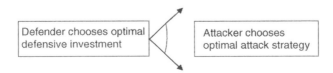

Figure 1: A sequential DA game.

Hausken and Levitin [7] similarly used game theory in their analysis of combined series/parallel systems where the components have different performance and reliability characteristics, and applied their model to an illustrative power-substation system. The objective of the defender in their model is to find optimal separation strategies for the elements within the system, in order to ensure that any single attack can damage only a subset of components.

Bier *et al.* [8] studied DA games in which a defender must allocate defensive resources to a collection of individual assets or "locations" and then the attacker chooses a location to attack. They concluded that the defender's problem gives rise to negative externalities between locations because increasing the resources allocated to one location increases the likelihood of attacks at other locations. In fact, the defender exploits these externalities to manipulate the attacker's behavior, by protecting the more valuable and vulnerable locations, in order to deflect attacks to locations that will be less damaging to the defender. It is important to note that due to the first-mover advantage, the defender in this model prefers his or her defensive allocation to be public rather than secret. This is because defense of high-valued targets not only reduces the success probability of attacks on those targets but also deflects attacks to less-valued targets.

By contrast, Dighe *et al.* [9] found conditions under which partial secrecy (i.e., disclosure of the total defensive investment but secrecy regarding the allocation of that investment to the various assets or locations) can be advantageous to the defender in a sequential DA game. This result is due to the fact that the success probability of an attack is a non-convex function of the level of defensive investment in their model. Pita *et al.* [10] took advantage of similar results to achieve more cost-effective protection in an application to allocation of guards and checkpoints at the Los Angeles International Airport. Moreover, Zhuang and Bier [3] found conditions under which secrecy and deception may be advantageous to the defender even in the absence of such non-convex success probabilities; their results suggest that secrecy and deception are more likely to be desirable when defense is only marginally justified (i.e., not so costly as to be clearly not worthwhile but not so cheap as to be obviously worth implementing).

Bier *et al.* [11] applied the model developed by Bier *et al.* [8] to the defensive budgets of the top 10 urban areas in the United States using various measures of target attractiveness to the attacker. In addition to expected fatalities and expected economic losses, they also used data on infrastructure (in particular, average daily bridge traffic and number of airport departures) as illustrative measures of target attractiveness.

Sequential DA models have also been applied to telecommunication networks. For example, Cox [12] focused specifically on resilient network design, in which an attempt to disrupt traffic leads to rerouting of the traffic. The defender first chooses a set of defensive measures, and the attacker then interdicts some number of links or nodes of the telecommunication network. The goal of the defender is to ensure that the network has sufficient capacity and path diversity so that service can continue with no disruption even after an attack of a given size.

2.3   Sequential AD games

Sequential AD games determine what an attacker should do if he gets to move first and how the defender should optimally respond to an observed attack. The sequence of play in such games is as follows: Given the attacker's constraints, the attacker launches an optimal attack; the defender then observes the attacker's strategy and the resulting damage, and identifies the best possible response. See Figure 2 for the sequence of decisions in a typical AD game.

In many such models, the attacker has the advantage of surprise, that is, deciding when, where, and how to attack. Due to this first-mover advantage, such AD games can be considered a worst-case situation from the viewpoint of the defender.

Many examples of sequential AD games in the literature deal with networked infrastructure. In particular, for example, network interdiction problems are a special case of sequential AD games, where the attacker maximizes the defender's minimum operating cost (see, for example, Kunturska et al. [13]). Such games can be used to identify and assess network vulnerabilities. Here, the attacker launches an optimal attack and disables some components of the network; the defender then determines how to optimally operate the network given its remaining capability.

For example, Israeli and Wood [14] developed an interdiction algorithm in which the attacker maximizes the shortest path on a directed power network. Similarly, Salmeron et al. [15] modeled the interdiction of critical system components (transmission lines, generators, and transformers) in an electric transmission system, using a heuristic algorithm to solve the attacker's optimal interdiction strategy (in other words, the most critical components in the network). The objective of the defender is to minimize the sum of generating and load-shedding costs. For the same problem, Bier et al. [16] used a greedy algorithm that interdicts the components with the maximum flow and obtained similar results to those of Salmeron et al. [15]. Salmeron et al. [17] improved on the heuristic algorithm in their earlier paper, with the result that they can generate faster and better solutions for considerably larger electric power grids. Sequential AD models have also been applied to oil supply chains [18], road-network vulnerability [19], and information systems [20].

In some interdiction problems, the defender can also interdict the attacker's network. For example, see Wood [21] for a defender interdiction problem where the defender minimizes drug trafficking in a capacitated network.

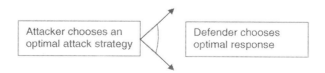

Figure 2: A sequential AD game.

2.4   Sequential DAD games

In sequential DAD games, the defender designs an optimal network before the attack, assuming that the attacker will launch an optimal attack, and the defender will then choose the best possible response to that attack. In other words, we can describe the interaction between the attacker and the defender in three phases:

1. Preattack (defender's network-design problem): The defender protects the infrastructure network (e.g., through hardening, redundancy, surveillance, pre-emption, and deterrence).
2. Attack: The attacker chooses and executes an optimal attack strategy.
3. Postattack (defender's best-response problem): The defender responds to the attack (e.g., by rerouting the flow through the network).

See Figure 3 for the sequence of decisions in a typical DAD game.

Yao *et al.* [22] defined sequential DAD models as including active defense (since the defender foresees an optimal attack and designs her network accordingly), rather than only passive defense (where the defender merely responds to an attack after it happens, as in sequential AD models). Yao *et al.* [22] also proposed a solution procedure for DAD games and applied this procedure to a problem involving defense of power networks.

Smith *et al.* [23] considered a sequential DAD game for a generic transportation or telecommunication network, in which an attacker attempts to minimize the maximum possible post-interdiction profit achievable by the defender. They considered two heuristic attack strategies (interdicting the arcs with the highest capacities or with the highest initial flows) but found that these did significantly less well than the optimal attack strategy. Note that this is different than the results in Bier *et al.* [16], where the maximum-flow heuristic attack strategy worked well. The reason for this difference is unclear, but it may be because the electricity networks in Bier *et al.* [16] are heavily capacity constrained, while the randomly generated networks in Smith *et al.* [23] generally have large excess capacity.

In Church and Scaparra [24], the goal of the defender is to first identify and then fortify (protect) critical facilities in a network of service facilities. The attacker wants to maximize the weighted average service distance for the entire system, where if service is lost at one facility, it will be provided by other facilities.

Figure 3: A sequential DAD game.

The authors tested their model for two moderate-sized cases and found that the solutions of their fortification problems contained at least one facility that was also part of the optimal interdiction strategy of the attacker.

Brown *et al.* [18] developed a decision-support system to identify the critical components in an electric power network. The system begins with a sequential AD model, as in Salmeron *et al.* [15] and Brown *et al.* [25], to identify the critical components in the network. However, it then identifies near-optimal defender hardening strategies, thus extending the model to a DAD game. Similarly, Bier *et al.* [16] also extended the AD game discussed in the Section 2.3 to include a hardening algorithm, in which the defender hardens a subset of the possible targets identified for interdiction. See Brown *et al.* [26] for a discussion of sequential DAD games and their potential application to bioterrorism.

2.5   Simultaneous DD games

Simultaneous DD games involve the defensive investments of multiple agents in a system, where the threat may sometimes be modeled as "exogenous" (i.e., unrelated to the defender decisions). Kunreuther and Heal [27] described these games as interdependent security games. In principle, defensive investments by any one agent can create either positive externalities (e.g., if one agent uses anti-virus software, reducing the risk to other agents) or negative externalities (e.g., if one target is hardened, deflecting attacks to other targets) for other agents.

Kunreuther and Heal [27] began by focusing on applications with positive externalities (e.g., vaccination, computer security, and baggage screening at airports). In such problems, if defense is low cost for any given agent, that agent will choose to invest in security (S), as shown in Figure 4; if defense is costly, agents will generally not invest (N). Interestingly, Heal and Kunreuther [28] found that there is a region (for intermediate investment costs) where there are multiple equilibria (either N,N or S,S); in other words, each player prefers to

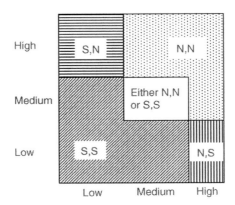

Figure 4: Security investment decision of two firms (modified from Ref. [28]).

choose whatever the other player chooses. This creates a need for mechanisms to coordinate the investment decisions of the various agents in order to achieve the social optimum. Kunreuther and Heal [27] suggested internalizing these externalities by coordination mechanisms (e.g., insurance, liability, fines or subsidies, regulations, third-party inspections, and recommendations by trade associations). Zhuang et al. [29] extended this basic model from a "snapshot" model (in which the threat is manifested immediately) to a time-dependent model (in which the threat is realized only over time). They found that in this case, the presence of a single myopic player in the game can make it undesirable for non-myopic players to invest in security, even when it would otherwise be in their interests to do so.

However, there can be also cases with negative externalities. For example, investing in the security of the aviation system may increase the risk to other modes of transportation. Similarly, investing in the security of the U.S. Postal Service may increase the threat to private mail carriers such as Federal Express [30].

Keohane and Zeckhauser [31] considered various types of externalities among potential victims as a result of the strategic nature of the terrorist threat. For example, if a tall building is hardened, this may either decrease the probability of an attack or decrease the consequence of an attack. This may endanger other buildings if the hardening deters attacks on the protected building, creating negative externalities for the owners of the other buildings. At another level, as the number of people exposed to a threat decreases (e.g., through protection of individual buildings), the attractiveness of the entire region to potential attackers may decrease, creating positive externalities for all residents of the region. Keohane and Zeckhauser [31] identified four relevant effects: discouragement of attacks (if protection against threat decreases the probability of attack, creating a positive local externality), diversion of attacks (if precautions shift the attack to other targets in the same location, creating a negative local externality), displacement of attacks (if local precautions shift the attack to other locations, creating a negative global externality), and finally containment (if protection against a threat benefits others, creating a positive global externality), as in the case of screening or vaccination [27].

Hausken [32] incorporated game theory into probabilistic risk analysis. He used two hypothetical infrastructure examples to illustrate series and parallel systems, respectively. For a series system, he borrowed the example of dams from Hirshleifer [33]. In this example, there is a circular island, where each citizen owns a "pie-shaped" slice or wedge of land. Storms may flood the island, in which case all citizens would be affected. The only protection is to build dikes around the entire island. Each citizen makes his own decision about how high of a dike to build on his slice of land. This creates positive externalities, since investment by any one citizen also benefits other citizens; in this case, each defender wishes to invest in defense only if other players also invest. In order to avoid the equilibrium where nobody invests, Hausken proposed that the defenders should coordinate their efforts so that everybody invests and everybody benefits.

For a parallel system, Hausken used the example of antimissile defense from Hirshleifer [33]. In this example, each citizen of a city may erect an antimissile defense battery on the outskirts of the city, again creating positive externalities (since any one citizen's defense also benefits other citizens). However, due to the parallel (or redundant) nature of the defences in this case, only a single successful defense is necessary to destroy an incoming missile. Therefore, the social optimum may be for only one citizen (or a small number of citizens) to erect defences. However, one equilibrium is that no citizen erects any defences, since they all want to shift the burden of defense to their neighbors.

3 Limitations of game-theoretic models

Although game-theoretic models provide a rigorous and mathematically sophisticated way of incorporating the actions of an intelligent and adaptive adversary into security decision making, they also have some limitations. In particular, real-world problems may not necessarily fit the assumptions that a standard game-theoretic model requires, as discussed in the following.

Rationality of the agents It may be unrealistic to assume that the attacker is perfectly rational and has unlimited computational ability. In particular, game-theoretic models disregard the fact that strategic reasoning (and the supporting calculations) requires minimum levels of skill (education and problem-solving ability) and resources (time, tools, computers, data, etc.), which might be either unavailable to attackers or too costly to be worthwhile. Thus, Ezell et al. [34] criticized game theory as being primarily a normative technique for determining how players should play in an idealized world, rather than a descriptive technique that represents how players might actually play. One possible way of addressing this limitation is by considering heuristic rather than optimal decision making by the attacker; see, for example, Bier et al. [16].

Common knowledge Many game-theoretic models rely on the assumption of common knowledge, in which all agents share the same understanding of the system, and also know the objective functions and payoffs of other agents, or at least prior distributions for the types of the other agents in a Bayesian game. See, for example, the discussion in Bier et al. [35]. In practice, however, it is a daunting task to determine agents' utility functions and payoffs; in fact, one reason for the existence of intelligence services is precisely because the defender may not know the attacker's preferences (and vice versa). However, Bayesian games can still be used when some players have incomplete information about the characteristics of other players.

Modeling challenges Most models in the literature assume that both the attacker and the defender have at least roughly the same objective function. It is also common to use linearized objective functions to simplify nonlinear models (such as linear DC load flow models to simulate nonlinear power flows); for example, see Brown et al. [25]. Another challenge is that the attacker's optimization problem is often discrete (e.g., whether to attack or which target to attack) rather than continuous, which can make the attacker's optimization problem difficult to solve; some techniques for solving such problems are discussed in Brown *et al.* [18].

Excessive conservatism   Ezell *et al.* [34] noted that in many game-theoretic models, the attacker's objective is assumed to be to maximize the consequences of an attack. This means that the optimal defender strategy in such games will typically be to defend against only the most severe possible attack(s). However, this may leave the defender vulnerable to lesser attacks that may be attractive to attackers with slightly different objective functions, due to insufficient defensive "hedging."

As a result of problems such as these, it is generally accepted that game theory does not always provide accurate predictions of how players behave empirically. Therefore, as an alternative to game theory, Ezell *et al.* [34] proposed the use of probabilistic risk analysis to represent attacker choices as uncertain events. However, Parnell *et al.* [36] noted that probabilistic risk assessment often involves dauntingly large numbers of hypothetical event sequences, with subjective probabilities that must be assessed by elicitation of expert judgment, even though terrorist attacks are so rare that subjective assessment of their likelihoods may be of limited accuracy. The National Research Council [37] also noted that probabilistic risk analysis may not be adequate for capturing the behavior of intelligent adversaries.

Parnell *et al.* [36] also argued that probabilistic risk assessment may understate the likelihood of severe events (like the attack on September 11) by treating the various steps or choices leading up to such an event as being probabilistically independent. By contrast, game-theoretic models avoid this pitfall by focusing on the purposive or intentional nature of the intelligent adversary's actions, rather than just assigning probabilities to those choices.

Cox [38] emphasized that it is not necessary to pick one of these methods over another and that game theory can in fact be integrated with risk analysis. For example, risk analysis can support game-theoretic models by providing probability distributions (rather than point estimates) of consequences for every pair of AD actions [35]; thus, Banks and Anderson [39] combined game theory and risk analysis in a bioterrorism example, in which they used risk analysis to generate reasonable probability distributions for the payoff matrices of various AD combinations for a smallpox threat. Similarly, Guikema [40] discussed cases in which game theory is incorporated into reliability analysis of complex systems. For additional discussions of the pros and cons of game theory for security, see Parnell *et al.* [41], Ezell and von Winterfeldt [42], and Guikema and Aven [43].

4   Conclusion

Game theory provides a rigorous mathematical way to account for the actions of intelligent adversaries, and as a result, game-theoretic models are being increasingly used in infrastructure security. In this chapter, we categorized different game-theoretic models in the literature on infrastructure security and provided illustrative examples.

Of course, as noted by Box and Draper [44], no model represents the real world perfectly. However, game-theoretic models can still yield useful insights into what both attackers and defenders may do if they take into account each other's actions and preferences.

Applying game theory to infrastructure networks of realistic size and complexity can still be challenging. However, with the advancement of computing technologies and algorithms, it will become increasingly feasible to solve complex infrastructure security problems using game theory.

References

[1] Von Neumann, J., Zur theorie der gesellschaftsspiele. *Mathematische Annalen*, **100**, pp. 295–320, 1928. Translated by S. Bargmann as On the theory of games of strategy in contributions. *Contributions to the Theory of Games IV*, eds Tucker, A. and Luce, R.D., *Annals of Mathematics Study*, **40**, Princeton University Press: New Jersey, pp. 13–42, 1957.

[2] Bier, V.M., Nagaraj, A., & Abhichandani, V., Protection of simple series and parallel systems with components of different values. *Reliability Engineering and System Safety*, **87(3)**, pp. 315–323, 2005.

[3] Zhuang, J. & Bier, V.M., Secrecy and deception at equilibrium, with applications to anti-terrorism resource allocation, *Defence and Peace Economics*, **22(1)**, pp. 43–61, 2010.

[4] Hausken, K., Bier, V.M., & Zhuang, J., Defending against terrorism, natural disaster, and all hazards (Chapter 4). *Game Theoretic Risk Analysis of Security Threats*, eds Bier, V.M. and Azaiez, M.N., Springer: New York, pp. 65–97, 2009.

[5] Patcha, A. & Park, J.M., A game theoretic formulation for intrusion detection in mobile ad hoc networks. *International Journal of Network Security*, **2(2)**, pp. 131–137, 2006.

[6] Azaiez, N. & Bier, V.M., Optimal resource allocation for security in reliability systems. *European Journal of Operational Research*, **181(2)**, pp. 773–786, 2007.

[7] Hausken, K. & Levitin, G., Minmax defense strategy for complex multi-state systems. *Reliability Engineering and System Safety*, **94**, pp. 577–587, 2009.

[8] Bier, V.M., Oliveros, S., & Samuelson, L., Choosing what to protect: Strategic defense allocation against an unknown attacker. *Journal of Public Economic Theory*, **9(4)**, pp. 563–587, 2007.

[9] Dighe, N., Zhuang, J., & Bier, V.M., Secrecy in defensive allocations as a strategy for achieving more cost-effective attacker deterrence. *International Journal of Performability Engineering*, special issue on System Survivability and Defense against External Impacts, **5(1)**, pp. 31–43, 2009.

[10] Pita, J., Jain, M., Western, C., Portway, C., Tambe, M., Ordóñez, F., Kraus, S., & Paruchuri, P., Deployed ARMOR protection: The application of a game-theoretic model for security at the Los Angeles International Airport. In *AAMAS-08 (Industry Track)*, Proceedings of the International Foundation for Autonomous Agents and Multiagent Systems, pp. 125–132, 2008.

[11] Bier, V.M., Haphuriwat, N., Menoyo, J., Zimmerman, R., & Culpen, A.M., Optimal resource allocation for defense of targets based on differing measures of attractiveness. *Risk Analysis*, **28(3)**, pp. 763–770, 2008.

[12] Cox, L.A. Jr., Making telecommunications networks resilient against terrorist attacks (Chapter 8). *Game Theoretic Risk Analysis of Security Threats*, eds Bier, V.M. and Azaiez, M.N., Springer: New York, pp. 175–198, 2009.

[13] Kunturska, U., Schmöcker, J., Fonzone, A., & Bell, M.G.H., Improving reliability through multi-path routing and link defense (Chapter 9), *Game Theoretic Risk Analysis of Security Threats*, eds Bier, V.M. and Azaiez, M.N., Springer: New York, pp. 13–32, 2009.

[14] Israeli, E. & Wood, K. Shortest-path network interdiction. *Networks*, **40**, pp. 97–111, 2002.

[15] Salmeron, J., Wood, K., & Baldick, R., Analysis of electric grid security under terrorist threat. *IEEE Transactions on Power Systems*, **19(2)**, pp. 905–912, 2004.

[16] Bier, V.M., Gratz, E.R., Haphuriwat, N.J., Magua, W., & Wierzbicki, K.R., Methodology for identifying near-optimal interdiction strategies for a power network transmission system. *Reliability Engineering and System Safety*, **92(9)**, pp. 315–323, 2007.

[17] Salmeron, J., Wood, K., & Baldick, R., Worst-case interdiction analysis of large-scale electric power grids. *IEEE Transactions on Power Systems*, **24(1)**, pp. 96–104, 2009.

[18] Brown, G.G., Carlyle, W.M., Salmerón, J., & Wood, K., Defending critical infrastructure. *Interfaces*, **36(6)**, pp. 530–544, 2006.

[19] Bell, M.G.H., Kanturska, U., Schmöcker, J.D., & Fonzone, A., Attacker–defender models and road network vulnerability. *Philosophical Transactions A*, **366**, pp. 1872–1893, 2008.

[20] Liu, D., Wang, X.F., & Camp, J., Game-theoretic modeling and analysis of insider threats. *International Journal of Critical Infrastructure Protection*, **1(1)**, pp. 75–80, 2008.

[21] Wood, R.K., Deterministic network interdiction. *Mathematical and Computer Modelling*, **17(2)**, pp. 1–18, 1993.

[22] Yao, Y., Edmunds, T., Papageorgiou, D., & Alvarez, R., Trilevel optimization in power network defense. *IEEE Transactions on Systems, Man and Cybernetics-Part C: Applications and Reviews*, **37(4)**, pp. 712–718, 2007.

[23] Smith, J.C., Sudargho, F., & Lim, C., Survivable network design under various interdiction scenarios. *Journal of Global Optimization*, **38(2)**, pp.181–199, 2007.

[24] Church, R.L. & Scaparra, M.P., Protecting critical assets: The r-interdiction median problem with fortification. *Geographical Analysis*, **39(2)**, pp. 129–146, 2007.

[25] Brown, G.G., Carlyle, W.M., Salmerón, J., & Wood, K., Analyzing the vulnerability of critical infrastructure to attack and planning defenses. *Tutorials in Operations Research*, pp. 102–123, 2005.

[26] Brown, G., Carlyle, W.M., & Wood, R., Optimizing Department of Homeland Security defense investments: Applying defender–attacker (–defender) optimization to terror risk assessment and mitigation (Appendix E). *Department of Homeland Security Bioterrorism Risk Assessment: A Call for Change*, The National Academies Press: Washington, DC, pp. 90–102, 2008.

[27] Kunreuther, H. & Heal, G., Interdependent security. *Journal of Risk and Uncertainty*, **26(2)**, pp. 231–249, 2003.

[28] Heal, G. & Kunreuther, H., Modeling interdependent risks. *Risk Analysis*, **27(3)**, pp. 621–634, 2007.

[29] Zhuang, J., Bier, V.M., & Gupta, A., Subsidies in interdependent security with heterogeneous discount rates. *The Engineering Economist*, **52(1)**, pp. 1–19, 2007.

[30] Bier, V.M., Choosing what to protect. *Risk Analysis*, **27(3)**, pp. 607–620, 2007.

[31] Keohane, N.O. & Zeckhauser, R.J., The ecology of terror defense. *Journal of Risk and Uncertainty*, **26(2)**, pp. 201–229, 2003.

[32] Hausken, K., Probabilistic risk analysis and game theory. *Risk Analysis*, **22(1)**, pp. 17–27, 2002.

[33] Hirshleifer, J., From weakest-link to best-shot: The voluntary provision of public goods. *Public Choice*, **41(3)**, pp. 371–386, 1983.

[34] Ezell, B.C., Bennett, S.P., von Winderfeldt, D., Sokolowski, J., and Collins, A.J., Probabilistic risk analysis and terrorism risk. *Risk Analysis*, **30(4)**, pp. 575–589, 2010.

[35] Bier, V.M., Cox, L.A., & Azaiez, M.N., Why both game theory and reliability theory are important in defending infrastructure against intelligent attacks (Chapter 1). *Game Theoretic Risk Analysis of Security Threats*, eds Bier, V.M. and Azaiez, M.N., Springer: New York, pp. 1–11, 2009.

[36] Parnell, G.S., Borio, L.L., Brown, G.G., Banks, D., & Wilson, A.G., Scientists urge DHS to improve bioterrorism risk assessment. *Biosecurity and Bioterrorism*, **6(4)**, pp. 353–356, 2008.

[37] National Research Council, *Department of Homeland Security Bioterrorism Risk Assessment: A Call for Change*, The National Academies Press: Washington, DC, 2008.

[38] Cox, L.A. Jr., Game theory and risk analysis. *Risk Analysis*, **29(8)**, pp. 1062–1068, 2009.

[39] Banks, D.L. & Anderson, S., Combining game theory and risk analysis in counterterrorism: A smallpox example. *Statistical Methods in Counterterrorism: Game Theory, Modeling, Syndromic Surveillance, and Biometric Authentication*, eds Wilson, G., Wilson, G.D., and Olwell, D.H., Springer: New York, pp. 9–22, 2006.

[40] Guikema, S.D., Game theory models of intelligent actors in reliability analysis (Chapter 2). *Game Theoretic Risk Analysis of Security Threats*, eds Bier, V.M. and Azaiez, M.N., Springer: New York, pp. 13–32, 2009.

[41] Parnell, G.S., Borio, L.L., Cox, L.A., Brown, G.G., Pollock, S., & Wilson, A.G., Response to Ezell and von Winterfeldt. *Biosecurity and Bioterrorism*, **7(1)**, pp. 111–112, 2009.

[42] Ezell, B.C. & Winterfeldt, D., Probabilistic risk analysis and bioterrorism risk. *Biosecurity and Bioterrorism*, **7(1)**, pp. 108–110, 2009.

[43] Guikema, S.D. & Aven, T., Assessing risk from intelligent attacks: A perspective on approaches. *Reliability Engineering & System Safety*, **95**, pp. 478–483, 2010.

[44] Box, G.E.P. & Draper, N.R., *Empirical Model-Building and Response Surfaces*, Wiley: New York, 1987.

Part III
Cybersecurity in Information and
SCADA Systems

Modelling, measuring and managing information technology risks

Stephen Elky
Deputy Director of Information Technology Services,
US Library of Congress, Washington, DC 20540

Abstract

An understanding of risk and the application of risk assessment methodology are essential to being able to efficiently and effectively create a secure computing environment. Unfortunately, this is still a challenging area for information professionals due to the rate of change in technology, the relatively recent advent and explosive growth of the Internet, and perhaps the prevalence of the attitude (or reality) that assessing risk and identifying return on investment is simply too hard to do. This chapter explores risk modelling, measurement and management.

Keywords: Risk, Threat, Threat-source, Vulnerability, Qualitative Risk Assessment, Quantitative Risk Assessment, Likelihood, Impact, Risk Mitigation, Risk Transference, Risk Acceptance, Risk Avoidance, Threat Zone, Plan of Action & Milestones

1 Introduction

The fundamental precept of information security is to support the mission of the organization. All organizations are exposed to uncertainties, some of which impact the organization in a negative manner. In order to support the organization, information technology (IT) security professionals must be able to help their organizations' management understand and manage these uncertainties.

Managing uncertainties is not an easy task. Limited resources and an ever-changing landscape of threats and vulnerabilities make completely mitigating all risks impossible. Therefore, IT security professionals must have a toolset to assist them in sharing a commonly understood view with IT and business managers concerning the potential impact of various IT security-related threats to the mission. This toolset needs to be consistent, repeatable, cost effective and reduce risks to a level that is deemed reasonable by the organization, rather than the individual.

Risk management is nothing new. There are many tools and techniques available for managing organizational risks. There are a myriad of tools under the moniker of Governance, Risk and Compliance (GRC). This chapter explores the issue of risk management with respect to information systems and seeks to answer the following questions:

- What is risk with respect to information systems?
- Why is it important to understand risk?
- How is risk assessed?
- How is risk managed?
- What are some common risk assessment/management methodologies and tools?

2   What is risk with respect to information systems?

Risk is the potential harm that may arise from some current process or from some future event. Risk is present in every aspect of our lives, and many different disciplines focus on risk as it applies to them. From the IT security perspective, risk management is the process of understanding and responding to factors that may lead to a failure in the confidentiality, integrity or availability of an information system. IT security risk is the harm to a process or the related information resulting from some purposeful or accidental event that negatively impacts the process or the related information.

Risk is a function of the *likelihood* of a given *threat-source* exercising a particular potential *vulnerability* and the resulting *impact* of that adverse event on the organization [1].

2.1   Threats

One of the most widely used definitions of threat and threat-source can be found in the National Institute of Standards and Technology's (NIST) Special Publication (SP) 800-30, *Risk Management Guide for Information Technology Systems*. NIST SP 800-30 provides the following definitions.

Threat: The potential for a threat-source to exercise (accidentally trigger or intentionally exploit) a specific vulnerability [2].

Threat-source: Either (1) intent and method targeted at the intentional exploitation of a vulnerability or (2) a situation and method that may accidentally trigger a vulnerability [2].

The threat is merely the potential for the exercise of a particular vulnerability. Threats in themselves are not actions. Threats must be coupled with threat-sources to become dangerous. This is an important distinction when assessing and managing risks, since each threat-source may be associated with a different likelihood, which, as will be demonstrated, affects risk assessment and risk management. It is often expedient to incorporate threat-sources into threats. The list below shows some (but not all) of the possible threats to information systems.

Table 1: Sample threats (including threat-sources)

Threat (including threat-source)	Description
Accidental disclosure	The unauthorized or accidental release of classified, personal or sensitive information
Acts of nature	All types of natural occurrences (e.g., earthquakes, hurricanes, tornadoes) that may damage or affect the system/application. Any of these potential threats could lead to a partial or total outage, thus affecting availability
Alteration of software	An intentional modification, insertion or deletion of operating system or application system programs, whether by an authorized user or not, which compromises the confidentiality, availability or integrity of data, programs, system or resources controlled by the system. This includes malicious code, such as logic bombs, Trojan horses, trapdoors and viruses
Bandwidth usage	The accidental or intentional use of communications bandwidth for other than intended purposes
Electrical interference/ disruption	An interference or fluctuation may occur as the result of a commercial power failure. This may cause denial of service to authorized users (failure) or a modification of data (fluctuation)
Intentional alteration of data	An intentional modification, insertion or deletion of data, whether by authorized user or not, which compromises confidentiality, availability or integrity of the data produced, processed, controlled or stored by data processing systems
System configuration error (accidental)	An accidental configuration error during the initial installation or upgrade of hardware, software, communication equipment or operational environment
Telecommunication malfunction/ interruption	Any communications link, unit or component failure sufficient to cause interruptions in the data transfer via telecommunications between computer terminals, remote or distributed processors, and host computing facility

2.2 Vulnerabilities

Once again, NIST SP 800-30 provides an excellent definition of vulnerability as it pertains to information systems.

Vulnerability A flaw or weakness in system security procedures, design, implementation or internal controls that could be exercised (accidentally triggered or intentionally exploited) and result in a security breach or a violation of the system's security policy [3].

Notice that the vulnerability can be a flaw or weakness in any aspect of the system. Vulnerabilities are not merely flaws in the technical protections provided by the system. Significant vulnerabilities are often contained in the standard operating procedures that systems administrators perform, the process that the help desk uses to reset passwords or inadequate log review. Another area where vulnerabilities may be identified is at the policy level. For instance, a lack of a clearly defined security testing policy may be directly responsible for the lack of vulnerability scanning.

Here are a few examples of vulnerabilities related to contingency planning/disaster recovery:

- Not having clearly defined contingency directives and procedures
- Lack of a clearly defined, tested contingency plan
- The absence of adequate formal contingency training
- Lack of information (data and operating system) backups
- Inadequate information system recovery procedures for all processing areas (including networks)
- Not having alternate processing or storage sites
- Not having alternate communication services

3   Why is it important to manage risk?

The principle reason for managing risk in an organization is to protect the mission and assets of the organization. Therefore, risk management must be a management function rather than a technical function.

It is vital to manage risks to systems. Understanding risk and, in particular, understanding the specific risks to a system allow the system owner to protect the information system commensurate with its value to the organization. The fact is that all organizations have limited resources, and risk can never be reduced to zero. So understanding risk, especially the magnitude of the risk, allows organizations to prioritize scarce resources.

4   Managing risk at the organizational level

Before you can manage risk at the IT system level, you have to be able to manage risks at the organizational level. Risk related to the operation and use of information systems is another component of organizational risk that senior leaders must address as a routine part of their ongoing risk management responsibilities. Organizational risk can include many types of risk (e.g., investment risk, budgetary risk, program management risk, legal liability risk, safety risk, inventory risk and the risk from information systems) [4].

Deciding upon the acceptable level of risk for the organization, sometimes called the risk tolerance, is the responsibility of upper management. While upper management needs to be advised on IT security risks by a specialist, the actual decision should always be made by upper management.

NIST defines a Risk Executive function that ensures risk decisions are made from an organizational perspective keeping in mind the mission and business functions. This function can be of one or more individuals who interact with senior management and IT security specialists to provide a holistic view of tolerable risk that will allow the organization to fulfil its mission in a cost-effective manner.

5   How is risk assessed?

Risk is assessed by identifying threats and vulnerabilities, then determining the likelihood and impact for each risk. It's easy, right? Unfortunately, risk assessment is a complex undertaking, usually based on imperfect information. There are many methodologies aimed at allowing risk assessment to be repeatable and give consistent results. Some of the leading methodologies are discussed in greater detail in Section 7.

Recall that threat is a potential likelihood that something bad will happen. This has historically proved very difficult to measure. The most meaningful data are statistics collected directly by the organization. If this is not available, there are some high-level indicators of likelihood that have been collected across the industry. The Consensus Audit Guidelines (CAG) identifies the top 20 effective controls. Since controls are applied against risks, the likelihood component can be inferred. While this does not give a concrete picture of likelihood, it does allow the organization to focus on the top observed risks. The CAG is based on the observed effectiveness of various security controls in preventing compromise. The CAG was developed by the Center for Strategic and International Studies, which included numerous U.S. government agencies along with experts from the banking and critical infrastructure communities.

Vulnerability is much easier to measure. It is the impact on the business if a particular weakness is exploited. For those vulnerabilities where the impact is very clear, the impact can be measured consistently. However, other vulnerabilities can have a range of impacts, from a minor annoyance to completely compromising the entire system. For these vulnerabilities, there are two basic schools of thought: prepare for the absolute worst case or prepare for the worst reasonable case. Both these approaches have their pros and cons. Absolute worst case may overstate the impact for a particular vulnerability, while worst reasonable case relies heavily on likelihood.

In addition, the reader is directed to read the U.S. Department of Commerce's, National Institute of Standards and Technology Interagency Report 7564, *Directions in Security Metrics Research* for an in-depth discussion on security metrics (http://www.nist.gov/customcf/get_pdf.cfm?pub_id=902180).

5.1   Quantitative risk assessment

Quantitative risk assessment draws upon methodologies used by financial institutions and insurance companies. By assigning values to information, systems, business processes, recovery costs and so on, impact, and therefore risk, can be measured in terms of direct and indirect costs. Mathematically, quantitative risk can be expressed as Annualized Loss Expectancy (ALE). ALE is the expected monetary loss that can be expected for an asset due to a risk being realized over a 1-year period.

$$ALE = SLE * ARO,$$

where

- Single Loss Expectancy (SLE) is the value of a single loss of the asset. This may or may not be the entire asset. This is the impact of the loss.
- Annualized Rate of Occurrence (ARO) is how often the loss occurs. This is the likelihood.

While utilizing quantitative risk assessment seems straightforward and logical, there are issues with using this approach with information systems. This previous discussion highlighted the difficulty of getting an accurate value for likelihood (i.e., ARO). Moreover, although the cost of a system may be easy to define, the indirect costs, such as the value of the information, lost production activity and the cost to recover, may be more difficult to determine.

Therefore, a large margin of error is typically inherent in quantitative risk assessments for information systems. This might not always be the case in the future. As the body of statistical evidence becomes available, trends can be extrapolated on past experience. Insurance companies and financial institutions make excellent use of such statistics to ensure that their quantitative risk assessments are meaningful, repeatable and consistent.

Quantitative risk measurement is the standard way of measuring risk in many fields, such as insurance, but it is not commonly used to measure risk in information systems. Two of the reasons claimed for this are (1) the difficulties in identifying and assigning a value to assets and (2) the lack of statistical information that would make it possible to determine frequency. Thus, most of the risk assessment tools that are used today for information systems are measurements of qualitative risk [5].

Currently, the relative difficulty of obtaining accurate and complete information limits the usage of quantitative risk assessments in IT security. Nonetheless, if the information is deemed reliable, a qualitative risk assessment is an extremely powerful tool to communicate risk to all levels of management.

5.2   Qualitative risk assessment

Qualitative risk assessments assume that there is already a great degree of uncertainty in the likelihood and impact values and define them, and thus risk, in somewhat subjective or qualitative terms. Similar to the issues in quantitative risk assessment, the great difficulty in qualitative risk assessment is defining the likelihood and impact values. Moreover, these values need to be defined in a manner that allows the same scales to be consistently used across multiple risk assessments.

The results of qualitative risk assessments are inherently more difficult to concisely communicate to management. Qualitative risk assessments typically give risk results of 'High', 'Moderate' and 'Low'. However, by providing the impact and likelihood definition tables and the description of the impact, it is possible to adequately communicate the assessment to the organization's management.

In a qualitative risk assessment, it is best not to use numbers when assessing risk. Managers, especially the senior-level managers who make decisions concerning resource allocation, often assume more accuracy than is actually conveyed when reviewing a risk assessment report containing numerical values. Recall that in a qualitative risk assessment, the likelihood and impact values are based on the best available information, which is not typically well grounded in documented past occurrences.

The concept of not providing any more granularity in risk assessment reports than was available during the assessment process is roughly analogous to the use of significant digits in physics and chemistry. Roughly speaking, significant digits are the digits in a measurement that are reliable. Therefore, it is impossible to get any more accuracy from the result than was available from the source data.

Identifying threats

As was alluded to in the section on threats, both threat-sources and threats must be identified. Threats should include the threat-source to ensure accurate assessment.

Some common threat-sources include the following:

- natural threats – floods, earthquakes, hurricanes;
- human threats – threats caused by human beings, including both unintentional (inadvertent data entry) and deliberate actions (network-based attacks, virus infection, unauthorized access);
- environmental threats – power failure, pollution, chemicals, water damage.

Some common threats were illustrated in Table 1 – partial list of threats with threat-sources taken into consideration.

Individuals who understand the organization, industry or type of system (or better yet all three) are key in identifying threats. Once the general list of threats has been compiled, review it with those most knowledgeable about the system, organization or industry to gain a list of threats that applies to the system.

A best practice is to compile a list of threats that are present across the organization and use this list as the basis for all risk management activities. As a major consideration of risk management is to ensure consistency and repeatability, an organizational threat list is invaluable.

Identifying vulnerabilities

Vulnerabilities can be identified by numerous means. Different risk management schemes offer different methodologies for identifying vulnerabilities. In general, start with commonly available vulnerability lists or control areas. Then, working with the system owners or other individuals with knowledge of the system or organization, start to identify the vulnerabilities that apply to the system. Specific vulnerabilities can be found by reviewing vendor websites and public vulnerability archives, National Vulnerability Database or NVD (http://nvd.nist.gov).

NVD is the U.S. government repository of standards-based vulnerability management data represented using the Security Content Automation Protocol (SCAP). This data enables automation of vulnerability management, security measurement and compliance. NVD includes databases of security checklists, security-related software flaws, misconfigurations, product names and impact metrics [6].

If they exist, previous risk assessments and audit reports are the best place to start to identify vulnerabilities.

Moreover, while the following tools and techniques are typically used to evaluate the effectiveness of controls, they can also be used to identify vulnerabilities:

- Vulnerability scanners – Software that can examine an operating system, network application or code for known flaws by comparing the system (or system responses to known stimuli) to a database of flaw signatures.
- Penetration testing – An attempt by human security analysts to exercise threats against the system. This includes operational vulnerabilities, such as social engineering.
- Audit of operational and management controls – A thorough review of operational and management controls by comparing the current documentation to best practices (such as ISO 17799, COBIT or NIST SP 800-53) and by comparing actual practices against current documented processes.

It is invaluable to have a base list of vulnerabilities that are always considered during every risk assessment in the organization. This practice ensures at least a minimum level of consistency between risk assessments. Moreover, vulnerabilities discovered during past assessments of the system should be included in all future assessments. Doing this allows management to understand that past risk management activities have been effective.

Relating threats to vulnerabilities

One of the more difficult activities in the risk management process is to relate a threat to a vulnerability. Nonetheless, establishing these relationships is a mandatory activity, since risk is defined as the exercise of a threat against a vulnerability. This is often called threat–vulnerability (T-V) pairing. Once again, there are many techniques to perform this task.

Not every threat-action/threat can be exercised against every vulnerability. For instance, a threat of 'flood' obviously applies to a vulnerability of 'lack of contingency planning' but not to a vulnerability of 'failure to change default authenticators'.

While logically it seems that a standard set of T-V pairs would be widely available and used, there currently is not one readily available. This may be due to the fact that threats, and especially vulnerabilities, are constantly being discovered and that the T-V pairs would change fairly often.

Nonetheless, an organizational standard list of T-V pairs should be established and used as a baseline. Developing the T-V pair list is accomplished by reviewing the vulnerability list and ensuring that all the vulnerabilities that that threat-action/threat can act against have been identified. For each system, the standard T-V pair list should then be tailored.

Defining likelihood

Determining likelihood is fairly straightforward. It is the probability that a threat caused by a threat-source will occur against a vulnerability. In order to ensure that risk assessments are consistent, it is an excellent idea to utilize a standard definition of likelihood on all risk assessments.

Be very careful in setting up the likelihood definitions. Table 2 shows a bell curve, with a Moderate being twice as significant as a Low or a High. This may be an unfair characterization for a particular organization that prefers to use a straight curve (Low: 0–33%, Moderate: 34–66%, High: 67–100%) or perhaps five levels of likelihood: Very Low, Low, Moderate, High and Very High. The most important thing is to make sure that the definitions are consistently used, clearly communicated, agreed upon and understood by the team performing the assessment and by organizational management.

Defining impact

In order to ensure repeatability, impact is best defined in terms of impact upon availability, impact upon integrity and impact upon confidentiality. Table 3 illustrates a workable approach to evaluating impact by focusing attention on the three aspects of information security. However, in order to be meaningful, reusable and easily communicated, specific ratings should be produced for the entire organization. Table 4 shows these specific values.

Table 2:   Sample likelihood definitions

	Definition
Low	0–25% chance of successful exercise of threat during a 1-year period
Moderate	26–75% chance of successful exercise of threat during a 1-year period
High	76–100% chance of successful exercise of threat during a 1-year period

Table 3:   Sample impact definitions

	Confidentiality	Integrity	Availability
Low	Loss of confidentiality leads to a limited effect on the organization	Loss of integrity leads to a limited effect on the organization	Loss of availability leads to a limited effect on the organization
Moderate	Loss of confidentiality leads to a serious effect on the organization	Loss of integrity leads to a serious effect on the organization	Loss of availability leads to a serious effect on the organization
High	Loss of confidentiality leads to a severe effect on the organization	Loss of integrity leads to a severe effect on the organization	Loss of availability leads to a severe effect on the organization

Table 4:   Examples of organizational effect

Effect type	Effect on mission capability	Financial loss/ damage to organizational assets	Effect on human life
Limited effect	Temporary loss of one or more minor mission capabilities	Under $5,000	Minor harm (e.g., cuts and scrapes)
Serious effect	Long-term loss of one or more minor or temporary loss of one or more primary mission capabilities	$5,000–$100,000	Significant harm but not life threatening
Severe effect	Long-term loss of one or more primary mission capabilities	Over $100,000	Loss of life or life threatening injury

It is vital to apply the impact definitions across the entire organization. In order to effect this, ensure that these definitions are supported by the Risk Executive function in the organization.

Assessing risk

Assessing risk is the process of determining the likelihood of the threat being exercised against the vulnerability and the resulting impact from a successful compromise. When assessing likelihood and impact, take the current threat environment and controls into consideration. Likelihood and impact are assessed on the system as it is operating at the time of the assessment. Do not

Table 5:   Sample risk determination matrix

		Impact		
		High	Moderate	Low
Likelihood	High	High	High	Moderate
	Moderate	High	Moderate	Low
	Low	Moderate	Low	Low

take any planned controls into consideration. Table 5 can be used to evaluate the risk when using a three-level rating system.

Following this logic, if likelihood and impact were evaluated on a Low, Moderate, High basis, risk would also be Low, Moderate or High.

If the risk assessment report does not clearly communicate the proper level of granularity, the number of impact and likelihood rating levels should be increased. Some organizations prefer to use a four- or even five-level rating for impact and likelihood. However, understand that the individual impact and likelihood levels must still be concisely defined.

6   How is risk managed?

Recall that the purpose of assessing risk is to assist management in determining where to direct resources.

6.1   Strategies for managing individual risks

There are four basic strategies for managing risk: mitigation, transference, acceptance and avoidance. Each will be discussed below.

Mitigation
Mitigation is the most commonly considered risk management strategy. Mitigation involves fixing the flaw or providing some type of compensatory control to reduce the likelihood or impact associated with the flaw. A common mitigation for a technical security flaw is to install a patch provided by the vendor. Sometimes the process of determining mitigation strategies is called control analysis.

Transference
Transference is the process of allowing another party to accept the risk on your behalf. This is not widely done for IT systems, but everyone does it all the time in their personal lives. Car, health and life insurance are all ways to transfer risk. In these cases, risk is transferred from the individual to a pool of insurance holders, including the insurance company. Note that this does not decrease the likelihood or fix any flaws, but it does reduce the overall impact (primarily financial) on the organization.

Acceptance

Acceptance is the practice of simply allowing the system to operate with a known risk. Many low risks are simply accepted. Risks that have an extremely high cost to mitigate are also often accepted. Beware of high risks being accepted by management. Ensure that this strategy is in writing and accepted by the manager(s) making the decision. Often risks are accepted that should not have been accepted, and then when the penetration occurs, the IT security personnel are held responsible. Typically, business managers, not IT security personnel, are the ones authorized to accept risk on behalf of an organization.

Avoidance

Avoidance is the practice of removing the vulnerable aspect of the system or even the system itself. For instance, during a risk assessment, a website was uncovered that let vendors view their invoices, using a vendor ID embedded in the HTML file name as the identification and no authentication or authorization per vendor. When notified about the web pages and the risk to the organization, management decided to remove the web pages and provide vendor invoices via another mechanism. In this case, the risk was avoided by removing the vulnerable web pages.

6.2   High-level risk management strategies

Managing every risk on an individual basis is costly and time consuming. Instead, focus on strategies to manage all the risks associated with the organization's IT systems rather than on the individual risks.

Managing risk using baselines

Continuing with the theme of measuring and managing risk in a consistent and repeatable manner, an organization should develop a baseline set of controls that will reduce risk to an acceptable level. However, not all information and business processes are equally valuable to the organization. As discussed earlier, organizational value of information and business processes is measured by the impact on the organization where the information or business process to be compromised. Therefore most organizations develop multiple baselines, corresponding to the different impact levels. NIST SP 800-53 defines three baselines corresponding to Low, Moderate and High impact.

The most effective risk management technique is avoidance. Requiring systems to comply with a baseline does not require tremendous analysis to determine if a system will operate at an acceptable level of risk. However, not all systems can implement every control in the baseline. In these cases, the experts must come together and analyse the situation, either establishing compensating controls or using one of the other three risk strategies, and grant an exception. Exceptions generally require greater resources (due to the additional analysis) but allow flexibility.

So manage risk by compliance where possible and by exception where necessary.

Using threat zones

Threat zones are a tool that can be used to tailor existing baselines to take into account attacks on certain systems are more likely. Attacks can be more likely due to the system placement. (Internet facing systems are subject to more frequent attacks than intranet servers that are not directly accessible from the Internet.) By defining threat zones and associating additional controls to systems within the threat zones, the systems can operate at a tolerable level of risk. While these additional controls could be added to the baseline, it might not be cost effective to deploy the controls for all systems in the entire enterprise (e.g., write-only logs).

Managing risk prior to deployment

Before deployment is the optimal time to reduce risk to the lowest level. Applying the baseline controls during development is typically orders of magnitude less costly as well as generally being more effective than building in additional controls after deployment.

The often maligned certification and accreditation process is merely testing the controls required by the baseline and a formal acceptance of risk by appropriate management. By including the baseline in the system requirements, implementing the baseline during the design/development/integration and testing the controls, systems with a set tolerance for known risk can be deployed.

This same process should be utilized for any additions or changes to the system before they are deployed.

Managing risk after deployment

After deployment, periodic exhaustive retesting of all the baseline controls has shown to be largely ineffective. Continuous monitoring of the system is the strategy that has proven to be most effective at managing risk. Continuous monitoring is the process of monitoring known attack vectors and operational processes that have been known to fail. Reviewing logs, patching the operating system and auditing account management are among the more effective continuous monitoring targets. The CAG is widely considered the seminal set of continuous monitoring targets.

6.3   Communicating risks and risk management strategies

Risk must also be communicated. Once risk is understood, risks and risk management strategies must be clearly communicated to organizational management in terms easily understandable to organizational management. Managers are used to managing risk; they do it every day. So present risk in a way they will understand. Do not use 'fear, uncertainty and doubt'. Instead, present risk in terms of likelihood and impact. Organizational management will more

Table 6:   Sample risk management

Risk	Risk description	Impact	Likelihood	Risk management strategy	Cost	Residual risk after implementing risk management strategy
Moderate	Failure in environmental systems (e.g., air conditioning) leaves systems unavailable	Failure in environmental controls could cause system to become unavailable for more than 48 hours	Past data indicate this happens once or twice annually	Implement a hot spare at the alternate site	$250,000	Low

readily understand and accept the findings and recommendations based on consistent terms rooted in facts.

With a quantitative risk assessment methodology, risk management decisions are typically based on comparing the costs of the risk against the costs of risk management strategy. A return on investment (ROI) analysis is a powerful tool to include in the risk assessment report. This is a tool commonly used in business to justify taking or not taking a certain action. Managers are very familiar with using ROI to make decisions.

With a qualitative risk assessment methodology, the task is somewhat more difficult. While the cost of the strategies is usually well known, the cost of not implementing the strategies is not, which is why a qualitative and not a quantitative risk assessment was performed. Including a management-friendly description of the impact and likelihood with each risk and risk management strategy is extremely effective. Another effective strategy is showing the residual risk after the risk management strategy was enacted (Table 6).

6.4   Implementing risk management strategies

A Plan of Action & Milestones (POAM) should be part of the risk assessment report presented to management. The POAM is a tool to communicate to management on the proposed and actual completion of the implementation of the risk management strategies.

The first step in implementing risk management strategies is to get management to approve the POAM. Afterwards, the various individuals and teams report upon their progress. This in turn is reported to management and tracked as part of the ongoing process of risk management.

Table 7:   Sample POAM

Risk	Risk Management strategy	POC	Resources required	Milestones	Target completion date
Failure in environmental systems (e.g., air conditioning) leaves systems unavailable	Implement a hot spare at the alternate site	Joe Smith	$100,000 hardware	Procure hardware & software	9/1
			$50,000 software	Install hardware	9/15
			$100,000 labour	Install software	10/1
				Configure system	10/15
				Test system	11/1

Table 7 illustrates a typical POAM. The POAM contains the risk, the risk management strategy, the Point of Contact (POC) responsible for implementing the strategy, the resources required and the various milestones that comprise the implementation. For each milestone, a target completion date is listed. Note that the POAM is a tool to communicate to management, rather than a project management plan.

7   What are some common risk assessment/management methodologies and tools?

There are numerous risk assessment/management methodologies and tools. The following methodologies and tools were developed for managing risks in information systems.

7.1   NIST methodology

NIST SP 800-30, *Risk Management Guide for Information Technology Systems*, is the U.S. Federal Government's standard. This methodology is primarily designed to be qualitative and is based upon skilled security analysts working with system owners and technical experts to thoroughly identify, evaluate and manage risk in IT systems. The process is extremely comprehensive, covering everything from threat-source identification to ongoing evaluation and assessment.

The NIST methodology consists of nine steps:

Step 1: System characterization
Step 2: Threat identification
Step 3: Vulnerability identification
Step 4: Control analysis
Step 5: Likelihood determination

Step 6: Impact analysis
Step 7: Risk determination
Step 8: Control recommendations
Step 9: Results documentation

7.2   OCTAVE®

The Software Engineering Institute (SEI) at Carnegie Mellon University developed the Operationally Critical, Threat, Asset and Vulnerability Evaluation (OCTAVE) process. The main goal in developing OCTAVE is to help organizations improve their ability to manage and protect themselves from information security risks. OCTAVE is workshop based rather than tool based.

This means that rather than including extensive security expertise in a tool, the participants in the risk assessment need to understand the risk and its components. The workshop-based approach espouses the principle that the organization will understand the risk better than a tool and that the decisions will be made by the organization rather than by a tool.

There are three phases of workshops. Phase 1 gathers knowledge about important assets, threats and protection strategies from senior managers. Phase 2 gathers knowledge from operational area managers. Phase 3 gathers knowledge from staff and develops the protection strategy.

7.3   FRAP

The Facilitated Risk Assessment Process (FRAP) is the creation of Thomas Peltier. It is based upon implementing risk management techniques in a highly cost-effective way. FRAP uses formal qualitative risk analysis methodologies using Vulnerability Analysis, Hazard Impact Analysis, Threat Analysis and Questionnaires. Moreover, FRAP stresses pre-screening systems and only performing formal risk assessments on systems when warranted. Lastly, FRAP ties risk to impact using the Business Impact Analysis as a basis for determining impact. Thomas Peltier has written a book on FRAP and several consulting companies, including Peltier Associates, teach FRAP.

7.4   GRC tools

Over the last few years, GRC tools have exploded onto the marketplace. Driven by government and statutory requirements these tools are capable of tracking compliance against standard and custom baselines. Moreover, some of these tools can directly measure compliance (SCAP is becoming more prevalent) and even enforce baselines.

8   Summary

In summary, successful and effective risk management is the basis of successful and effective IT security. Due to the reality of limited resources and nearly unlimited threats, a reasonable decision must be made concerning the allocation of resources to protect systems. Risk management practices allow the organization to protect information and business process commensurate with their value. To ensure the maximum value of risk management, it must be consistent and repeatable, while focusing on measurable reductions in risk. Establishing and utilizing an effective, high-quality risk management process and basing the information security activities of the organization on this process will lead to an effective information security program in the organization.

References

[1] U.S. Department of Commerce, National Institute of Standards and Technology Special Publication 800-30, *Risk Management Guide for Information Technology* Systems (July 2002), page 8. http://csrc.nist.gov/publications/nistpubs/800-30/sp800-30.pdf

[2] U.S. Department of Commerce, National Institute of Standards and Technology Special Publication 800-30, *Risk Management Guide for Information Technology Systems* (July 2002), page 12. http://csrc.nist.gov/publications/nistpubs/800-30/sp800-30.pdf

[3] U.S. Department of Commerce, National Institute of Standards and Technology Special Publication 800-30, *Risk Management Guide for Information Technology Systems* (July 2002), page 15. http://csrc.nist.gov/publications/nistpubs/800-30/sp800-30.pdf

[4] U.S. Department of Commerce, National Institute of Standards and Technology Special Publication 800-39, *Managing Risk from Information Systems*. Gaithersburg, MD, available at http://csrc.nist.gov/publications/nistpubs/800-39/SP800-39-final.pdf.

[5] Horton, T. *Managing Information Security Risks*. http://gigabytedownloads.com/accessing/Horton_Thomas_Managing_Information_Security_Risks_ebook.rar

[6] Department of Homeland Security National Vulnerability Database. Washington DC, available at http://nvd.nist.gov/.

Trustworthiness evaluation of critical information infrastructures

Stefan Winter, Daniel Germanus, Hamza Ghani, Thorsten Piper,
Abdelmajid Khelil & Neeraj Suri
TU Darmstadt, Germany

Abstract

Information technology (IT) is increasingly applied in the domain of critical infrastructure protection (CIP). As CIP mechanisms are often tightly coupled with components of the critical infrastructure (CI) they are intended to protect, they become critical for the dependable and secure operation of the CI itself. A comprehensive trustworthiness (i.e., dependability and security) evaluation of IT-based CIP mechanisms is of equal importance as the expected CI protection gain, in order to weigh off the benefits and risks of IT-based CIP. In this chapter, we overview common types of trustworthiness evaluations and discuss the application of specific approaches for trustworthiness evaluations of CI and CIP components in two EU-funded projects.

Keywords: Critical Information Infrastructure Protection, Trustworthiness Evaluation

1 Introduction

Critical infrastructures (CIs) are important assets of our modern society as our everyday life largely depends upon their continuous provision of correct service. The incorrect operation of CIs poses a risk to the public safety and security, necessitating effective protection mechanisms.

A first step toward CI protection (CIP) is accomplished through CI monitoring and control, provided by a Critical Information Infrastructure (CII). Being an integral part of the CI, CIP mechanisms that are implemented via the CII require protection themselves, as improper or malicious usage may provoke hazardous consequences resulting in threats to public safety and security or in considerable financial loss. Therefore, Critical Information Infrastructure Protection (CIIP) has become indispensable, and CIIP mechanisms are in turn required to fulfill strict dependability and security requirements. To this end, trustworthiness evaluations provide means to verify and assess to which degree these requirements are fulfilled and, thus, take a vital part in the protection of CIs. This chapter provides an overview on trustworthiness evaluation approaches and their application to ensure the trustworthy operation of both CIIs (implicitly CIP mechanisms and CIs) and CIIP mechanisms.

In the remainder of this chapter, we introduce a taxonomy of dependability and security evaluation approaches along with a high-level discussion of the most commonly applied approaches in Section 2. In Sections 3 and 4, we exemplify the application of such evaluation methods in two CI-related EU FP7 [1] projects and conclude the chapter with a summary in Section 5.

2   Dependability and security evaluation approaches

The two fundamental questions related to an evaluation attempt are as follows:

1. *What* are the attributes to be evaluated?
2. *How* can the considered properties be evaluated (efficiently)?

The answer to the first question denotes the *aspect* under which the evaluation takes place. Constituting the evaluation aspect in dependability and security evaluations, *dependability* and *security* are high-level concepts that are hard or even impossible to evaluate directly in an arguably valid manner. Most evaluation attempts, therefore, focus on one or more specific dependability and security *attributes*. The second question targets the evaluation methodology. As soon as the attributes (according to which an evaluation is conducted) are chosen, suitable metrics and the respective evaluation methods need to be derived.

Throughout this section, we will introduce attributes of the high-level dependability and security concepts along with fundamental distinctions in evaluation attempts, which we will refer to as *dimensions* according to which dependability and security evaluations can be described. We will then provide a high-level overview of widely applied dependability and security evaluation methods according to this taxonomy.

2.1   A taxonomy for evaluation approaches

Dimension 1: Dependability/security attributes   We adopt the dependability and security notions from Avizienis et al. [2], as this taxonomy has gained widespread acceptance in the dependable computing community. *Dependability* as a high-level concept is defined as the ability to deliver service that can justifiably be trusted, where the *service* that a system delivers denotes its perceived behavior and *correct service delivery* denotes a service implementing the intended system function.

Dependability comprises a number of attributes [2].

- *Availability*: Readiness for correct service
- *Reliability*: Continuity of correct service

- *Safety*: Absence of catastrophic consequences on the system's operational environment (especially on its users)
- *Integrity*: Absence of improper system alterations
- *Maintainability*: Ability to undergo modifications and repair

   Security comprises availability, integrity, and *confidentiality* (the absence of unauthorized information disclosure) such that it concurrently provides

- availability for authorized actions only,
- confidentiality, and
- integrity, as defined above, with "improper" meaning unauthorized.

Dimension 2: Process versus product evaluations   When attempting to evaluate a system, there are two fundamentally distinct approaches. Either the development *process* of that system is evaluated (e.g., for ensuring service *correctness by construction*) or the resulting *product*, that is, the system implementation. The advantage of evaluating (and often certifying) a development process is that it can be done before or during the actual development. Unfortunately, good processes do not necessarily imply the development of good products (which ultimately provide the services their users depend on), as many critics have pointed out (e.g., [3, 4, 5]), and is also not applicable to already deployed legacy systems or off-the-shelf components, for which the required information on their development process may be unavailable [5]. For these reasons, the evaluation approaches selected for discussion in Section 2 are all considering product evaluations.

Dimension 3: Online versus off-line evaluations   Evaluations with respect to certain system properties can be conducted either online or off-line. *Online* refers to evaluations taking place during the actual operation of the system, that is, after its deployment. *Off-line*, in contrast, refers to evaluations that take place while the system is not (yet) operating in its intended operational environment, for example, when the system is executed in a test bench.

Dimension 4: Intrusiveness   The *intrusiveness* of an evaluation approach is indicated by the required degree of access to the system under evaluation (SUE). Three distinct access levels are commonly considered:

- *Black-box access*: If the SUE is considered a black box, no information except for its interface specifications is available to the evaluator.
- *Grey-box access*: For grey-box access, the SUE is considered a composition of black-box components. The interface specifications of the SUE and its black-box components as well as the composition's "layout", that is, information on how the individual components are interconnected to form the composition, are assumed to be available to the evaluator.
- *White-box access*: In white-box evaluation approaches, all information on the system's implementation is assumed to be available, including all source code of software components, detailed information about the applied hardware, and so on.

Between the defined grey- and white-box assumptions, there are several intermediate levels, for example, where all hardware components are black boxes and all software components are white boxes.

Dimension 5: Analytical versus experimental evaluations *Analytical* approaches attempt to gain evidence by stating requirements in a formal language and prove their fulfillment (or nonfulfillment) by formally deriving arguments or counterarguments from the system's implementation or a model thereof. *Experimental* approaches derive evidence from comparing the results of controlled system execution samples (experiments) with expected results derived from the system's requirements specification.

There are two more common approach types in this dimension. *Simulation* denotes the imitation of behavior, *emulation* the imitation of processes that lead to the exhibition of behavior. Simulations and emulations serve two purposes in system evaluations.

1. *Simulation/emulation of the SUE*: In the case of simulations, the evaluation is reduced to the behavior of the system as defined in its specification. As only a model of the actual system is being evaluated, this type of evaluation is not suited for verifying properties of the implementation against its specification but for validating the system specification against requirements imposed by its operational environment. Emulations are applicable for the same purpose in white- and grey-box scenarios, where individual components of the SUE can be either simulated or their actual implementations can be integrated.
2. *Simulation/emulation of the operational environment*: The behavior of the system's operational environment is modeled and simulated/emulated. The system's implementation is evaluated in this simulated/emulated operational environment.

2.2   Common evaluation approaches and applications

The conceptual similarities of dependability and security (cf. [2] and Dimension 1 in Section 2.1 for an overview) facilitate using the same techniques for dependability and security evaluations.

Subsequently, we will give an overview of three widely applied classes of evaluation approaches: testing, formal verification, and runtime monitoring. Each of them covers the range of attributes that were introduced in Section 2.1 to a different extent, and not all of them fit every purpose. In the following, we introduce dependability benchmarking as a method to compare the evaluation results of different systems with each other.

Dynamic testing
Dynamic testing is an intuitive evaluation approach. In order to determine whether a system does what it is intended to do the way it is intended to do it, the system is "tried out" by executing *test cases*. Test cases specify operational

conditions and stimuli that the SUE is exposed to as well as SUE's expected reaction to these stimuli. When a test case is executed, the SUE is exposed to the specified conditions and stimuli; its reaction is monitored and compared with the expected reaction. Dynamic testing is therefore an experimental evaluation technique.

Dynamic testing can in principle be performed off-line or online. The latter is usually not advisable for multiple reasons, the most relevant for CIIP evaluations being that the actual reaction of a SUE in a test-case execution is unknown. If a system is, for instance, found to be unsafe in an online evaluation, this means that it exposes unsafe behavior during actual operation, implying catastrophic consequences on its operational environment.

Dynamic testing can be performed with all possible degrees of access to the SUE. Test cases can be derived from interface specifications as well as from implementation details and, thus, all stimuli exposure and reaction monitoring can be performed according to the respective access levels.

Although in theory applicable to all dependability and security attributes, dynamic testing is particularly widespread for evaluations of certain attributes, for example, *stress testing* for availability or *correctness* and *robustness testing* for reliability.

The major issue with any evaluation attempt utilizing dynamic testing is the amount of evidence that can justifiably be drawn from such an evaluation. Exhaustive testing is commonly infeasible due to resource constraints (cf. [6]), and therefore only a comparatively small number of experiments can be performed. Actual evidence can only be derived for the concrete test cases used for performing the evaluation.

Formal verification
Formal verification aims at providing mathematical proofs of the fulfillment or nonfulfillment of dependability- and security-related properties by the SUE. After specifying a mathematical model of the SUE and expressing verifiable properties in formal logic, techniques to prove that the model satisfies the properties are applied. As they are operating on SUE models that are invariant with respect to operational conditions, formal verification approaches are analytical and performed off-line.

In order to provide justifiable dependability or security evidence, formal verification requires an accurate SUE model. Therefore, white-box-level access is usually advisable, making these approaches difficult to apply to legacy or off-the-shelf SUEs.

The applicability of formal verification is in general not limited to specific dependability or security attributes, as long as their fulfillment or nonfulfillment can be expressed in a formal specification language.

Contrary to dynamic testing, formal verification provides complete evidence about the presence or absence of dependability or security-related SUE properties (if the verification succeeds). However, the scope of formal verification is limited due to computability and size constraints (e.g., the state-space explosion problem in model checking) causally determined by the model's complexity.

Runtime monitoring

Runtime monitoring approaches monitor dependability- and security-relevant characteristics of a deployed SUE during its actual operation and, hence, is an online approach. Runtime monitoring is not analytical, as it is not operating on a model of the SUE or its operational environment. It is an experimental evaluation approach to the degree that the SUE's operation is performed in a controlled manner.

Runtime monitoring necessitates the instrumentation of the SUE with monitoring components, which is in general viable for any type of access level to its implementation. However, the utility of a runtime monitoring attempt depends on the provided degree of access to the SUE. Assume that the reliability of some black-box SUE is subject to evaluation by runtime monitoring. The functional specification of the SUE is known and can be applied to verify the monitored behavior at the SUE's interfaces. While such an attempt is capable of *detecting* unreliable behavior, the derived evidence about the SUE's unreliability does not provide means for its *prevention*. However, if grey- or white-box access to the SUE is provided, it can be instrumented with monitors for the detection of erroneous states that eventually lead to a reliability violation detectable at the SUE's interfaces. In this case, a dependability violation at the black-box level can be prevented, if a higher degree of access for instrumentation is provided.

The applicability of runtime monitoring for different dependability and security attributes depends on the availability of appropriate metrics according to which monitoring mechanisms can be implemented. An illustrative example of this relationship is provided in Section 3.

Evidence from runtime monitoring is restricted to the specific operational conditions the deployed SUE is being exposed to. In particular, no "proven in use" evidence can be derived through runtime monitoring, as it vanishes with even slight changes of the operational environment, such as the advent of new cyber attacks.

Dependability benchmarking

Unlike testing, formal verification, and runtime monitoring, dependability benchmarking does not refer to a distinct class of evaluation approaches. Instead, it applies techniques from the aforementioned evaluation classes to provide a standardized set of measures for the assessment and comparison of different systems or components, with the intent to characterize their behavior in the presence of faults in a generic and reproducible way. This is accomplished by conducting the benchmark in a uniform and standardized test environment, in which the set of measures, the approaches, and the conditions under which these measures are obtained are identical.

The FP5 and FP7 EU projects DBench [7] and AMBER (Assessing, Measuring, and Benchmarking Resilience) [8] constitute two noted contributions in the area of dependability benchmarking. Within the DBench project, a conceptual framework as well as an experimental environment for benchmarking the depend-ability of commercial-off-the-shelf (COTS) components and COTS-based systems were developed. Furthermore, a report presenting the concepts, specifications, and guidelines for dependability benchmarking, as well as a set of dependability benchmark prototype tools, was published by the project.

The AMBER project focuses on the synthesis of a research agenda for assessing, measuring, and benchmarking (AMB) resilience as input for the EU FP7. Moreover, AMBER aims to foster the European research efforts of resil-ience measuring and benchmarking in computer systems and components by coordinating studies in this area.

3   On the evaluation of Financial Infrastructure Protection (FIP)

In this section, we introduce important aspects of the evaluation of FIP. Regard-ing the object of evaluation, we differentiate between two levels: the financial critical infrastructure (FCI) itself and the protection middleware utilized to assure its security. These constitute two CIs to be evaluated. We will discuss the different facets of FIP with respect to the dimensions we have presented in Section 2.1.

3.1   FCI: Trustworthiness evaluation trends

A financial infrastructure usually refers to the collection of banks, financial institutions, and insurance companies that constitute the backbone for the world economy. At the same time, today's complex and highly connected financial environment triggers a multitude of trust and information security concerns. As several public statements by government institutions worldwide demonstrate [9,10], the sector is of high value and constitutes a symbolic target for potential cyber attacks. From a historical perspective, we mainly identify three eras in the FCI trustworthiness strategies progress.

In the first era, the FCI institutions were widely isolated and interconnected only through proprietary networks and systems. Accordingly, the trustworthi-ness of these system islands was mostly ensured by isolation. System availability and data consistency were the major drivers for protection. The design of local financial IT systems underwent rigid evaluation, testing, and verification. From a process-related perspective (cf. Dimension 2 in Section 2.1), a financial IT system needs to be developed in such a way that it complies with the specific information security goals of the FCI. The Information Technology Infrastructure Library (ITIL) [11], for example, which constitutes a body of rules and a frame-work for IT development, is a de facto standard for conducting and assessing the development of IT solutions that meet the specific trustworthiness require-ments. Software trustworthiness testing techniques are utilized as experimental evaluation techniques in order to evaluate the quality of protection (QoP) and the dependability of financial IT systems. The interested reader can refer to a wide range of techniques described in the literature [12,13]. Analytical techniques such as formal verification [14] are also being applied to assess the dependability of financial IT solutions.

The subsequent (still continuing) era is characterized by FCI institutions being pushed, through the spread of new technologies as well as cost-efficiency concerns, to provide access to their transactional systems via the Internet and to mobile customers. Here the main goal with respect to trustworthiness of the FCI is to ensure security through minimal and strictly secure data and service access from outside of the FCI. Trustworthiness assurance is considered as a prestige project, and it is a matter of competition rather than collaboration among FCI institutions. Technically, the assurance of the system's trustworthiness is mainly driven by rigorous development processes and runtime monitoring.

The third emergent (already started) era is characterized by (a) immensely increased interconnections of FCIs and (b) the appearance of new distributed and coordinated cyber attacks. Accordingly, more and more FCI participants recognize the large benefit from cooperative defense schemes established across institutions within the FCI. Data export should be minimal and adhering to strict specific requirements (privacy, anonymity issues). The cooperation is technically supported by the provision of an external trustworthy platform (fully decoupled from the internal IT infrastructure) for information dissemination and distributed collaborative event detection. In the remainder of this section, we will focus on this collaboration protection platform, which we refer to as Financial Infrastructure Protection.

3.2   FIP trustworthiness requirements and key components

Usually, the FCI is considered a grey-box system according to the terminology we introduced in Section 2.1 (Dimension 4) for the collaborative platform. Each trustworthiness evaluation approach should take this restriction into consideration and provide a solution that requires a minimalistic amount of data from the financial institutions. In addition, the FIP evaluation is required to be driven online (e.g., runtime monitoring) as well as off-line utilizing forensics and auditing techniques [15], for example.

For the financial institutions, it is important to have a reliable data source that is providing evaluation results continuously at runtime so that they have the possibility to react to the potential exploitation of security deficiencies. The FP7 EU project CoMiFin [16] (see Section 3.3) meets this crucial requirement in the sense that it provides real-time metric calculations and off-line metrics aggregations in order to assist the financial institutions in conducting their online as well as off-line periodic trustworthiness analytical activities. It is also important to objectively measure the same trustworthiness attributes for the CoMiFin infrastructure itself as it equally constitutes a CI. This issue will be discussed in the following subsections.

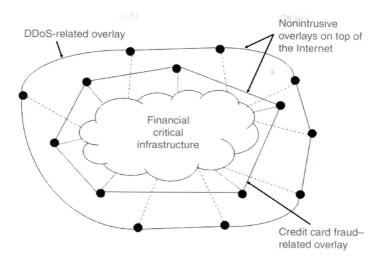

Figure 1: Nonintrusive overlays.

3.3   FIP example: CoMiFin as a FCI wrapper

In order to meet the specific and rigorous requirements of FCIs with respect to enhancing the QoP and evaluating the level of this enhancement, a novel collaborative approach has been developed within CoMifin. It consists of developing a communication middleware for sharing security-relevant information (e.g., security alerts, specific metrics about alerts) among financial institutions in order to enhance the QoP of the FCI. Taking into consideration the role that the CoMiFin infrastructure will play in enhancing the QoP of the FCI, and being aware of the sensibility of the data shared among CoMiFin participants, CoMiFin itself can be perceived as a CI. Figure 1 depicts CoMiFin's basic idea of deploying a nonintrusive overlay on top of the existing FCI in order to meet its rigid privacy requirements.

In this approach, the financial institutions have the full control on the data that they want to share with the other participating institutions. Data can be preprocessed and anonymized before being disseminated through the overlay. The overlay network is also utilized for cooperatively detecting distributed large-scale attacks that cannot be easily detected by one financial institution on its own. Furthermore, the overlay is utilized for monitoring and assessment purposes. We describe the metric-based monitoring and evaluation activities utilizing the overlay later in this section. CoMiFin gives the financial institutions the possibility to build groups that have shared topics of interest. If a collection of banks is interested in sharing information about Distributed Denial of Service (DDoS) attacks or credit card fraud, for example, they can deploy a dedicated overlay for sharing information or alerts related to this topic. Hereby, the thrust of the CoMiFin approach is to evaluate and ensure the trustworthiness of the overlays on top of untrustworthy Internet communication. The interested reader is referred to [17] for a comprehensive description of this concept.

3.4 Metric-based FIP trustworthiness evaluation

The assessment of several trustworthiness attributes is needed in order to give financial institutions the possibility to permanently monitor whether the required level of trustworthiness is actually reached or not. Security and dependability are complex terms that embody the principal attributes introduced in Section 2.1. Evaluating the trustworthiness attributes within the FCI constitutes an important task of CoMiFin. For this purpose, a large number of trustworthiness metrics are defined in order to assess the overall level of trustworthiness. Furthermore, the parameters defining the required level of QoP are determined in terms of Service Level Agreements (SLAs). Within CoMiFin, appropriate trustworthiness metrics from state-of-the-art literature [18,19,20] as well as new CoMiFin specific metrics are utilized. In the following, we introduce some basic trustworthiness metrics that are being applied within CoMiFin: In order to quantify the level of anonymity, for example, several metrics have been proposed such as k-anonymity [21]. K-connectivity is an important metric that can be measured in order to evaluate the network connectivity degree and hence the reliability and availability degree of the communications [22]. In order to determine the quality of the used proactive techniques, the quality of failure prediction is to be evaluated. The following metrics, for which other terms can be also applied, are used in the context of CoMiFin: precision p = number of correct alarms/number of alarms and recall r = number of correct alarms/number of failures.

For the security, several low-level metrics can be calculated, such as the availability (in percentage) of secure communication channels like https, anonymization of user credentials, and other personal data. The runtime monitoring of trustworthiness attributes is based on these predefined metrics (amongst others), which are in general SLA oriented. The general metrics monitoring scheme and methodology used within CoMiFin comprises the following steps: (a) sensing quantitatively predefined trustworthiness attributes of the overlay network at runtime, (b) comparing the current values with the predefined SLA thresholds, (c) triggering alarms and suggesting corrections in case of SLA violations, and (d) utilizing aggregated, historical metrics for ulterior, off-line evaluation.

4 On the evaluation of CIIP

Subject to a widespread CII flavor are Supervisory Control and Data Acquisition (SCADA) systems. SCADA systems provide system operators with a real-time or close-to-real-time view of the CI and means to modify the CI if necessary. These are often found in, but not limited to, CIs in industrial processes like the power grid.

Dependable and secure SCADA system operation is required to maintain a corresponding CI in a dependable and secure way. The INSPIRE research project [23] investigates resilience increasing mechanisms for CIIs. The project focussed on availability, confidentiality, integrity, and reliability attributes. Confidentiality is required to shield SCADA system internals from unauthorized individuals. Interconnected SCADA systems might be comprised of competing companies or public/private sector coalitions and require that only subsets of their data are shared [24]. This could be either by virtue of legislation or due to business secrets. Availability, reliability, and integrity of the SCADA system are demanded to provide secure CI operation; for example, availability and reliability address timely and continuous SCADA message reception and processing, and integrity addresses the inability to inject or modify SCADA messages.

Evaluations of the CI processes reflected by CIIs exceed the scope of this chapter. Therefore, we will focus on product evaluations with respect to the previously introduced dependability and security attributes from the INSPIRE research project.

Runtime monitoring is being applied to detect incidents that violate a CII's trustworthiness, where the degree of access to CII components determines the maximum level of intrusiveness possible for the CII monitoring component. In the following, we concentrate on SCADA systems that evolved from proprietary and insulated systems toward distributed systems using COTS software and hardware components [25]. Consequent on the interconnection of many CIs, large-scale SCADA network topologies emerged, and their messages are frequently transmitted via multipurpose networks, such as the Internet. The transmission of sensitive or time-critical data through public networks raises protection needs.

The remainder of this section focusses on cyber threats to SCADA systems, that is, attacks or faults that potentially harm the CI by perturbing the SCADA system and how these perturbations can be mitigated through SCADA system runtime monitoring. Two probable perturbation scenarios are (i) node crashes and (ii) illicit SCADA data modifications. The node crash scenario may result from intentional or unintentional behavior and thereby involve dependability and security attributes. The second scenario addresses solely security attributes. Intentional actions have to be taken on behalf of an attacker for illicit SCADA data modification, as accidental modifications are usually prevented by error-detecting codes. To counteract the previously introduced perturbations, CIIP mechanisms are required.

4.1 Design requirements for CIIP

CIIP approaches to mitigate the previously introduced perturbation scenarios need to be scalable, minimally intrusive, interoperable, frugal, and of course, provide a protection enhancement. Scalability is important for the CIIP mechanisms to support large-scale networks with thousands of data points, for example, in power plants or interconnected SCADA topologies. Hardware or software access to SCADA systems may be limited; therefore, the solution should be minimally intrusive, that is, integration needs to be viable without source code access and without a dedicated hardware infrastructure. Interoperability is beneficial in interconnected SCADA systems to cover many different system types without the need for comprehensive adaption for each kind of system. Resource frugality addresses legacy SCADA system support because field devices might come with sparse resources.

4.2 Peer-to-Peer (P2P)-based CIIP

We propose a P2P overlay to address the given problem [26]. P2P technology functions as a middleware that manages routing and storage functionality and provides a simple service interface. A middleware approach is favorable for the integration of systems without source code access. Furthermore, structured P2P protocols [27,28] are scalable up to millions of peers and thereby satisfy the requirement to fit into large-scale interconnected topologies. Also, P2P technology masks heterogeneity by providing each peer with simple and symmetric interfaces. Structured P2P protocols require only few resources in terms of data storage or computation cycles, which satisfies the resource frugality requirement. The proposed middleware-based solution does not require an additional dedicated hardware infrastructure and thereby satisfies the minimally intrusiveness requirement. Moreover, it can coexist on many of the present SCADA nodes. The node-level architecture is shown in Figure 2. The middleware intercepts SCADA communication using a listener component, extracts the intercepted SCADA payload according to a given SCADA model, and hands the payload over to the P2P subsystem. The introduction of an additional software layer may lead to undesired interference with the existing SCADA application, which results in timeliness violations or denial of service at the worst. Several mechanisms exist for the adaption of the P2P overlay to circumvent bandwidth shortages in the underlay network [29]. Also, system operators may tune P2P protocol parameters to achieve noninterference.

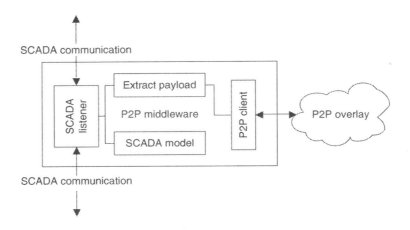

Figure 2: Architecture of P2P-based CIIP.

The P2P-based CIIP middleware monitors the intercepted SCADA traffic. The SCADA listener may deduce the frequency of SCADA sensor messages either from observations or via the SCADA model and might indicate overdue messages. Furthermore, the middleware layer monitors and compares SCADA payloads to detect integrity violations. Based upon these two monitoring mechanisms, two mitigation strategies have been developed that address the previously defined perturbation scenarios.

4.3   Mitigation strategy for node crashes

Path redundancy and adaptive routing protocols are primary ingredients to anticipate the effects of a node crash. Yet, most routing protocols do not allow adaption at rates that meet the close-to-real-time SCADA requirements. P2P overlay networks exploit path redundancy and may thereby provide alternate paths to surround crashed nodes. Therefore, as a preventive countermeasure, the P2P-based CIIP mechanism requests messages from the overlay in case SCADA messages are overdue or the connection between SCADA stations is broken.

4.4   Mitigation strategy for illicit SCADA data modification

Our approach exploits the data replication mechanism of structured P2P protocols to mitigate illicit SCADA data modification. Every time a SCADA node receives data from a sensor or actuator, the same SCADA data payload is also requested from the P2P overlay. The assumption is that an attacker has limited prevalence and cannot modify all replicated SCADA data copies. This mechanism is also a preventive countermeasure and provides security monitoring since the indication of data differences, originating from varying peers or the underlying SCADA nodes, helps in a trustworthiness evaluation.

4.5   Evaluation of P2P-based CIIP

Two measures have been defined for assessing the effectiveness of the given mitigation strategies. For the node crash scenario, a *recovery* rate specifies how many SCADA messages that were indicated overdue could be retrieved via the P2P-based CIIP. Furthermore, the illicit SCADA data modification scenario's effectiveness is rated using a *discovery* rate, specifying how many inconsistent payloads have been discovered. The evaluation according to Section 2 is a product-centric, online, minimally intrusive, and experimental approach. Both measures provide a meaningful basis to evaluate the SCADA system's availability, reliability, and integrity.

  The introduction of an additional software layer into a CII inevitably raises the question if the additional layer does not interfere with the CII in a negative way. Especially, bandwidth consumption is a crucial point, since the availability and timeliness requirements of the SCADA system may be violated if the additional layer for CIIP consumes too much network or computational resources.

Therefore, the approach's suitability in terms of traffic requirements needs to be assessed.

The traffic consumption using two widespread P2P protocols, namely, Chord [27] and Kademlia [28], for the P2P-based CIIP approach was evaluated using simulations. The configuration of the simulated SCADA system was as follows: The number of SCADA nodes ranged between 8 and 512. Each SCADA node had 64 data sources (e.g., sensors) connected to it. Data sources were sending their messages in random but fixed intervals between 1 s and 30 s to their associated SCADA node, which forwarded the data to a SCADA server. The network topology consisted of SCADA nodes (being peers at the same time) at the edge and a router mesh in between.

Based on properties of structured P2P networks, the traffic consumption scales with the number of peers. Therefore, upper bounds for traffic requirements can be determined according to the SCADA applications messaging behavior, the chosen P2P protocol, and its configuration parameters. Having an upper bound determined, it is straightforward to decide if the additional CII layer is not interfering with the SCADA application. Also, simulations have shown that the proposed mitigation strategies help to recover (node crash scenario) and discover (illicit data modification scenario) up to 95% of the incidents.

5 Conclusion

Modern societies entail an increasing reliance on CIs. Therefore, the need arises to protect CIs from the consequences of operational perturbations or deliberate threats. As a consequence, the accurate and quantitative assessment of the trustworthiness level of CIs constitutes a key objective for both the public and private sectors.

A key aspect for a CI's protection is the vitality and robustness of its closely linked CII. Sophisticated requirements on behalf of operating corporations, operational environments, and the CII's application software behavior arise. Trustworthiness is demanded for all constituting CII building blocks as well as the compound system. Throughout this chapter, we have provided a classification of contemporary approaches to trustworthiness evaluations of computer systems according to fundamental properties, which determine their applicability to CII and CIIP evaluations. The application of specific approaches has been discussed for two ongoing FP7 EU research projects, namely, CoMiFin and INSPIRE.

Acknowledgments

This research is partially funded by the EU projects CoMiFin and INSPIRE. This work was also supported by CASED (www.cased.de). The authors wish to thank their project colleagues for their collaboration.

References

[1] European Commission CORDIS FP7, http://cordis.europa.eu/fp7/home_en.html, accessed 02/2011.

[2] Avizienis, A., Laprie, J., Randell, B., & Landwehr, C., Basic Concepts and Taxonomy of Dependable and Secure Computing. *IEEE Transactions on Dependable and Secure Computing*, **1(1)**, pp. 11–33, 2004.

[3] Voas, J., Can Clean Pipes Produce Dirty Water? *IEEE Software*, **14(4)**, pp. 93–95, 1997.

[4] McDermid, J.A., Software Safety: Where's the Evidence? *Proceedings of 6th Australian Workshop on Industrial Experience with Safety Critical Systems and Software (SCS '01)*. Australian Computer Society, Inc: Darlinghurst, Australia, pp. 1–6, 2001.

[5] Redmill, F., Analysis of the COTS Debate. *Safety Science*, **42(5)**, pp. 355–367, 2004.

[6] Huang, J.C., An Approach to Program Testing. *ACM Computing Surveys*, **7(3)**, pp. 113–128, 1975.

[7] DBench, http://www.laas.fr/DBench/, accessed 08/2010.

[8] AMBER, http://www.amber-project.eu/, accessed 08/2010.

[9] EU Commission, http://cordis.europa.eu/fetch?CALLER=PROJ_ICT&ACTION=D&CAT=PROJ&RCN=85446, accessed 09/2011.

[10] USGA-Office, Critical Infrastructure Protection—Efforts of the Financial Services Sector to Address Cyber Threats. Technical report, United States General Accounting Office, 2003.

[11] ITIL, http://www.itil.org/, accessed 02/2011.

[12] Wysopal, C., Nelson, L., Zovi, D., & Dustin, E., *The Art of Software Security Testing*. Symantec Press: Upper Saddle River, NJ, 2007.

[13] Graham, D., van Veenendaal, E., Evans, I., & Black, R., *Foundations of Software Testing*. Cengage Learning Business Press, London, 2006.

[14] Bjesse, P., What Is Formal Verification? *ACM/SIGDA*, **35**, p. 1, 2005.

[15] Peisert, S., Bishop, M., & Marzullo, K., Computer Forensics in Forensis. *ACM SIGOPS Operating Systems Review*, **42(3)**, pp. 112–122, 2008.

[16] CoMiFin-Consortium, http://www.comifin.eu, accessed 02/2011.

[17] Lodi, G., Baldoni, R., Elshaafi, H., Mulcahy, B. P., Csertàn, G., & Gönczy, L., Trust Management in Monitoring Financial Critical Information Infrastructures. *Proceedings of the 2nd International Conference on Mobile Lightweight Wireless Systems-Critical Information Infrastructure Protection Track*, Barcelona, Spain, May 10–12, 2010.

[18] Jaquith, A., *Security Metrics: Replacing Fear, Uncertainty, and Doubt*. Addison-Wesley Professional: Upper Saddle River, NJ, 2007.

[19] Reussner, R. & Firus, V., Basic and Dependent Metrics, in R. Reussner, I. Eusgeld, & F. C. Freiling (eds), *Dependability Metrics: Advanced Lectures*. Springer-Verlag: Berlin, Heidelberg, pp. 37–38, 2008.

[20] Eusgeld, I., Fraikin, F., Rohr, M., Salfner, F., & Wappler, U., Software Reliability, in R. Reussner, I. Eusgeld, & F.C. Freiling (eds), *Dependability Metrics: Advanced Lectures*. Springer-Verlag: Berlin, Heidelberg, pp. 104–125, 2008.

[21] Kelly, D.J., Raines, R.A., Grimaila, M.R., Baldwin, R.O., & Mullins, B.E., A Survey of the State-of-the-Art in Anonymity Metrics. *NDA '08: Proceedings of the 1st ACM Workshop on Network Data Anonymization*. ACM: New York, pp. 31–40, 2008.

[22] Zhang, H. & Hou, J.C., Asymptotic Critical Total Power for k-Connectivity of Wireless Networks. *IEEE/ACM Transactions on Networking*, **16(2)**, pp. 347–358, 2008.

[23] D'Antonio, S., Khelil, A., Romano, L., & Suri, N., Increasing Security and Protection of SCADA Systems through Infrastructure Resilience. *International Journal of System of Systems Engineering*, **1(4)**, pp. 401–413, 2009.

[24] Dionysiou, I., Gjermundrod, H., Germanus, D., Khelil, A., Suri, N., Bakken, D.E., & Hauser, C., Leveraging the Next-Generation Power Grid: Data Sharing and Associated Partnerships. *Proceedings of the First IEEE Conference on Innovative Smart Grid Technologies (ISGT) Europe*, Göteberg, Sweden, October 11–13, 2010.

[25] Krutz, R.L., *Securing SCADA Systems*. Hungry Minds Inc, Wiley Publishing, Inc. Indianapolis, 2006.

[26] Germanus, D., Khelil, A., & Suri, N., Increasing the Resilience of Critical SCADA Systems Using Peer-to-Peer Overlays. *Proceedings of the First International Symposium on Architecting Critical Systems (ISARCS)*, Springer, number 6150 in LNCS, pp. 161–178, 2010.

[27] Stoica, I., Morris, R., Karger, D., Kaashoek, M.F., & Balakrishnan, H., Chord: A Scalable Peer-to-Peer Lookup Service for Internet Applications. *Proceedings of SIGCOMM '01*, ACM, pp. 149–160, 2001.

[28] Maymounkov, P. & Mazières, D., Kademlia: A Peer-to-Peer Information System Based on the XOR Metric. *IPTPS '01: Revised Papers from the First International Workshop on Peer-to-Peer Systems*. Springer-Verlag: London, pp. 53–65, 2002.

[29] Small, T., Li, B., & Liang, B., Outreach: Peer-to-Peer Topology Construction Towards Minimized Server Bandwidth Costs. *IEEE Journal on Selected Areas in Communications*, **25(1)**, pp. 35–45, 2007.

Network resilience

Luigi Coppolino, Salvatore D'Antonio & Luigi Romano
University of Naples Parthenope, Naples, Italy

Abstract

Generally speaking, resilience is the ability of a system to provide an acceptable level of service even in the face of faults and challenges to normal operation. In this chapter, focus is on two specific categories of challenges, namely, (i) cyber attacks and (ii) technology changes. We present a number of resilience-enhancing techniques, which are suitable for a wide variety of current and future Critical Infrastructures (CIs). We do so in a practice-oriented view and with respect to some of the most widely used and/or emerging network technologies for building CIs, specifically satellite networks, IP-based systems, and Wireless Sensor Networks. The techniques have been implemented in a distributed architecture, which integrates four main functions: monitoring, detection, diagnosis, and remediation. The ideas and results presented in this chapter are part of the lessons we have learned in INTERSECTION and INSPIRE, two FP7 projects we have been involved in. Additional information is available on the websites of the projects.

Keywords: Critical Infrastructure Protection, SCADA, Monitoring, Detection, Diagnosis, Remediation

1 Introduction

Resilience is an (relatively recently) abused word, in a number of fields. A sensible definition of resilience in computer networking is the one given by the ResiliNets research initiative [1]: "Resilience is the ability to provide and maintain an acceptable level of service in the face of faults and challenges to normal operation." In this chapter, we will refer to the above definition of resilience, in the context of Critical Infrastructures (CIs) and with emphasis on two specific categories of challenges, namely, (i) cyber attacks and (ii) technology changes.

The reason why we decided to focus on cyber attacks is that we are witnessing a dramatic increase of external-borne security incidents, while internal incidents are basically stable and accidental incidents have increased only slightly (most probably, such a slight increase is mainly due to the increased complexity of the equipment, which results in more operator mistakes and interactions faults in general) [2]. In particular, the shared communication infrastructure has become an obvious target for disrupting a Supervisory Control and Data Acquisition (SCADA) network. For example, an attacker may exploit a vulnerability of the wireless trunk of a SCADA communication infrastructure to prevent real-time delivery of SCADA messages, which would result in the loss of monitoring information or even of the ability to control entire portions of the SCADA system. Evidence is showing that current CIs are exposed to major security risks. As an example, in [3] it is reported that Cyberspies have penetrated the U.S. electrical grid and installed malicious software programs that could be used to disrupt the system. The recent Internet worm Stuxnet specifically targeting SIEMENS WinCC SCADA systems [4] is another remarkable example of the vulnerability of current CIs. The worm exploits systems running WinCC SCADA systems configured with the default hardcoded password. Changing the password is not a viable option, since it could interrupt communications between the WinCC software and the database and interfere with the operations. Thus, SIEMENS recommended not to change the password for guaranteeing business continuity. Even worse, when SIEMENS released a new tool for finding and removing the malicious software, along with a full-fledged security update for its SCADA management products, it was found that removing the worm might harm industrial systems. More precisely the company warned its users to contact the customer center with the following note: "As each plant is individually configured, we cannot rule out the possibility that removing the virus may affect your plant in some way" [5]. Finally, if one gets an opportunity to talk privately to the personnel in charge of information technology (IT) security at electric utility companies or at the Department of Homeland Security, they say that they are extremely worried about security exposure of their SCADA systems [6].

The reason why we decided to focus on technology changes is that new technologies are being increasingly used for building CIs, with major impacts on the security level, and it will be even more so in the future. Traditional CIs were intrinsically secure systems, due to a combination of factors, some of which are briefly described in the following:

- They consisted (almost exclusively) of special purpose devices, which were based on proprietary technologies.
- Individual sub-systems operated almost in isolation; that is, they did not interact with the external world, with the exception of the system being controlled.
- They were largely based on dedicated (as opposed to shared) communication links.
- They massively relied on proprietary (as opposed to open) communication protocols.

These trends have been largely subverted, and it will be even more so in the future. First, to achieve interoperability, open communication protocols are being increasingly used, thus exposing SCADA systems to the same vulnerabilities that threaten general purpose IT systems. Second, Wireless Sensor

Networks (WSNs) have become an integral part of a wide variety of CIs, for a number of reasons [7], both technical (WSN technology has the potential of significantly improving the sensing capabilities of SCADA sub-systems [8,9] as well as the resilience of the overall SCADA architecture [10,11]) and political (governments around the world have recognized the importance of WSNs as a key technology for the protection of CIs and have issued formal directives – as well as funded specific programs – for favoring the development of WSN technology in the context of CI protection [12,13]). Third, Commercial Off-the-Shelf (COTS) components are being massively used for implementing SCADA systems [14]. Fourth, sub-systems are being connected using the infrastructure of the corporate Local Area Network (LAN), or even Wide Area Network (WAN) links, possibly including the public Internet as well as wireless/satellite trunks.

The typical architecture of current CIs has a hierarchical structure, which integrates heterogeneous devices and network trunks, also via shared network connections.

As it is apparent from the figure, there are multiple paths for accessing a CI. The US-CERT review [6] identifies several attack patterns to break into a CI, in particular (i) evading the firewall protection typically in place to isolate the business LAN from the Internet and the control LAN from the business LAN;

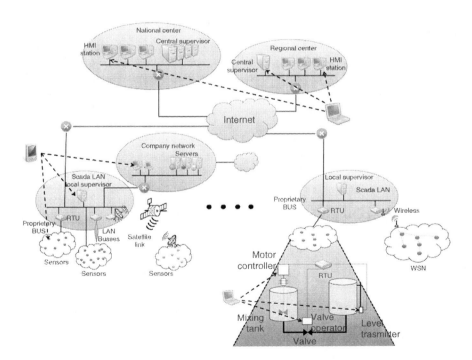

Figure 1: Alternative communication paths into and out of a typical architecture of a next generation CI.

(ii) exploiting the dial-up access typically available for Remote Terminal Unit (RTU) control and management, which typically requires no authentication or a password for authentication; (iii) exploiting the connection reserved to vendor support; (iv) exploiting database links typically used for logging actions of the production control system; (v) gaining tight control over neighboring utilities by a peer-to-peer connection to the control system; (vi) flooding the control system LAN; (vii) sending commands directly to the sensors/actuators, which generally accept any properly formatted command; (viii) exporting the human–machine interface (HMI) screen, as an example with a reverse virtual network computing (VNC) connection, hence obtaining the complete control guaranteed by the operator control panel; (ix) manipulating the data in the database; and (x) conducting a man-in-the-middle attack, which allows the attacker to manipulate both the stream of commands toward the sensors/actuators and the data gathered from the periphery.

In the INTERSECTION [15] and INSPIRE [16] projects, we have investigated the vulnerabilities stemming from the aforementioned attack patterns and developed effective techniques for detecting, diagnosing, and countering the effects of attacks to a CI.

In the remainder of this chapter, we illustrate a variety of resilience-enhancing techniques that are suitable for current and future CIs. We do so in a practice-oriented view and with respect to specific network technologies. More precisely, the rest of the chapter is organized as follows. In Section 2 we present a distributed system comprising a number of components, whose operation is orchestrated in order to actually improve the resilience of the communication network supporting a typical CI. Section 3 illustrates how intrusion detection techniques can be used to protect satellite networks against cyber attacks that exploit vulnerabilities affecting satellite networks. Section 4 illustrates how intrusion detection and remediation techniques can be used to protect an IP-based network segment against Distributed Denial of Service (DDoS) attacks. Section 5 illustrates how tight integration of detection, diagnosis, and reconfiguration techniques can be used to effectively protect a CI consisting of a WSN zone and an IP-based network segment. Finally Section 6 closes the chapter with our final remarks.

We emphasize that most of the ideas and results presented in this chapter are part of the lessons we have learned from two FP7 projects, namely, INTERSECTION and INSPIRE. Additional information is available on the websites of the projects.

2   A component-based framework for improving network resilience in CIs

In this section we present the conceptual architecture of a distributed system comprising a number of components, whose operation is orchestrated in order to actually improve the resilience of the communication network supporting a

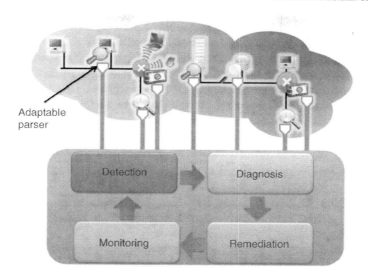

Figure 2: Main functional blocks of the resilience-enhancing distributed framework.

typical CI. The functional modules of the resilience-enhancing framework are depicted in Figure 2.

The choice of a distributed system was motivated by the possibility of separating concerns among a well-defined set of entities, each conceived to deal with a particular aspect of the problem. This has two important advantages: First, it simplifies the task of each involved entity; second, it allows a deeper specialization of each module (which can thus be modified without necessarily affecting the performance of the overall system).

The framework encompasses four main functions: monitoring, detection, diagnosis, and remediation. Monitoring aims at gathering and aggregating status data from diverse parts of a communication: both wired and wireless sensors, RTUs, historians, and supervisory stations. In order to cope with the heterogeneity of the formats of such data, grammar-based adaptable parsers [17] are employed to translate raw events to an intermediate format, so that they can be merged in a single data stream for further analysis and processing. Therefore, data provided by monitoring probes disseminated throughout the network are parsed and then used to feed the detection components, each adopting a different approach for detecting intrusions/faults. The output of each detection module is processed by a diagnoser, which is in charge of (i) clearly identifying the causes of the attacks/faults, (ii) accurately estimating their consequences on individual system components, and (iii) selecting the most suitable technique to treat the detected intrusion/fault among the implemented remediation mechanisms. The basic idea is to use an evidence-accruing fault/intrusion tolerance system to choose and carry out one out of multiple recovery/reconfiguration strategies, depending upon the perceived severity and/or on the adjudged nature of the fault/attack.

The framework [18] naturally lends itself to a context-aware deployment of the available resources, thus allowing a more effective placement of the different system modules. Dynamic deployment of the distributed system components is actually needed in order to ensure both flexibility of the architecture and resilience in the face of changes in network technologies, application services, and traffic conditions.

In the following sections, we show how the proposed framework can be used to detect, diagnose, and remediate cyber attacks against a CI that uses diverse network infrastructure technologies.

3   Intrusion detection and reaction in satellite networks

In this section we illustrate how intrusion detection techniques can be used to protect satellite networks against cyber attacks that exploit vulnerabilities affecting the so-called Performance-Enhancing Proxies (PEPs) [19]. PEPs are key elements of the transmission control protocol (TCP) accelerators, which are located at the edges a typical geostationary satellite link [20], for improving the performance of the TCP connections.

The major drawback when running PEP is the violation of the TCP end-to-end paradigm. In fact, PEP receives TCP segments, forwards them to the TCP receiver, and sends local acknowledgments (ACKs) to the TCP sender. The rationale of the use of PEP is to make the growth of the TCP congestion window faster and then to increase the actual transmission rate, which is affected by the ACK reception timing.

In the target scenario, the use of PEP allows to achieve a relevant improvement of the network performance [21]: TCP sender experiences a Round-Trip Time (RTT) lower than 1 ms or at most few ms instead of more than 500 ms experienced in case of an end-to-end TCP connection.

In this context, a PEP intentional or unintentional failure occurring after having sent an ACK and before checking the proper delivery of the corresponding packet to the actual receiver leads to an irreversible violation of the end-to-end reliability (Figure 3).

As an example of attack exploiting PEP vulnerabilities, let us assume that an end-system uses a satellite link to download a file from an FTP (file transfer protocol) server. In order to perform the file transfer, the user terminal creates a TCP connection with the FTP server in order to set up an end-to-end reliable byte stream. However, PEP agents installed at the edges of the satellite link split the end-to-end TCP connection into three "sub-connections" in order to improve TCP performance:

1. A sub-connection from the FTP client to the satellite terminal running standard TCP,
2. A sub-connection from the satellite terminal to the satellite gateway running an optimized TCP version, and
3. A sub-connection from the satellite gateway to the FTP server running standard TCP.

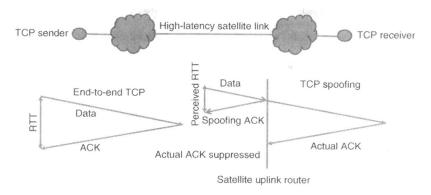

Figure 3: TCP spoofing application over satellite.

TCP splitting is transparent to the TCP end-points: The TCP server believes that received ACKs come directly from the TCP client, which is receiving packets successfully. In the following, we describe what actually happens if PEPs are used while setting up a TCP connection:

- An end-to-end TCP three-way handshake is performed in order to set up a connection between the client and the server; the exchanged packets have the TCP SYN flag on.
- Three different sub-connections are created and managed by the PEP agents.
- Each PEP uses a local cache to store the sent packets, which have not been acknowledged yet; the motivation is to allow possible retransmissions in case some packets get lost.

In this network scenario, a malicious user accesses PEP running in proximity of the satellite gateway and installs a malware application, which drops all the TCP packets from the PEP to the client network. Although there is nothing wrong experienced by the FTP server, that is, the TCP sender, the TCP connection will be kept open in order to allow the reception of a packet notifying the successful execution of the file transfer. That packet, instead, will not be generated and, thus, the TCP sender will become aware of the failure of the file transfer after a certain time period whose value depends on both TCP and application timers. The effect of the described attack is that the FTP client is not allowed to download the file.

   In this scenario, attack detection relies on the use of two detection tools disseminated throughout the network to be protected. The first tool, called SYN detector, runs on satellite gateway and keeps track of the active TCP connections. The second tool, referred to as TCP traffic analyzer, runs on the access routers of the client and the server network, and is in charge of monitoring all the TCP connections having nodes of the satellite network as source or destination. The TCP traffic analyzer measures to total amount of transferred bytes for each active TCP connection. Both SYN detector and TCP traffic analyzer collect TCP/IP statistics and forward them to a detection module that implements the attack detection logic. Outputs of the detection module are forwarded to the diagnostic module, which evaluates whether the detected anomaly can be considered as an attack or not. If an attack is detected, an alarm is generated.

The remediation module sends a control message to the PEP of the satellite terminal under attack, which causes its shutdown. Therefore, the PEP-related attack is counter-measured by removing the PEP from the network scenario, which implies a degradation of the network performance and the perceived quality of service. An attack report is produced and sent to the satellite network administrator. The report describes the pattern of the attack and is aimed to support network administrator in order to properly configure the PEP.

4 Detection and remediation of a distributed attack over an IP-based network

In this section we illustrate how intrusion detection and remediation techniques can be used to protect an IP-based network segment against DDoS attacks.

Usually, a DDoS attack abuses network protocols in order to saturate the resources of a network server, thus preventing legitimate users from using the provided service. Attackers usually attempt to consume the limited resources of the victim without directly violating it.

A common way to perform a DDoS attack is to take control of other hosts that are then used by the attacker to perpetrate the distributed attack.

A typical DDoS attack scenario involves several components widely distributed throughout the network: a "master," who initiates and orchestrates the distributed attack; several "agents," or "zombies," who receive commands from the master and launch the real attack; and a target node, which represents the victim of the attack.

An attacker, who intends to perpetrate a DDoS attack against a web-based component of a CI, first needs to "recruit" the necessary computing power. Indeed, the greater the available computing power, the greater the effects of the attack, since the capability of the attacker to saturate the victim's resources increases. For this reason, the attacker needs to opportunely violate several hosts, in order to recruit them as "accomplices." There exist several ways of compromising agent nodes: A trojan horse could be exploited, allowing the attacker to download an agent on the violated machine. Weaknesses in the software code that accepts remote connections can also be exploited for the recruitment process.

Once the victim has been identified, the attacker launches the attack by running the attack code on the master host. The master communicates with agents in order to instruct them about the attack to perform against the target by means of common packet flooding procedures. The distributed flooding is properly orchestrated by the master, in order to amplify the effects of the DDoS attack. Let us assume that each agent perpetrates a SYN FLOODING attack on the victim host. SYN FLOODING is a well-known type of attack, wherein the agent sends a succession of TCP SYN requests to the victim without completing the tree-way handshake process with the expected ACK message. Since the victim reserves memory for handling the connection associated with every TCP synchronization request, such attack can rapidly saturate the victim host's resources if the SYN request-sending rate exceeds the threshold defined by the time-out mechanism for the synchronization process on the server site.

In the INTERSECTION project, we have developed techniques that can effectively detect a DDoS attack to a CI and mitigate its effects. Such techniques have been implemented in a prototype system, which has been validated using the TFN2K tool for simulating a DDoS attack. TFN2K consists of two modules: a command-driven client to be installed on the master host and a daemon program for the agent host. TFN2K exploits four different flooding mechanisms for attacking the target: SYN FLOODING, UDP flooding, PING flooding, and SMURF attack. The target just consists of a host running a web server application, while the master and several agents running TFN2K modules represent the distributed attack system. To make the deployment scenario more realistic, the agents were placed in distinct network sites within the testbed infrastructure. Target host and master will also be placed in different networks.

The detection process is performed by monitoring the system at two different levels: A detection module analyzes traffic metrics and compares their values with specific patterns of activities and alerts the diagnostic module if anomalies are detected; the host-level probe monitors the target machine by controlling operating system parameters and identifies anomalous values of such parameters, which are symptoms of the ongoing attack. The diagnostic module correlates these two classes of symptoms and spots a SYN FLOODING attack. Then, it sends an alarm to the remediation module. The level of confidence of the decision-making process depends on the magnitude of the symptoms and on the presence of both classes of symptoms.

Network monitoring probes are disseminated throughout the network in order to effectively observe the evidences of the distributed attack.

The remediation process is initiated with the reception of an alert event from the diagnoser. According to the event type, network policy, and available remediation strategies, the remediation module selects the remediation strategy to be implemented. In the case of a DDoS attack, typical policy will combine general amelioration in the form of rate-limiting traffic filtering with a more focused remedy based on creating a white list to clients that return a correctly formed SYN-ACK. After pushing out the remedy, the remediation points are continually monitored for the amount of traffic they discard. If it falls below a policy-determined threshold, it will withdraw the remedy.

5   Diagnosis-driven reconfiguration of WSNs

In this section, we illustrate how tight integration of detection, diagnosis, and reconfiguration techniques can be used to effectively protect a CI consisting of a

WSN zone and an IP-based network segment. By diagnosis, we mean the capability of (i) clearly identifying the causes of the attacks and (ii) accurately estimating their consequences on individual system components.

The WSNs are often used in a physically semi-protected but nevertheless hostile environment, meaning one where people interested in altering the normal operation of the network can have physical access to the sensors, compromise them, or place equipment, such as intruder nodes, within the sensor network.

A well-known attack that can be launched by an intruder node against the WSN is commonly referred to as Sleep Deprivation Attack. This attack can be launched in a variety of ways depending on the particular routing protocol and its specific implementation. As an example, it is possible to send many broadcast routing packets. In this case, the attack is amplified if the fake routing packets force some nodes to change their parents, as in this case each fooled node will notify the change to all its neighbors, generating more traffic. Another way to conduct the attack is by sending unnecessary routing requests (RREQ) or by sending forged routing reply (RREP) packets that force the creation of loops in the WSN. In this case, due to the loops, packets are forwarded and stay alive for a longer time, hence resulting in unnecessary retransmissions and additional route messages. In the deployed scenario, we used a WSN composed of several Cross-Bow [22] IRIS motes and an MIB520 USB programming board. Sensors were equipped with TinyOS 2.x [23] and use Collection Tree Protocol (CTP) [24]. The attacker was exploiting a vulnerability of the CTP protocol [25] to conduct a Sleep Deprivation Attack by storing and forwarding multiple times a legitimate packet.

The attack has two negative effects on the WSN: (i) the discharge of batteries of all the nodes along the route (the path identified by triple arrows in Figure 4) from the malicious node to the base station and (ii) a denial of service for those nodes whose path toward the base station (identified with the symbol "×" in Figure 4) crosses the attacked overloaded path to the base station.

In a realistic scenario, all the packets reaching the base station are forwarded to a proxy, which in turn forwards them, on a TCP/IP channel, to the application server for the data delivery to the actual consumer (Figure 5). Every data packet generated by a node and reaching the base station is encapsulated into the payload of a TCP packet and sent to the application server via a virtual private network (VPN). In case of an attack, all the packets sent by the malicious node will reach the application server, which will recognize them as valid packets, as they are duplicates of valid packets, thus resulting in a manipulated view of the field. A smarter attack can use this behavior to attack the CI without generating extremely high duplicate packet rates, hence evading the intrusion detection system (IDS) for the WSN, but still compromising the application connected to the sensor network.

In order to detect this and other WSN-targeted attacks, it is necessary to correlate alerts generated by a WSN-aware IDS and probes deployed in the traditional IP network.

In [22], we presented a Hybrid IDS for WSN. The proposed solution relied on cooperation between IDS Local Agents and an IDS Central Agent. Each IDS

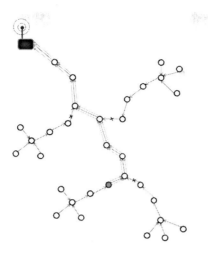

Figure 4: A Sleep Deprivation Attack results in (i) the discharge of batteries for all the nodes under attack (those part of the path with triple arrows) and (ii) a DoS (Denial of Service) for the node in branches connected to the attacked nodes.

Figure 5: The deployment scenario includes a WSN, a proxy forwarding messages from/to the WSN, an application server visualizing collected data. Two probes gathering data from the WSN and the application server complete the deployment.

Local Agents run in sensor nodes and operates with an anomaly-based approach. The IDS Central Agent is deployed in the PC connected to the base station and correlates, with a signature-based approach, alerts thrown by the IDS Local Agents to other control information collected from the network.

It is possible to correlate (Figure 5) alarms given by the WSN-specific IDS and results given by an application-level probe for detecting the described attack. The WSN-specific IDS generates alarms based on the analysis of the network and periodically (e.g., every minute) calculates the packet generation rate at every node. Such data are sent in Internet Protocol Flow Information Export (IPFIX) [26] format to the correlation module, which analyzes them together with alarms triggered by the application-level probe for packet arrival rates at the application server higher than a threshold value defined in the training stage.

By correlating the data gathered by the two probes, the diagnostic module is able to detect the Sleep Deprivation Attack and even to identify the ID of the malicious node. The identity of the ID of the malicious node can be exploited while applying remediation and recovery actions. The reaction module is in charge of triggering reaction strategies. Strategies are selected from a list of possible options, reordered based on their effectiveness with respect to the diagnostic results (e.g., attacker ID, level of damage, and class of attack), and finally sequentially applied until the attack is stopped. Examples of possible reaction strategies for the described attack are (sorted by effectiveness) as follows:

- Over the air reprogramming of the malicious node
- Switching off (i.e., setting to sleep mode) the malicious node
- Isolation of the malicious node and if necessary manual shut down and reprogramming of the node

Based on the results of the applied strategies, the diagnostic report is iteratively updated.

6   Conclusions

Generally speaking, resilience is the ability of a system to provide an acceptable level of service even in the face of faults and challenges to normal operation. In this chapter, focus was on two specific categories of challenges, namely, (i) cyber attacks and (ii) technology changes.

With respect to the aforementioned challenges, the lesson we learned is that achieving network resilience in a sophisticated CI is only possible if four key functions – namely, monitoring, detection, diagnosis, and remediation – are effectively integrated in a high-performance distributed architecture. We presented a number of resilience-enhancing techniques, which are suitable for a wide variety of current and future CIs. We did so in a practice-oriented view and with respect to specific network technologies, namely, satellite networks, IP-based systems, and WSNs. We first presented the conceptual architecture of the resilience-enhancing distributed system. We then illustrated how intrusion detection techniques can be used to protect satellite networks against cyber attacks that exploit vulnerabilities affecting satellite networks. We also discussed how intrusion detection and remediation techniques can be used to protect an IP-based network segment against DDoS attacks. Finally, we illustrated how tight integration of detection, diagnosis, and reconfiguration techniques can be used to effectively protect a CI consisting of a WSN zone and an IP-based network segment.

The ideas and results presented in this chapter are part of the lessons we have learned in INTERSECTION and INSPIRE, two FP7 projects we have been involved in. Additional information is available on the websites of the projects.

Acknowledgments

The research leading to these results has received funding from the European Community's Seventh Framework Programme (FP7/2007-2013) under Grant Agreement No. 225553 (INSPIRE project) and Grant Agreement No. 216585 (INTERSECTION project).

References

[1] The "ResiliNets" Research Initiative, available at https://wiki.ittc.ku.edu/resilinets_wiki/index.php/Main_Page (last accessed 05/08/2010).

[2] Byres, E. & Eng, P. Who Turned Out the Lights? Security Testing for SCADA and Control Systems. CanSecWest Conference, Vancouver, 2006.

[3] Beech, E. Cyberspies Penetrate Electrical Grid: Report. Reuters Top Ten News Stories, Wednesday April 8, 2009. [Online] Available at http://www.reuters.com:80/article/topNews/idUSTRE53729120090408 (last accessed 01/06/2010).

[4] Available at http://news.cnet.com/8301-27080_3-20011159-245.html (last accessed 05/08/2010).

[5] Available at http://www.computerworld.com/s/article/9179551/Siemens_Removing_SCADA_worm_may_harm_industrial_systems (last accessed 05/08/2010).

[6] USA Computer Emergency Readiness Team, Control Systems Security Program: Overview of Cyber Vulnerabilities, available at http://www.us-cert.gov/control_systems/csvuls.html (last accessed 05/08/2010).

[7] Roman, R., Alcarza, C., & Lopez, J. The Role of Wireless Sensor Networks in the Area of Critical Information Infrastructure Protection. Information Security Technical Report, Vol. 12, No. 1, 2007, pp. 1363–4127.

[8] Ye, W. & Heidemann, J. Enabling Interoperability and Extensibility of Future SCADA Systems. Technical Report ISI-TR-625, USC/Information Sciences Institute, November 2006.

[9] Wolmarans, V. & Hancke, G. Wireless Sensor Networks in Power Supply Grids. SATNAC 2008, Wild Coast Sun, September 2008.

[10] Bai, X., Meng, X., Du, Z., Gong, M., & Hu, Z. Design of Wireless Sensor Network in SCADA System for Wind Power Plant. Proceedings of the IEEE International Conference on Automation and Logistics, Qingdao, China, September 2008.

[11] He, Z.Y., Zhang, J., Li, H.W., Bo, Z.Q., Zhang, H.P., & Nie, Q.W. An Advanced Study on Fault Location System for China Railway Automatic Blocking and Continuous Transmission Line. IET 9th International Conference on Developments in Power Systems Protection, DPSP, Glasgow, 2008.

[12] U.S. Government: US National Plan for Research and Development in Support for CIP. April 8, 2005. [Online] Available at http://www.dhs.gov/xlibrary/assets/ST_2004_NCIP_RD_PlanFINALApr05.pdf (last accessed 02/06/2010).

[13] Bopping, D. CIP in Australia. First CI2RCO Critical Information Infrastructure Protection Conference, Rome, March 2006.

[14] Critical Foundations: Protecting America's Infrastructures. Report of the President's Commission on Critical Infrastructure Protection. [Online] Available at http://www.fas.org/sgp/library/pccip.pdf (last accessed 31/05/2010).

[15] INTERSECTION project website: http://www.intersection-project.eu/ (last accessed 05/08/2010).

[16] INSPIRE project website: http://www.inspire-strep.eu (last accessed 05/08/2010).

[17] Campanile, F., Cilardo, A., Coppolino, L., & Romano, L. Adaptable Parsing of Real-Time Data Streams. 15th Euromicro Conference on Parallel, Distributed and Network-Based Processing (PDP '07), Naples, Italy, 2007, pp. 412–418.

[18] Coppolino, L., D'Antonio, S., Elia, I.A., & Romano, L. From Intrusion Detection to Intrusion Detection and Diagnosis: An Ontology-Based Approach. Book: Software Technologies for Embedded and Ubiquitous Systems, Vol. 5860/20090020 – ISSN 0302-9743 – pp. 192–202.

[19] SatLabs: Interoperable PEP (I-PEP) Transport Extensions and Session Framework for Satellite Communications: Air Interface Specification. October 2005. (http://satlabs.org/pdf/1-PEP_Specification_Issue_1a.pdf).

[20] Partridge, C. & Shepard, T.J. TCP/IP Performance over Satellite Links, *IEEE Network*, Vol. 11, No. 5, September/October 1997, pp. 44–49.

[21] Caini, C., Firrincieli, R., Marchese, M., De Cola, T., Luglio, M., Roseti, C., Celandroni, N., & Portontì, F. Transport Layer Protocols and Architectures for Advanced Satellite Networks, *International Journal of Satellite Communications and Networking*, Vol. 25, No. 5, January 2007, pp. 1–26.

[22] CrossBow. Available at http://www.xbow.com (last accessed 05/08/2010).

[23] Fonseca, R., Gnawali, O., Jamieson, K., & Levis, P. TinyOS Enhancement Proposals 119: Collection. February 9, 2006. [Online] Available at http://www.tinyos.net/tinyos-2.x/doc/html/tep119.html (last accessed 01/06/2010).

[24] Gnawali, O., Fonseca, R., Jamieson, K., Moss, D. & Levis, P. Collection Tree Protocol. Proceedings of the 7th ACM Conference on Embedded Networked Sensor Systems (SenSys), Berkeley, CA, 2009.

[25] Coppolino, L., D'Antonio, S., Romano, L., Spagnuolo, G., "An Intrusion Detection System for Critical Information Infrastructures using Wireless Sensor Network technologies," Critical Infrastructure (CRIS), 2010, *Procedings of the 5th International Conference on*, pp. 1–8, Beijing 20–22 Sept. 2010, ISSBN. 978-1-4244-8080-7.

[26] The IPFIX Status Page. Available at http://tools.ietf.org/wg/ipfix/ (last accessed 05/08/2010).

Wireless sensor networks for critical infrastructure protection

P. Langendoerfer[1], L. Buttyán[2], A. Hessler[3], C. Casteluccia[4],
A. Casaca[5], A. Alkassar[6] & E. Osipov[7]
[1]IHP Microelectronics, 15236 Frankfurt (Oder), Germany
[2]BME CrySyS Lab, Budapest, Hungary
[3]NEC Labaratories, 69115 Heidelberg, Germany
[4]National Institute for Research in Computer Science and Control,
75013 Paris, France
[5]IST/INESC, 1000-029 Lisbon, Portugal
[6]Sirrix, 66123 Saarbrücken, Germany
[7]Luleå University of Technology, SE-971 87 Luleå, Sweden

Abstract

In this chapter we analyse the applicability of Wireless Sensor Networks (WSNs) as a potential building block to increase the dependability of critical infrastructures. The main focus is on the security aspects of WSNs which are used to support the control application of critical infrastructure. After a brief introduction which provides an overview and motivation for the work, a threat analysis, including details on the attacker model, attacker objective and potential attacks, is provided. A thorough state-of-the-art analysis for WSNs is also provided; this is used to identify open research issues, which are then briefly introduced in the conclusion section.

Keywords: Wireless Sensor Networks, Critical Infrastructure, Dependability, Security

1 Introduction

Critical Infrastructures (CIs) such as transportation and energy distribution networks are essential to our society; for this reason they are expected to be available 24 hours a day, 365 days a year. Critical Infrastructure Protection (CIP) requires monitoring mechanisms that enable reliable failure and attack detection as early as possible. These failures may have a number of causes, including, but not limited to, bad weather conditions or natural disasters, while attacks may range from mere vandalism to terrorist activities. Real-world examples of such failures include the failure of the energy distribution network due to heavy snowing in Munsterland, North-Western Germany,[1] in 2005, and the disruption of telecommunication services by the intentional cutting of some optical fibres in Morgan Hill, northern California,[2] in April 2009. More recently a computer worm code-named Stuxnet against control systems[3] was reported in July 2010. It raised international concern, as it has been a very sophisticated virus, targeting exclusively CIs.

Since many CIs have a large geographical span, CIP monitoring mechanisms must be scalable; in this context, Wireless Sensor Networks (WSNs) naturally arise as a potential solution. Specifically, WSNs can be relatively easily deployed at large scale to cover large geographic regions, and as they are normally built from low-cost devices, they provide a very cost-efficient monitoring solution without requiring additional infrastructure.

Another advantage of such deployments is that the distributed nature of a WSN increases the survivability of the network in critical situations. This improved resiliency is achieved because a large-scale WSN is much less likely to be affected in its entirety by failures or attacks [1,2]. In very critical situations, partially functioning WSNs may still provide sufficient information about the CI that will help the operator to prevent further damage and begin the recovery process.

It is, however, important to note that the usefulness of WSNs for CIP is primarily determined by the dependability of the WSN itself. A WSN that fails to report a faulty condition would prevent the CI operator from carrying out the appropriate maintenance that may fix the problem before the consequences affect the CI. System aspects, such as redundancy, integrity, real-time behaviour, as well as security and availability, are essential requirements to make the WSN, and hence the monitoring services that it provides, dependable.

The use of WSNs has significant impact on the dependability of the CI control system and the CI itself. In particular, it is well known that wireless communication channels are more vulnerable to environmental noise and hence are in general less reliable than wired links. Moreover, wireless channels are also vulnerable to attacks such as jamming, injection of forged data and eavesdropping that are more difficult to carry out in a wired environment, where access to the communication links are physically limited.

The two examples of attacks against CI, that is, the vandalism in northern California and the criminal attack against control systems, highlight the importance of appropriate security features to be included in the overall system.

The rest of this chapter is structured as follows. In Section 2, we introduce a threat analysis for CI when WSNs are used as part of the CI control system. We then provide in Section 3 a thorough survey of the state of the research in

[1] http://schneechaos-muensterland.de/home/
[2] http://www.morganhilltimes.com/news/255181-vandals-cut-phone-and-internet-cable-cause-headaches-for-residents-businesses-and-law-enforcement
[3] http://www.zeit.de/2010/34/T-Stuxnet-Trojaner

the area of WSNs related to challenges identified in the threat analysis part. The chapter ends with an introduction of research topics needed to increase the dependability of WSNs in such a way that they can be used as a building block to increase CI dependability.

2   Security threat analysis

The objective of this section is to carry out a threat analysis of WSNs in the context of CI applications, which includes both the identification of vulnerabilities related to this communication technology and the estimation of their risk of being exploited. It is important to understand that we are considering potential applications of WSNs in CIs in general and not a particular, well-specified system. In other words, we are not analysing an already existing system, but to some extent, we are looking into the future and investigating how such a system may potentially look like and what vulnerabilities it may entail. Consequently, the analysis will be rather high level. For the threat analysis we consider that the WSN becomes part of a control loop, where it is important to continuously and reliably deliver data from the sensors to the control centre and from the control centre to the actuators.

2.1   Adversary models

We distinguish different classes of adversaries in terms of their available resources. In particular, we identify the following three classes of adversaries depending on the amount of resources that they can invest into attacking the system:

Poor   Poor adversaries have no or very limited amount of resources both in terms of technical knowledge and money to invest. In terms of equipment, they may obtain commercially easily available devices, such as a laptop computer. However, they have no particular experience and knowledge in (mis)using those equipments to mount malicious attacks. As a representative of this class, one may think of kids playing around with a laptop and trying to interfere with the operation of the system in a rather *ad hoc* and non-premeditated manner. The main objectives could be vandalism and to disturb the operation of the system.

Clever   Clever adversaries have limited monetary resources, but they are technically highly skilled. In terms of equipment, they may obtain some special devices that are typically available in a university laboratory environment (e.g., laptops, evaluation boards, oscilloscopes etc.), or they can craft special devices for their needs using a limited budget (e.g., a wireless sniffer with a sensitive antenna). In addition, they are fully aware of how the system operates and how the protocols used in the WSN work. As representatives of this class, one may think of a university student or a network engineer. The main objective of an attack is disrupting the operation of the control system partly or entirely.

Rich   Rich adversaries have substantial monetary resources that they can use to buy very specialized equipments and are technically skilled professionals. Clearly, these are the most dangerous adversaries that can carry out premeditated, carefully organized and large-scale attacks. A representative of this class would be a criminal or terrorist organization. The main objectives of this adversary type could be to completely disable the operation of the system, to create a false impression that the system works properly when, in reality, it does not (i.e., deception), and to gather sensitive information about the CI.

2.2   Risk assessment

In the risk estimation, we used three levels to quantify the risk (low, medium and high), and we determined the level in each case, by taking into account the objectives of the given adversary as well as the difficulty to carry out the given attack and its expected amount of damage. Thus, an easy-to-mount attack, which prevents at least parts of the system to operate correctly, for example, jamming, is of high risk independently of the type of attacker. Attacks which have limited impact such as dismounting or stealing sensors are considered to have a low risk only, except for the rich attacker type. The results of our analysis are summarized in Table 1 below, where we collected the estimated risks of the attack types and adversary type.

As it can be seen from the table, the risk of the attacks that require physical access (e.g., destruction, stealing and relocating nodes or sensors) depends on how easy or difficult it is to physically approach the nodes or the sensors. If

Table 1: Summary of the risk analysis (L: low, for example, difficult attack or limited impact; M: medium, for example, feasible attack, some impact; H: high, for example, simple attack, high impact)

Attack type/adversary model>	Poor	Clever	Rich
Physical destruction of nodes	M/L	M/L	H/M
Dismounting and stealing nodes	M/L	H/L	H
Dismounting and relocating sensors	L	L	M
Sensor input manipulation	L	L	M
Jamming	H	H	H
Eavesdropping	M	H	H
Replay of protocol messages	L	H	H
Injection of crafted protocol messages	L	H	H
Corruption of stored data	n/a	n/a	n/a
Remote code injection	L	M	M
Installing rogue software on nodes	L	M	H
Deployment of rogue nodes	L	H	H

physical access is possible, then these attacks are easy to carry out, and hence, they have a rather high risk; otherwise their risk is rather low. However, many of the attacks that do not require physical access, but can be carried out remotely due to the wireless communication medium, are always easy for a capable attacker to carry out, and hence, in general, they have a high risk. In particular, we must mention jamming, eavesdropping, replay and injection of protocol messages, and deployment of rogue nodes, which are attacks with a high associated risk given a serious adversary with knowledge or monetary resources. Modifying the behaviour of the nodes by remote code injection or attacking the code update procedures is also possible, although we estimated the risk somewhat lower. Given the fact that a CI might be targeted by terrorists or organized crime, the development of means to prevent attacks of the rich attacker types is essentially needed.

3   Survey of the state of the art

In order to identify research results as well as open issues in the field of WSN, we extended the security tomography developed in the UbiSec&Sens[4] project. The main idea of our dependability tomography is to partition a complete WSN into smaller junks such as the sensor nodes themselves or the protocol layers. Then we extended the resulting structure with dependability issues such as energy management which have significant influence on the dependability of the WSN and consequently also on the CI; see Figure 1.

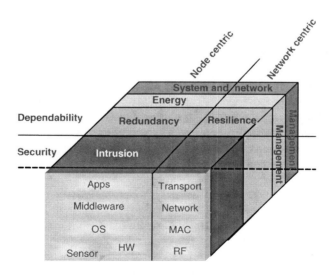

Figure 1: WSN dependability tomography.

---

[4] www.ist-ubisecsens.org/

3.1 Sensor node protection

Node configuration Optimal configuration of sensor node software has been researched in recent years on different abstraction layers: on the operating system, middleware and compiler levels. The two former approaches allow for reconfiguration at run-time, whereas the latter aims at optimizing the start-up configuration. Some operating systems (e.g., Contiki [3], SOS [4] and MagnetOS [5]) allow for code updates at run-time. The middleware approaches can be divided into adaptive middleware approaches that allow for exchange of components [6–8] and approaches that are based on the virtual machine concept [9,10]. Some middleware compilers [11–14] are designed to build middleware for safety critical embedded systems. The only approach of a middleware compiler for WSN we know of was published in [15].

The sensor node presented in [16] is enhanced with self-diagnosing features, which enable it to verify the current status of all connected components as well as its own physical conditions. In addition, the sensor node is equipped with a special hardware sensing layer around the node. This sensing layer uses a number of accelerators to determine the current orientation of the node, and it is able to detect possible impacts. This method produces much overhead in hardware and energy costs, but it is very interesting for applications in hazard environments and for intrusion detection.

Operating system dependability Several embedded operating systems for sensors have been developed in the past few years: TinyOS [17], MANTIS [18], Contiki [3], SOS [4]. However, none of them provide operating system protection (i.e., protection of the operating system from the applications) because many microcontrollers do not offer hardware support for that. It is, therefore, difficult to create reliable sensor network software that runs safely on these systems. TinyOS has recently been improved by providing efficient memory and type safety [19]. The optimizations proposed in [19] ensure that array and pointer errors are caught before they can corrupt the RAM. Another approach is called t-kernel [20], which improves resistance to application faults by providing a software virtual memory and software separation of the kernel and application spaces. This is achieved by modifying the binary code on the fly.

Detection of node compromise Krauss *et al.* presented two efficient hardware-based attestation protocols for detecting compromised cluster heads [21]. In this work, cluster heads are equipped with a Trusted Platform Module. A cluster node can verify the trustworthiness of the cluster head using the Trusted Platform Module as a trust anchor and therefore validate whether the system integrity of the cluster head has not been tampered with. Seshadri *et al.* proposed a software-based attestation technique (SWATT) to verify the memory contents of embedded devices and to establish the absence of malicious changes in the memory contents [22]. In SWATT, the attestation verifier is physically distinct from the sensor in order to avoid the usage of special secure hardware: without secure hardware, a compromised sensor cannot be trusted to verify itself correctly. SWATT uses a challenge-response protocol between the verifier and the sensor. The design of SWATT ensures that the sensor can return the correct answer only if its memory contents are correct.

Secure code update   Most of current code update solutions assume a trusted environment and focus on the authentication of the code sent by the base station. For example, Deng *et al.* proposed to secure code updates using Merkle hash trees [23]. Dutta *et al.* proposed a similar scheme to secure Deluge, the TinyOS remote programming system [24]. Seshadri *et al.* are looking at the other side of the problem: how can the base station have the guarantee that the node has updated its code [25]. They proposed Secure Code Update By Attestation (SCUBA), a scheme based on ICE (Indisputable Code Execution), a primitive that can guarantee untampered execution of code even on a compromised node.

3.2   Dependable sensor networking

Node deployment and network bootstrapping   While many research papers assume that sensor nodes are deployed in a random manner (e.g., thrown out of an aircraft), we believe that in the majority of the civilian applications, and in particular when applied to CIs, sensor nodes are deployed systematically. This has the advantage that the positions of the nodes (including the base stations and special communication relays) can be optimized for maximum sensing coverage, reduced energy consumption and increased network lifetime [26,27]. Besides these basic objectives, previous research [28–31] has also investigated how to deploy the nodes in a fault-tolerant manner, meaning that the network can tolerate random node and link failures. However, no prior work has considered intentional attacks that disable nodes or communication links in the context of node deployment strategies.

Key set-up   Securing some basic functions of the sensor network, such as routing and clustering, requires that neighbouring nodes share some cryptographic key material. Many protocols have been proposed to set-up those keys (see [32] for an overview). A common characteristic of most of these protocols is that they require key pre-distribution, that is, the installation of some keys in the nodes before their deployment. This pre-installed key material can be a master key that is used to set up pair-wise keys right after the deployment of the network and forgotten afterwards [33] or a fraction of a large set of random keys (or polynomial shares) that are used to derive pair-wise keys between the nodes in a probabilistic manner [34–37]. A different approach is proposed by Anderson, Chan and Perrig in [38] that does not require the pre-distribution of keys; however, the security of the set-up phase is somewhat weaker in this approach. Their idea is that each node broadcasts a key in clear text to all its neighbours, assuming that malicious nodes can only overhear the messages in their own neighbourhood. Therefore, if the number of malicious nodes present during the set-up phase is small, the number of keys that they can overhear is also small.

The main disadvantage of the scheme proposed in [33] is that the set-up phase is vulnerable, whereas the main disadvantage of the probabilistic key pre-distribution schemes [34–37] is that they require a large amount of memory in the sensor nodes. The problem with the scheme proposed in [38] is that it does not guarantee the authenticity of the keys, and it requires a very low density (1–3%) of malicious nodes present during the set-up phase.

Energy-efficient reliable MAC (media access control) protocols WSN MAC protocols have been mainly dominated by two main protocol families or their combinations [39]: Carrier Sense Multiple Access (CSMA) and Time Division Multiple Access (TDMA). Unlike in Wireless Local Area Network (WLANs), MAC protocols for WSNs are focused on energy management issues, maximizing the sleep periods while still keeping acceptable packet delivery delays. CSMA-based protocols present some specific sources of inefficiency, such as idle listening, collisions, message overhearing and control packets overhead. TDMA protocols, however, are well suited to avoid these problems [40] but require tight synchronization, have reduced flexibility to handle uneven or changing topologies as well as irregular multi-hop communication patterns, often requiring complex and sometimes message-intensive slot assignment algorithms to guarantee collision and interference-free slot schedules. Usual assumptions for proposed MAC protocols are single channel communication, the absence of node mobility and the low bit-rate and soft quality of service requirements of sensor data [41,42]. Streaming of higher bit-rate multimedia data (e.g., audio, still images and video) in so-called Wireless Multimedia Sensor Networks (WMSNs) has led to more recent proposals of multichannel MAC protocols. Virtual-Multiple Input Multiple Output (MIMO) schemes have also been proposed, where nodes in close proximity form a cluster, each node operating as a single antenna element, sharing information and thus simulating the operation of a multiple antenna array [42].

Resilient clustering and routing Clustering and routing protocols determine where data will flow in the sensor network or, in other words, which nodes will have to forward data packets on behalf of other nodes. For this reason, both clustering and routing have a major effect on the energy consumption of the nodes and, hence, on the lifetime of the network. Not surprisingly, clustering and routing were intensively studied in the sensor network research community, and literally hundreds of energy-efficient cluster formation and routing protocols were proposed in the literature (see [43] and [44] for surveys on sensor network clustering and routing protocols, respectively). However, less attention has been paid to the dependability of these protocols. While some research has been carried out on fault-tolerant clustering [45] and on securing cluster head election protocols [46], fault tolerance and security have not been considered jointly in the context of clustering. In case of routing, most of the sensor network routing protocols have been designed in such a way that they can tolerate or recover from random node and link failures (i.e., they are inherently fault tolerant). At the same time, there has only been a relatively small amount of work on securing sensor network routing protocols against intentional attacks (see [47] for an overview of existing proposals). In addition, some approaches to secure routing try to ensure that the routing state of the nodes (e.g., their routing tables) is always consistent [48], but this turns out to be very difficult, if not impossible, to achieve in general.

Reliable and secure transport protocols   The well-known TCP protocol presents significant inefficiencies when employed without considerable modification in WSNs. This has led to the development of reliable transport protocols that are better suited for WSNs. WSN transport protocols can be broadly classified in two main functions [49]: reliability and congestion control. In WMSNs, where sensing data may consist of audio and image/video streaming, the integration between congestion control, reliable delivery and quality of service (QoS) is paramount and must be traded off against energy efficiency [42]. Only a few proposed transport protocols integrate more than one of these functionalities [50]. The development of transport protocols that are able to support in-network data fusion in WMSNs is also an area that is not completely explored. Finally, the reliable transport protocols that have been proposed so far for WSNs badly fail in case of malicious attacks, and securing them is a completely unexplored area of research.

Network coding   Network coding was introduced in the seminal paper of Ahlswede *et al.* [51], where its advantage over traditional routing was shown. However, practical applications of network coding to reduce the number of messages in wireless networks have started to appear only recently [52]. Besides optimizing the throughput, network coding techniques can also be applied to increase redundancy and therefore the reliability of transmissions [53]. However, network coding might also increase the damage that originates from malicious nodes. Some techniques for ensuring security with network coding have been studied [54,55], though not in the context of WSN.

Topology hiding techniques   Traffic analysis and identification of nodes that play special roles in the network can be exploited by an adversary to increase the efficiency of an attack against the WSN. For instance, a larger amount of damage can be caused by disabling base stations or cluster head nodes than by destroying ordinary sensor nodes. For this reason, techniques to prevent traffic analysis and hide the role of the nodes in the network can be very beneficial. Related prior work in this field includes some papers on anonymous routing in mobile *ad hoc* networks [56–59] that try to hide who the real communicating partners are; however, those networks have usually more resources than sensor networks. There are some papers [60,61] that consider the problem of hiding the location of the source of reported events in sensor networks, but those works do not attempt to solve the problem of hiding the nodes that play special roles in the network. The problem of traffic analysis in sensor networks is considered in [62], where a suite of decorrelation countermeasures are described aiming at disguising the location of a base station. The proposed basic countermeasures include hop-by-hop re-encryption of the packets and decorrelation between their reception and forwarding times.

In addition, elaborated mechanisms are described that introduce randomness into the packet routes. However, the proposed countermeasures induce a considerable message overhead and, thus, decrease the network lifetime.

3.3 Dependable sensor network services

Fault-tolerant middleware Graceful degradation is a concept that a system continues operation even in the event of a failure. Furthermore, once the requirements for providing the full service are no longer met, the WSN should possibly not fail completely but reduce the functionality with growing severity of the damage. Routing protocols for sensor networks already consider mechanisms that increase the robustness [63]. However, current protocols for an elementary WSN service such as secure data aggregation, for example [64,65], do not tolerate any node failure.

Fault-tolerant event detection The algorithm introduced in [66] provides a distributed approach of regional event extraction based on majority voting of nodes. This algorithm was only simulated and tested on a strictly organized sensor network architecture. The sensor architecture in [67] promises optimal event detection but uses a kind of majority voting too. Even though single events are not explicitly considered, it at least provides a good algorithm to choose a proper neighbourhood for the fusion role. This algorithm takes energy resources of nodes as well as detection efficiency into account to determine an appropriate size of the neighbourhood. This makes the algorithm potentially suitable for sensor networks. Another distributed algorithm that manages a sensor network due to the accessibility of sensor nodes is proposed in [68]. It offers a fault-tolerant infrastructure that is able to cope with failed nodes. The drawback of this solution is the need of special managing nodes which are equipped with more resources than normal sensing nodes to administrate a certain region. Thus failures in those nodes unavoidably lead to loss of a part in the network and produce enormous overhead for reconfiguration. Moreover, the presented fault-tolerant architecture was only simulated and not implemented so far. In contrast to the already mentioned approaches [69], introduces a fault-tolerant approach that exploits heterogeneous redundancies. Based on the simple idea to have more measurements available than variables in the equation that must be satisfied, they are able to substitute some faulty measurements by correct ones from other sources. That means different measurements acquired from different sources, so-called heterogeneous devices, can be compared to determine and correct faulty measurements. In terms of expected advancements in sensor technology, the use of heterogeneous sensor redundancies will become widely accepted sooner or later.

In order to improve the reliability of data, measured sensor data between available sensor nodes within a given range can be compared. In addition, this method principally allows detecting faulty sensor nodes and correcting false measurements. In [70] a fault-tolerant fusion role is used to combine several binary sensor measurements in a fusion centre, by determining the minimum hamming distance between all data. A similar approach is given in [69] where probability data is used to smooth probably faulty sensor measurements. In almost the same manner the data fusion algorithms presented in [71] adjust detected faulty measurements to the most confidential values in their neighbourhood. All presented solutions smooth probably faulty measurement and hence are not well suited for reliable event detection. Furthermore they do not present a distributed approach and are used in predefined network architectures with restricted regional expansion only.

Secure and dependable distributed data storage   Considering data storage within a WSN is a recent topic and research concentrated mainly on the distribution and localization of data [72] without considering node failures. TinyPEDS [73] stores information persistently by storing a duplicated copy in a distant WSN region. With the double memory consumption, this allows robustness against one node failure, or a local WSN failure, respectively. Network coding techniques can generalize this approach. Besides the aforementioned benefits for transmission, network coding can also be used to increase the ratio of dependability of data storage and memory usage [74]. Codes for an optimized storage in WSN have also been proposed [75]. Another way to increase the ratio of dependability and memory consumption is compression. For a WSN, compression techniques that do not need coordination between nodes are desirable. This can be achieved with distributed source coding following the Slepian–Wolf theorem (see [76] for the case of WSNs).

Intelligent energy management   Most of the proposed energy management approaches consider the higher levels of the communication stack. The development of an efficient MAC [77,78] and routing protocol [44] is considered as the most important issue for the network designers. Also, the problem of providing data dissemination [79,80] and data aggregation [81] in WSN received a lot of attention. On the physical level, novel node architectures [82,83] along with the use of dedicated, power-optimized, radio and digital parts have been proposed [84,85]. In the case of high-performance WSNs, the voltage and frequency scaling is proposed as a technique that targets both the static and the dynamic power to some extent [86,87]. Power gating [88] is also considered as a possible low-power solution, but it is rarely explored in papers related to WSNs.

4   Conclusions and identification of further research topics

The field of WSNs has developed with an exciting pace from merely pure research to a more or less ready-to-use technology which is going to be applied in various areas. WSNs will become the glue between a CI and the Information and Communication Technology (ICT) infrastructure which monitors and controls the CI. A dependable WSN can keep up the information flow in critical situations, because WSNs are by design fault tolerant up to a certain level, and thus make the information flow independent of the wired-based control system. WSNs are an ideal technology to inexpensively monitor and manage information about CIs over large areas. Even though the research community has made tremendous achievements within the past years regarding the self-X features of WSNs as well as with respect to WSN security, a sufficiently high level of dependability of WSNs is still unsatisfactory. In application areas as CIP wired connections are the reference. Here WSNs have to deal with severe constraints such as limited resources and publicly shared medium. In addition some of the essentially needed core features are still contradicting: strong security vs long lifetime, reliable data transfer vs lifetime, low-cost vs stronger processing resources and so on. In order to resolve this area of conflicts and to make WSNs a building block for applications that require high level of dependability, open issues on all protocol layers related to security and reliability have to be investigated. This also holds true for the software deployed on wireless sensor nodes such as operating systems. In addition designing dependable systems under severe constraints, as it is the case for WSNs, is a highly complex task, so we also recommend further research in the field of design methodologies and tools. To conclude, Table 2 indicates open issues in comparison to the state of the art given in Section 3.

Table 2: Open research issues

Research area	Open research issues
WSN design requirements and methodologies	• Developing an innovative system engineering methodology including tool support for analysis and synthesis phases
Node configuration	• Tool support for determining initial node configuration • Two-layer approach – very efficient lower layer extending the Operating System (OS) and programmable virtual machine on top to provide run-time configurations of the node and service running on the nodes
Key set-up	• Designing pair-wise key establishment protocol without key pre-distribution needed, which reduces the number of nodes that can be impersonated and works reliable with higher percentage of malicious nodes than existing approaches
OS dependability	• Applying microkernel technology and virtualization techniques in order to enable strong separation properties • Mechanisms for trusted bootstrapping will be developed
Node compromise	• Tailoring SWATT techniques for WSN • Analysis of existing software solutions and development of new software or co-design (SW/HW) solutions
Secure code update	• Investigation of secure code update solutions that ensure multilateral security • Support for incremental code update in case sensor nodes are not homogeneously configured

Node deployment and network bootstrapping	• Identification of appropriate failure and adversary models • Derivation of theoretical optima for node deployment • Development of approximation algorithms
Energy-efficient MAC protocols	• Design of new QoS supporting and energy-efficient MAC protocols • Investigation of cross-layer approaches to mobility management
Resilient clustering and routing	• Joint consideration of security and fault tolerance • Investigation of design principles for routing protocols that tolerate random failures and detect and recover from inconsistencies caused by malicious attacks
Reliable and secure transport protocols	• Investigation of algorithms that find best trade-off between reliability and QoS • Cross-layer integration of transport, routing and energy management functions • New approaches to protect reliable transport protocols against malicious attacks
Topology hiding	• Investigation of fundamental trade-off between topology hiding and overhead, delay introduced by topology hiding • Development of means to hide cluster heads and aggregator nodes inside the WSN
Fault-tolerant event detection	• Techniques that enable independent and randomly distributed wireless devices to self-organize into a fault-tolerant architecture • Analysis of overhead incurred and means to keep it minimal
Secure and dependable distributed data storage	• Investigation of network coding technologies to extend distributed data storage, for example, for middleware • Design of new codes and coding strategies
Intelligent energy management	• Combination of existing strategies into an energy management matrix • Vertical energy management at node level • Horizontal energy management in nodes vicinity to enhance the situation awareness of the energy management algorithms
Sensor architecture for CIP	• Monitoring of substations via local reliable and secure WSNs • Improvement of sensor deployment, increase the flexibility of measurements and no single point of failure • Increases of the protection capabilities of the energy distribution network

Acknowledgements

The research leading to these results has received funding from the European Community's Seventh Framework Programme (FP7/2007-2013) under Grant Agreement No. 225186 (www.wsan4cip.eu).

The information in this document is provided 'as is', and no guarantee or warranty is given that the information is fit for any particular purpose. The use of the information is at the sole risk and liability of the user.

References

[1] R. Roman, C. Alcaraz & J. Lopez, The Role of Wireless Sensor Networks in the Area of Critical Information Infrastructure Protection, Information Security Technical Report, Vol. 12, No. 1, pp. 24–31, Elsevier Advanced Technology. ISSN: 1363-4127, November 2007.

[2] J. Lopez, J. A. Montenegro & R. Roman, Service-Oriented Security Architecture for CII Based on Sensor Networks, 2nd International Workshop on Security Privacy and Trust in Pervasive and Ubiquitous Computing (SecPerU'06), IEEE Press, Lyon, France, June 2006.

[3] A. Dunkels, B. Grönvall & T. Voigt, Contiki – A Lightweight and Flexible Operating System for Tiny Networked Sensors, IEEE Workshop on Embedded Networked Sensors, November 2004.

[4] C.-C. Han, R. K. Rengaswamy, R. Shea, E. Kohler & M. Srivastava, SOS: A Dynamic Operating System for Sensor Networks, ACM Conference on Mobile Systems, Applications, and Services (Mobisys), Seattle, WA, USA, 2005.

[5] H. Liu, T. Roeder, K. Walsh, R. Barr & E. G. Sirer, Design and Implementation of a Single System Image Operating System for Ad Hoc Networks, ACM Conference on Mobile Systems, Applications, and Services (MobiSys), 2005.

[6] A. Murphy & W. Heinzelman, "MiLAN: Middleware Linking Applications and Networks," TR795, University of Rochester, 2002.

[7] Q. Han and N. Venkatasubramanian, Autosec: An Integrated Middleware Framework for Dynamic Service Brokering. IEEE Distributed Systems Online, Vol. 2, No. 7, pp. 518–535, 2001.

[8] P. J. Marrón, D. Minder, A. Lachenmann & K. Rothermel, TinyCubus: A Flexible and Adaptive Cross-Layer Framework for Sensor Networks, Technical Report TR 481, Computer Science Department, ETH Zurich, 2005.

[9] P. Levis & D. Culler, Mate: A Tiny Virtual Machine for Sensor Networks, International Conference on Architectural Support for Programming Languages and Operating Systems, San Jose, CA, 2002.

[10] C. Fok, G. Roman & C. Lu, Mobile Agent Middleware for Sensor Networks: An Appl ication Case Study, IEEE Conference on Information Processing in Sensor Networks (IPSN), UCLA, Los Angeles, CA, USA, 2005.

[11] A. Brown, J. Conallen & D. Tropeano, Introduction: Models, Modeling, and Model-Driven Architecture (MDA). Model-Driven Software Development, Springer Verlag, pp. 1–16, 2005.

[12] J. Hatcliff, W. Deng, M. Dwyer, G. Jung & V. Prasad, Cadena: An Integrated Development, Analysis, and Verification Environment for Component-Based Systems, 25th International Conference on Software Engineering, Portland, OR, USA, 2003.

[13] J. Stankovic, R. Zhu, R. Poornalingam, C. Lu, Z. Yu, M. Humphrey & B. Ellis, VEST: An Aspect-Based Composition Tool for Real-Time Systems, IEEE Real-Time Applications Symposium, Toronto, Canada, 2003.

[14] K. B. Arvind, Applying Model-Driven Development to Distributed Real-Time and Embedded Avionics Systems. *International Journal of Embedded Systems*, Special issue on Design and Verification of Real-Time Embedded Software, 2005.

[15] P. Langendoerfer, S. Peter, K. Piotrowski, R. J. C. Nunes & A. A. Casaca, Middleware Approach to Configure Security in WSN, ERCIM Workshop on e-Mobility, Workshop Proceedings, ISBN: 978-972-95988-9-0, Coimbra, Portugal, 2007.

[16] S. Harte, A. Rahman & K. M. Razeeb, Fault Tolerance in Sensor Networks Using Self-Diagnosing Sensor Nodes, IEE International Workshop on Intelligent Environments, University of Essex, Colchester, UK, June 2005.

[17] J. Hill, R. Szewczyk, A. Woo, S. Hollar, D. Culler & K. Pister, System Architecture Directions for Networked Sensors, International Conference on Architectural Support for Programming Languages and Operating Systems (ASPLOS), Cambridge, UK, November 2000.

[18] S. Bhatti, J. Carlson, H. Dai, J. Deng, J. Rose, A. Sheth, B. Shucker, C. Gruenwald, A. Torgerson & R. Han, MANTIS OS: An Embedded Multithreaded Operating System for Wireless Micro Sensor Platforms. *ACM Mobile Networks and Applications*, Vol. 10, No. 4, 2005.

[19] N. Cooprider, W. Archer, E. Eide, D. Gay & J. Regehr, Efficient Memory Safety for TinyOS, ACM Conference on Embedded Networked Sensor Systems (SenSys), Sydney, NSW, Australia, November 2007.

[20] L. Gu & J. A. Stankovic, t-Kernel: Providing Reliable OS Support for Wireless Sensor Networks, ACM Conference on Embedded Networked Sensor Systems (SenSys), Boulder, CO, USA, 2006.

[21] C. Krauss, F. Stumpf & C. Eckert, Detecting Node Compromise in Hybrid Wireless Sensor Networks Using Attestation Techniques, European Workshop on Security and Privacy in Ad-Hoc and Sensor Networks (ESAS), Cambridge, UK, July 2007.

[22] A. Seshadri, A. Perrig, L. van Doorn & P. Khosla, SWATT: SoftWare-Based ATTestation for Embedded Devices, IEEE Symposium on Security and Privacy, Oakland, CA, May 2004.

[23] J. Deng, R. Han & S. Mishra, Secure Code Distribution in Dynamically Programmable Wireless Sensor Networks, International Conference of Information Processing for Sensor Networks (IPSN), Nashville, TN, USA, 2006.

[24] P. Dutta, J. Hui, D. Chu & D. Culler, Securing the Deluge Network Programming System, International Conference of Information Processing for Sensor Networks (IPSN), Nashville, TN, USA, 2006.

[25] A. Seshadri, M. Luk, A. Perrig, L. van Doorn & P. Khosla, SCUBA: Secure Code Update by Attestation in Sensor Networks, ACM Workshop on Wireless Security (WiSe), Los Angeles, CA, September 2006.

[26] X. Bai, S. Kumar, D. Xuan, Z. Yun & T. H. Lai, Deploying Wireless Sensors to Achieve Both Coverage and Connectivity, ACM Symposium on Mobile Ad-Hoc Networking and Computing (MobiHOC), Florence, Italy, 2006.

[27] Y. Shi & Y. T. Hou, Approximation Algorithm for Base Station Placement in Wireless Sensor Networks, IEEE Conference on Sensor, Mesh, and Ad Hoc Communications and Networks (SECON), San Diego, CA, June 2007.

[28] W. Zhang, G. Xue & S. Misra, Fault-Tolerant Relay Node Placement in Wireless Sensor Networks: Problems and Algorithms, IEEE Conference on Computer Communications (Infocom), Anchorage, AL, USA, 2007.

[29] X. Han, X. Cao, E. L. Lloyd & C. -C. Shen, Fault-Tolerant Relay Node Placement in Heterogeneous Wireless Sensor Networks, IEEE Conference on Computer Communications (Infocom), Anchorage, AL, USA, 2007.

[30] A. Kashyap, S. Khuller & M. Shayman, Relay Placement for Higher Order Connectivity in Wireless Sensor Networks, IEEE Conference on Computer Communications (Infocom), Barcelona, Catalunya, Spain, 2006.

[31] O. Younis, M. Krunz & S. Ramasubramanian, A Framework for Resilient Online Coverage in Sensor Networks, IEEE Conference on Sensor, Mesh, and Ad Hoc Communications and Networks (SECON), San Diego, CA, June 2007.

[32] S. A. Camtepe & B. Yener, Key Distribution Mechanisms for Wireless Sensor Networks: A Survey, Technical Report, Rensselaer Polytechnic Institute, 2005.

[33] S. Zhu, S. Setia & S. Jajodia, LEAP: Efficient Security Mechanisms for Large-Scale Distributed Sensor Networks, ACM Conference on Computer and Communications Security (CCS), Washington, DC, USA, October 2003.

[34] L. Eschenauer & V. D. Gligor, A Key-Management Scheme for Distributed Sensor Networks, ACM Conference on Computer and Communications Security (CCS), Washington, DC, USA, November 2002.

[35] H. Chan, A. Perrig & D. Song, Random Key Predistribution Schemes for Sensor Networks, IEEE Symposium on Security and Privacy, Oakland, CA, 2003.

[36] W. Du, J. Deng, Y. S. Han & P. K. Varshney, A Pairwise Key Pre-Distribution Scheme for Wireless Sensor Networks, ACM Conference on Computer and Communications Security (CCS), Washington, DC, USA, October 2003.

[37] D. Liu & P. Ning, Establishing Pairwise Keys in Distributed Sensor Networks, ACM Conference on Computer and Communications Security (CCS), Washington, DC, USA, October 2003.

[38] R. Anderson, H. Chan & A. Perrig, Key Infection: Smart Trust for Smart Dust, International Conference on Network Protocols (ICNP), Berlin, Germany, October 2004.

[39] K. Langendoen & G. Halkes, Energy-Efficient Medium Access Control, In R. Zurawski (ed.), *Embedded Systems Handbook*, CRC Press, August 2005, Available online at: http://pds.twi.tudelft.nl/~koen/publications.php.

[40] M. Nunes, A. Grilo & M. Macedo, Interference-Free TDMA Slot Allocation in Wireless Sensor Networks, 32nd IEEE Conference on Local Computer Networks (IEEE LCN 2007), Dublin, Ireland, October 2007.

[41] M. Ali, U. Saif, A. Dunkels, T. Voigt, K. Römer, K. Langendoen, J. Polastre & Z. Uzmi, Medium Access Control Issues in Sensor Networks, *ACM Computer Communication Review*, Vol. 36, No. 2, April 2006.

[42] I. Akyildiz, T. Melodia & K. Chowdhury, A Survey on Wireless Multimedia Sensor Networks. *Computer Networks*, Vol. 51, No. 4, pp. 921–960, March 2007.

[43] A. A. Abbasi & M. Younis, A Survey on Clustering Algorithms for Wireless Sensor Networks. *Computer Communications*, Vol. 30, No. 14–15, pp. 2826–2841, 2007.

[44] J. N. Al-Karaki & A. E. Kamal, Routing Techniques in Wireless Sensor Networks: A Survey. *IEEE Wireless Communications*, Vol. 11, No. 6, pp. 6–27, 2004.

[45] F. Kuhn, T. Moscibroda & R. Wattenhofer, Fault-Tolerant Clustering in Ad Hoc and Sensor Networks, IEEE Conference on Distributed Computing Systems (ICDCS), Lisbon, Portugal, 2006.

[46] K. Sun, P. Peng, P. Ning & C. Wang, Secure Distributed Cluster Formation in Wireless Sensor Networks, Annual Computer Security Applications Conference (ACSAC), Miami Beach, FL, USA, 2006.

[47] G. Acs, L. Buttyán & I. Vajda, Provably Secure On-Demand Source Routing in Mobile Ad Hoc Networks. *IEEE Transactions on Mobile Computing*, Vol. 5, No. 11, 1533–1546, 2006.

[48] G. Ács, L. Buttyán & I. Vajda, Modelling Adversaries and Security Objectives for Routing Protocols in Wireless Sensor Networks, ACM Workshop on Security in Ad Hoc and Sensor Networks (SASN), 2006.

[49] C. Wang, K. Sohraby, B. Li, M. Daneshmand & Y. Hu, A Survey of Transport Protocols for Wireless Sensor Networks. *IEEE Network*, Vol. 20, No. 3, pp. 34–40, May/June 2006.

[50] B. Marchi, A. Grilo & M. Nunes, DTSN – Distributed Transport for Sensor Networks, Proceedings of the IEEE Symposium on Computers and Communications (ISCC'07), Aveiro, Portugal, 2007.

[51] R. Ahlswede, N. Cai, S. -Y. R. Li & R. W. Yeung, Network Information Flow, *IEEE Transactions on Information Theory*, IT-46, Vol. 46, pp. 1204–1216, 2000.

[52] S. Katti, H. Rahul, W. Hu, D. Katabi, M. Médard & J. Crowcroft, XORs in the Air: Practical Wireless Network Coding, SIGCOMM 2006, Pisa, Italy, pp. 243–254, 2006.

[53] K. Misra, S. Karande & H. Radha, INPoD: In-Network Processing over Sensor Networks Based on Code Design, IEEE Secon, San Diego, CA, USA, June 2007.

[54] D. Charles, J. Kamal & K. Lauter, Signatures for Network Coding. Information Sciences and Systems, CISS 2006, IEEE, pp. 857–863, 2006.

[55] S. Jaggi, M. Langberg, S. Katti, T. Ho, D. Katabi & M. Médard, Resilient Network Coding in the Presence of Byzantine Adversaries, INFOCOM'07, IEEE, pp. 616–624, 2007.

[56] J. Kong & X. Hong, ANODR: Anonymous On-Demand Routing with Untraceable Routes for Mobile Ad-Hoc Networks, ACM Symposium on Mobile Ad Hoc Networking and Computing (MobiHoc), Annapolis, MD, USA, 2003.

[57] Y. Zhang, W. Liu & W. Lou, Anonymous Communications in Mobile Ad Hoc Networks, IEEE Conference on Computer Communications (INFOCOM), Miami, FL, USA, 2005.

[58] S. Seys & B. Preneel, ARM: Anonymous Routing Protocol for Mobile Ad Hoc Networks, IEEE Workshop on Pervasive Computing and Ad Hoc Communications (PCAC), Vienna, 2006.

[59] I. Aad, C. Castelluccia & J. P. Hubaux, Packet Coding for Strong Anonymity in Ad Hoc Networks, IEEE SecureComm, Baltimore, MD, August 2006.

[60] P. Kamat, Y. Zhang, W. Trappe & C. Ozturk, Enhancing Source Location Privacy in Sensor Network Routing, IEEE Conference on Distributed Computing Systems, Columbus, OH, USA, 2005.

[61] A. Durresi, V. Paruchuri, M. Durresi & L. Barolli, A Hierarchical Anonymous Communication Protocol for Sensor Networks, International Conference on Embedded and Ubiquitous Computing (EUC), Nagasaki, Japan, 2005.

[62] J. Deng, R. Han & S. Mishra, Decorrelating Wireless Sensor Network Traffic to Inhibit Traffic Analysis Attacks, *Elsevier Pervasive and Mobile Computing Journal*, Special Issue on Security in Wireless Mobile Computing Systems, Vol. 2, No. 2, April 2006.

[63] G. Barrenechea, B. Beferull-Lozano & M. Vetterli, Lattice Sensor Networks: Capacity Limits, Optimal Routing and Robustness to Failures, IPSN'04, ACM Press, Berkeley, CA, USA, pp. 186–195, 2004.

[64] H. Chan, A. Perrig & D. Song, Secure Hierarchical In-Network Aggregation in Sensor Networks, ACM CCS, New York, pp. 278–287, 2006.

[65] M. Manulis & J. Schwenk, Provably Secure Framework for Information Aggregation in Sensor Networks. *Computational Science and Its Applications (Part I), ICCSA 2007*, LNCS 4705, Springer, Berlin Heidelberg, Germany, pp. 603–621, 2007.

[66] B. Krishnamachari, S. S. Iyengar, Efficient and Fault-Tolerant Feature Extraction in Sensor Networks, 2nd Workshop on Information Processing in Sensor Networks, IPSN '03, Palo Alto, CA, April 2003.

[67] X. Luo, M. Dong & Y. Huang, Optimal Fault-Tolerant Event Detection in Wireless Sensor Networks, 13th European Signal Processing Conference, Antalya, Turkey, 2005.

[68] L. B. Ruiz, I. G. Siqueira, L. B. Oliveira, H. C. Wong, J. Marcos, S. Nogueira, A. Antonio & F. Loureiro, Fault Management in Event-Driven Wireless Sensor Networks, Proceedings of the 7th ACM International Symposium on Modeling, Analysis and Simulation of Wireless and Mobile Systems, Venice, Italy, 2004.

[69] F. Koushanfar, M. Potkonjak & A. Sangiovanni-Vincentelli, Fault Tolerance in Wireless Ad Hoc Sensor Networks. *IEEE Sensors*, Vol. 2, pp. 1491–1496, June 2002.

[70] T.-Y. Wang, Y. S. Han, P. K. Varshney & P.-N. Chen, Distributed Fault-Tolerant Classification in Wireless Sensor Networks. *IEEE Journal on Selected Areas in Communications*, Vol. 23, No. 4, pp. 724–734, April 2005.

[71] T. Sun, L.-J. Chen, C.-C. Han & M. Gerla, Improving Data Reliability via Exploiting Redundancy in Sensor Networks, Technical Report TR040037, UCLA CSD, 2004.

[72] S. Shenker, S. Ratnasamy, B. Karp, R. Govindan & D. Estrin, Data-Centric Storage in Sensornets. *ACM SIGCOMM Computer Communications Review*, Vol. 33, No. 1, pp. 137–142, 2003.

[73] J. Girao, D. Westhoff, E. Mykletun & T. Araki, TinyPEDS: Tiny Persistent Encrypted Data Storage in Asynchronous Wireless Sensor Networks. *Elsevier Ad Hoc Journal*, Vol. 5, No. 7, pp. 1073–1089, September 2007.

[74] S. Acedanski, S. Deb, M. Médard & R. Koetter, How Good Is Random Linear Coding Based Distributed Networked Storage? NetCod, Riva del Garda, Italy, 2005.

[75] A. Kamra, V. Misra, J. Feldman & D. Rubenstein, Growth Codes: Maximizing Sensor Network Data Persistence, ACM SIGCOMM, Pisa, Italy, September 2006.

[76] C. Tang, C. S. Raghavendra & V. K. Prasanna, An Energy Efficient Adaptive Distributed Source Coding Scheme in Wireless Sensor Networks, IEEE International Conference on Communications (ICC '03), Anchorage, AK, USA, May 2003.

[77] W. Ye, J. Heidemann & D. Estrin. An Energy-Efficient MAC Protocol for Wireless Sensor Networks, Proceedings of the IEEE Infocom, New York, USC/Information Sciences Institute, IEEE, pp. 1567–1576, June 2002.

[78] T. van Dam & K. Langendoen, An Adaptive Energy-Efficient MAC Protocol for Wireless Sensor Networks, Proceedings of the 1st International Conference on Embedded Networked Sensor Systems, Los Angeles, CA, 5–7 November 2003.

[79] W. R. Heinzelman, A. Chandrakasan & H. Balakrishnan, Energy-Efficient Communication Protocol for Wireless Micro Sensor Networks, Proceedings of 33rd Hawaii International Conference on System Sciences, Hawaii, 2000.

[80] L. Lee, Data Dissemination for Wireless Sensor Networks, 10th IEEE International Symposium on Object and Component-Oriented Real-Time Distributed Computing (ISORC'07), Santorini Island, Greece, 2007.

[81] M. Ahmed, S. Krishnamurthy, S. K. Dao & R. H. Katz, Optimal Selection of Nodes to Perform Data Fusion in Wireless Sensor Networks, Proceedings of SPIE, Vol. 4396, Battlespace Digitization and Network-Centric Warfare, Raja Suresh (ed.), pp. 53–64, Orlando, FL, USA, August 2001.

[82] M. Hempstead, N. Tripathi, P. Mauro, G.-Y. Wei & D. Brooks, An Ultra Low Power System Architecture for Sensor Network Applications, 32nd Annual International Symposium on Computer Architecture, Madison, WI, USA, pp. 208–219, June 4–8, 2005.

[83] J. L. Hill & D. E. Culler, System Architecture for Wireless Sensor Networks, PhD dissertation, University of California, Berkeley, CA, 2003.

[84] J. Rabaey et al., PicoRadios for Wireless Sensor Networks: The Next Challenge in Ultra-Low-Power Design, IEEE ISSCC, San Francisco, CA, USA, pp. 200–201, July 2002.

[85] B. H. Calhoun, D. C. Daly, N. Verma, D. Finchelstein, D. D. Wentzloff, A. Wang, S.-H. Cho & A. P. Chandrakasan, Design Considerations for Ultra-Low Energy Wireless Microsensor Nodes. *IEEE Transactions on Computers*, Vol. 54, No. 6, pp. 727–740, June 2005.

[86] T. Burd, T. Pering, A. Stratakos & R. Brodersen, A Dynamic Voltage-Scaled Microprocessor System, *IEEE International Solid-State Circuits*, Conference Digest of Technical Papers, Vol. 35, No. 11, pp. 1571–1580, November 2000.

[87] A. P. Chandrakasan, R. Min, M. Bhardwaj, S. Cho & A. Wang, Power Aware Wireless Microsensor Systems, Keynote Paper ESSCIRC, Florence, Italy, September 2002.

[88] H. Jiang, M. Marek-Sadowska & S. R. Nassif, Benefits and Costs of Power-Gating Technique, ICCD, San Jose, CA, USA, pp. 559–566, 2005.

Part IV
Monitoring and Surveillance Technologies

Intelligent video surveillance

Rita Cucchiara[1], Andrea Prati[2] & Roberto Vezzani[1]
[1]Department of Information Engineering, University of Modena and Reggio Emilia, Italy
[2]Department of Engineering Science and Methods, University of Modena and Reggio Emilia, Italy

Abstract

Safety and security reasons are pushing the growth of surveillance systems, for both prevention and forensic tasks. Unfortunately, most of the installed systems have recording capability only, with quality so poor that makes them completely unhelpful. This chapter will introduce the concepts of modern systems for Intelligent Video Surveillance (IVS), with the claim of providing neither a complete treatment nor a technical description of this topic but of representing a simple and concise panorama of the motivations, components, and trends of these systems. Different from CCTV systems, IVS should be able, for instance, to monitor people in public areas and smart homes, to control urban traffic, and to identity assessment for security and safety of critical infrastructure.

Keywords: Video Surveillance, Object Detection and Tracking

1 Introduction

This chapter will introduce the concepts of modern systems for Intelligent Video Surveillance (IVS), with the claim of providing neither a complete treatment nor a technical description of this topic, but of representing a simple and concise panorama of the motivations, components and trends of these systems.

There exist several definitions of the term *surveillance*. Among them, one interesting definition is that *surveillance concerns models, techniques, and systems for acquiring information about the 3-D external world, detecting targets along the time and space, recognizing interesting or dangerous situations, generating real-time alarms recording meaningful data about the controlled scene* [1]. The explosion of requests of surveillance systems for *protecting critical infrastructures* is due to the need for security that has followed recent catastrophic events, such as September 11, 2001. These events have contributed to the dissemination of advanced technologies, including *video surveillance*, able, for instance, to monitor people in public areas and smart homes, to control urban traffic, and to assess people identity for security and safety [2]. Recently, the term *video analytics* has also been extensively used to indicate the capability of automatically analyzing videos to detect and determine temporal events.

Thanks to the nature and richness of the provided information, cameras are widespread as the most used devices for monitoring and protecting critical infrastructures. In recent years, there has been a profound change in the way cameras and video surveillance have been used, moving from passive instruments for monitoring and storing images to *active tools for the prevention and the prompt reaction* in the case of abnormal or interesting events, leading to the so-called IVS. Until a few years ago, in fact, the major control centers of the police worldwide used the multitude of cameras only to monitor the various sites of interest and to manually detect areas at risk or events of interest, thus assisting the action of colleagues on site. This enormous (and often unnecessary) amount of information was then stored and used for criminal investigations and forensic activity in support of judges, with serious problems, however, of information retrieval (the typical "needle in the haystack"). It has been estimated that the continued presence of a human observer in private U.S. agencies costs approximately $150,000 per year. Finally, several studies in the psychology of perception agree that human attention degrades below the limit of acceptability after only 22 minutes of active video monitoring [3].

The recent advanced systems for video surveillance are often referred as *multimedia surveillance systems* [4]. The adjective *multimedia* is normally referred to systems and services conceived for human end users for accessing and using multimedia data. Applied to video surveillance, this term does not refer only to a system with the output in a multimedia format, but this system is also capable to collect, process in real time, correlate, and handle multimedia data coming from different sources (image, video, sensors, audio, etc.).

The leaning toward active and intelligent tools has dramatically increased the research activity in video surveillance over the past 5 years. In fact, the development of hardware and software solutions in complex and real scenarios is far from being straightforward. In addition, the diffusion of cameras over the major cities of the world to protect critical infrastructures calls for the use of *active multicamera systems* [5], which exploit distributed multiple cameras to provide redundant information and different viewpoints, even if they pose architectural and development issues.

Thus, a real-world IVS application usually requires a good integration and replication of a large plethora of modules (which will be detailed in the next section): *integration* in order to face compound problems and *replication* to manage more than one video source at the same time. Research interests have thus migrated from simple integration calls for specific solutions for handling camera handoff (to pass tracked objects between cameras' fields of view), methods for determining the best view given the scene's context, and sensor-fusion algorithms to best exploit a given sensor or sensor modality's strengths.

Leading companies in surveillance have proposed their own integrated frameworks, specially focusing on reliability, extendibility, and scalability aspects. For example, IBM S3 [6] is an open and extensible framework for performing real-time event analysis. New detection capabilities can be included by adding plug-ins to the low-level system (SSE, Smart Surveillance Engine), while all the fusion tasks are provided at the high level (MILS, Middleware for Large-Scale Surveillance). Similarly, ObjectVideo proposed the VEW system [7], developed starting from the prototype made under the VSAM (Video Surveillance and Monitoring) program [8]. Sarnoff Corporation proposed a fully integrated system called *Sentient Environment*, which can detect and track multiple humans over a wide area using a network of stereo cameras.

The ideal IVS system should have the following requirements:

- *Security*: The system should be capable to work also in challenging environments (due, for instance, to weather conditions or heat). It should also provide trustful data, with a certain guarantee of authenticity and protection against tampering, video manipulation, and so on.
- *Privacy*: Accessibility to raw video feeds is the way of disseminating data from camera systems. In some cases, live videos are streamed directly on the web, posing serious problems regarding privacy. Even in the case of video data directly accessible from authorized operators, potential misuses of these data are possible, and more dedicated solutions to protect privacy should be adopted [9].
- *No overstraining data*: As above mentioned, operators are overcommitted to watch tens of cameras at one time and are easily distracted by this huge amount of information (not to mention the distraction given by PTZ—Pan Tilt Zoom—cameras). Keeping a single person tracked in a single camera or even when moving between cameras can be a very challenging operation.
- *Flexibility*: The system must be designed to be easy to extend with new cameras and sensors, and with new functionalities. It should also be pluggable onto existing infrastructures, both in terms of cameras, data communication, and processing power.

The following section of this chapter will briefly introduce the main components of the architecture of an IVS system and report some examples of applications related to research projects in the world.

2 Architecture of an IVS system

This section will briefly describe the main components of an IVS system. Independent from the application, some IVS tasks are almost unavoidable, although their execution order and their mutual feedback can be designed in different ways, according to the architecture of the system and the peculiarities of the application itself. For instance, some systems first identify moving objects and then classify them to select only useful targets (e.g., vehicles or people); others, instead, provide target detection at the beginning and then they track selected objects only. Apart from some initial image enhancement and image processing steps, in any IVS system we can identify the following steps, even if their order can be different:

- *Foreground/object detection*: This task is devoted to detect what is of interest in the scene, in order to localize it and then track it along time. Typically, motion is an important cue and background is of no interest. For this reason, in stationary cameras this task is always provided by background suppression, where fixed, not moving areas are automatically separated from moving (foreground) areas. In more general scenarios with moving cameras or without a reference image, segmentation according with motion fields, color, texture, and so on have been adopted. Since the surveillance system detects and can be interested on vehicles, animals in addition to people, hereinafter the more general term of *moving object* is often used (see [10,11]).
- *Moving object tracking*: This task exploits time coherency to follow the same object along the time and the space. The dichotomy of tracking-by-detection or detection-by-tracking is still open [12]. When detection is easily provided in stationary camera, *appearance-based tracking* models working at pixel level are preferable (e.g., [13]). However, a complete survey on the topic was provided by Yilmaz *et al.* [14].
- *Object recognition*: This task consists of exploiting model coherency to provide object identification and classification, discerning between vehicles, people, bicycles, and so on, or even with a finer classification that can include the object identification (such as in the case of face recognition for identifying people). This problem was initially underestimated in surveillance since the type of objects is often predefined within the application (e.g., vehicles on road or people in an office), but it is mandatory in real scenarios, especially in the protection of critical infrastructures.
- *Scene understanding*: This high-level task is less defined than the previous ones and typically depend on the application. Some examples include the recognition of actions, events, and behaviors; the analysis of object trajectories in the scene; the estimation of crowd flows; and so on. This is typically the final step, and new generations of IVS systems must integrate a final step of high-level reasoning to assess the situation, infer possible dangerous or interesting events, and generate alarms.
- *Data fusion*: This optional task consists of fusing information coming from different sensor/camera sources to provide better detection and tracking, or to enlarge and enrich the recognition and understanding of the scene. As mentioned above, this task is becoming more popular due to the wide distribution of cameras and sensors for security purposes. In fact, the natural evolution of standard surveillance systems goes in the direction of enlarging the data availability using more cameras in parallel and consequently more processing modules for providing the previously discussed steps. In all these situations, data fusion is mandatory.

3   Examples of applications

3.1   LAICA project

Among the possible critical infrastructures, cities are the first that come in mind, given the high density of population and possible threat targets. This scenario, often referred to as *urban surveillance*, is one of the most challenging since the city is a complex entity with people and numerous sources of data/noise. The regional project LAICA (acronym for Laboratorio di Ambient Intelligence per una Città Amica—in English, Laboratory of Ambient Intelligence for a Friendly City) has been a 2-year (2005–2006) project funded by Regione Emilia-Romagna, Italy for a total budget of over 2 million euros and that involved universities, industries, and public administrations for a total of about 320 man-months.

The main objective of LAICA project is to explore the Ambient Intelligence (AmI) capabilities in a medium-sized Italian city such as Reggio Emilia. LAICA partners aim at defining innovative models and technologies for AmI in urban environments and at studying and developing advanced services for the citizens and the public officers in order to improve personal safety and prevent crimes. Multimedia and multimodal data have been collected from different sources, such as cameras, microphones, textual data about the traffic, the security, and the general situation of the city. The processed information has been made available to both police control centers and citizens by means of a dedicated Web site.

The foreseen services should be provided by a set of prototypal systems, as for instance, a system for the automatic monitoring of pedestrian subways by means of mobile and low-power audio and proximity sensors [15], a system that generates a feedback in pedestrian crossing systems to select the best duration of the green signal for the crossing [16], and a system for the automatic monitoring of public parks with a plethora of cameras (both fixed and PTZ) [17], also accounting for privacy issues [9].

The monitoring of public areas is more properly related to the topic of this chapter and requires the exploitation of multiple cameras for enhancing the security of people. Unfortunately, multiple cameras are useless if uncorrelated. The exploitation of the multiple viewpoints to correlate data from multiple cameras is often called *consistent labeling*, referring to the fact that the label/ identity of moving objects is made consistent not only *over time* (as in the case of tracking from a single camera) but also *over space* (in the sense of different cameras). Often cameras' fields of view are disjoint, due to installation and cost constraints. In this case, the consistent labeling should be based on appearance only, basing the matching essentially on the color of the objects [18].

If the fields of view are overlapping, consistent labeling can exploit geometry-based computer vision, as we did in LAICA by proposing a novel method, called HECOL (Homography and Epipolar-Based COnsistent Labeling) [19]. The method takes into account both geometrical and shape features in a probabilistic framework. Homography and epipolar lines are computed to create relationships between cameras. When a new object is detected, the system checks the

Figure 1: Examples of the HECOL system.

mutual correspondence of people using the axis of the objects precisely warped in the other field of view using epipolar lines. It accounts for the matching of the warped axis and the shapes of people. This makes the method particularly robust against segmentation errors and allows to disambiguate groups of people.

Figure 1 shows some examples of results of HECOL from a public park in Reggio Emilia.

3.2   THIS project

Transportation systems (fuel supply, railway network, airports, harbors, and inland shipping) are assets that are essential for the functioning of a society and economy and thus are critical infrastructures that can be effectively protected by an active surveillance system.

The European project THIS—Transport Hub Intelligent Video System (2010–2011)—deals with both new research approaches and concrete solutions for the safety and the security of transport hubs. THIS is carried on with the support of the Prevention, Preparedness and Consequence Management of Terrorism and Other Security-Related Risks Programme, European Commission, Directorate-General Justice, Freedom and Security.

In particular, the project THIS addresses automatic behavioral analysis through video processing, focused on crowded scenarios. THIS aims at a system performing human behavioral analysis, detaching what is usual from what is not, providing a reactive and hopefully proactive control task, preventing terroristic attacks or crime situations in public place. In order to learn what is normal or not, THIS proposes to use statistical inference enriched with contextual information. For example, "starting to run" in an exit zone could be abnormal and suspicious, but it becomes normal if the person is trying to reach a closing gate.

New computer vision technologies and software tools will be included in current available surveillance systems, equipped with web interfaces to be friendly managed by public operators. The final objective is to test research and emerging industrial solutions in real contexts to give a concrete answer to the possibility to prevent crime or terroristic attacks in public places, focusing the attention of the operators on meaningful situations in real time.

To evaluate the effectiveness of the developed system and to perform a preliminary requirement analysis, a number of use cases have been defined at the beginning of the project. These use cases are designed in order to serve three basic scenarios:

1. *Human interaction*, which deals with interactions among humans that need further investigation (e.g., people hugging and shaking hands, people quarrelling/fighting, etc.);
2. *Suspicious behavior*, which focuses on the detection of abnormal behaviors that could be indicators of potential criminal or terroristic incidents (e.g., individual running without an obvious reason, frequent visitor detection, abnormal trajectory analysis, etc.);
3. *Suspect surveillance*, which considers the continuous tracking of a suspected individual using the fixed cameras of a transport hub, which requires technologies such as consistent labeling [19], people reidentification [20], and so on.

The surveillance platform under development has been conceived to be as much flexible, customizable, and general as possible. Typical video surveillance systems consist at least of a single camera, connected with an embedded or general purpose computer with local or remote storage, display resources and related computer vision software. When more than one single camera processing is active at the same time, as usual in surveillance of critical infrastructure such as transport hubs, more knowledge about the scene can be obtained from the combination of the single outputs.

The overall surveillance tracking system can be seen as a set of clusters of overlapping cameras. Each node consists of a single camera processing, embedding the traditional single view stack of tasks. Inside each cluster, a strong interaction among nodes guarantees the consistent labeling by means of geometrical and appearance constraints. Information coming from each cluster are then merged and managed by a higher level processing [21]. The resulting framework is a three-layer architecture as depicted in the topmost part of Figure 2.

In addition to the tracking, a complete surveillance system should include several high-level modules to cope with the recognition and understanding points. Face detection, face recognition, action analysis, and event detection are some

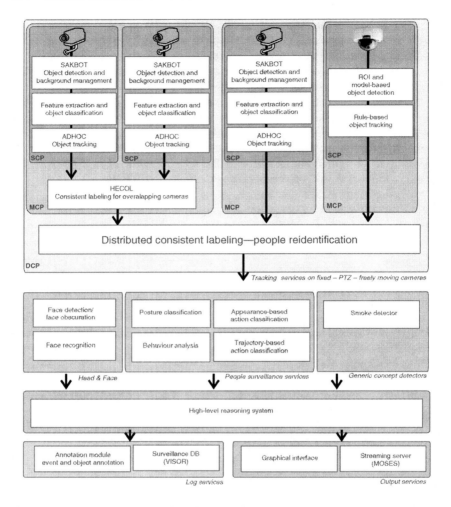

Figure 2: Multilayer and multiservice surveillance framework under development within the surveillance project THIS.

examples of functionalities of automatic people surveillance systems. Other modules can be added depending on the application and/or the research environment.

Some of these tasks should or could be performed on a subset of the installed cameras only or with a particular time schedule. Moreover, the same task (e.g., face detection) can be carried on using different techniques. A wide surveillance system should be able to take into account all these requirements. To this aim, THIS project proposes a Service-Oriented Architecture to model each system functionality, with an event-driven communication schema supporting this plethora of services. In Figure 2 a schema of the framework is reported, and in Table 1 the main services implemented in the prototype are described.

Table 1: List of the main surveillance services implemented in the framework.

People classifier	The HoG-based people classifier [22] is implemented as a service to detect people among the set of tracks, whenever they appear in the scene
Face detector	Two different face detectors are implemented in the framework: the well-known Viola & Jones of the OpenCV library and the face detection library by Kienzle *et al.* [23]
Posture classifier	The frame-by-frame posture of each person can be classified by means of the visual appearance. The implemented posture classification is based on projection histograms and selects the most likely posture among standing, sitting, crouching, and laying down [24]
Appearance-based action recognition	The action in progress is detected using features extracted from the appearance data. Walking, waving, and pointing are some examples of the considered actions. Two different approaches have been selected and implemented: The first is based on Hidden Markov Models, [25] and the second on action signature [26]
Trajectory-based action recognition	People trajectories (i.e., frame-by-frame positions of the monitored tracks) embed information about the people behavior; in particular, they can be used to detect abnormal paths that can be related to suspicious events. A trajectory classifier has been added in the system following the algorithm described in [27]
Smoke detector	The smoke detection algorithm proposed in [28] has been integrated in the system. The color properties of the object are analyzed accordingly to a smoke reference color model to detect if color changes in the scene are due to a natural variation or not. The input image is then divided in blocks of fixed sized and each block is evaluated separately. Finally a Bayesian approach detects whether a foreground object is smoke
Video streaming	MOSES (MObile Streaming for vidEo Surveillance) is a streaming system proposed by Gualdi *et al.* [29] that supports video streaming in different conditions, aiming at low-latency transmission over limited-bandwidth networks. In addition, the video stream is provided with a sufficient quality to be correctly analyzed by both human-based or computer-based video surveillance layers

3.3   Other examples

To complete the list of all the research projects or possible applications related to IVS is a paramount effort, which is out of the scope of this chapter. However, some of these are specifically related to the protection of critical infrastructures and will be here briefly introduced.

In the field of surveillance of cities and urban environments in general, besides the LAICA project already mentioned, it is worth mentioning the project UrbanEye[1] funded by the European commission within the Fifth Framework Programme (FP) and devoted to provide a comparative overview of institutional contexts of CCTV (Closed-Circuit TV) systems in Austria, Denmark, Germany, Hungary, Norway, Spain, and the United Kingdom by textual interpretation of policy documents, legislation, and the analysis of media talks in selected print media. The CAVIAR[2] project in Sixth FP also addressed the so-called city center surveillance aiming to provide semiautomatic analysis of videos for preventing nighttime crime and antisocial behavior problems, such as drunkenness, fights, vandalism, breaking and entering shop windows, and so on.

Also Seventh FP is really focused on the security research, and several projects have already been accepted. For instance, the VANAHEIM (Video/Audio Networked surveillance system enhAncement through Human-cEntered adaptIve Monitoring) project has started in February 2010 and will last 42 months. This project will address the study of innovative surveillance components for monitoring critical infrastructures such as underground transportation systems. Another example is the recent SUPPORT (Security UPgrade for PORTs) IP European project that started in June 2010 (and will last 48 months). SUPPORT is addressing potential threats on passenger life arising from intentional unlawful attacks on port facilities. The overall benefit will be the secure and efficient operation of European ports, enabling uninterrupted flows of cargo and passengers while suppressing attacks on high-value port facilities, illegal immigration, and trafficking of drugs, weapons, and illicit substances.

Also international communities, especially from United States, have demonstrated much interest in the use of IVS for surveillance of critical infrastructures. Among the many, one interesting example is the use of a multicamera IVS system for monitoring a public sport event, such as the SuperBowl XXXVII in 2003 in San Diego, CA. The research team of Prof. Mohan Trivedi at UCSD developed a system called DIVA (Distributed Interactive Video Arrays) [5] used to detect humans and animals in visually cluttered scenes on a 24-hour basis (using also a thermal camera) and to analyze the traffic flow on a road nearby stadium. Finally, an omnicamera in downtown San Diego has been used to simultaneously monitor traffic conditions and estimate the crowd size.

---

[1] http://www.urbaneye.net/index.html
[2] http://homepages.inf.ed.ac.uk/rbf/CAVIAR/caviar.htm

From the above list of research projects, it should be clear that the application of IVS systems for the protection of critical infrastructures is becoming more and more popular worldwide, thanks to the advances in the computer vision and pattern recognition technologies.

4   Conclusions

Surveillance of wide areas with several connected cameras integrated in the same automatic system is no more a chimera, but modular, scalable, and flexible architectures are mandatory to manage them. The explosion of requests of IVS systems for different scenarios leads research activity to explore many different dimensions in terms of both architectural issues and algorithms for scene recognition and interpretation.

Thus, many synergic fields spanning from hardware embedded systems, sensor networks, computer architecture on one side to image processing, computer vision, pattern recognition, and computer graphics on the other should be tightly integrated to cope with real-time surveillance applications and to provide reliable and effective answers to the security needs of critical infrastructures.

The most promising research directions in this field include the implementation of surveillance algorithms on embedded systems (to be applied on forests of small yet smart sensors), the higher level of understanding of the scene (to bridge the gap between the human operator and the IVS system), and the intelligent human–computer interfaces for forensic applications (which can guarantee an easy-to-use and fast retrieval of semantically meaningful information).

References

[1] R. Cucchiara & A. Prati, "Multicamera, distributed and heterogeneous sensor systems: Architectures and algorithms for people surveillance," *Proceedings of the First Workshop on Sensor- und Datenfusion—Architekturen und Algorithmen*, Berlin, Germany, 2009.

[2] G. Bocchetti, F. Flammini, C. Pragliola, & A. Pappalardo, "Dependable integrated surveillance systems for the physical security of metro railways," *Proceedings of the Third ACM/IEEE International Conference on Distributed Smart Cameras (ICDSC 2009)*, Como, Italy, 2009, pp. 1–7.

[3] S. Fleck & W. Strasser, "Towards secure and privacy sensitive surveillance," *Proceedings of ACM/IEEE International Conference on Distributed Smart Cameras (ICDSC 2010)*, Atlanta, GA, USA, 2010, pp. 126–132.

[4] R. Cucchiara, "Multimedia surveillance systems," *Proceedings of the Third ACM International Workshop on Video Surveillance and Sensor Networks (VSSN 2005)*, Singapore, 2005, pp. 3–10.

[5] M.M. Trivedi, T.L. Gandhi, & K.S. Huang, "Distributed interactive video arrays for event capture and enhanced situational awareness," *IEEE Intelligent Systems*, vol. 20, 2005, pp. 58–66.

[6] Y.-li Tian, L. Brown, A. Hampapur, M. Lu, A. Senior, & C.-fe Shu, "IBM smart surveillance system (S3): Event-based video surveillance system with an open and extensible framework," *Machine Vision and Applications*, vol. 19, 2008, pp. 315–327.

[7] N. Haering, P. Venetianer, & A. Lipton, "The evolution of video surveillance: An overview," *Machine Vision and Applications*, vol. 19, 2008, pp. 279–290.

[8] R.T. Collins, A.J. Lipton, T. Kanade, H. Fujiyoshi, D. Duggins, Y. Tsin, D. Tolliver, N. Enomoto, O. Hasegawa, P. Burt, & L. Wixson, "A system for video surveillance and monitoring," *Technical Report of Camegie Melion University (CMU)*, CMU-RI-TR-00-12, 2000.

[9] R. Cucchiara, A. Prati, & R. Vezzani, "A system for automatic face obscuration for privacy purposes," *Pattern Recognition Letters*, vol. 27, 2006, pp. 1809–1815.

[10] M. Piccardi, "Background subtraction techniques: A review," *Proceedings of IEEE SMC 2004 International Conference on Systems, Man and Cybernetics*, The Hague, The Netherlands, 2004, pp. 3099–3104.

[11] R.J. Radke, S. Andra, O. Al-Kofahi, & B. Roysam, "Image change detection algorithms: A systematic survey," *IEEE Transactions on Image Processing*, vol. 14, 2005, pp. 294–307.

[12] M. Andriluka, S. Roth, and B. Schiele, "People-tracking-by-detection and people-detection-by-tracking," *Proceedings of IEEE Conference on Computer Vision and Pattern Recognition (CVPR 2008)*, Anchorage, Alaska, USA, 2008, pp. 1–8.

[13] T. Zhao & R. Nevatia, "Tracking multiple humans in complex situations," *IEEE Transactions on Pattern Analysis and Machine Intelligence*, vol. 26, 2004, pp. 1208–1221.

[14] A. Yilmaz, O. Javed, & M. Shah, "Object tracking: A survey," *ACM Computing Surveys*, vol. 38, 2006, p. 13.

[15] P. Zappi, E. Farella, & L. Benini, "A PIR-based wireless sensor node prototype for surveillance applications," *Proceedings of European Workshop on Wireless Sensor Networks (EWSN 06)*, Zurich, Switzerland, 2006, pp. 26–27.

[16] A. Broggi, R.L. Fedriga, & A. Tagliati, "Pedestrian detection on a moving vehicle: An investigation about near infrared images," *Intelligent Vehicles Symposium, 2006 IEEE*, Meguro-ku, Japan, 2006, pp. 431–436.

[17] S. Calderara, R. Cucchiara, & A. Prati, "Group detection at camera handoff for collecting people appearance in multi-camera systems," *Proceedings of the IEEE International Conference on Video and Signal Based Surveillance (AVSS'06)*, Sydney, NSW, Australia, 2006, p. 36.

[18] R. Vezzani, D. Baltieri, & R. Cucchiara, "Pathnodes integration of standalone particle filters for people tracking on distributed surveillance systems," *Image Analysis and Processing—ICIAP 2009*, P. Foggia, C. Sansone, and M. Vento, eds, Springer Berlin/Heidelberg, Germany, 2009, pp. 404–413.

[19] S. Calderara, A. Prati, & R. Cucchiara, "HECOL: Homography and epipolar-based consistent labeling for outdoor park surveillance," *Computer Vision and Image Understanding*, vol. 111, 2008, pp. 21–42.

[20] M. Farenzena, L. Bazzani, A. Perina, V. Murino, & M. Cristani, "Person re-identification by symmetry-driven accumulation of local features," *Proceedings of IEEE Conference on Computer Vision and Pattern Recognition*, San Francisco, CA, USA, 2010, pp. 2360–2367.

[21] R. Vezzani & R. Cucchiara, "Event-driven software architecture for multi-camera and distributed surveillance research systems," *Proceedings of the First IEEE Workshop on Camera Networks—CVPRW*, San Francisco, CA, 2010, pp. 1–8.

[22] N. Dalal & B. Triggs, "Histograms of oriented gradients for human detection," *Proceedings of the 2005 IEEE Computer Society Conference on Computer Vision and Pattern Recognition (CVPR05)*, IEEE Computer Society, Washington, DC, 2005, pp. 886–893.

[23] W. Kienzle, G. Bakir, M. Franz, & B. Scholkopf, "Face detection—efficient and rank deficient," *Advances in Neural Information Processing Systems*, vol. 17, 2005, pp. 673–680.

[24] R. Cucchiara, C. Grana, A. Prati, & R. Vezzani, "Probabilistic posture classification for human-behavior analysis," *IEEE Transactions on Systems, Man, and Cybernetics—Part A: Systems and Humans*, vol. 35, 2005, pp. 42–54.

[25] R. Vezzani, M. Piccardi, & R. Cucchiara, "An efficient Bayesian framework for on-line action recognition," *Proceedings of the IEEE International Conference on Image Processing*, Cairo, Egypt, 2009.

[26] S. Calderara, R. Cucchiara, & A. Prati, "Action signature: A novel holistic representation for action recognition," *IEEE*, Santa Fe, NM, 2008.

[27] S. Calderara, A. Prati, & R. Cucchiara, "Learning people trajectories using semi-directional statistics," *Proceedings of Sixth IEEE International Conference on Advanced Video and Signal Based Surveillance (AVSS)*, Genova, Italy, 2009.

[28] P. Piccinini, S. Calderara, & R. Cucchiara, "Reliable smoke detection system in the domains of image energy and color," *6th International Conference on Computer Vision Systems, Vision for Cognitive Systems*, Santorini, Greece, 2008.

[29] G. Gualdi, A. Prati, & R. Cucchiara, "Video streaming for mobile video surveillance," *IEEE Transactions on Multimedia*, Santorini, Greece, vol. 10, 2008, pp. 1142–1154.

Audio surveillance

Stavros Ntalampiras
*Artificial Intelligence Group, Electrical and Computer Engineering
Department, University of Patras, Rio, Greece*

Abstract

This chapter deals with a relatively new application domain of the generalized
sound recognition technology, audio surveillance. The particular branch of computational auditory scene analysis aims at detecting acoustic events that may be
indicative of catastrophic situations (e.g., gunshot, scream, etc.) in timely fashion.
In general, this kind of systems is meant to help the authorized personnel through
a decision support interface toward taking the appropriate actions for minimizing
the effect of the hazard. This chapter provides a thorough analysis on the way that
the generalized audio recognition technology can be adapted to the needs of audio
surveillance. The acoustic parameters and the pattern recognition algorithms
that can be used for the specific domain are explained. Subsequently, this work
provides a representative picture of the bibliography and discusses several aspects
that could be of interest with respect to future directions. Lastly, it mentions
several privacy concerns along with conclusions, where the merits of surveillance
frameworks that are based on heterogeneous modalities are emphasized.

Keywords: Computational Auditory Scene Analysis, Sound Event Detection,
Audio Pattern Recognition, Civil Safety

1 Introduction

Nowadays surveillance is becoming a common practice in various environments,
like stores, agencies, and so on. Detection of situations that may include any type
of danger (human injuries, damage of properties, etc.) is of particular importance
for civil safety. As a result, there is a need for unattended space monitoring,
which has motivated the signal processing community toward experimenting
with various frameworks. Surveillance systems are typically based on the visual modality since the information they capture may provide an accurate picture
of the region of interest [1]. However, there are several problems that need to
be handled, like the field of view of the sensor network for capturing the entire
region as well as the fact that several scenes may look normal even though an

atypical situation is in progress. On top of that the acoustic modality can capture information that may be difficult or even impossible to obtain by any other means. The basic advantages of the acoustic sensors over the visual ones are (a) lower computational needs during information processing and (b) the illumination conditions of the space to be monitored and/or possible occlusions do not have an immediate effect on sound.

In this chapter, *audio surveillance* includes capturing the audio information of a particular space and processing the incoming sequence toward detecting sound events that are indicative of catastrophic situations, that is, atypical sound events, for example, scream, gunshot, explosion, and so on. This definition clearly states that audio surveillance primarily constitutes a branch of the generalized sound recognition technology. The particular technology is a part of the scientific domain, which is often called computational auditory scene analysis (CASA), and aims at a complete description of the region of interest based solely on the acoustic modality. A complete description typically includes localization, enumeration, separation, and recognition of all the included acoustic emissions. Sound recognition has many interesting applications, which can be categorized as follows:

• Voice activity detection (VAD): The principal goal of a VAD algorithm is to segment an audio signal into speech and nonspeech parts. This process is to assist a speech/speaker recognition system by elaborating on speech segments alone, thus improving its performance.
• Applications as regards to processing of musical signals: Over the past decade, this application category has attracted the interest of a relatively large number of researchers [2–4]. It includes applications such as music transcription, identification of music genre, recognition of performer, indexing and retrieval of musical data, and so on.
• Applications as regards to processing of bioacoustic signals: This special kind of audio signals belongs to very different frequency ranges. Animal vocalizations may be employed for mate attraction, territorial defense, and so on. There exists a variety of applications, like tracking of animals, monitoring of endangered species, biodiversity indexing [5–7], and so on.
• Applications of machine acoustics signal processing: This area encompasses processing of acoustic signals emitted by solids (e.g., metal, rock, ceramic, etc.) when they are subjected to stress. These emissions can be characteristic of internal fracture and/or deformation. The associated applications are non-destructive testing, fault detection and function control, maintenance services [8,9], and so on.
• Context recognition: The specific application domain essentially comprises the recognition of the physical environment around a device, including identification of relevant sound events as well as recognition of the activity of the user. Context recognition gives the ability to a device to alter its functions according to the surrounding environment [10]. Other applications are memory extension [11], environment recognition for robots [12], acoustic surveillance [13], and so on.

This chapter is organized as follows: Section 2 focuses on the domain of generalized sound recognition as seen from the scope of audio surveillance. Section 3 provides an overview of the literature along with evaluation methodologies that are usually employed. Subsequently, Section 4 mentions some privacy concerns, while conclusions are drawn in Section 5.

2   Sound recognition for audio surveillance

The domain of audio recognition is currently dominated by techniques that are mainly applied to speech technology [14]. This fact is based on the assumption that all audio streams can be processed in a common manner, even if they are emitted by different sources. In general, the goal of generalized audio recognition technology is the construction of a system that can efficiently recognize its surrounding environment by solely exploiting the acoustic modality. Every sound source exhibits a consistent acoustic pattern that results in a specific way of distributing its energy on its frequency content. This unique pattern can be discovered and modeled by using statistical pattern recognition algorithms. Similarly, an audio surveillance system models and subsequently identifies the spectral patterns of atypical sound events. However, there exists a variety of obstacles that need to be tackled when such a system operates under real-world conditions. When we have to deal with a large number of different sound classes, the recognition performance is decreased. Moreover, the categorization of sounds into distinct classes is sometimes ambiguous (an audio category may overlap with another), while composite real-world sound scenes can be very difficult to analyze. This fact has led to solutions that target specific problems, while a generic system is still an open research subject.

A typical sound recognition system as regards to classification of N sound categories is depicted in Figure 1. Initially, the audio signal passes through a preprocessing step, which usually includes mean value removal and gain normalization. This stage is to remove inconsistencies for facilitating the parameterization step. Preprocessing is of particular importance with respect to acoustic surveillance toward avoiding any loss of information. DC offset appears in the case where a waveform has unequal quantities in the positive and negative spaces. Our scope is the signal to have its middle point at zero for obtaining the maximum dynamic range. Furthermore, it is usual for an abnormal sound event to demonstrate the "clipping" effect. Gain normalization scales the audio data so that the amplitude of the respective waveform is increased to the maximum level without introducing any type of distortion. Subsequently, the signal is segmented into frames of predefined size using a windowing technique (e.g., Hamming). Then the hypothesis is made that inside a particular frame the characteristics of the audio signal are stationary. Moreover, an overlap is usually inserted with respect to adjacent frames for smoothing any discontinuities. Various frame and overlap sizes have been reported in the literature (30–200 ms). The optimal choice depends on the specifics of the particular application, while it should

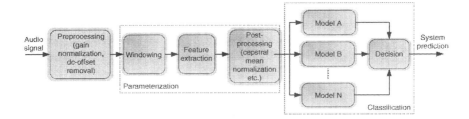

Figure 1: A sound recognition system as regards to classification of N sound categories.

be made after extensive experimentations. Afterwards, a feature extraction methodology is applied onto each frame. Feature extraction is a data reduction procedure, while its purpose is to summarize the audio segments using low-dimensional vectors. These vectors should capture the most relevant information with respect to a specific classification task. It should be noted that the inclusion of nonrelevant information may result in decreased performance. For example, in the audio surveillance case when one has to classify between explosions and screams, one should use features that are able to capture the differences between these two types of signals, for example, Mel frequency cepstral coefficients (MFCC) and features based on the Teager energy operator [15]. The following feature sets, which are typically used for sound recognition, can be employed for the special case of audio surveillance:

- MFCC: They originate from the speech/speaker recognition field. Their basic purpose is to mimic the human auditory system to some extent. More specifically, during their computation the nonlinearity of pitch perception as well as the nonlinear relationship between intensity and loudness are considered. In combination with their low computational cost, they have become the standard choice for many speech-related tasks, such as language identification, emotion recognition, and so on.
- The block diagram with respect to MFCC's extraction is depicted in Figure 2. Initially the signal is cut into frames of small duration (20–40 ms) based on the Hamming window technique. At this stage, a hop-size of 10 ms is usually employed. Afterwards the short-time Discrete Fourier Transform (DFT) is calculated for each frame using a predefined number of points (e.g., 256 or 512). A triangular filter bank elaborates on the outcome of the DFT. Subsequently, the data are logarithmically spaced and the Discrete Cosine Transform (DCT) is applied for exploiting its energy compaction properties.
- MPEG-7 low-level descriptors (LLD) [16]: MPEG-7 provides a set of standardized tools for automatic multimedia content description and offers a degree of "explanation" of the information meaning. It eases navigation of audio data by providing a general framework for efficient audio management. Furthermore, it includes a group of fundamental descriptors and description schemes

Figure 2: Extraction of MFCC.

for indexing and retrieval of audio data. Seventeen temporal and spectral descriptors that are useful for generalized sound recognition are used within the MPEG-7 audio standard. Several of them are quite simplistic (e.g., Audio Power) while others mainly target music processing (e.g., the ones that belong to the timbral group). The LLDs that may be proven effective as regards to the task of audio surveillance are as follows:

a) *Audio spectrum envelope*: This series of features belong to the basic spectral descriptors and is derived for the generation of a reduced spectrogram of the original audio signal. It is a log-frequency power spectrum and calculated by summing the energy of the original power spectrum within a series of logarithmically distributed frequency bands using a predefined resolution.

b) *Audio spectrum centroid*: The center of the log-frequency spectrum's gravity is given by this descriptor. Omitting power coefficients bellow 62.5 Hz (which are represented by a single coefficient) makes able the avoidance of the effect of a nonzero DC component.

c) *Audio spectrum spread*: The specific LLD is a measure of signal's spectral shape and corresponds to the second central moment of the log-frequency spectrum. It is computed by taking the root mean square deviation of the spectrum from its centroid.

d) *Audio spectrum flatness*: This descriptor is a measure of how flat a particular portion of the spectrum of the signal is and represents the deviation of the signal's power spectrum from a flat shape. The power coefficients are taken from nonoverlapping frames, while the spectrum is typically divided into ¼-octave resolution logarithmically spaced overlapping frequency bands. The ASF is derived as the ratio of the geometric mean and the arithmetic mean of the spectral power coefficients within a band.

The next stage of the sound recognition methodology, which is illustrated in Figure 1, is the post-processing of the extracted features. Techniques for normalizing the cepstral coefficients and/or the dynamic range are usually included. Both can be proven helpful for acoustic surveillance since they may reduce the dereverberation effects that usually appear when it comes to real-world conditions. Moreover, they can help during the classification stage, since they allow for a better comparison of the underlying characteristics that are exhibited by the novel data with the ones of the training data.

Another type of post-processing that can be used concurrently targets at projecting the feature coefficients onto a low-dimensional space. These processes try to keep only a small amount of the feature coefficients, which include their most important information. Even though feature projection facilitates the classification stage (since high-dimensional data tend to lead to a sparse representation), one should take extra care in order not to discard important information. The dimensionality reduction techniques that are proposed by the MPEG-7 audio standard are singular value decomposition, principal component analysis, nonnegative factorization, and independent component analysis. These can be used for audio surveillance tasks while keeping in mind that their majority are data depended approaches, which means that a large deviation between the train and test data may lead to disappointing recognition accuracy.

As a general comment on signal parameterization with respect to the area of audio surveillance, we claim that the features that provide a description of the spectrum are the most useful ones since the Fourier transform can efficiently characterize pressure waves. We believe that the MFCCs can provide a strong basis for the formulation of an effective feature set. MPEG-7 LLDs that characterize the signal in a different way can be appended. Their selection depends on the needs of the specific application. In addition, descriptors derived from the wavelet domain can also be used since their combination with the spectral ones have been shown to lead to improved recognition accuracy as regards to generalized sound classification [17]. The particular domain has not been fully explored as regards to atypical sound event detection, and we think that it could be very interesting for future research. Finally, our suggestion is to employ the DCT for the post-processing of the final feature vector since it is almost as efficient as the data-driven approaches at a much lower computational cost.

The final step of Figure 1 is the classification. The classifiers that are currently employed by the audio recognition community can be divided into two categories: discriminative and nondiscriminative. The discriminative ones try to approximate a boundary between the categories of the training data. Some examples are the polynomial classifier [18], multilayer perceptron [19], and Support Vector Machines (SVMs) [20]. On the opposite side, the generative approaches, which are the main class of the nondiscriminative classifiers, try to estimate the underlying distribution of the training data. They include Gaussian mixture models (GMMs) [21], hidden Markov models (HMMs) [22], and probabilistic neural networks (PNN) [23]. Other nondiscriminative approaches are the k-nearest neighbors (k-NN) [24] and the learning vector quantization (LVQ) [25]. In addition, several hybrid classification schemes have been reported in the literature [26–28], which exploit the merits of the two types of classification approaches. The majority of the audio surveillance frameworks that exist in the literature are based on generative approaches since these approaches tend to provide high recognition rates. However, there is still room for improvement and the most promising way to achieve higher performance is the development of hybrid methods. This kind of methods can be adjusted so as to satisfy the requirements of a specific application and potentially provide improved results.

3   A representative picture of the related literature

This section intents to provide a representative picture of what has been developed so far in the area of audio surveillance (see also Table 1). The emphasis of previous approaches is mainly placed on the classifier, the feature extraction process, the training data, and the number of classes. The system of Ntalampiras *et al.* [29] exploits the advantages of maximum a posteriori adaptation as well as diverse feature sets that allow detection of scream, normal speech, background environment, gunshot, and explosion sound events. The authors report results after a continuous operation for three subsequent days while using three types of environmental noise (metro station, urban and military environment). Their database was formed by using a combination of professional sound effect collections. Valenzise *et al.* [30] presented a surveillance system for gunshot and scream detection and localization in a public square. Forty-nine features were computed in total and given as an input to a hybrid filter/wrapper selection method. Its output was used to build two parallel GMMs for identifying screams from noise and gunshots from noise. Data were drawn out from movie sound tracks, Internet repositories, and people shouting at a microphone while the noise samples were captured in a public square of Milan. An interesting application, crime detection inside elevators, was explained in [31]. Their approach relied on time-series analysis and signal segmentation. Consistent patterns were discovered and the respective data were used for training one GMM for each one of the eight classes using low-level features. The data set contained recordings of suspicious activities in elevators and some event-free clips while they reported detection of all the suspicious activities without any misses. A gunshot detection method under noisy environments was explained in [32]. Their corpus consisted of data that were artificially created from a set of multiple public places and gunshot sound events extracted from the national French public radio. Widely used features were employed, including MFCC for constructing two GMMs with respect to gunshot and normal class using data of various Signal-to-Noise Ratio (SNR) levels. In [33] the issue of detection of audio events in public transport vehicles was addressed by using both a generative and a discriminative method. The audio data were recorded using four microphones during four different scenarios, which included fight scenes, a violent robbery scene, and scenes of bag or mobile snatching. They used GMM and SVM while their feature set was formed from the first 12 MFCC, energy, derivatives, and accelerations. Vacher *et al.* [34] presented a framework for sound detection and classification for medical telesurvey. Their corpus consisted of recordings made in the CLIPS laboratory, files of the "Sound Scene Database in Real Acoustical Environment" (Real World Computing Partnership* (RCWP) Japan). They used wavelet-based cepstral coefficients to train GMMs for eight sound classes while their system was evaluated under different SNR conditions. A hierarchical classification scheme that identified

---

* http://tosa.mri.co.jp/sounddb/indexe.htm

Table 1: Various approaches on the task of acoustic surveillance.

Reference	Atypical sound classes	Model adaptation	Classifier	Features	Database
Ntalampiras et al. [29]	Scream, gunshot, and explosion	MAP adaptation of GMMs	GMM	MFCC, MPEG-7, CB-TEO, Intonation	Large audio corpora from professional sound effects collections
Valenzise et al. [30]	Scream and gunshot	–	GMM	Temporal, spectral, cepstral, correlation	Movie soundtracks, Internet, and people shouts
Radhakrishnan & Divakaran [31]	Banging and non-neutral speech	–	GMM	MFCC	Elevator recordings
Clavel et al. [32]	Gunshot	–	GMM	MFCC, spectral moments	CDs for the national French public radio
Rouas et al. [33]	Shout	Adaptive threshold for sound activity detection	GMM, SVM	Energy, MFCC	Recorded during four scenarios
Vacher et al. [34]	Scream and glass break	–	GMM	Wavelet-based cepstral coefficients	Laboratory recordings and RCWP
Atrey et al. [35]	Shout	–	GMM	ZCR, LPC, LPCC, LFCC	Recorded in office corridor
Ito et al. [36]	Glass clash, scream, fire cracker	Adaptive threshold for abnormal sound event detection	GMM	MFCC, Power	Recorded under laboratory conditions

normal from excited sound events was described in [35]. The authors used four audio features for training GMMs, each one associated with one node of the classification tree. The audio was recorded for around two hours in the real environment (office corridor) and included talk, shout, knock, and footsteps. In [36] the authors use a multistage schema based on GMMs that "learns" the normal sounds and subsequently detects events that exhibit large differences from the normal ones. A procedure for automatic determination of the threshold that differentiates between normal and abnormal sounds is also reported. Their feature vector includes the 16 first MFCCs and the power along with the corresponding derivatives while their experiments took place on recordings made under laboratory conditions.

It is argued that previous research in the specific domain is far from concluding on a common framework as, for example, in the case of speech/speaker recognition where the classifier and the feature extraction process is more or less established (i.e., GMMs and HMMs as classifiers and variations of spectral features as input). The difficulty basically lies on the next three facts:

1. An atypical situation is not a well-defined category (e.g., laughter vs cry vs scream).
2. There are many cases where there is a thin line between a typical and an atypical situation (e.g., gunshot vs explosion).
3. The microphone can be located far from the source of the acoustic incident; therefore, reverberation and acoustic events belonging to an almost unrestricted range of classes may become the input to the microphone.

As a general conclusion, we can point out the fact that statistical-based approaches are used by the majority of the authors, while for each article the feature set is chosen so as to fit the needs of the specific application. An interesting direction to follow would be the establishment of frameworks that include hybrid methods during the pattern recognition phase, such as the combination of generative and discriminative approaches. Furthermore, because of the unavailability of real-world atypical audio data that include extreme emotional manifestations and abnormal sound events, the novelty detection methodology [37], which is only partially explored in [36], could be proven useful.

3.1 Evaluation of audio surveillance frameworks

The present section comments on a highly important issue of audio surveillance frameworks, that is, the evaluation methodology. The establishment of a common evaluation metric is critical toward making a reliable comparison between different surveillance approaches. This kind of frameworks essentially includes single or multiple detection problems. A typical representation technique of the performance of a detector is the receiver operating characteristic curve (ROC curve). An example of a ROC curve is illustrated in Figure 3. In this case, the true-positive rate ($R_{TP} = TP/(FN + TP)$), percentage of the correct classified test

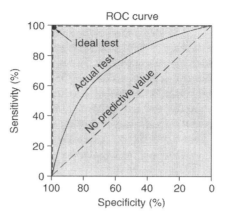

Figure 3: The ROC curve. The more the curve is in the upper left corner, the better is the detection system. The threshold T is increased from left to right. If the threshold is zero, every test case is classified as TRUE, thus the Sensitivity is one but the Specificity is zero (lower left corner); if the threshold is maximal, all test cases are classified as FALSE, thus the curve ends in the upper right corner. The optimal value for a threshold T is the one for which the curve is next to the upper left corner. The dashed line indicates the performance of a system that just is guessing (50% detection rate in a two class-problem). Source: Image Characteristics and quality, Terry Sprawls, www.sprawls.org.

cases from all of those that are "positive" in reality) is plotted in relation to the false-positive rate ($R_{FP} = FP/(FP + TN)$, percentage of test cases that are "negative" in reality and wrongly classified as "positive" by the detector) in dependence of a parameter, typically a threshold. This is done if an adjustable threshold T in the detection system is responsible for the decision "detected" or "not detected", and the optimal value for this threshold, a maximal quotient, should be found.

Although this type of error analysis provides useful information, it is believed that the Detection Error Tradeoff (DET) curves that comprise an adapted version of ROC curves should be used. A typical DET curve is depicted in Figure 4. The DET curves as introduced by the National Institute of Standards and Technology [38] can be viewed as presenting the trade-off between two error types: missed detections and false alarms. The point where the average of the missed detection and false alarm rates is minimized is the optimal point, that is, the one that should be used during the operation of the system. The specific average essentially is the cost function of a DET curve. There are two important things to note about the DET curve. First, in the case that the resulting curves are straight lines, it can safely be assumed that the underlying likelihood distributions from the system are normal. Second, the diagonal $y = -x$ on the normal deviate scale represents random performance. With a large number of targets and roughly equal occurrences of all nontargets, the overall performance is effectively represented.

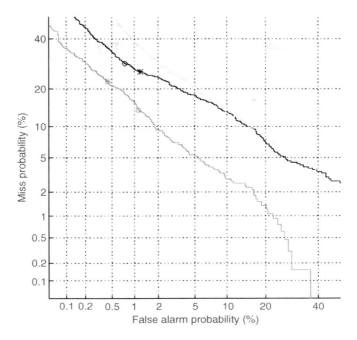

Figure 4: The DET curves can be viewed as presenting the trade-off between two error types: missed detections and false alarms. The "circles" on the curves indicate the optimal decision cost for a system, and the "starts" indicate the actual decision cost at the selected operational point (threshold, etc.). Source: Reference [38].

Unlike the standard ROC curve, the DET curves are approximately linear curves that are easily observable and suitable for presenting performance results where trade-offs of two error types are involved. Furthermore, the production of a DET curve requires a common scale for the likelihood of each event, which is a desirable property in many applications. Finally, the DET curve may include a number of special points to facilitate performance analysis, such as a specific false alarm or a miss detection rate.

4 Privacy

Acoustic sensors are sometimes perceived as invasive, especially when the subject of attendance is human. Therefore, privacy issues need to be fully taken into account while constructing an audio surveillance system. The research conducted in the specific scientific area is based and motivated by the next presuppositions:

- Threatening situations such as crime and terrorist acts in large urban areas are not fictitious scenarios but real facts that require special attention and measures.

Moreover, the knowledge that public spaces are being secured by intelligent monitoring is expected to discourage the manifestation of such acts.

- Surveillance, in general, is not in conflict with the law, and it is common practice in stores, agencies, airports, and so on, where the need for increased security justifies the installation of video cameras.

- Unattended autonomous surveillance is much less "invasive" as it precludes human interference from the interpretation of the sensor's information as well as data broadcasting at any stage of the inference process. Therefore, it restricts human processing as well as unscrupulous circulation of personal data. As the right to privacy is claimed by more and more people, unattended surveillance ensures that the interpretation of the sensors information does not involve unauthorized human interference at any stage of the inference process.

- The main task of unattended surveillance is to identify in time the sensed situation and deliver the necessary warning messages to an authorized officer. It does not involve any other kind of uncontrolled action or initiative in part of the machine. In addition, the microphones are not used to identify individuals or to interpret spoken words or sentences.

It is believed that compliance with the above four points ensure that the privacy of all individuals is not to be compromised at any stage of the processing chain of an audio surveillance framework. Therefore, such frameworks can play a significant role with respect to civil safety [39].

5   Conclusion

Unattended space monitoring based on the acoustic modality comprises an effective tool toward scene analysis for detection of catastrophic situations. This chapter provided an overview of the technology that lies behind the specific scientific area, a descriptive review of the literature along with several privacy issues that need special attention. Although it is not possible to identify a general purpose feature set as well as the recognition technique that performs best for all surveillance applications, the usage of MFCCs as the starting point is suggested. MPEG-7 LLDs as well as other application-specific parameters can be appended at a second stage for improving classification accuracy. With respect to the pattern recognition part, the HMM approach is a reasonable choice since they offer satisfying detection results in many audio classification applications. Furthermore, a synthetic scheme that employs the complementary properties of the generative (e.g., GMM) and discriminative (e.g., SVM) classifiers can be employed.

Throughout this chapter, some directions for future research were suggested, which concentrate on acoustic signal processing. Another interesting direction to be explored is the combination of the acoustic sensors with other heterogeneous ones. The acoustic modality can play either a stand-alone role or be used in parallel with other modalities toward obtaining an enhanced analysis of the scene of interest. The information from heterogeneous sensors, which is both comple-mentary and redundant, aims at surpassing the weaknesses of each modality in dealing with coverage of the sensed area and its response to occlusion, noise, and differing environmental conditions. These sensors can be complementary in two different ways:

1. The combination of different sensors' reports can be merged into a single but more complete piece of information.
2. Information gained from one sensing modality can be used to validate observa-tions and/or aid the processing chain of the others.

For example, a network of proximity indicators can efficiently detect and count the number of people. However, this type of sensor gives no information about the height of the people involved or their appearance. Estimates of height, color of clothes, and appearance can be generated using observations from a monoc-ular camera. However, if there are shadows or low/time varying lighting con-ditions or occlusion due to another person, the camera (which also generates ambiguity due to depth) will sense reflected light so that the image will be a product of both intrinsic skin reflectivity and external incident illumination and will, therefore, return poor results. Moreover, variations in ambient illumination will enlarge the within-class variability of any statistical classifier, thus severely degrading classification performance of subjects, behavior, and interaction. The detection of human presence and the complementary data of height but not of color can be provided by the infrared camera that detects the thermal emission of bodies (which is an intrinsic measurement that can be isolated from exter-nal illumination) and, therefore, works under low-light conditions. Acoustic data picked up by a microphone array and their associated time-frequency signatures can return bearing and location measurements as well as provide information for scene interpretation. To summarize, a dispersed network of multimodal sensors allows complementary views about the state of the environment to be deduced that would be unavailable to either sensor working alone.

References

[1] Haritaoglu, I., Harwood, D., & Davis, L., W4: Real-time surveillance of people and their activities. *IEEE Transactions on Pattern Analysis and Machine Intelligence*, **22(8)**, pp. 809–830, 2000.
[2] Eronen, A., & Klapuri, A., Musical instrument recognition using cepstral coefficients and temporal features. Proceedings of the ICASSP'00, Istanbul, pp. 753–756, 2000.
[3] Tzanetakis, G. & Cook, P., Musical genre classification of audio signals. *IEEE Transactions on Speech and Audio Processing*, **10(5)**, pp. 293–302, 2002.
[4] FitzGerald, D., Coyle, E., & Lawlor, B., Sub-band independent subspace analysis for drum transcription. Proceedings of the DAFX'02, Hamburg, pp. 65–69, September 2002.

[5] Ashiya, T., Hagiwara, M., & Nakagawa, M., IOSES: An indoor observation system based on environmental sounds recognition using a neural network. *Transactions of the Institute of Electrical Engineers of Japan*, **116-C(3)**, pp. 341–349, 1996.

[6] Gillespie, D. & Chappell, O., An automatic system for detecting and classifying the vocalizations of harbour porpoises. *Bioacoustics*, **13**, 37–61, 2002.

[7] Hennig, R.M., Acoustic feature extraction by cross-correlation in crickets. *Journal of comparative physiology. A Neuroethology, sensory, neural, and behavioral physiology*, **189**, pp. 589–598, 2003.

[8] Dimla, D.E., Jr, Lister, P.M., & Leighton, N.J., Neural network solutions to the tool condition monitoring problem in metal cutting. A critical review of methods. *International Journal of Machine Tools Manufacturing*, **37(9)**, pp. 1219–1240, 1997.

[9] Diei, E.N. & Dornfeld, D.A., Acoustic emission sensing of tool wear in face milling. *Transactions of ASME, Journal of Engineering for Industry*, **109**, pp. 234–240, 1987.

[10] Peltonen, V., Computational auditory scene recognition. Master of Science Thesis, Department of Information Technology, Tampere University of Technology, Tampere, 2001.

[11] Vemuri, S., Schmandt, C., Bender, W., Tellex, S., & Lassey, B., An audio-based personal memory aid. Proceedings of the 6th International Conference Ubiquitous Computing, Ubicomp'04, Tokyo, pp. 400–417, 2004.

[12] Chu, S., Narayanan, S., Jay Kuo, C.-C., & Matarić, M.J., Where am I? Scene recognition for mobile robots using audio features. Proceedings of the ICME'06, Ischia, pp. 885–888, 2006.

[13] Ntalampiras, S., Potamitis, I., & Fakotakis, N., On acoustic surveillance of hazardous situations. Proceedings of the ICASSP '09, Taipei, pp. 165–168, 2009.

[14] Foote, J.T., An overview of audio information retrieval. *ACM-Springer Multimedia Systems*, **7(1)**, pp. 2–11, 1999.

[15] Zhoun, G., Hansen, J.H.L., & Kaiser, J.F., Nonlinear feature based classification of speech under stress. *IEEE Transactions on Speech and Audio Processing*, **9(3)**, pp. 201–216, 2001.

[16] Casey, M., MPEG-7 sound recognition tools. *IEEE Transactions on Circuits and Systems for Video Technology*, **11(6)**, pp. 737–747, 2001.

[17] Ntalampiras, S., Potamitis, I., & Fakotakis, N., Exploiting temporal feature integration for generalized sound recognition. *EURASIP Journal on Advances in Signal Processing*, article ID: 807162, **2009**, 2009.

[18] Specht, D.F., Generation of polynomial discriminant functions for pattern recognition. *IEEE Transactions on Electronic Computers*, **16**, pp. 308–319, 1967.

[19] Rosenblatt, F., The perceptron: A probabilistic model for information storage and organization in the brain. *Psychological Review*, **65**, pp. 386–408, 1958.

[20] Vapnik, V.N., *The Nature of Statistical Learning Theory*, New York: Springer, 1995.

[21] Peltonen, V., Tuomi, J., Klapuri, A., Huopaniemi, J., & Sorsa, T., Computational auditory scene recognition. Proceedings of the ICASSP'02, Orlando, pp. 1941–1944, May 2002.

[22] Casey, M., General sound classification and similarity in MPEG-7. *Organised Sound*, **6(2)**, pp. 153–164, 2001.

[23] Bolat, B. & Kucuk, U., Musical sound recognition by active learning PNN. *Lecture Notes in Computer Science, vol. 4105/2006, Multimedia Content Representation, Classification and Security*, ISSN:0302-9743, Springer Berlin/Heidelberg, pp. 474–481, 2006.

[24] Essid, S., Classification of audio signals: Machine recognition of musical instruments. Seminars, CNRS-LTCI, 2006.

[25] Yella, S., Gupta, N.K., & Dougherty, M., Pattern recognition approach for the automatic classification of data from impact acoustics. Proceedings of the AISC'2006, Palma De Mallorca, pp. 144–149, 2006.

[26] Dietterich, T., An experimental comparison of three methods for constructing ensembles of decision trees: Bagging, boosting, and randomization. *Machine Learning*, **40(2)**, pp. 139–157, 2000.

[27] Kittler, J., Hatef, M., Duin, R., & Matas, J., On combining classifiers. *IEEE Transactions on Pattern Analysis and Machine Intelligence*, **20(3)**, pp. 226–239, 1998.

[28] Alkoot, F.M. & Kittler, J., Experimental evaluation of expert fusion strategies. *Pattern Recognition Letters*, **20(11)**, pp. 11–13, 1999.

[29] Ntalampiras, S., Potamitis, I., & Fakotakis, N., An adaptive framework for acoustic monitoring of potential hazards. *EURASIP Journal on Audio, Speech and Music Processing*, article ID: 594103, **2009**, 2009.

[30] Valenzise, G., Gerosa, L., Tagliasacchi, M., Antonacci, F., & Sarti, A., Scream and gunshot detection and localization for audio-surveillance systems. Proceedings of the Advanced Video and Signal-Based Surveillance, London, pp. 21–26, September 5–7, 2007.

[31] Radhakrishnan, R. & Divakaran, A., Systematic acquisition of audio classes for elevator surveillance. *SPIE Image and Video Communications Processing*, **5685**, pp. 64–71, 2005.

[32] Clavel, C., Ehrette T., & Richard, G., Event detection for an audio-based surveillance system. Proceedings of IEEE International Conference on Multimedia and Expo, Amsterdam, pp. 1306–1309, July 2005.

[33] Rouas, J.-L., Louradour, J., & Ambellouis, S., Audio events detection in public transport vehicles. Proceedings of IEEE Intelligent Transportation System Conference, Toronto, pp. 733–738, 2006.

[34] Vacher, M., Istrate, D., Besacier, L., Serignat J.-F., & Castelli, E., Sound detection and classification for medical telesurvey. Proceedings of International Conference of Biomedical Engineering, Innsbruck, pp. 395–399, 2004.

[35] Atrey, P.K., Maddage, N.C., & Kankanhalli, M.S., Audio based event detection for multimedia surveillance. Proceedings of International Conference on Acoustics, Speech and Signal Processing, Toulouse, pp. 813–816, May 2006.

[36] Ito, A., Aiba, A., Ito, M., & Makino, S., Detection of abnormal sound using multistage GMM for surveillance microphone. Proceedings of the Fifth International Conference on Information Assurance and Security, Xian, pp. 733–736, August 18–20, 2009.

[37] Markou, M. & Singh, S., Novelty detection: A review. *Signal Processing, Elsevier*, **83(12)**, pp. 2481–2497, 2003.

[38] Martin, A., Doddington, G., Kamm, T., Ordowski, M., & Przybocki, M., The DET curve in assessment of detection task performance. Proceedings of the Eurospeech, Rhodos, pp. 1895–1898, September 1997.

[39] Bocchetti, G., Flammini, F., Pappalardo, A., & Pragliola, C., Dependable integrated surveillance systems for the physical security of metro railways. Proceedings of the 3rd ACM/IEEE International Conference on Distributed Smart Cameras, Como (Italy), pp. 1–7, August 30 to September 2, 2009.

Terahertz for weapon and explosive detection

Megan R. Leahy-Hoppa
JHU, Applied Physics Laboratory, Laurel, MD 20723, USA

Abstract

Terahertz (THz) technology has experienced large growth within the past 20 years. Advances in technology have enabled a variety of applications of THz spectroscopy and imaging within the civilian and military arenas. Security applications have come to light as plastic explosives have been shown to be spectrally distinct in the THz spectral region. In addition, THz radiation has the ability to differentiate hidden objects below many types of clothing. As technology has progressed, more compact systems have been designed and commercial systems have become available for a rapid transition from the research laboratory to real-world applications. This review describes the THz spectroscopy and imaging applications as applied to both weapons and explosive detection.

Keywords: Terahertz Spectroscopy, Terahertz Imaging, Sub-millimeter Wave, Explosive Detection, Security, Weapons Detection

1 Introduction

Terahertz technology has experienced tremendous growth in the past 30 years. Although there have been many advances with respect to the many facets underlying this technology, progress has not been without controversy. There are difficulties that must be addressed or overcome in order to best utilize the technology for security applications, which include weapon and explosive detection. Recognition that no sensor or sensor technology is the absolute solution to any complex detection problem is paramount to accepting that the technology may be a part of a tiered solution to security applications.

The terahertz region of the spectrum, sometimes referred to as the sub-millimeter wave band, is most commonly thought to be from 100 GHz to 10 THz. For spectroscopic investigations, inter- and intramolecular resonances can be seen at room temperature in solids. Many dielectrics including most clothing material and plastic packaging material are transparent or semitransparent to terahertz radiation, which enables nondestructive evaluation of concealed objects and materials. Terahertz radiation is nonionizing and typical powers in the systems currently available, both electronic and optical in nature, fall within the current guidelines set forth by the American National Standards Institute's (ANSI) Safe Use of Lasers and the IEEE Standard for Safety Levers with Respect to Human Exposure to Radio Frequency Electromagnetic Fields and are therefore safe for human exposure according to the guidelines [1].

One of the major problems to overcome with the use of the technology is the opacity and attenuation of THz radiation in the atmosphere. Fortunately, many security applications can use close-range standoff sensors, minimizing the path of the THz radiation through the atmosphere. Although attenuation in the atmosphere can be 1 to 10 dB/km [2], there are a multitude of applications that can benefit from the use of THz technology in the short standoff range of distances. Additional hurdles include increasing the source power and the sensitivity of the detectors, which leads to enhanced overall signal-to-noise ratio (SNR) of the system.

2   Terahertz technology

2.1   Overview

The terahertz frequency band lies between the microwave and far-infrared regions of the spectrum, which has traditionally been thought of as 100 GHz to 10 THz in frequency or 3 mm to 30 μm in wavelength. In addition, 1 THz is equivalent to 46 K in temperature or 4 meV in energy. Blackbodies and graybodies (non-ideal blackbodies) radiate well in the THz region of the spectrum, although these are incoherent sources of radiation. Coherent emission and detection methods were developed in the early 1980s and continue their development today.

Both optical and electronic methods of THz generation and detection exist for exploitation of the terahertz frequency band. There are both broadband sources, for example, optical rectification and photoconduction with ultrafast (femtosecond) laser pulses, and narrowband sources. Narrowband sources can be either electronic, for example, upconversion of microwave oscillators, backward wave oscillators (BWOs), and carcinotrons, or optical in nature, for example, gas THz lasers, quantum cascade lasers, and nonlinear photomixing of two continuous wave (CW) lasers. A comprehensive description of these and other optical and electronic methods of THz generation can be found in [3,4].

THz detection also has a variety of techniques for time-domain and spectral analysis. As thermal (incoherent) background is large in comparison with many of the THz sources mentioned earlier, sensitive detection techniques are imperative. Cryogenic thermal detectors are commonly used to reduce the large thermal background, but cryogenic temperatures are not easy to maintain in real-world applications. Heterodyne detectors can be used for high spectral resolution. Pyroelectric detectors and Golay cells can also be used. For pulsed detection techniques, free-space electro-optic and photoconductive sampling are two common techniques. Again, a comprehensive description of these and other techniques for THz detection can be found in [3,4].

Both optical and electronic techniques come with their own sets of benefits and drawbacks. While many optical techniques can generate broadband THz radiation in a single measurement, electronic techniques can provide higher power within a narrow band, which can then be swept through the desired frequencies. Single frequency optical sources also exist, for example, Quantum Cascade Lasers and terahertz gas lasers. Traditional time-domain THz spectroscopic techniques require ultrafast lasers; however, they provide the full spectrum available in a single scan, which can be obtained through standard Fourier transform techniques.

Optical properties of materials also make the use of THz technology attractive. Materials such as plastics, cardboard, and cloth (natural and synthetic fibers) are at least partially transmissive to THz radiation. Hidden objects can be seen beneath multiple layers of clothing [5] (see Figure 1). Hidden objects can also be seen within shoes (see Figure 2) using THz time-domain spectroscopy, which implies that concurrent imaging and spectroscopic information can be obtained through time domain spectroscopy. Through-container non-destructive imaging can also be performed on certain container types, such as those made of plastic and cloth, e.g., luggage (see Figure 3) and shipping boxes. Metallic containers cannot be interrogated with THz radiation, limiting the types of containers which can be searched.

2.2   THz systems

Both spectroscopic and imaging systems can be built with the previously mentioned sources and detectors. Single frequency (or several distinct frequency)

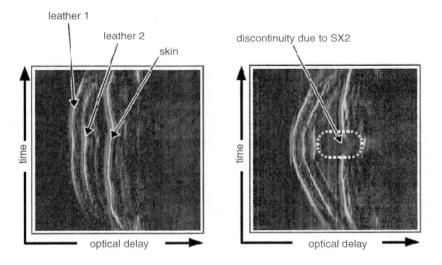

Figure 1: THz reflection through two layers of leather with (right) and without (left) the plastic explosive SX2 hidden below. Adapted from reference [5].

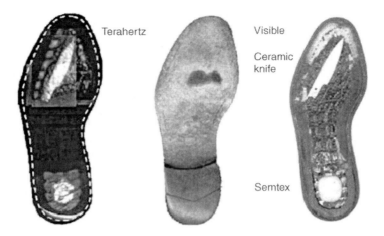

Figure 2: THz (left) and visible image (middle and right) of objects hidden in the sole
of a shoe. A ceramic knife and piece of plastic explosive (Semtex) can be
seen in the visible and THz images. Image courtesy of Teraview, Ltd [6].

systems tend to be more suited for imaging applications where the differences
between surface reflections can be seen, for example, between a human and a
knife or gun hidden under clothing.

THz systems range from large table-top optical systems to small (laptop-sized)
commercial systems. Large optical systems commonly found in research laboratories often employ single or multiple lasers that occupy the better part of a large
optical table. Ultrafast laser systems (femtosecond pulsed lasers) are commonly
made of two to three lasers depending on whether the output of the oscillator is
amplified. Photomixing systems are often equivalent in size to ultrafast pulsed
laser systems with two large lasers occupying an optical table. Smaller commercial systems, such as those from Picometrix or Zomega Terahertz Corporation,
are available employing fiber lasers that are considerably more compact.

Commercial electronic systems such as those from Virginia Diodes or the
BWOs, such as those from Microtech Instruments, Inc., are not as large as the
laser systems; however, they are most powerful at the lowest frequencies and
quickly lose power at higher frequencies as the conversion efficiency of the frequency multipliers directly affects the output power.

Imaging systems are both active and passive. Passive imaging systems are
anomaly detectors, for example, Thruvision T4000 and T5000 [8]. These systems
exploit the difference in emissivity and reflectivity between humans and other materials. Since the THz waves can penetrate through clothing, unlike in the infrared,
the THz radiation will reflect from the human surface and other objects under the clothing, enabling an image to be constructed. Plastic, ceramic, or metallic objects hidden beneath the clothing will appear different from the human since those objects
emit and reflect ambient THz radiation differently from humans. Depending on the

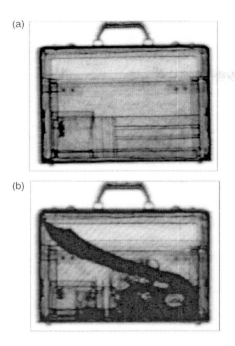

Figure 3: Transmission THz image using a 0.2 THz CW system: (a) an empty
leather briefcase; (b) leather briefcase containing knife and benign
objects such as a compact disc, a video cassette, audio cassette, and pens.
Adapted and reprinted with permission from reference [7]. Copyright
2005, American Institute of Physics.

sensitivity of the detector, solids, powders, and liquids may be detected by these
passive anomaly detectors. Although THz radiation is nonionizing and has been
shown to be safe for human exposure under the current safety guidelines [1], passive technologies are more attractive than active systems in certain applications.

Active imaging systems range from single frequency or several frequency
systems to broadband systems that can perform spectroscopy in addition to imaging.
There are laser-based, time-domain spectroscopy and imaging systems as well as
CW laser systems. Active systems are similar to passive systems in their ability
to detect plastics, ceramics, and so on under concealed conditions, for example,
clothing, plastic, and cardboard; however, they can achieve higher resolution.

3   Terahertz for weapons detection

THz imaging has applicability to security screening for weapons detection. Both
active and passive systems can differentiate between a concealed weapon under
clothing and the human background. Much emphasis has been placed on security
applications for THz imaging in recent years due to the ability to use off-the-shelf

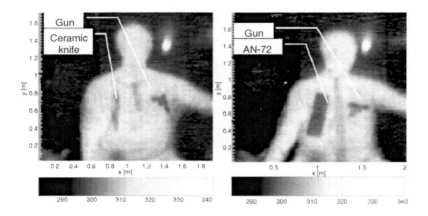

Figure 4: Passive THz image with 8-mm spatial resolution at the target. The bright spot in the background is used for radiometric temperature calibration. The colorbars at the bottom of the images indicate absolute radiometric temperature scale for each image. Adapted with permission from reference [18].

technology at power levels safe for human exposure [1] coupled with its ability to penetrate clothing and other nonmetallic materials. Interest as a research topic is being actively pursued in both the academic and commercial communities [5,9–19].

As stated earlier, for passive systems, there is a difference in the emissivity and reflectivity between the human and concealed nonhuman objects that can be detected as an anomaly. As there are numerous examples of THz applications for weapons detection, a few representative examples of the capabilities of THz technology in this arena will be discussed. Luukanen et al. [18,19] have developed a system for real-time passive indoor THz imaging (see Figure 4). Their detector design uses either Nb- or NbN-based detectors and has 8-mm spatial resolution with only 10-msec pixel integration time. Their frequency range covered by these detectors is 0.2–3.6 THz. These detectors are microbolometers, however, and require cryogenic cooling.

Jacobs et al. [12] examined human observer performance against a wide variety of test objects with a 640-GHz imaging system (see Figure 5 for a representative image at 640 GHz). Test articles ranged from small hidden items such as a lighter and cell phone to larger objects that included a metal pipe bomb and a block of explosive simulant. Their findings show that object identification appears more difficult with an active system than with a passive infrared detection. They noted, however, that active images contain more specular reflection than the corresponding passive system. The problem of specular reflections, though, can be partially mitigated through preprocessing of the data before it is shown to the observer.

The group at Picometrix, led by D. Zimdars [20,21], has developed fiber-pigtailed THz time-domain spectroscopic instrumentation. This system is capable of both collecting spectroscopic information and building imaging information from the time-domain signal. The added functionality of collecting spectroscopic

Figure 5:   640 GHz image (left) of a person with a concealed toy gun and a visible image with the gun exposed for visual aid. Adapted with permission from reference [12].

information while imaging provides possible identification of explosive material, for example, as there are unique signatures in the THz region of the spectrum for many plastic explosives, as will be discussed in the following section. Figure 6 shows an example of both transmission and reflection spectroscopy for imaging of luggage.

4   Terahertz for explosive detection

A large body of research on explosives detection with THz technology has been and continues to be built within the THz community. A recent review article [22] provides insight into both solid and gas phase spectroscopy that has been performed to identify spectral signatures of explosives. Many explosive compounds have unique spectral signatures in the THz region of the spectrum (see Figure 7). Both neat explosives and plastic explosive compounds, which contain other possible confusant materials, are represented in this set of spectra. For example, from the spectra of (b) and (c), it can be seen that the plastic explosive PE4 contains the explosive RDX from the signature at 0.8 THz. This 0.8 THz signature of RDX has been used across a variety of explosives as a unique identifier as other explosives do not contain the same signature that has been attributed to phonon modes within the crystalline structure. The signatures of the neat and plastic explosives have been demonstrated by a side variety of research groups adding to the validity of the spectral signatures [23–31]. Not only has a multitude of experimental work been performed but also theoretical calculations of the spectra [32–36].

In addition to the research associated with the identification of spectral signatures of neat and plastic explosives as in [23–31], Chen et al. [28] (see Figure 8) have also examined explosives and related compounds (ERCs) in both transmission and diffuse reflection geometries. The bulk of THz spectroscopy that has been performed on ERCs has incorporated a transmission geometry where the THz beam

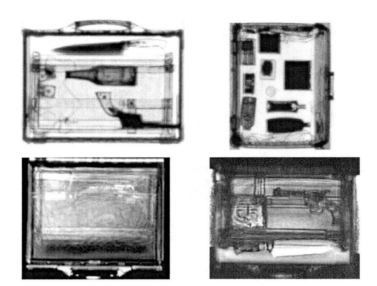

Figure 6: THz transmission and reflection images (not to relative scale). (Top left) THz transmission image of an attaché case; (top right) THz transmission image of suitcase with dimensions 30 inches × 20 inches × 13 inches, image of contents of the box; (bottom left) THz reflection image of attaché case—return is from the top of the attaché case; (bottom right) THz reflection image of attaché case—return is from the interior of the case showing a knife and pistol, which were both located under a jacket. Adapted with permission from reference [21].

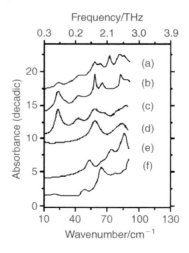

Figure 7: THz absorption spectrum for (a) Semtex H, (b) PE4, (c) RDX, (d) PETN, (e) HMX, and (f) TNT. Plots (a)–(e) are vertically offset for clarity. Adapted with permission from reference [23].

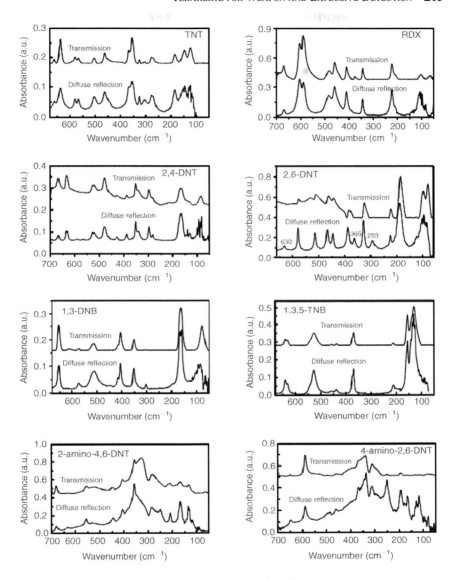

Figure 8: Comparison of transmission and diffuse reflectance spectra of ERCs. Spectra have been vertically shifted for clarity. Adapted with permission from reference [28].

passes through the sample material and the detector is on the opposite side of the sample as the source. Although this technique is used more often than a reflection geometry, it is less practical from an application standpoint. In most applications, the signal will require collection from reflections or scatter off the target of interest, whether package, container, or human. THz reflection spectroscopy has been

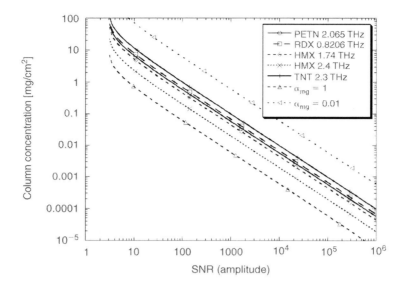

Figure 9: Detection limit for three different neat explosives as a function of SNR. Adapted and reprinted from reference [25], Copyright (2007), with permission from Elsevier.

performed, for example, by the group of X.-C. Zhang at Rensselaer Polytechnic Institute (RPI) [28,37,38], our group at Johns Hopkins University Applied Physics Laboratory (JHU/APL) [38–42], and others [43–48]. As can be seen in the spectra in Figure 8, the diffuse reflectance spectra are comparable to the transmission spectra. Signatures of the ERCs, at specific frequencies, can be identified and used for spectral fingerprinting in this region.

From the spectral signatures, our research group at JHU/APL has been able to measure the absolute absorptivities and molecular cross sections [25] facilitating the determination of the SNR needed for varying concentrations of explosive material (see Figure 9). For given applications, it may be known whether trace or bulk material is the target of interest, which would make possible the appropriate choice of instrumentation. Often the spectra obtained from THz measurements are relative in nature, and absolute absorptivities are not obtained. This work was a critical contribution to the field, bringing to forefront the need for absolute measurements to be obtained.

5   Discussion

As mentioned earlier, it is also possible to combine the spectroscopic and imaging capabilities of this technology to obtain pixel-by-pixel spectroscopic information while building an image (e.g., see Figure 1 [5]). This combination facilitates both a determination of object detection (anomaly detection) and the identification of the material. This will allow users to determine if the anomaly that is detected is a threat, for example, explosive or other contraband, such as narcotics, or if the anomaly is benign, permitting the person, container, or luggage to continue without further scrutiny. Many of the detection techniques currently employed in security applications today require a multilayered approach to narrow down whether a potential threat is in fact a threat or a benign material that appears similar to the potential threat material. For example, consider security at a typical airport, where first you pass through a metal detector; if alarmed, you then pass to a secondary screening for more thorough metal detection and/or a pat down by a security officer. If a THz system could image the person in real time, the metallic and nonmetallic objects on a person could be identified as possible threat objects and further data processing could determine if the object was a cell phone or a block of plastic explosive in the person's jacket. This tool can be employed in an already layered security arena to assist or replace some of the current technologies in place. In addition, when baggage is screened before being placed on the airplane, if anomalous objects are detected, it is common for screening personnel to open the luggage and look by hand at the contents. If THz spectroscopic imaging was performed, the anomaly could be detected and the spectroscopic signatures can be compared with a library of potential threats to determine whether further action is necessary.

Current commercial systems do have the capability to perform this spectroscopic imaging, but as the technology itself is still relatively new, being commercialized within the past decade, slow adoption has taken place. Continued development and funding is imperative for the commercial products to be fully developed into the products that meet the specific needs of varied security applications.

With the existing limits of commercial and prototype systems, there have been demonstrations of the use of terahertz technology for real-time security applications with both people screening [5,6], for example, under clothing and within shoe, and container screening [7,21], for example, luggage and shipping boxes. While these systems are not currently widely used in existing security applications, the research has shown the potential benefit to security applications for active terahertz imaging systems. In addition, passive THz systems [8,18] are similar to existing passive millimeter wave imagers [49] currently in use around the world. Overall, terahertz technology in its current state can be a useful addition to an integrated security system. Continued development and advancement of the technology will provide added benefits to the security community while also benefitting the scientific community as a whole.

Acknowledgments

The author acknowledges useful discussions with R. Osiander, J. Miragliotta, and M. J. Fitch. The author also acknowledges JHU/APL for funding to prepare the manuscript.

References

[1] Berry, E., Walker, G. C., Fitzgerald, A. J., Zinov'ev, N. N., Chamberlain, M., Smye, S. W., Miles, R. E., & Smith, M. A., Do in vivo terahertz imaging systems comply with safety guidelines. *Journal of Laser Applications*, **15**, pp. 192–198, 2003.

[2] Appleby, R., Passive millimetre-wave imaging and how it differs from terahertz imaging. *Philosophical Transactions of the Royal Society of London. Series A: Mathematical, Physical and Engineering Sciences*, **362**, pp. 379–393, 2004.

[3] Ferguson, B. & Zhang, X.-C., Materials for terahertz science and technology. *Nature Materials*, **1**, pp. 26–33, 2002.

[4] van der Weide, D., Applications and outlook for electronic terahertz technology. *Optics and Photonics News*, **14**, pp. 48–53, 2003.

[5] Baker, C., Tribe, W. R., Lo, T., Cole, B. E., Chandler, S., & Kemp, M. C., People screening using terahertz technology. *Proceedings of SPIE*, **5790**, pp. 1–10, 2005.

[6] www.teraview.com.

[7] Karpowicz, N., Zhong, H., Zhang, C., Lin, K.-I., Hwang, J.-S., Xu, J., & Zhang, X.-C., Compact continuous-wave subterahertz system for inspection applications. *Applied Physics Letters*, **86**, p. 054105, 2005.

[8] www.thruvision.com.

[9] Federici, J. F., Barat, R., Gary, D., & Zimdars, D., THz standoff detection and imaging of explosives and weapons. *Proceedings of SPIE*, **5727**, pp. 123–131, 2005.

[10] Jacobs, E., Driggers, R. G., Krapels, K., De Lucia, F. C., & Petkie, D., Terahertz imaging performance model for concealed weapon identification. *Proceedings of SPIE*, **5619**, pp. 98–107, 2004.

[11] Kemp, M. C., Taday, P. F., Cole, B. E., Cluff, J. A., Fitzgerald, A. J., & Tribe, W. R., Security applications of terahertz technology. *Proceedings of SPIE*, **5070**, pp. 44–52, 2003.

[12] Jacobs, E. L., Moyer, S., Franck, C. C., DeLucia, F. C., Casto, C., Petkie, D. T., Murrill, S. R., & Halford, C. E., Concealed weapon identification using terahertz imaging sensors. *Proceedings of SPIE*, **6212**, pp. 62120J-62121–62120J-62129, 2006.

[13] Gerecht, E., Gu, D., Yngvesson, S., Rodriguez-Morales, F., Zannoni, R., & Nicholson, J., HEB heterodyne focal plane arrays: A terahertz technology for high sensitivity near-range security imaging systems. *Proceedings of SPIE*, **5790**, pp. 149–160, 2005.

[14] Federici, J. F., Gary, D., Barat, R., & Zimdars, D., THz standoff detection and imaging of explosives and weapons. *Proceedings of SPIE*, **5781**, pp. 75–84, 2005.

[15] Murrill, S. R., Jacobs, E. L., Moyer, S. K., Halford, C. E., Griffin, S. T., De Lucia, F. C., Petkie, D. T., & Franck, C. C., Terahertz imaging system performance model for concealed-weapon identification. *Applied Optics*, **47**, pp. 1286–1297, 2008.

[16] Liu, H. B., Zhong, H., Karpowicz, N., Chen, Y. Q., & Zhang, X.-C., Terahertz spectroscopy and imaging for defense and security applications. *Proceedings of the IEEE*, **95**, pp. 1514–1527, 2007.

[17] Song, Q., Zhao, Y. J., Redo-Sanchez, A., Zhang, C. L., & Liu, X. H., Fast continuous terahertz wave imaging system for security. *Optics Communications*, **282**, pp. 2019–2022, 2009.

[18] Luukanen, A., Gronberg, L., Helisto, P., Penttila, J. S., Seppa, H., Sipola, H., Dietlein, C. R., & Grossman, E. N., An array of antenna-coupled superconducting microbolometers for passive indoors real-time THz imaging. *Proceedings of SPIE*, **6212**, p. 62120Y, 2006.

[19] Luukanen, A., Gronberg, L., Helisto, P., Penttila, J. S., Seppa, H., Sipola, H., Dietlein, C. R., & Grossman, E. N., Passive Euro-American Terahertz Camera (PEAT-CAM): Passive indoors THz imaging at video rates for security applications. *Proceedings of SPIE*, **6548**, p. 654808, 2007.

[20] Zimdars, D., Fiber-pigtailed terahertz time domain spectroscopy instrumentation for package inspection and security imaging. *Proceedings of SPIE*, **5070**, pp. 108–116, 2003.

[21] Zimdars, D., White, J., Stuk, G., Chernovsky, A., Fichter, G., & Williamson, S. L., Time domain terahertz detection of concealed threats in luggage and personnel. *Proceedings of SPIE*, **6212**, p. 62120O, 2006.

[22] Leahy-Hoppa, M., Fitch, M., & Osiander, R., Terahertz spectroscopy techniques for explosives detection. *Analytical and Bioanalytical Chemistry*, **395**, pp. 247–257, 2009.

[23] Tribe, W. R., Newnham, D. A., Taday, P. F., & Kemp, M. C., Hidden opject detection: Security applications of terahertz technology. *Proceedings of SPIE*, **5354**, pp. 168–176, 2004.

[24] Leahy-Hoppa, M. R., Fitch, M. J., Zheng, X., Hayden, L. M., & Osiander, R., Wideband terahertz spectroscopy of explosives. *Chemical Physics Letters*, **434**, pp. 227–230, 2007.

[25] Fitch, M. J., Leahy-Hoppa, M. R., Ott, E. W., & Osiander, R., Molecular absorption cross-section and absolute absorptivity in the THz frequency range for the explosives TNT, RDX, HMX, and PETN. *Chemical Physics Letters*, **443**, pp. 284–288, 2007.

[26] Baker, C., Lo, T., Tribe, W. R., Cole, B. E., Hogbin, M. R., & Kemp, M. C., Detection of concealed explosives at a distance using terahertz technology. *Proceedings of the IEEE*, **95**, pp. 1559–1565, 2007.

[27] Barber, J., Hooks, D. E., Funk, D. J., Averitt, R. D., Taylor, A. J., & Babikov, D., Temperature-dependent far-infrared spectra of single crystals of high explosives using terahertz time-domain spectroscopy. *Journal of Physical Chemistry A*, **109**, pp. 3501–3505, 2005.

[28] Chen, Y., Liu, H., Fitch, M. J., Osiander, R., Spicer, J. B., Shur, M., & Zhang, X.-C., THz diffuse reflectance spectra of selected explosives and related compounds. *Proceedings of SPIE*, **5790**, pp. 19–24, 2005.

[29] Chen, J., Chen, Y., Zhao, H. J., Bastiaans, G. J., & Zhang, X.-C., Absorption coefficients of selected explosives and related compounds in the range of 0.1–2.8 THz. *Optics Express*, **15**, pp. 12060–12067, 2007.

[30] Fan, W. H., Burnett, A., Upadhya, P. C., Cunningham, J., Linfield, E. H., & Davies, A. G., Far-infrared spectroscopic characterization of explosives for security applications using broadband terahertz time-domain spectroscopy. *Applied Spectroscopy*, **61**, pp. 638–643, 2007.

[31] Fan, W. H., Zhao, W., Chen, G. H., Burnett, A. D., Upadhya, P. C., Cunningham, J. E., Linfield, E. H., & Davies, A. G., Time-domain terahertz spectroscopy and applications on drugs and explosives. *Proceedings of SPIE*, **6840**, pp. 68400T68401–68400T68408, 2007.

[32] Allis, D. G., Prokhorova, D. A., Fedor, A. M., & Korter, T. M., First principles analysis of the terahertz spectrum of PETN. *Proceedings of SPIE*, **6212**, p. 62120F, 2006.

[33] Allis, D. G., Prokhorova, D. A., & Korter, T. M., Solid-state modeling of the terahertz spectrum of the high explosive HMX. *Journal of Physical Chemistry A*, **110**, pp. 1951–1959, 2006.

[34] Allis, D. G., Zeitler, J. A., Taday, P. F., & Korter, T. M., Theoretical analysis of the solid-state terahertz spectrum of the high explosive RDX. *Chemical Physics Letters*, **463**, pp. 84–89, 2008.

[35] Clarkson, J., Smith, W. E., Batchelder, D. N., Smith, D. A., & Coats, A. M., A theoretical study of the structure and vibrations of 2,4,5-trinitrotoluene. *Journal of Molecular Structure*, **648**, pp. 203–214, 2003.

[36] Hu, Y., Huang, P., Guo, L. T., Wang, X. H., & Zhang, C. L., Terahertz spectroscopic investigations of explosives. *Physics Letters A*, **359**, pp. 728–732, 2006.

[37] Liu, H., Chen, Y., Bastiaans, G. J., & Zhang, X. -C., Diffuse fresnel reflection spectroscopy of explosive RDX studied by THz time-domain spectroscopy. *Proceedings of IEEE*, **2**, pp. 588–589, 2005.

[38] Liu, H. B., Chen, Y. Q., Bastiaans, G. J., & Zhang, X.-C., Detection and identification of explosive RDX by THz diffuse reflection spectroscopy. *Optics Express*, **14**, pp. 415–423, 2006.

[39] Leahy-Hoppa, M. R., Fitch, M. J., & Osiander, R., Terahertz reflection spectroscopy for the detection of explosives. *Proceedings of SPIE*, **6893**, p. 689305, 2008.

[40] Dikmelik, Y., Fitch, M. J., Osiander, R., & Spicer, J. B., The effects of rough surface reflection on terahertz time-domain spectroscopy. *Optics Letters*, **31**, pp. 3653–3655, 2006.

[41] Fitch, M. J., Dodson, C., Chen, Y., Liu, H., Zhang, X. -C., & Osiander, R., Terahertz reflection spectroscopy for explosives detection. *Proceedings of SPIE*, **5790**, pp. 281–288, 2005.

[42] Osiander, R., Fitch, M. J., Leahy-Hoppa, M., Dikmelik, Y., & Spicer, J. B., Signature and signal generation aspects of explosive detection using terahertz time-domain spectroscopy. *International Journal of High Speed Electronics and Systems*, **18**, pp. 295–306, 2008.

[43] Zurk, L. M., Sundberg, G., Schecklman, S., Zhou, Z., Chen, A., & Thorsos, E. I., Scattering effects in terahertz reflection spectroscopy. *Proceedings of SPIE*, **6949**, p. 694907, 2008.

[44] Zimdars, D. & White, J. S., Terahertz reflection imaging for package and personnel inspection. *Proceedings of SPIE*, **5411**, pp. 78–83, 2004.

[45] Zimdars, D., White, J., Stuk, G., Sucha, G., Fichter, G., & Williamson, S. L., Time domain terahertz imaging of threats in luggage and personnel. *International Journal of High Speed Electronics and Systems*, **17**, pp. 271–281, 2007.

[46] Zimdars, D., High speed terahertz reflection imaging. *Proceedings of SPIE*, **5692**, pp. 255–259, 2005.

[47] Shen, Y. C., Taday, P. F., Newnham, D. A., & Pepper, M., Chemical mapping using reflection terahertz pulsed imaging. *Semiconductor Science and Technology*, **20**, pp. 254–257, 2005.

[48] Jepsen, P. U. & Fischer, B. M., Dynamic range in terahertz time-domain transmission and reflection spectroscopy. *Optics Letters*, **30**, pp. 29–31, 2005.

[49] www.brijot.com.

Structural health monitoring

R. Mason[1], L. Gintert[1], S. Sweeney[2], R. Lampo[2],
K. Chandler[3], & J. Chandler[3]
[1]*Concurrent Technologies Corporation, Largo, FL 33773, USA*
[2]*Materials and Structures Branch, United States Army Engineer
Research and Development Center, Construction Engineering Research
Laboratory, Champaign, IL 61826-9005, USA*
[3]*Chandler Monitoring Systems, Inc., Lawrenceville, GA 30043, USA*

Abstract

The monitoring of infrastructure for structural integrity continues to be a critical need. The potential for structural failure—due to phenomena related to material and component degradation over time (corrosion) as well as instantaneous occurrences such as earthquakes and terrorist attacks—is a growing concern as bridges and buildings are becoming older yet more heavily used. Structural integrity concerns are traditionally addressed through regular inspection of the structure, which may include visual, dye penetrant, ultrasonic, and/or radiographic nondestructive test methods. These methods are capable of detecting most defects of concern to authorities, but some of the methods may not detect defects (such as corrosion or cracks) in structural members that are completely hidden, and none of them are able to determine (in a single measurement) if a defect is actively growing. As a result, standard inspection techniques may not find defects that are likely to compromise integrity and could instead focus attention on defects that, while readily detectable, may be harmless to the overall health of the structure. State-of-the-art and emerging sensor technology approaches are available that can assess structural integrity in real time. Furthermore, these technologies can be integrated into a comprehensive remote monitoring system that can continuously assess the structural health of a building or a bridge, facilitating the rapid repair of potential issues.

Keywords: Structural Health Monitoring, Structural Health Management, Bridges, Corrosion, Infrastructure, Sensors, Fiber Bragg Gratings.

1 Introduction

The structural health of infrastructure has become an increasing area of concern in recent years, as age, aggressive environments, and increased traffic volume have taken their toll on many structures. The potential for catastrophic failure of bridges in particular has instigated studies and surveys of bridge structural health, which provide a grim picture. In December 2008 the United States (U.S.) Department of Transportation (DOT) reported that, of over 601,000 U.S. highway bridges in inventory, as many as 151,000 may be either structurally deficient or functionally obsolete [1]. The criticality of the situation is underscored when one considers that a number of these bridges may be fracture critical (i.e., they may contain a single component whose failure could lead to failure of the entire structure). These studies, as well as incidents such as the catastrophic collapse of the Interstate 35 (I-35) West Bridge over the Mississippi River in Minneapolis, MN in August 2007, have refocused public attention upon the age and condition of bridges within the nation's infrastructure. Steel bridges have become a specific concern in recent years, as metal fatigue can combine with corrosion damage to accelerate bridge health deterioration. Conditions like these have been implicated in several recent failures of steel bridges [2]. Of 503 U.S. bridges that failed over an 11-year period, 100 were found to be due to corrosion [3]. Failure may be exacerbated by catastrophic occurrences such as earthquakes, tidal waves, landslides, and terrorist attacks.

It is recognized that organizations responsible for infrastructure maintenance are constrained to some degree by current state-of-the-art inspection equipment and techniques. The engineering investigation following the collapse of the I-35 Bridge highlighted the fact that conventional inspection techniques employed during the routine assessment of steel bridges—including visual, dye penetrant, ultrasonic, and/or radiographic nondestructive testing methods—may not be capable of detecting cracks in hidden or nearly inaccessible areas (such as those in built-up structures) and may also be unable to determine if a crack in a critical location or component is actively growing.

In view of the above issues, there is an urgent need to examine and assess the latest state-of-the-art technologies and approaches to the remote monitoring of the degradation of critical infrastructure by means of strategically positioned sensors, reliable data acquisition systems, and advanced analytical software. A number of sensor technologies are available that can meet this need. Furthermore, innovative structural health monitoring (SHM) systems can incorporate several different types of sensor technologies into a single interactive system. When properly implemented on a structure, these SHM systems can provide advance warning of a growing structural problem as well as an opportunity for repair before catastrophic failure. Such a system has recently been envisioned [3], designed [4,5], and implemented on a bridge structure [6].

2   Structural evaluation

Before initiating the design of an integrated sensor system for a structure, it is essential to conduct a structural evaluation of the as-built structure. This evaluation is necessary not only to establish the current structural health of the

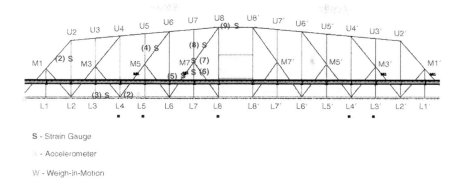

S - Strain Gauge

- Accelerometer

W - Weigh-in-Motion

Figure 1: Government Bridge schematic with installed sensor placement.

structure (as a baseline) but also to determine any critical failure points, load paths, and so on. This evaluation will also establish optimum areas for sensor placement.

For example, previous work to design and implement a SHM system on two bridges [4–6] was initiated with the structural analyses of the bridges to establish the current load rating, critical members, expected structural response, and any other identified characteristics necessary for the design of the SHM system for each bridge. To accomplish this, structural engineers evaluated both bridges based on three-dimensional finite element models; separate structural analyses were required for each bridge. In addition, available bridge inspection reports and maintenance reports were reviewed. Optimum sensor placement was then determined from the analyses. Using this methodology, the locations of the desired sensors for the swing span of one of the bridges, the Government Bridge at Rock Island Arsenal, IL, was developed. This bridge consists of two levels: a lower level for highway traffic and an upper level for trains. A diagram of the optimum sensor locations for the SHM system on the Government Bridge is presented in Figure 1.

Several points of interest were derived from the analyses. It was found that additional sensors (possibly two or three strain gages) would be useful to determine railroad and highway floor beam stress levels, since some of these are fracture critical members. A weigh-in-motion sensors/system was also found to be useful to determine the weight of the train while on either track.

3   Sensor selection

The sensors employed within a SHM system will be dependent upon the size, age, condition, environment, and unique needs of the structure. A number of sensor types are available to monitor and manage the structural health of infrastructure as described in the following sections.

Figure 2: COTS accelerometer.

3.1   Accelerometers

Acceleration measurement is a useful tool in SHM. These measurements are typically determined using accelerometers, placed at specific points on the structure such that the natural frequencies and vibration mode shapes can be determined. Changes in modal response, vibration, and inclination can then be measured as a function of time. Modal response in particular is an excellent method for determining changes in the overall structural behavior of bridges, in that changes in the bridge's natural frequency may be indicative of damage to the structure [3]. A commercial off-the-shelf (COTS) accelerometer is presented in Figure 2 [3].

3.2   Strain sensors

An assessment of strain, to monitor tensile and compressive loading in critical structural members of the superstructure, can be derived using strain gages adhered directly to the structure. Important data related to stresses in critical bridge members, particularly those that are not redundant, can be obtained using strain gages.

3.3   Tilt sensors

Tilt sensors are employed to determine rotational displacement on free-standing structural members such as bridge piers. Movement at piers and expansion joints is measured and monitored using tiltmeters. COTS tiltmeters attached to a bridge structure are presented in Figure 3 [7].

3.4   Displacement sensors

Deflection/displacement sensors can be employed to measure movement between structural members, such as displacement between deck joints and

Figure 3: COTS tiltmeters attached to bridge structure.

displacements at bridge bearings. Measured deflections, like strain readings, are helpful in determining whether a structure is responding as expected and can serve as an early warning if unanticipated trends are observed.

3.5   Corrosion sensors

A number of COTS corrosion sensing technologies are available for monitoring corrosion and material degradation of structures. In general, three types of corrosion monitoring technologies have been considered for infrastructure applications [3]: linear polarization resistance (LPR) sensors, electrical resistance (ER) sensors, and test coupon racks.

The LPR technique involves the application of a small voltage (or polarization potential) to an electrode in solution. By measuring the resulting current, a corrosion rate can be derived. While this technique can provide a snapshot of how the material is degrading in real time, the disadvantage of LPR sensors is that they are designed for relatively clean, aqueous, electrolytic environments. Monitoring the portion of bridge piers that are underwater would be an optimal application for LPR sensors, whereas the monitoring of above water portions might not. The interpretation of the data can also be complex. In general, LPR is easy to use as a qualitative signal of general corrosion phenomena such as coating deterioration but not corrosion rate [8].

Conversely, ER corrosion sensors can be used to measure atmospheric corrosion rates. ER sensors measure the change in Ohmic resistance of a corroding metal element exposed to the atmosphere. The action of corrosion on the surface of the element produces a decrease in its cross-sectional area, with a corresponding

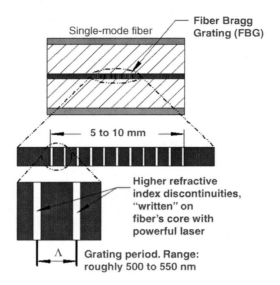

Figure 4: Diagram of fiber-optic cable with FBGs.

increase in its ER. The increase in resistance can be related directly to metal loss, and this loss as a function of time is by definition the corrosion rate.

An assessment of atmospheric corrosion can also be made using a test rack of metallic coupons that are exposed to the subject environment. Bare metal coupons mounted on a polymer sample card (using nonmetallic fasteners that suspend the samples above the card) can be employed to assess the visual onset of corrosion. Additional information can be obtained by removing the test coupon racks at regular intervals and analyzing the coupons for mass loss and residual surface contaminants using methods such as ASTM G11 [9] and ASTM B825 [10], respectively.

While corrosion sensors using other electrochemical techniques such as electrochemical impedance spectroscopy and zero-resistance ammetry have been developed, they have not yet been demonstrated for infrastructure applications.

3.6　Fiber Bragg Gratings (FBGs)

FBG technology can be employed as simple, low-cost, high-sensitivity sensors for infrastructure. FBGs are "mirrors" that are photo-imprinted into a fiber-optic cable that is bonded to (or embedded in) a structure. A diagram of FBGs within fiber-optic cable is presented in Figure 4 [4].

Each FBG sensor has a specific wavelength and measures a specific parameter. When a laser light source is used to project light through the fiber, a portion of the light is reflected back from the FBG. As this wavelength changes over time due to temperature and/or stress of the fiber, each FBG sensor returns information on these parameters as a function of the state of the structure [11]. The nature of FBG sensors makes them well suited for outdoor infrastructure monitoring; they consume lower power than standard sensor systems and are immune to electromagnetic effects, corrosion, and most chemicals. Optical sensors have been previously demonstrated for infrastructure applications using this technique [12–14]. The utility of using FBG sensors to assess the structural health of buildings damaged by earthquakes or terrorist attacks was envisioned as early as 2004 [15].

The versatility of FBG sensors lends them to a number of useful applications with respect to the SHM system. An assessment of strain can be derived using FBG strain gages adhered directly to the bridge structure [6]. In addition, FBG tilt sensors can be employed to determine rotational displacement in bridge piers, and FBG deflection/displacement sensors can be used to measure displacement between deck joints and displacements at bridge bearings.

3.7 Acoustic emission sensors

Acoustic emission (AE) technology detects and monitors ultrasonic waves produced by materials when they undergo cracking [3,4,11]. As these ultrasonic waves can travel great distances, AE sensors are capable of inspecting the entire monitored area for defects, covering beams, gussets, stringers, and hidden structural members. The technique has been thoroughly demonstrated for the structural health assessment of bridge systems by Carlyle [16–20] and others.

Under past efforts [6], AE sensors were used to identify active crack growth in selected pins used to connect truss members on the Government Bridge. The AE portion of the SHM system consisted of piezoelectric sensors and specialized signal processing to separate, in real time, the acoustic defect signal from typical traffic noise. At each pin, sensors actively listened for distress or cracking. In addition, the sensor actively emitted a signal (ping) at regular intervals in order to detect cracks or changes in the pin connectors.

3.8 Additional technologies

SHM systems placed on infrastructure can incorporate additional monitoring technologies such as video cameras [21]. Cameras can be placed on and around the structure to allow remote viewing and to save video images when an event is triggered. The video cameras can be set in such a way as to allow remote viewing of the length of the structure as well as the main navigation channels. If an event is triggered, the cameras can automatically zoom in on the affected area and begin recording. Video capture from the remote computer can be made possible through the SHM software (see Section 4.1).

Laser-based measuring systems have been employed to monitor the vibration of bridge systems under road traffic conditions [21]. These systems simply measure the position of the laser on a sensitive screen and record changes in two-dimensional space.

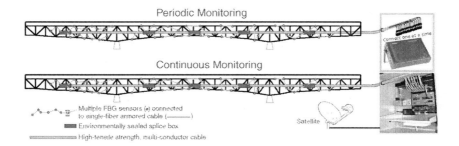

Figure 5: SHM system installation on bridge structure.

It is envisioned that future SHM systems will incorporate technologies that have yet to be fully embraced and are therefore currently used only on a handful of applications. These include ground-penetrating radar, thermography, and impact echo as well as emerging technologies such as tiny sensors enabled by microelectromechanical systems (MEMS) and nanotechnology. These future SHM systems could also incorporate mesh or cloud data networks [22].

4   System design and integration

Two SHM systems were designed to acquire and process data from two bridges under past work [6]. On each bridge, relevant sensor technologies (primarily FBG but also incorporating AE and corrosion sensors) were incorporated into a single interactive system. Sensors were placed along the bridges in a unique, unobtrusive "single trunk" design, in which cabling from all sensors is part of a single large bundle running along the length of the bridge. This design greatly reduced required space and took advantage of the FBG technology's ability to transmit data over long distances. A diagram of the SHM system implemented on a bridge structure in two monitoring configurations (periodic and continuous) is presented in Figure 5.

Cabling is significantly reduced for FBG sensors compared to traditional sensors. In both of the above scenarios, data is gathered from the individual sensors, sent through the cable, and transmitted through the data acquisition and analysis system (see Section 4.1) to the satellite dish where it is transmitted to the responsible parties for review.

For one of the bridges, the aforementioned Government Bridge, the overall intent of the SHM system was to monitor corrosion and detect structural irregularities and/or changes to the bridge span. The SHM system for this bridge was therefore designed to monitor modal response (accelerometers), strain response (strain gages), acoustic response (AE sensors), and corrosion (ER sensors and metal coupons). It is noted that the SHM system on this bridge was designed to operate while the swing span is in any operating position as well as while it is in motion.

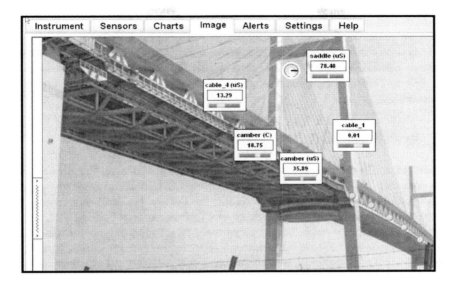

Figure 6: Example of GUI for bridge SHM system.

4.1   Data acquisition

The control system for the integrated SHM system must provide data integration, analysis, and output for all sensors incorporated into the sensor system. The control system generally consists of two major components: a data recorder and analysis system located on the structure for recording and performing the analysis, and a remote computer to store data, perform additional analysis, send alerts via e-mail and telephone, and serve as a Web-based access portal for visualizing the data and generating reports.

Typical SHM software consists of a graphic user interface (GUI) compatible with a standard operating system. The software records and archives the data as it is generated. While standard GUIs may employ simple graphical sensor readouts, such graphs are often difficult to interpret by untrained viewers. A more useful and simple methodology would be to provide a real-time graphical presentation of the data in an innovative "color code" system. Rather than provide a typical data readout that must be interpreted and understood before action can be taken, the system would simply show a photograph or diagram of the monitored structure overlaid with a color code—green, yellow, or red—for each sensor. An example of this innovative GUI is presented in Figure 6.

In this way the software performs real-time analysis of the structure for the purpose of detecting potential problems or safety concerns. The system allows two-way communication between the data recorder and analysis system on each structure and the remote computer such that programming and querying of instrumentation may be performed remotely. If any sensor area maintains a yellow/red status, or if an event is triggered, the system automatically transmits warnings to designated personnel via e-mail and cell phone so that the overall data can be reviewed and an appropriate response can be quickly determined. The SHM software should also be able to access archived video footage as well as control the pan feature of video cameras (if used) and capture live video on demand.

5   Review and interpretation of the data

Once the SHM system has been implemented on a structure, the data should be reviewed frequently to monitor the readings from the sensors and manage the overall health of the structure. While the system has built-in warnings to alert users when significant events or changes occur (see Section 4.1), occasional monitoring to make sure the system is functioning properly should also occur. The readings should be monitored periodically by maintenance personnel as well as by structural engineers who can direct the appropriate precautionary measures on an as-needed basis.

It should be noted that the implementation of such a system will likely incur additional costs in identifying the current state of the structure (in addition to the initial structural analyses mentioned in Section 2) as well as tuning the structural models used to determine triggers and conditions so that warning thresholds are properly set. This process will occur as the results are interpreted and understood as a function of time and will likely be a unique process for each structure. Recent studies [6] have demonstrated that data must be collected and analyzed for as much as a year to fully understand the effects of environmental factors such as thermal strains and movements, water levels, winds, rain, and so on.

6   Summary

Existing sensor technologies can be integrated into a comprehensive SHM system for the remote monitoring of the structural integrity of critical infrastructure. The SHM system is intended to provide advance warning of a growing structural problem as well as an opportunity for repair before catastrophic failure. The capabilities of such systems, and the potential benefits for future possible application, continue to be of keen interest to both government and civilian organizations. As such, it is anticipated that SHM systems will continue to be considered for bridges, buildings, and similar load bearing structures.

Acknowledgments

The aforementioned past work [4–6] was funded by the U.S. Army Engineer Research & Development Center, Construction Engineering Research Laboratory (ERDC-CERL) through the U.S. Office of the Secretary of Defense. The authors wish to recognize the sponsors of the U.S. Department of Defense Corrosion Prevention and Control Program:

- Office of Under Secretary of Defense, Office of Corrosion Policy and Oversight (Director, Mr. Dan Dunmire)
- Deputy Assistant Secretary of the Army Acquisition Policy and Logistics (Army Corrosion Control Prevention Executive, Mr. Wimpy D. Pybus)
- Assistant Chief of Staff for Installation Management (Mr. David Purcell)
- Headquarters, U.S. Army Installation Management Command (Mr. Paul Volkman)

The authors also wish to acknowledge the contributions of the Bridge SHM Team members who have put forth considerable time and effort to support the tasks outlined in this chapter. The authors would specifically like to recognize

- Mr. Vincent Chiarito, Mr. Henry Diaz-Alvarez, and Dr. Paul Mlakar, U.S. Army ERDC, Geotechnical and Structures Laboratory
- Mr. Larry Cranford and Dr. Doug Neale, Mandaree Enterprises Corporation
- Dr. William O'Donnell, Mr. Tony Hedderman, Mr. Don Shaw, and Mr. Jeremy Himes, O'Donnell Consulting Engineers Inc.
- Dr. John Carlyle, Carlyle Consulting
- Dr. Scott Wade, Monash University
- Mr. R. Kirk Gallien, P.E., P.T.O.E., Louisiana Department of Transportation
- Mr. Mitchell K. Carr, Mississippi Department of Transportation
- Mr. Christian Hawkinson, P.E., Rock Island Arsenal Directorate of Public Works

Finally, the authors wish to recognize the significant contributions of Mr. Vincent Hock, U.S. Army ERDC-CERL, in the planning and execution of this activity.

References

[1] Accelerating Improvement, *Engineering News-Record*, McGraw-Hill, April 13, 2009, page B2.
[2] Riggs Larsen, K., New Legislation Focuses on Extending the Life of Highway Bridges. *Materials Performance*, August 2008.
[3] Sweeny, S., Lampo, R., & Hock, V., Remote Structural Monitoring and Corrosion Degradation Modeling of Bridges. 2008 U.S. Army Corrosion Summit, Clearwater, FL, February 2008.
[4] Mason, R. *et al.*, A Novel Structural Health Management Approach for Steel Bridges, U.S. Army Corrosion Summit, Clearwater Beach, FL, February 2009.
[5] Mason, R. *et al.*, A Novel Integrated Monitoring System for Structural Health Management of Military Infrastructure, 2009 DoD Corrosion Conference, Washington, DC, August 2009.
[6] Mason, R. *et al.*, Implementation of a Novel Structural Health Management System for Steel Bridges, U.S. Army Corrosion Summit, Huntsville, AL, February 2010.

[7]   Sorgenfrei, D., Structural Health Management (SHM) of Steel and Composite Bridges, *Proceedings of the Workshop on Structural Health Management of Steel and Composite Bridges*, Washington, DC, USA, May 2008.

[8]   Scully, J., Corrosion Rate Monitoring on Bridge Structures—Theory, *Proceedings of the Workshop on Structural Health Management of Steel and Composite Bridges*, Washington, DC, USA, May 2008.

[9]   ASTM G1, Standard Practice for Preparing, Cleaning, and Evaluating Corrosion Test Specimens, ASTM International, West Conshohocken, PA, 1990 (reapproved 1999).

[10] ASTM B825, Standard Test Method for Coulometric Reduction of Surface Films on Metallic Test Samples, ASTM International, West Conshohocken, PA, 2002 (reapproved in 2008).

[11] Yolken, H. & Matzkanin, G., Recent Trends in Structural Health Monitoring Technologies, *AMMTIAC Quarterly*, Advanced Materials, Manufacturing, and Testing Information Analysis Center, Rome, NY, Vol. 3, No. 4, pp. 3–6.

[12] Kersey, A., Monitoring Structural Performance with Optical TDR Techniques, *Symposium and Workshop on Time Domain Reflectometry in Environmental, Infrastructure, and Mining Applications*, Northwestern University, Evanston, IL, September 17–19, 1994 (Washington, D.C.: U.S. Bureau of Mines, 1994), pp. 434–442. USBM special publication SP 19–94.

[13] Udd, E. *et al.*, Fiber Optic Sensors for Infrastructure Applications, Oregon Department of Transportation Report No. FHWA-OR-RD-98-18, February 1998.

[14] Paolozzi, A. *et al.*, FBG Sensors for Composite Material and Bridge Monitoring: Some Applications, concept paper, 2008.

[15] Hong-Nan LI & Liang Ren, Recent Progress on Structural Health Monitoring by Fibre Optic Sensor in Civil Engineering, *3rd China-Japan-US Symposium on Structural Health Monitoring and Control*, Dalian, China, October 13–16, 2004.

[16] Pollock, A. & Carlyle, J., Acoustic Emission for Bridge Inspection—Application Guidelines, Final Report, Contract DTFH61-90-C-0049, Federal Highway Administration, Washington, DC, June 1995.

[17] Carlyle, J., Acoustic Emission Monitoring of the I-205 Willamette River Bridge, Phase Report, Contract DTFH61-90-C-0049, Federal Highway Administration, Washington, DC, April 1993.

[18] Carlyle, J., Acoustic Emission Monitoring of the I-10 Mississippi River Bridge, Phase Report, Contract DTFH61-90-C-0049, Federal Highway Administration, Washington, DC, January 1993.

[19] Carlyle, J. & Leaird, J., Acoustic Emission Monitoring of the I-80 Bryte Bend Bridge, Phase Report, Contract DTFH61-90-C-0049, Federal Highway Administration, Washington, DC, October 1992.

[20] Carlyle, J. & Ely, T., Acoustic Emission Monitoring of the I-95 Woodrow Wilson Bridge, Phase Report, Contract DTFH61-90-C-0049, Federal Highway Administration, Washington, DC, September 1992.

[21] Bien, J. *et al.*, Dynamic Load Tests in Bridge Management, Transportation Research Circular, Supplement Number E-C053, Transportation Research Board of the National Academies, July 2003.

[22] Friedland, I., The FHWA Bridge Program and Structural Monitoring of Highway Bridges, *Proceedings of the Workshop on Structural Health Management of Steel and Composite Bridges*, Washington, DC, USA, May 2008.

Networks of simple sensors for detecting emplacement of improvised explosive devices

Neil C. Rowe, Ahren A. Reed, Riqui Schwamm, Jeehee Cho,
Jose J. Flores & Arijit Das
US Naval Postgraduate School, Monterey, CA 93943, USA

Abstract

Detection of improvised explosive devices is difficult and requires a wide spectrum of strategies. Detection during emplacement is the best hope. Nonimaging sensors provide several advantages over cameras in expense, robustness, and processing simplicity for this task. We describe experiments with inexpensive commercial sensors and show how data can be combined to provide monitoring for suspicious pedestrian behavior at a 1–10 meter scale. Our approach preanalyzes terrain to rate likelihood of emplacement. We install sensors and monitor the terrain, seeking direct clues to suspicious behavior such as loitering and odd sounds such as excavation. We also use sensor data to track people by inferring their probability distributions and use this to detect significant accelerations and atypical velocity vectors, both of which can indicate suspicious behavior. We describe experiments we have conducted with a prototype sensor network of eight kinds of sensors, from which it appears that motion and sonar sensors are the most helpful for this task.

Keywords: Improvised Explosive Device, IED, Emplacement, Sensors, Networks, Suspicion, Terrain, Probability, Anomaly.

1 Introduction

Improvised explosive devices (IEDs) are an increasing threat to both civilians and militaries. These are mine-like explosives, often manually detonated, and are ideal weapons for insurgencies. IEDs have been particular threats to the US military in Iraq and Afghanistan since 2003 (Advanced Professional Education and News Service [1]). Typically, they are emplaced along roads frequented by targets and at locations such as bridges that cannot be detoured.

IEDs are inexpensive to produce, can be used anywhere, and can be very effective. Detection once emplaced is very difficult even with sophisticated remote-sensing techniques. But emplacement necessarily involves some unusual and suspicious actions with some degree of abnormal concealment. Detecting emplacement is our best chance for locating IEDs on a local (1–50-foot) scale. With enough sensors at critical locations, we can do it autonomously and transmit data wirelessly. If evidence of emplacement is strong enough, security personnel can be dispatched to investigate. Challenges are in choosing the sensors, their deployment, and what software should look for.

2 Clues to IED emplacement

IED emplacement is a kind of criminal behavior in public. Criminal behavior occurs more in publicly owned and unowned areas (Brower [2]; Bolz, Dudonis, and Schulz [3]) and is localized by assessing the trade-off between opportunity and risk, as for instance by burglars (Brown and Altman [4]). Opportunity is affected by the likelihood that victimizable targets will move through an area. Risk depends on the number of criminals working together and the likelihood of discovery of the criminal activity either by active surveillance (as by law enforcement) or inadvertent observation by bystanders; the latter is affected by the sense of personal interest in reporting, the extent of investment in the concept of reporting, the ability to identify the activity as suspicious, and the feeling of control by the bystander (Newman [5]).

This means that the main clues to IED emplacement are suitability of the location, anomalousness of the behavior, occurrence of goal-changing behavior, and coordinated activity. Suitability of the location is based on emplacement difficulty, concealability, and ability to escape. Anomalies can be in time, location, speed, manner, and other properties of the behavior. Most automated surveillance systems address only anomalies, but this creates significant numbers of false alarms, since many legitimate activities are anomalous, such as repairing a road. Goal-changing behavior is a clue since most people in a public area are passing through and tend to be consistent in their speed, direction, and manner of motion; significant changes suggest changing of goals (Rowe [6]), reflecting concealment of intentions or opportunism. Finally, unusually coordinated activity can be suspicious.

2.1 Cameras versus nonimaging sensors

Most work on detecting suspicious behavior has used video surveillance data (Bak *et al.* [7]; Barbara *et al.* [8]; Wiliem *et al.* [9]). But it has several disadvantages. Cameras are subject to occlusion of view and sensitivity to the angle of view; they do not work as well at night and in storms; images require time and power to transmit; image analysis requires substantial processing and can make many kinds of mistakes; and images risk violation of privacy more than nonimaging sensors. In view of the seriousness of the IED threat, it is important to also exploit other modalities for detecting suspicious behavior.

Nonimaging sensors provide a relatively independent source of information to supplement image data. In addition, deception is easier to see with nonimaging sensors because it is more difficult for people to control less-visible aspects of their behavior (Vrij [10]).

A disadvantage of nonimaging sensors is that the strength of many signals like audio, sonar, and magnetic ones is inversely proportional to the square of the distance from the source, whereas images have resolution inversely proportional to the distance. However, IED emplacements are very unevenly distributed and tend to cluster at "choke points" in traffic, like bridges, culverts, road narrowings, and road intersections. At such locations, we only need to provide coverage within a radius of 3 meters, which we can do well with nonimaging sensors.

2.2   Prior probabilities for emplacement

A variety of methods have been used for assessing likelihoods of IEDs at a location (Fong and Zhuang [11]; Li, Bramsen, and Alonso [12]; Parunak, Sauter, and Crossman [13]). Poisson models can work well, but the base rate will vary considerably with the terrain. Our approach to estimating these base rates is, following the above analysis, to assess factors based on traffic density, suitability of the terrain for emplacement, potential concealability of emplacement and triggering, ability to escape after emplacement or triggering, and degree of community support for emplacement.

Video of an area of interest can be recorded over representative periods of time from a fixed camera position and orientation. Traffic patterns can be found by automatically analyzing the video to find the moving objects. Our primary interest is pedestrians (Rowe [6]) in a planar area. We divide the ground plane shown in the camera view into bins and count the number of occurrences of the feet of people in each bin. Bins with unusually high counts represent choke points. We also compute the average velocity vector for each bin so we can note anomalies. We do this by mapping directions to a range of 0–180 degrees to account for bidirectional nature of paths (by doubling the velocity angle, averaging it, and then halving the angle). Traffic statistics do differ with time of day, day of week, and week of year, and we should calculate averages for a variety of them.

Figure 1 shows some example terrain, and Figure 2 indicates by the size of circles the corresponding counts of human presence. Figure 2 was made from six videos of 30 minutes each taken during the day on six separate days and shows a view from above for bins of 1.5 meters by 1.5 meters, where the size of a circle is proportional to its count. The camera location was the origin of the coordinate system, and the line through the camera and parallel to the up-and-down path through the center of the courtyard was the vertical axis.

Terrain suitability is another factor in the probability of emplacement. It is easiest to conceal an IED by burying it, and it is easiest to bury it in unpaved

Figure 1: Example computed background image for video.

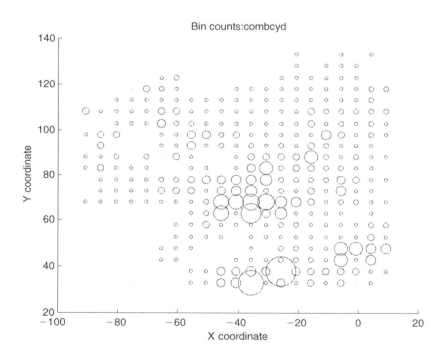

Figure 2: Bin counts for the terrain in Figure 1 as viewed from above.

bare ground. So we create an array corresponding to the 5 foot by 5 foot traffic bins representing terrain suitability. But all the area within a blast radius of bare ground is also dangerous, so we must "blur" the array by averaging values with those of their neighbors. The left image of Figure 3 shows the resulting IED suitability for the data in Figure 2, where brighter means more suitable.

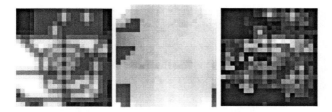

Figure 3: Terrain suitability, mobility, and calculated overall likelihood of terrain in Figure 1 for IED placement.

Another factor is the concealment opportunity. IEDs tend to be emplaced where partial concealment of the act is possible, and triggermen prefer concealed locations nearby. We calculate the first kind of concealment as follows:

$$c(x, y) = (1/M) \sum_{k=0}^{M-1} (1/b(x, y, 2\pi k/M)),$$

where b gives the distance in the map plane of the nearest occluding obstacle from (x, y) in the direction of its third argument (Rowe et al. [14]). Concealment was not a significant factor for the terrain of Figure 1.

Other factors are mobility, nearness to home, and distinguishability. Mobility on the terrain matters because IED emplacers prefer to get away quickly after emplacement, and IED triggerman need to get away quickly after detonation, as any criminals. We estimate mobility from the square root of the ratio of the amount of area that can be covered in 15 seconds from a given location to the amount of area that can be covered on unobstructed terrain (Rowe et al. [14]). The middle image in Figure 3 shows the estimated mobility for the terrain of Figure 1. Criminals also prefer familiar areas close to their homes but not too close (Rossmo [15]), and this should apply to IEDs. In addition, the location of a triggered IED needs to be distinctive enough for triggerman to recognize when the target is over it, and for locals to avoid a non-triggered mine-like IED, so areas without landmarks are poor locations for IEDs.

These factors for location are generally independent of one another. Thus, the arrival rate of the Poisson process for IED occurrence can be modeled as proportional to the product of their rates, or as

$$r = K r_B r_T r_C r_M r_H r_D,$$

where r_B is the base traffic rate of the location, r_T is the terrain factor, r_C is the concealment factor, r_M is the mobility factor, r_H is the home-base factor, and r_D is the distinguishability factor. The right image of Figure 3 shows our combined analysis of the terrain of Figure 1 viewed from above, where brighter means higher IED probability.

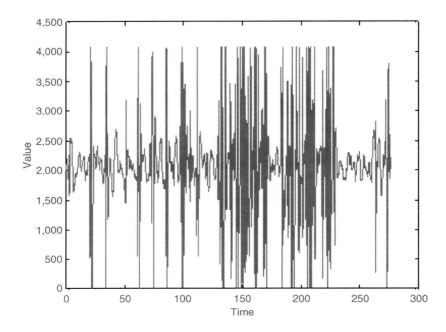

Figure 4: Motion sensor signal during an experiment with transits followed by loitering.

2.3   Anomalous behavior

Evidence of emplacement behavior can come from sensors. Most people transit public areas with a straight trajectory of constant speed (nonaccelerating). This will create a single local extremum of the signal with most sensors. Suspicious behavior will tend to show many local extrema in a short period. Figure 4 shows an example of a motion sensor (360-degree infrared) mounted near the center of the circle in Figure 1, where the horizontal axis is time in seconds. A subject passed the sensor on a nonaccelerating trajectory seven times (seconds 10–120), then loitered within a meter of the sensor (seconds 140–230). The difference in behavior can be measured by the number of values over 3,000 in a time period.

Ranging sensors such as radar and sonar provide a different kind of clue. Figure 5 shows data from an inexpensive sonar for the same experiment as that of Figure 4. The default value due to ground reflection can be seen to be 500, corresponding to about 1.5 meters. Again we see a considerable number of low readings during loitering, measurable as the rate of low values per unit time.

Some clues to suspicious behavior are negative (i.e., they are clues to non-suspicious behavior), such as sounds of speech and vehicles, since they suggest the presence of normal activities and witnesses. Other clues come from more detailed categorization of a signal such as gaits observed by audio or

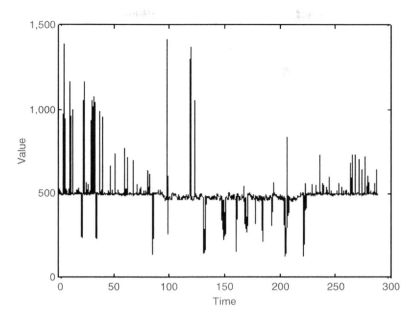

Figure 5: Sonar values for the same experiment as Figure 4.

vibration sensors. Most human footsteps are regular events, 0.4–0.8 seconds apart (Sabatier and Ekimov [16]). Unusually fast gaits suggest running, unusually slow gaits suggest carrying something heavy, and uneven gaits suggest loitering. All are suspicious. Stopping or starting suddenly is also suspicious and is usually signaled by an unusually strong footstep necessary for deceleration or acceleration.

It is important to look for anomalies at several different scales of time and space, an important principle in geographical criminology (Brantingham *et al.* [17]). So we should look for average rates over 5-second intervals as well as over 0.5-second intervals, and odd behavior should be rounded to the nearest point on a 5-foot grid as well as the nearest point on a 0.5-foot gird.

2.4   Goal changing and coordinated activity

Goal changing, signaled by changes in speed, direction, gait, or sounds, is another clue to possible emplacement behavior. That is because deception is often associated with goal changing (Vrij [10]) and emplacement almost necessarily must be deceptive.

Detection of goal changing from velocity vectors requires tracking of people over a period of time. This is more difficult with nonimaging sensors than with video but can be done well when occurrences of people are relatively infrequent as in rural areas. We infer a probability distribution of human presence from each sensor value over a threshold. Figure 6 shows the distributions we inferred

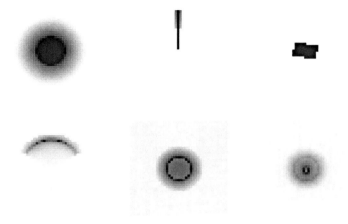

Figure 6:   Probability distributions of location associated with the sensors used in our experiments.

in our experiments for motion, directional-infrared, and pressure-strip sensors in the first row, and sonar, vibration, and audio (footstep) sensors in the second row. In each case, the sensor was oriented to the north, an inch represents 4 meters, and darkness indicates increased probability.

To find tracks, we multiply the probability distributions for sensor values above their thresholds in a fixed time window (one of 0.5 seconds seemed to work well) to get a cumulative distribution in the map plane. We then fit the centroids of probability distributions over time to line segments in spacetime of the form $x = c_1t + c_2$, $y = c_3t + c_4$. Figure 7 shows an example path in spacetime as fit by four sensor processors with six functioning sensors each. Least-squares fitting of segments is done by recursive splitting until contiguous segments are found with sufficiently good fit; then collinear contiguous segments are merged. Sufficiently strong discontinuities in the paths can be considered suspicious. The spacing of times for fitting can be 0.5 seconds apart (to detect gait wobbling) to 3 seconds (to detect wandering and stopping) to 10 seconds (to detect loitering). Figure 7 was obtained from data of four sensor locations, and smoother paths can be obtained by using more sensors.

Changes in behavior patterns of a person can also be suspicious, particularly those involving rare behaviors. Examples of behavior patterns are two people walking together, two people talking while stationary, a person stopping to examine an object, placing an object, removing an object, and excavation behavior. We can use a case-based approach to classify behaviors using the average velocity and acceleration vectors in different time spans (Rowe et al. [14]).

Detection of coordinated activity (such as an organized riot) requires more data fusion then the aforementioned types of suspicious activity since interesting coordination can be widely separated. So it mostly must be done at a base

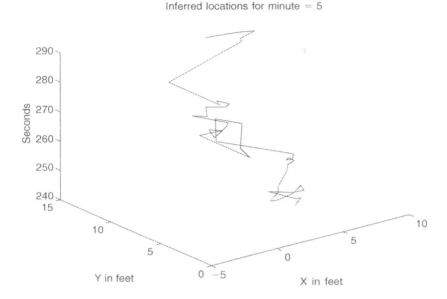

Figure 7: Example inferred path in spacetime of a single pedestrian crossing the sensor field.

station collecting data from a reasonably large area. However, coordinated activity near a single sensor processor can also be noted, such as

- significant accelerations at nearly the same time but different locations,
- similar rare behaviors at dispersed locations, and
- projected arrivals at the same time and location (suggesting a planned meeting).

We can find the first two by hashing the data onto a limited set of bins representing time intervals and looking for bins with unusually large counts. To find similar destinations, we project paths in spacetime based on current velocity vectors and note spacetime bins that have large totals.

3   Sensor management

Since prior probabilities of IEDs vary widely, a "greedy" algorithm for sensor placement is preferable to a placement on a uniform grid:

1. Obtain from security experts a distribution $r(x,y)$ of the *a priori* likelihood of an IED at a location.
2. Place a processor at the global maximum of all locations where it can be placed and assign one sensor of each of the available types to it.
3. Recalculate $r(x,y)$, zeroing its values around the last placement point.

4. Return to Step 2 if processors are unassigned.
5. At each processor location, position and orient its sensors to cover the most area.

This algorithm will be optimal whenever the number of potential targets is finite, targets can be covered by a single processor, and targets are further apart than the maximum coverage radius of a sensor. Such conditions often hold in rural areas such as Afghanistan where IEDs tend to be placed on bridges and culverts.

What measures can we take to prevent IED emplacers from vandalizing the sensor network? We can easily detect tampering in progress from the network data. Proactively, we can conceal or camouflage the sensors and processors, as by burial in the ground, embedding within concrete, or camouflaging as electrical power equipment. While attackers could use metal detectors to find sensors, this is as tedious and time consuming as attempts to find IEDs themselves, and searching would be highly suspicious in itself. We could make it harder by deploying many decoy sensors. Ploys such as exploding dye packs can tag people who tamper with the equipment. Sensor network designers have an advantage in time and resources on IED emplacers, so they can be clever.

Power consumption is a key issue with distributed sensors, and communications require significant power. Our approach entails that only suspicious behavior need be reported to a base station if coordinated activity is unlikely, and suspicious behavior will be rare. Prior probabilities for each sensor's range and sensor thresholds can be downloaded in advance to the sensor processors. Then distributions of location can be calculated by each processor from the reports it receives from its sensors, and anomalous and goal-changing phenomena can be noted locally. If it is useful to compare data between particular neighbor processors, as on a long bridge, wired connections or Bluetooth networking can be used. But longer term tracking, such as for loitering in a 100-foot area, requires coordinated analysis at a base station through broadband communications. Bundling of transmissions so they are sent infrequently when no suspicious behavior is detected will also save power.

How do we handle deliberate attempts to overtax the sensor network by large amounts of suspicious behavior? This is best recognized at the base station. Transmissions of repeated occurrences of similar data can be aggregated and summarized statistically to reduce bandwidth. Of course, overtaxing the sensor network is suspicious and deserves investigation too.

4   Experiments

We conducted experiments with a variety of sensors deployed in both indoor and outdoor public areas. Terrain preanalysis used data obtained from monitoring the area for 30-minute periods at several times a day. Usage was calculated for 1.5 meter by 1.5 meter bins, which balanced adequate counts with adequate localization. Laptop computers ran sets of four to eight sensors each. Sensors other than microphones came from Phidgets (http://www.phidgets.com) and used their software as well as interface hardware. The sensor cables averaged 1.5 meters in length, and sensors had a 3-meter range on average, so we could monitor an area of about 100 square meters with one set. The Phidgets sensors we used were motion (broad-range infrared), photocell-type infrared, sonar (1–5 meters), pressure-strip, light-intensity, magnetic, and vibrational. Of these, the motion and sonar sensors performed best at finding possible IED-emplacement behavior, but both signals were noisy and needed to be averaged over time. The pressure-strip and infrared sensors were good when they fired but missed many transits due to their narrow location coverage. The light-intensity sensor could recognize people in a short range, but it saturated easily outdoors and needed to have its light input cut by 90% before it could contribute. The vibrational sensor was too sensitive to wind to be useful, and the magnetic sensor was insufficiently sensitive to detect anything useful.

The microphones were standard cardioid microphones attached with Icicle preamplifiers to the laptops. Audio and vibrational signals were low-pass filtered to remove frequencies higher than 200 hertz (Rowe, Reed, and Flores [18]). Following Sabatier and Ekimov [16], positive peaks of sufficient height and width were identified as candidate footsteps, and then candidates not in sequences of 0.4–0.8 seconds apart of length 3 were ruled out. We also looked for other loud unrepeated sounds, since they can indicate excavation behavior, and looked for speech as a negative clue to suspicious behavior. Audio analysis caught things that the other sensors did not, but it produced many false alarms.

Figure 8 shows inferred locations of suspicious activity (the dots) in the representative 9/17/10 experiment in which we used seven sets of sensors plus two additional microphones and tested a variety of suspicious behavior. Figure 9 shows five suspiciousness factors and their averages over time (in seconds), smoothed over 10-second periods; heights on the graphs were adjusted to obtain better visual separation. The five factors were those found most effective during earlier experiments: the terrain likelihood, the suspiciousness of the acceleration norm, the compatibility of the velocity with observed trends, the anomalousness of the motion readings, and the anomalousness of the sonar readings. The system was successful at recognizing suspicious behavior during times 380–450 (dropping and picking up a bag), 690–740 (digging with a shovel), 770–810 (loitering plus normal activity), and 860–910 (loitering plus normal activity). The system was unsuccessful at recognizing the loitering alone at 450–650, but this may be due to an airplane passing overhead at 540.

The terrain factor was unhelpful because of the kinds of suspicious activity we focused on, but all the other factors were helpful. In general, performance of our implementation at finding obvious suspicious behavior was excellent, but tracking made mistakes due to the limits on the number of sensors and their area of coverage due to cable lengths. Most tracking mistakes occurred when subjects were outside the convex hull containing the sensors, so we recommend that be made as large as possible in a deployment.

Figure 8: Assessment of locations of suspicious behavior (small dots) for the 9/17/10 experiment.

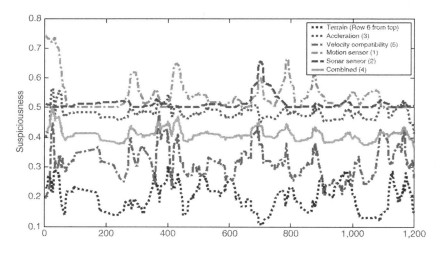

Figure 9: Suspiciousness factors over time for 9/17/10 experiment.

5   Conclusions

We have shown that IED-emplacement behavior can be detected by relatively simple nonimaging sensors. It does require a careful prior analysis of location likelihood, and we must reason at every time step about both potentially suspicious behavior and the probability distributions of location implied by the sensor values. This is a relatively novel approach that should provide some diversity in our defenses against these serious threats.

Acknowledgments

This work was supported by the US National Science Foundation under Grant 0729696 of the EXP Program. The opinions expressed are those of the authors and do not represent those of the US government.

References

[1] Advanced Professional Education and News Service, *IEDs—Improvised Explosive Devices (CD-ROM)*. Washington, DC: Progressive Management, 2010.

[2] Brower, S., Territory in urban settings. In Altman, I., Rapoport, A., and Wohlwill, J. (Eds), *Human Behavior and the Environment*. New York: Plenum, vol. 4, pp. 179–208, 1980.

[3] Bolz, F., Dudonis, K., & Schulz, D., *The Counterterrorism Handbook: Tactics, Procedures, and Techniques*. Boca Raton, FL: CRC Press, 2002.

[4] Brown, B. & Altman, I., Territoriality and residential crime: A conceptual framework. In Brantingham, P. J. and Brantingham, P. J. (Eds), *Environmental Criminology*. Beverly Hills, CA: Sage, pp. 57–76, 1981.

[5] Newman, O., *Defensible Space: Crime Prevention through Urban Design*. New York: Macmillan, 1972.

[6] Rowe, N., Interpreting coordinated and suspicious behavior in a sensor field. Proceedings of the Military Sensing Symposium Specialty Group on Battlespace Acoustic and Seismic Sensing, Magnetic and Electric Field Sensors, Laurel, MD, August 2008.

[7] Bak, P., Rohrdantz, C., Leifert, S., Granacher, C., Koch, S., Butscher, S., Jungk, P., & Keim, D., Integrative visual analytics for suspicious behavior detection. Proceedings of the IEEE Symposium on Visual Analytics Science and Technology, Atlantic City, NJ, pp. 253–254, October 2009.

[8] Barbara, D., Domeniconi, C., Duric, Z., Fillippone, M., Mansgield, R., & Lawson, E., Detecting suspicious behavior in surveillance images. Workshops of IEEE International Conference on Data Mining, Pisa, Italy, pp. 891–900, December 2008.

[9] Wiliem, A., Madasu, V., Boles, W., & Yarlagadda, P., A context-based approach for detecting suspicious behaviors. Proceedings of Digital Image Computing: Techniques and Applications, Melbourne, VIC, Australia, pp. 146–153, December 2009.

[10] Vrij, A., *Detecting Lies and Deceit: The Psychology of Lying and the Implications for Professional Practice*. Chichester, UK: Wiley, 2000.

[11] Fong, S. & Zhuang, Y., A security model for detecting suspicious patterns in physical environment. Proceedings of the Third International Symposium on Information Assurance and Security, Manchester, UK, pp. 221–226, August 2007.

[12] Li, H., Bramsen, D., & Alonso, R., Potential IED threat system (PITS). IEEE Conference on Technologies for Homeland Security, Boston, MA, pp. 242–249, May 2009.

[13] Parunak, H., Sauter, J., & Crossman, J., Multi-layer simulation for analyzing IED threats. Proceedings of the IEEE Conference on Technologies for Homeland Security, Boston, MA, pp. 323–330, May 2009.

[14] Rowe, N., Houde, J., Kolsch, M., Darken, C., Heine, E., Sadagic, A., Basu, A., & Han, F., Automated assessment of physical-motion tasks for military integrative training. Proceedings of the Second International Conference on Computer Supported Education, Valencia, Spain, April 2010.
[15] Rossmo, D., *Geographic Profiling*. Boca Raton, FL: CRC Press, 2000.
[16] Sabatier, J., & Ekimov, A., A review of human signatures in urban environments using seismic and acoustic methods. Proceedings of the IEEE Conference on Technologies for Homeland Security, pp. 215–220, May 2008.
[17] Brantingham, P., Brantingham, P., Vajihollahi, M., & Wuschke, K., Crime analysis at multiple scales of aggregation: A topological approach. In Weisburd, D., Bernasco, W., and Bruinsma, G., *Putting Crime in Its Place: Units of Analysis in Geographic Criminology*. New York: Springer, pp. 87–108, 2009.
[18] Rowe, N., Reed, A., & Flores, J., Detecting suspicious motion with nonimaging sensors. Proceedings of the Third IEEE International Workshop on Bio and Intelligent Computing, Perth, WA, Australia, April 2010.

Part V
Security Systems Integration and Alarm Management

Security systems design and integration

F. Garzia
INFOCOM Department, SAPIENZA – University of Rome, Italy

Abstract

The security of a critical infrastructure is strongly dependent on the use of integrated technological systems; any weakness of the latter involves a weakness of the former. For this reason the design and the implementation of highly integrated, efficient and reliable security systems is a mandatory task. The purpose of this chapter is to illustrate and discuss in short the basic security installations such as intrusion detection, access control, video surveillance and their integration by means of telecommunication subsystems.

Keywords: Security Systems, Integrated Systems

1 Introduction

In order to satisfy in an efficient way the security needs of a critical infrastructure it is necessary to use physical security, security procedures and security systems, all of them integrated together to generate a whole security management system [1,2].

Security installations have actually reached a high performance and reciprocal integration level that it would be better to define them as *security systems* [3–5].

Due to the impressive evolution of security systems, a deep knowledge of physics, electronics, computer science, telecommunications, installations, and systems engineering is required to design and integrate them correctly.

A security system, to operate correctly, must be designed, installed, used, and maintained with a proper knowledge and skill.

For this reason it is necessary to have a good acquaintance of the subjects mentioned above, together with a certain practical experience, to face directly the problems and the risks on the field [5].

Often the security systems are approached without a proper skillness that gives, as results, bad performing systems that are not adapt to face concrete risks. Security systems are aimed at protecting people and material and immaterial goods from voluntary attacks. Safety systems, on the contrary, are aimed at protecting people and material and immaterial goods from incidental events.

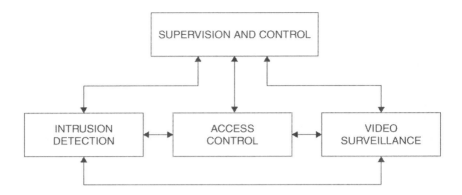

Figure 1: General block diagram of an integrated security system.

Security systems are very often used as safety systems. In fact a video camera can be used by a fire detection system to verify if a flame is present in a certain alarmed zone to avoid the risk of sending safety personnel directly. In the same way an access control system can forbid entrance in a dangerous zone.

Security systems are mainly composed of intrusion detection, access control and video surveillance, integrated together by means of a telecommunication system to exchange information reciprocally and with proper supervision consoles that are located at a distance from the controlled critical infrastructure, reaching optimal performances (Figure 1) [3–5].

Security systems can be drawn according to a basic scheme where the following elements are present:

- field components (intrusion detection sensors, access control readers, video cameras, etc.),
- manage and control panels of the different field components,
- telecommunication network between the field components and the control panels,
- telecommunication network between the different control panels or between the control panels and the consoles of the supervision and control system, and
- consoles of the supervision and control system.

Integrated security systems must be designed to guarantee a high reliability and availability using a high redundancy. In particular, they must be endowed with a completely autonomous electrical supply system.

2   The intrusion detection system

Intrusion detection systems represent a useful and reliable means to control and prevent unauthorized access in a given zone to avoid criminal actions.

If they are well designed, realized and maintained they can avoid events such as thefts, vandalism, sabotages, and spy actions that could compromise safety of people or could damage material and immaterial goods.

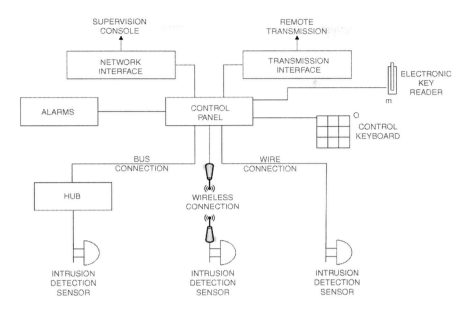

Figure 2: Block diagram of an intrusion detection system.

Every critical infrastructure is characterized by peculiar features that must be carefully analyzed and satisfied to obtain the desired results from the intrusion detection system.

The existence of plenty of available techniques for intrusion detection can sometimes generate confusion. The mentioned techniques, on the contrary, if they are well integrated, can generate a variety of solutions that can face most of the risks.

As shown in Figure 2, the intrusion detection system is composed of a central control panel and a series of field sensors connected to it by means of wire connections, wireless connections, or by hub/bus connections. The control panel executes particular programs as a function of its status, date, time, alarm zones, and so on. It is connected to the alarms, to control keyboard, and to electronic key readers for control panel activation/deactivation. The control panel is also connected to a transmission interface for remote communication and to a network interface for the connection with the supervision consoles.

Because of their importance, a more detailed description of the sensors is given in the following.

2.1   Sensors

Sensors are devices capable of using a particular physical phenomenon (mechanical, acoustic, electrical, magnetic, electromagnetic, light, temperature, etc.) to detect the presence of intruders inside an environment.

The kind of sensor depends on the environment to be protected and on the material that composes it. It is very important for the designer to acquire all the information related to the critical infrastructure that must be protected before starting with the design of the system. It is therefore important to acquire vital information such as kind of activity, number of people present, working time, value of goods to be protected, building material used, heating methods and devices, cooling methods and devices, use of environments, objects located in the environments, position of doors and windows, and other useful parameters.

There exist a great number of sensors basing their working principle on different effects.

Sensors can be divided into two groups: internal sensors and external sensors. Internal sensors are generally more numerous, simpler, more reliable, and cheaper with respect to the external sensors due to the less restrictive environmental working conditions.

External sensors are generally more robust and more expensive with respect to the internal sensors, and they need a more accurate maintenance. They are generally coupled with physical barriers so that they can reveal intrusion attempts while the barriers [1] keep the intruder outside the critical infrastructure to be protected.

Each mentioned group can be divided into four groups, defined kind of the sensors, which describe the kind of coverage of the sensors themselves. They are as follows:

1. Punctual
2. Linear
3. Superficial
4. Volumetric

A simple switch installed on a door to protect its opening can be considered as an example of punctual sensor. In this case an alarm is generated only if the door is opened or forced.

An infrared beam, such as the one installed on the door of lifts, can be considered as a linear sensor. In this case an alarm is generated only when the beam is interrupted.

A microphone sensor installed on a surface, such as a glass or a wall, can be considered as an example of superficial sensor. In this case an alarm is generated if the microphone reveals a noise or a vibration coming from the controlled surface.

A microwave sensor that saturates an environment with its emission, checking the reflected wave emitted by moving people, can be considered as a volumetric sensor. In this case an alarm is generated only if a moving intruder is revealed inside the protected environment.

The orders of sensors can be further divided into subgroups, represented by active sensors and passive sensors.

Active sensors generate and inject into the environment a particular physical field (ultrasound, microwave, infrared, etc.) and check the reflected field to reveal the presence of an intruder. Passive sensors check only a particular field without generating any field inside the environment. Due to the need of generating an active field, active sensors are characterized by a greater electrical consumption with respect to the passive sensors.

The subgroups can be further divided into families: the sensors belonging to the same family are characterized by the same working principle but differ for physical aspect and functionalities. Examples of families are magnetic switch, passive infrared sensors, microwave sensors, ultrasound sensors, and so on.

The families can be sometimes divided into subfamilies. For example, the magnetic switch can be divided into single-pole magnetic switch for low risk, double-pole magnetic switch for medium risk, triple-pole magnetic switch for high risk.

The most important division of sensors is the one between internal sensors and external sensors that are illustrated in the following.

2.2   Internal sensors

Internal sensors are generally simpler, more little and less robust with respect to the external sensors. Since they do not have to face the severe environmental conditions present in the external environment, their computing sections operate with a reduced level of noise, guaranteeing a higher sensibility and performance.

To be sure that an internal sensor works according to its better performance, it is necessary to consider the following checklist:

- environmental conditions: operative temperature range, exposition to direct sun radiation or through windows, exposition to natural or forced fanning, operative humidity range, presence of dust or particles in the air, vibration of the structure where the sensor must be installed, classification of surfaces of the room as a function of their absorbing and reflecting behavior;
- physical conditions: position with respect to furniture, walls, and so on to ensure maximum coverage and to avoid blinding of the sensors; position with respect to test and maintenance activities; position with respect to sabotage and damaging actions; protection from incidental damaging;
- operative conditions: presence of heat emitting devices; presence of heat convective devices; presence of air diffusing sources; presence of electromagnetic interference sources such as electrical transformers, radio transmitters, and so on; crossing of beams emitted by the sensors through windows, doors, walls, and so on;
- security conditions: maximum reliability of sensors; visibility of sensors; accessibility of sensors during not-armed time; security of electrical supply, wires, and control panel installation.

The main sensors for internal use are represented by the following:

- Magnetic switch (punctual, passive)
- Aggression prevention switch (punctual, passive)

- Glass sensors (superficial, passive)
- Piezoelectric sensors (superficial or volumetric, passive)
- Microphone sensors (superficial or volumetric, passive)
- Inertial sensors (punctual, passive)
- Step sensors (superficial, passive)
- Passive infrared sensors (volumetric, passive)
- Ultrasound sensors (volumetric, active)
- Microwave sensors (volumetric, active)
- Double technology sensors (volumetric, active + passive)
- Infrasound sensors (volumetric, passive)

2.3   External sensors

External sensors are generally exposed to severe environmental conditions such as rain, ice, snow, storm, lightning, fog, mist, and so on. For this reason they must be characterized by a high quality, and they must be selected and installed with a particular care.

They are anyway characterized by interesting performances.

They need a certain time before revealing an intruder, due to the need for screening the external disturbs.

They reduce the risk of attack of the protected critical infrastructure, the risk of vandalism actions and represent a valid deterrent effect when they are well visible.

To ensure the correct working of an external sensor, it is necessary to consider the following checklist:

- environmental considerations: more than 10-centimeter-high grass in the electronically protected zone, bushes located in the operative area of the sensors, leaves accumulation during autumn season, tree branches moving inside the operative area of the sensors, soil movement due to the root actions of trees subjected to wind;
- weather considerations: snowdrift, wind, lightning, fog, dew, intense hot or cold, rain, dust, sand, soil drying;
- human factors: children playing near sensors, vandalism, voluntary disturbance of sensors;
- environmental conditions: electromagnetic interference by aerial lines, buried devices, radio transmitters, welding devices, and so on; traffic vibrations;
- security considerations: device positioning, sensors positioning and shadow zones, kind of electrical supply, backup autonomy, electrical insulation, kind of used wires, skill of the system operator and cost of the related service, length of the revealing zone per sensor, organization of the controlled zones, length of cables, voltage supplied, position of electrical transformers.

The main external sensors are represented by the following:

- Fluid pressure sensors (superficial, passive)
- Optical fiber sensors (superficial, active/passive)

- Capacitive sensors (superficial, active/passive)
- Geophonic sensors (superficial, passive)
- Active infrared sensors (superficial, active)
- Microwave sensors (volumetric, active)
- Taut wire sensors (linear, passive)
- Piezoelectric cable sensors (superficial, passive)

3   The access control system

Access control systems manage the entrance/exit of people and vehicles in a given critical infrastructure. They can increase in a significant and determinant way the security level, ensuring the entrance only to authorized people and vehicles, and storing related information properly.

The choice of the correct system is not a simple operation since every critical infrastructure is characterized by peculiar features, and the system must correctly satisfy them.

The choice of a system depends mainly on the use of critical infrastructure and related security level, number of entrances and exits to be controlled, maximum time allowed for entrance authorization, total number of people, users' profile, finality of the system.

The systems can be characterized by

- high security level, for a limited number of entrances/exits and for a limited number of users who have already been controlled before. Typical high security sites are represented by research laboratories, military sites, nuclear plants, and so on;
- medium security level, for a discrete number of entrances/exits and for a numerous number of users. Typical medium security sites are represented by factories, offices, and so on;
- low security level, to prevent vandalism actions and entrances of nonprofessional thefts. Typical medium security sites are represented by residential centers, offices, and so on.

Access control systems increase the privacy level in a significant way, but they are not able to stop people outside the critical infrastructures, which is a typical duty of physical barriers [1].

These systems increase the security level, in particular way, during working time, deciding who can get in and where, how frequent, and which zone one can enter, but the systems cannot manage what happens inside the controlled critical infrastructure, and they are vulnerable to the connivance of internal people.

The differences between the access control system and the normal closed door are represented by the capabilities of

- identifying the key between thousands of other keys, allowing or denying the entrance without altering the closing device;

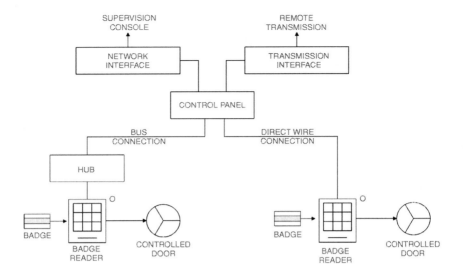

Figure 3: Block diagram of an access control system.

- storing the information of the place where the entrance takes place and the related identity of entering person;
- rapid programming and availability of high performances;
- controlling the state of the door, checking if it is opened or closed;
- interfacing with other systems to guarantee advanced features.

All access control systems are based on the principle of recognition of a proper device or card or a proper biometric feature such as face, fingerprint, voice, handprint, iris, retina, handwritten sign, and so on. This information is acquired by a proper reader that computes it, checks its validity, and transmits it to the central unit to be properly stored. If the read information is correctly validated, the system sends an opening command to the controlled door to enable the entrance of people or vehicles.

As it is possible to see from Figure 3, the access control system is composed by a central control panel and a series of readers connected to the control panel by means of wire connections or by hub/bus connections. The badge readers are also connected to the door-opening mechanism. The control panel executes particular programs as a function of the user profile, his or her status, the date, the time, the entrance zones, and so on. The control panel is also connected to a transmission interface for remote communication and to a network interface for connection with the supervision consoles.

The readers can generally work in a stand-alone way; that is, all authorized user profiles are stored inside it. When a user presents his or her credentials, the reader checks locally if the user is authorized and eventually opens the door, communicating this operation to the control panel through the communication network. This modality is very useful in case of lost of communication since the reader can operate locally without communicating every time with the control panel, ensuring a high operation reliability.

The choice of a given system must be made keeping in mind the feature of the considered critical infrastructure, the environment, and the desired security level.

Access control is also very useful in emergency situation, when it is necessary to evacuate a given area: In this case, thanks to its counting capabilities, it is possible to know how many people are in the area to be evacuated.

The most of access control systems are based on the following:

- alphanumeric keyboard
- cards or badges (magnetic strip, radio frequency, Wiegand effect, infrared, bar code, holography, microchip, etc.)
- cards + PIN (Personal Identification Code)
- biometric (recognition of face, fingerprint, handprint, iris, retina, voice, handwritten, sign, etc.)
- mixed systems
- license plate recognition for vehicles entrance

4   The video surveillance system

Video surveillance represents a cheap and reliable means to control and prevent voluntary attacks to critical infrastructures [2].

The primary scope is to offer the vision of remote areas to prevent dangerous situations and to store the related images and videos to reconstruct, in seconds, any kind of event.

Video surveillance is also very useful in avoiding voluntary damage of the property and vandalism events.

It can integrate with other security systems (intrusion detection and access control) and with safety systems (fire detection and extinguishing) to provide a remote vision of desired areas.

Video surveillance provides a remote vision to security operators, allowing them a real-time vision in different remote areas at the same time. It allows

- remote control for security reasons;
- remote control of dangerous zones where dangerous elements, such as toxic material, radioactive material, inflammable material, explosive material, and so on, could compromise the safety of people and goods;
- discrete control of a given area for investigation purposes;
- simultaneous control of multiple areas by a single operator, such as when it is necessary to control a moving person in a wide and crowded area (airport, station, etc.): In this case, a single operator can follow the suspected person using more cameras at the same time;
- recording of criminal events for law judgment.

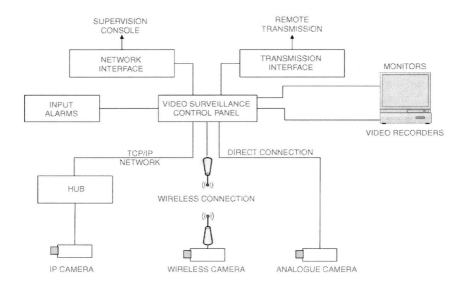

Figure 4: Block diagram of a video surveillance system.

As it is possible to see from Figure 4, the video surveillance system is composed of a central control panel and a series of field cameras connected to the control panel by means of wire connections, wireless connections or by hub/bus connections (digital communication network is illustrated in the next paragraph). The control panel executes particular programs as a function of its status, the date, the time, the alarm zones, and so on. It is connected to the monitors (traditional cathode tube, Liquid Crystal Display or LCD, plasma, etc.), to video recorders, to control keyboards, and to electronic inputs to be connected, for example, to the intrusion detection system and access control system to activate the related vision of the alarmed areas. Thanks to the control panel, it is possible to control which camera must be visualized in the desired monitor or which recorded image must be visualized. The system may be composed of auxiliary devices such as video splitters, which show on a unique monitor different images organized as an array; motion detectors, which give an alarm if there is a moving object in a selected video zone; pan-tilt-zoom controllers, to move remote cameras thanks to proper motion mechanisms; and so on. The control panel is also connected to a transmission interface for remote communication and to a network interface for the connection with the supervision consoles.

Actual video surveillance systems can be analog or digital.

In analog systems the cameras generate an analog output video signal that is distributed all over the video surveillance system. Two main analog video signal standards are used in the world: CCIR/PAL (used in Europe and other countries), capable of reproducing 50 half-frames per second, each frame composed by 625 lines, and EIA/NTSC (used in United States and other countries), capable of reproducing 60 half-frames per second, each frame composed of 525 lines. The total bandwidth of the video signals is of about 5 MHz in CCIR/PAL and of about 4.2 MHz in EIA/NTSC. The standard amplitude of the video signal is equal to 1 V_{pp}. The video signals are composed, for historical reasons, of a luminance signal, responsible for grey scale vision, and of a crominance signal, responsible for color vision. The crominance signal is partially overlapped to the luminance signal in its higher part of the spectrum: The crominance signal in CCIR/PAL standard is carried by a proper carrier centered around 4.434 MHz, while the crominance signal in NTSC/EIA standard is carried by a proper carrier centered around 3.579 MHz. Because of the bandwidth necessary, the video signal must be carried by proper coaxial cables to avoid external interference and signal irradiance. A good quality cable can carry a video signal unto a few hundred meters: Over that distance the signal becomes too weak to be handled without any amplification device. Further, the coaxial cable must be installed far away from energy cables and disturbing sources to preserve the quality of video signal. In critical infrastructures such as railway and road galleries, where the distances to be reached can be very long, the coaxial cable is not sufficient, and it is necessary to use proper electronics/light converters to inject the video signal into an optical fiber that can carry it for distance up to different kilometers, where it is converted in its original form using a reciprocal light/electronics converter. If the distance to be reached is around 1 kilometer, it is possible to use proper converters, on both sides of connection, that allow to use an UTP (Unshielded Twisted Pair) cable, which is more flexible and easier to be installed with respect to the coaxial cable.

In digital systems the cameras generate a digital output video signal that is distributed all over the video surveillance system using generally a TCP/IP protocol (which is illustrated in the following), basing on an Ethernet standard, on a digital network. Recent technology also allows to use wireless digital cameras based on 802.11X standard, which can connect to an access point (connected to the fixed network) if the distance is less than about 100 meters. Digital cameras generally produce a digital signal composed of 25 frames per second (fps) with a variable resolution as a function of the requested performance. The video flow can be properly compressed using compression algorithms such as MPEG-2 (Moving Pictures Expert Group), MPEG-4, H-264, and so on. In the digital case, the velocity varies from some Mbit/s with full frames flow, full resolution uncompressed video up to few hundreds of bit/s with reduced frames flow, low resolution, and compressed video. A simple PC or workstation, endowed with a proper software, can be used, at the same time, as control panel and video recorder, working as a stand-alone video surveillance system. The great advantage of digital cameras is that they can use an existing network, reducing the installation cost. Because of the necessity of high bandwidth for each camera and of the possibility of external and internal voluntary attacks to the network, it is strongly recommended to use a separate and dedicated network for high security applications.

Actually both analog and digital video signals are recorded in digital form on proper video recorders that allow to visualize the desired images without interrupting the recording activity, contrary to the no longer used analog video recorders. Furthermore, the digital video recorders use compression algorithms to store video that allow to reduce memory occupation, greatly increasing the recording time.

Both analog and digital cameras use solid state CCD (Charge Coupled Device) elements to convert light information in electrical information. These elements are characterized by reduced dimensions, high sensibility, and reduced electrical consumptions. Another advantage is represented by their sensibility to near infrared radiation, which allows a clear night vision if the scene is properly enlightened by infrared sources.

5   The communication network

The communication network represents the backbone of integrated security systems.

The general network model of ISO/OSI (International Organization for Standardization/Open System Interconnection) encompasses seven levels: physical, data link, network, transport, session, presentation, and application (Figure 5). Each level makes different duties, which are not shown here for brevity, totally separated with respect to the other levels. In the most common and used TCP/IP (Transfer Control Protocol/Internet Protocol) model, the presentation and session levels are absent, without compromising the functionality of the network that uses it.

Ethernet is a very common standard for the data link level allowing local area network (LAN) to reach velocity of hundreds of Mbit/s using twisted pair, coaxial cable, and optical fiber as physical medium (Layer 1).

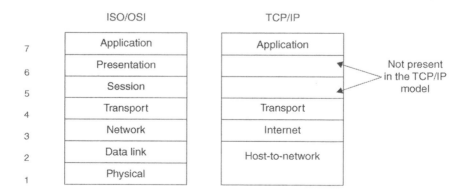

Figure 5: Architecture of ISO/OSI and TCP/IP layered models.

Thanks to the existence of devices such as hubs, switches, bridges, routers, and gateways it is possible to create the desired performances network based generally on TCP/IP protocol and Ethernet standard.

Network transportation capabilities must be designed and tailored according to the information flow that must be carried inside the security integrated systems, ensuring, at the same time, a high reliability.

Different network architectures can be used according to specific user needs. The most common are the so-called "redundant double optical fiber loop network" and the "dense connected double center network," which are shown in Figures 6 and 7, respectively.

In the first case, the optical backbone uses two loops, so that the interruption of a part or of a whole loop is properly recovered, generating a new path, using the other loop. In this way, the main loop guarantees high reliability and availability. The two loops composing the high redundancy loop do not follow the same path, since any voluntary or accidental cut of one loop cable of the net does not interrupt the other cable. The security data flows move on the optical loop backbone. They are diverted toward the desired point exiting or entering

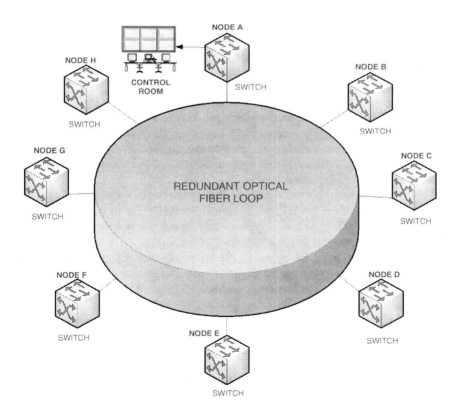

Figure 6: Block diagram of a typical double optical fiber-based loop network.

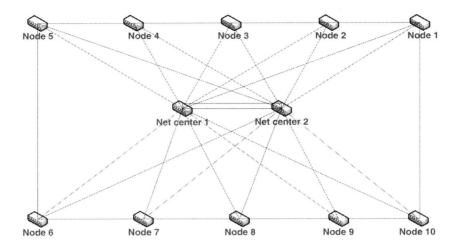

Figure 7: Block diagram of a typical double center, densely connected network.

through proper Add/Drop Multiplexer (Add/Drop Mux) nodes that spill in or out the traffic from the main high velocity loop toward the secondary reduced velocity net.

In the densely connected double center network two redundant centers are present, properly located in protected rooms. In this way, any accidental failure of a center is immediately recovered by the other. Each focal zone is endowed by a proper redundant switch connected to the main backbone via four different links: two of them are directed toward the centers and the others toward the switches of adjacent focal zones.

The two centers of the net are connected by means of a double optical fiber. Each connection of the net follows different physical paths so that the interruption of a link (voluntary or not) is immediately recovered by the other links. This kind of architecture guarantees a high level of reliability.

Particular care must be given to the calculation of the required network bandwidth. The network must be designed considering the situation where all the critical events take place at the same time and therefore all the cameras and sensors are active. In this situation, the maximum information flow over the network is present, and this last parameter must be used to design the required network bandwidth as a function of the network architecture.

Integrated security systems can be endowed by a mobile wireless communication system allowing fast spread of security information and a rapid response of personnel involved in emergency situations. This system must be strongly integrated with the other components of system. The critical issues for wireless systems are mainly related to the vulnerability of the electromagnetic signals.

6   Integration of security systems: The supervision and control system

When a plenty of security systems, located in different places of the critical infrastructure, are present, it is unproposable to actuate a manual management, and it is absolutely necessary to integrate them to create a whole system.

Integrated security systems allow the supervision and the control of the single subsystem in a simplified and automatic way, even if the subsystems are installed at a great distance, thanks to the communication capabilities of the network.

These systems allow the supervision and control not only of security systems but also of safety systems, allowing performances that are superior with respect to the single subsystems.

The integration is generally made at field level, directly between the different control panels, and at higher level, by means of the supervision and control system. Sometimes also other installations, such as electrical, air conditioning, elevators, and so on, are integrated, generating the so-called building automation systems that are capable of managing whole buildings both in ordinary and emergency conditions. They allow the full control of a critical infrastructure from any point of view from one or more local or remote consoles, unifying alarm signaling, management and control procedures, optimizing and reducing the human resources necessary for security and maintenance.

The integration of the security subsystem must be made through a proper coordination of the subsystem design with security procedures and security personnel needs, improving the use of different components to fully use their functional features.

During the integration process, it is necessary to consider properly the reliability of the components and the features of the final users. In fact, very often, an integrated system fails due to the failure of a low-quality component such as a simple communication connector. In the same way, highly integrated systems, which generate an elevate volume of information, are not designed for a given user profile, overcharging him with a plenty of signalings and reducing his level of attention and generating stress.

A well-designed integrated system must be characterized by a series of filters and automatic procedures that work automatically, activating proper programs and requesting the user actions only in strictly necessary situations and guiding him through his duties by means of proper help menus.

The general scheme of an integrated security is divided into three fundamental components: field subsystems, communication network, and central system.

Field subsystems are represented by the different control panels of the different installations (intrusion detection, access control, video surveillance) (Figure 8). These control panels take care of the different subsystems management and control, exchanging information between them and with the higher level supervision and control system. It is strongly recommended to divide

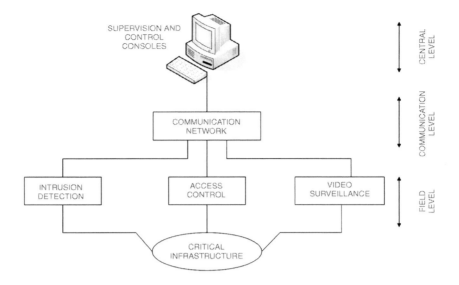

Figure 8: Basic architecture of an integrated security system.

a single subsystem into different control panels, so that a failure of one of them does not compromise the correct working of the whole subsystem, increasing its reliability and guaranteeing full functionalities in case of failure of communication network.

The communication network takes care of information carriage from the field toward high-level system and vice versa. It uses specific architecture and protocol, as it was shown before, as a function of the features of the different control panels and control and as a function of their relative distance. The network takes care of executing a secure and reliable communication. It can be composed of different architectures, if it connects the different control panels, since the information generated by them are generally of different kind and characterized by different transmission velocities. The network can connect control panels and central consoles separated by a great distance: In this last case, the network takes care of data homogenization and transmission through a wide band digital mean. The network must guarantee that all the information reach, without errors and in the desired time interval, the final destination as a function of the performances of the integrated system.

The central system is composed of one or more consoles that can be totally autonomous or can be connected reciprocally, both through a dedicated network and through the integrated system network. The consoles can work as signaling terminals or as operative terminals, allowing any kind of operation as a function of user profile. Generally a single console is dedicated to system programming and maintenance. The use of two redundant consoles is strongly recommended so that, in case of failure of one console, the other console allows the full control of the integrated system.

7   Conclusions

The security management in complex contexts, such as the critical infrastructures, needs a detailed risk analysis of threats and dangers that must be faced and a correct study, design, and realization of an efficient integrated security system capable of integrating the different security functionalities and, at the same time, ensuring the maximum reciprocal interaction of the different systems involved.

In this way, it is possible to realize a powerful and versatile integrated security system that guarantees a high level of security services for the interested critical infrastructures.

Future evolution of security integrated system is directed toward the digital world with particular attention to the wireless field. Video surveillance is migrating toward the digital technology with an intensive use of digital (IP cameras), megapixel (high-resolution), and wireless cameras, and the future video surveillance systems are becoming totally digital systems. New communication protocols are giving life to new generation sensors and new communication modalities that improve the performances of integrated security system aimed at the protection of critical infrastructures.

References

[1] Garcia, M. L., *The Design and Evaluation of Physical Protection Systems*, Butterworth-Heinemann, Burlington, MA, 2001.

[2] Bocchetti, G., Flammini, F., Pappalardo, A., & Pragliola, C., "Dependable integrated surveillance systems for the physical security of metro railways," Proceedings of 3rd ACM/IEEE International Conference on Distributed Smart Cameras (ICDSC 2009), Como (Italy), pp. 1–7.

[3] Garzia, F., Sammarco, E., & Cusani, R., "Integrated access control system for ports," Safety & Security Engineering III, WIT Press, Southampton (UK), pp. 313–323, 2009.

[4] Contardi, G., Garzia, F., & Cusani, R., "The integrated security system of the Senate of the Italian Republic," IEEE International Carnahan Conference on Security Technology, Zurigo (Svizzera), pp. 111–118, 2009.

[5] Garzia, F., Sammarco, E., Cusani, R., "The integrated security system of the Vatican City State", *International Journal of Safety & Security Engineering*, WIT Press, Vol. 1, No. 1, pp. 1–17, 2011, DOI: 10.2495/SAFE-V1-N1-1-17.

Multisource information fusion for critical infrastructure situation awareness

D. L. Hall

College of Information Sciences and Technology, Pennsylvania State University, University Park, PA, USA

Abstract

Protection of critical infrastructures requires understanding the state or situation of physical infrastructure components as well as monitoring the cyber domain and the human landscape. Achieving this situation awareness involves fusion of heterogeneous information from physical sensors as well as information from human observers. Historically, the information fusion problem evolved from traditional areas such as military situation assessment. These applications involved processing sensor data using a variety of techniques, ranging from signal and image processing to pattern recognition, state estimation and automated reasoning. Recently, four new trends have emerged: (1) rapid spread of cell phones and associated global communications that enable humans to act as *ad hoc* observers, (2) interest in observing and characterizing the human landscape as well as the physical landscape, (3) advances in human–computer interactions which facilitate human participation in the fusion and reasoning process and (4) collaborative tools which support distributed team decision-making and analysis. This chapter introduces the concept of information fusion, describes recent trends and discusses its application to critical infrastructure security.

Keywords: Multi-sensor Data Fusion, Participatory Sensing, Situation awareness

1 Introduction

Rapid developments in communications and the evolving Internet infrastructure including web-based information sensors have provided the ability to link data from multiple sources to enhance individuals' understanding of their environment, better predict events and improve the allocation of resources. Participatory sensing [1], the integration of a real-time human sensor network with static sensors, is based on the increased use of mobile hand-held devices by the general public to create awareness of the human surroundings. It allows the mapping and studying of the environmental impact on humans, connects seemingly unrelated events and improves the discernment of wide impact phenomena.

Multi-sensor data fusion uses humans' innate ability to sense and understand their surroundings in combination with data generated by more traditional sensors. This new 'soft sensing' increases the understanding of the human terrain (i.e., the complex interactions and trends among a specific human population) while using humans' capabilities to understand their surroundings to offer a more complete picture of an environment or a target's interaction with its local surroundings. This was quite evident in the human 'public reports' sharing information about the Iranian regime's crackdown on the opposition demonstrators after the June 2009 elections. Other examples of participatory sensing include Ushahidi's website [2] for worldwide reporting of information about environmental crises, political upheavals and other events. While 'soft sensing' has inherent problems, including everything from the uncertainty of human behaviour and personal biases to issues of privacy and second-order effects such as rumour generation, there remains a viable data set for functional modelling.

2 Joint Directors of Laboratories (JDL) data fusion process model

Before proceeding to discuss the new trends in information fusion, it is helpful to provide a brief review of the history and state of the art of data fusion. We distinguish between *data fusion*, focused on fusion of data from physical sensors such as radar, Light Detection and Ranging (LIDAR), acoustic arrays and so on, and *information fusion*, which includes information from human reports and from the web. An enormous amount of research in data fusion has been conducted in support of military applications such as target tracking, target identification, situation assessment and threat assessment [3–5]. This research has led to the development of engineering guidelines for system development [6], development of techniques focused on database issues in fusion systems [7], surveys of commercial off-the-shelf (COTS) software for implementing fusion systems [8] and multiple-process models [9].

The most well-known process model for understanding data fusion is the JDL process model. The original model was created in 1991 by the JDL Data Fusion Working Group led by Frank White [10] and subsequently revised by Steinberg, Bowman and White [11]. Details of the model are described in [3] and [5]. A top-level view of the model is shown in Figure 1.

At the top level the model prescribes six basis 'levels' of fusion. These include the following:

Level 0 fusion (data or source pre-processing) – It involves processing data from sensors (e.g., signals, images, hyper-spectral images, vector quantities or scalar data) to prepare the data for subsequent fusion.
Level 1 fusion (object refinement) – It seeks to combine data from multiple sensors or sources to obtain the most reliable estimate of the object's location,

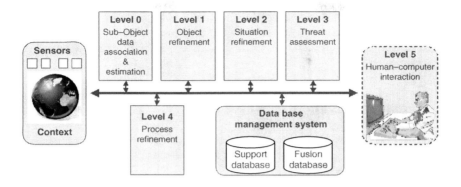

Figure 1: Top level of the JDL data fusion process model [3].

characteristics and identity. We speak here of an object (such as observing a physical object such as an airplane), but we could also fuse data to determine the location and identity of activities, events or other geographically constrained entities of interest.

Level 2 fusion (situation refinement) – Level 2 processing uses the results of Level 1 processing and seeks to develop a contextual interpretation of their meaning. This often entails understanding how entities are related to their environment, the relationship among different entities and how they interrelate.

Level 3 fusion (threat refinement/impact assessment) – Level 3 processing concerns projecting the current situation into the future to determine the potential impact of threats associated with the current situation. Level 3 processing seeks to draw inferences about possible threats, courses of action (in response to those perceived threats) and how the situation changes based on our changing perceptions. Techniques for Level 3 fusion are similar to those used in Level 2 processing, but they also include simulation, prediction and modelling.

Level 4 fusion (process refinement/resource management) – Level 4 processing is a meta-process (viz. a process that addresses a process). In particular, Level 4 processing 'observes' the ongoing data fusion process (the other levels of processing) and seeks to make the fusion process better (more accurate, more timely and more specific) by redirecting the sensors or information sources, changing the control parameters on other fusion algorithms or selecting which algorithm or technique is most appropriate to the current situation and available data.

Level 5 processing (human–computer interaction/cognitive refinement) – The Level 5 process seeks to optimize how the data fusion system interacts with one or more human users. The Level 5 process seeks to understand the needs of the human user and respond to those needs by appropriately focusing the fusion system attention on things that are important to the user.

It must be made clear that these 'levels' of fusion are defined simply for communications purposes. In actual data fusion systems, these processes are interleaved and overlap. The intent of the model is to assist in communications about data fusion functions and processing. References [3–5] provide details on these data fusion levels and associated algorithms and techniques for automated processing.

3   Comments on the state of the art

A general discussion of the state of the art of information fusion is provided by Hall and Jordan [12]. A brief summary of that review is provided below.

Level 0: Source refinement – Level 0 processing is commonly performed using advanced signal and image processing techniques. A wide variety of commercial tools are available to support this function. Emerging research is being conducted in automated semantic labelling of signal and image data [13], non-orthogonal signal processing and initial investigations of the characterization of human observers. A continuing challenge is absolute registration of image data (high accuracy mapping of image plane coordinates to geo-spatial referents). New 3-D sensors such as flash LIDAR create both challenges and opportunities.

Level 1: Object refinement – Level 1 processing involves applications such as target tracking and identification. This is a very old problem dating back to the creation of the method of least squares by Gauss to support orbit determination of asteroids. Current practices tend to explicitly separate the correlation from the estimation problem and use a wide variety of estimation techniques, ranging from Kalman filters to particle filters [14], multiple hypothesis tracking [15,16] and emerging methods such as random set theoretic methods [17]. Challenges in target tracking involve situations in which a target is erratically manoeuvring, in a dense tracking environment (with multiple targets), in a poor observing environment with low signal-to-noise or related challenges. Level 1 processing also involves automatic target recognition and characterization. Common techniques include machine learning, pattern recognition and automated reasoning [18]. Some efforts are underway to use methods such as intelligent agents and fuzzy logic methods [19]. Current challenges include situations in which there is limited or no training data (to train the pattern recognition methods), lack of context-based information and limited or weak link between observed characteristics of a target or event and the inherent *identity* of the target or event.

Level 2: Situation refinement – This is a challenging problem in which we seek to understand an evolving situation perhaps involving multiple targets, events or activities in the context of their environment. Current methods have sought to use automated reasoning methods (e.g., knowledge-based rule systems, neural networks, case-based reasoning, intelligent agents or other methods) [20–22]. To date there has been limited progress in developing effective cognitive models and translating those models into effective automated reasoning schemes.

The most recent methods for situation refinement involve representation of data and inter-relationships using graph theory, including so-called dirty graphs, in which relationships can exhibit uncertainty or imprecision [23].

Level 3: Threat refinement – This is analogous to Level 2 processing but is focused on the future, seeking to predict future threats or situations and understanding their potential impact. This is very domain specific. Except for physically modelled systems such as target motion, very limited predictive models exist. There are some efforts to use hybrid reasoning techniques in which information from historical data is mined and used in combination with contextual reasoning by human analysts and model predictions.

Level 4: Process refinement – This process is a meta-process which seeks to monitor the ongoing fusion effort and make refinements to improve the resulting inferences. For systems involving controllable sensors and communications links, robust optimization methods based on operations research perform well. Challenges occur when there is limited control over the information sources, a weak link between the observables and desired fusion results, and if there are confounding issues such as deception, adaptive adversaries and limited resources such as communications. There are particular challenges when humans are used as information sources. Not only is it difficult to task *ad hoc* observers, but the very act of requesting information can bias the observer's results. Recent research has used concepts from electronic market systems [24] and intelligent agents as proxies for bidding for resources.

Level 5: Cognitive refinement – As fusion systems transition from a situation in which humans are considered to be passive users of the fusion results to hybrid systems in which humans are actively engaged in observation, pattern matching, context-based reasoning and collaboration, the Level 5 area becomes increasingly important. Rapid advances in human–computer interface (HCI) technologies have been demonstrated in areas such as 3-D immersive displays, haptic interfaces, 3-D sound and direct computer/brain interfaces. As a result, it is anticipated that new concepts for human/data interaction will emerge. Creative HCI research is needed to adapt fusion systems to the needs of individual users and to promote the mitigation of known human cognitive biases and illusions. There is limited work on 'crowd-sourcing' of analysis (e.g., using virtual world technologies) and on *ad hoc* analysis [12].

4 Human-centric information fusion

Hall and Jordan [12] describe the concept of human-centred information fusion (illustrated in Figure 2) and identify four new trends in information fusion.

The key trends include the following.

The domain of interest is changing – Traditional data and information fusion systems have focused on observing and characterizing the physical domain or landscape. For critical infrastructures this might translate into monitoring the machinery or equipment in a factory or power plant or monitoring the condition

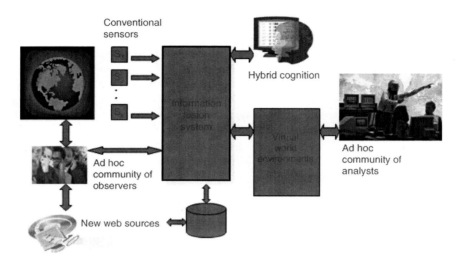

Figure 2: Concept of human-centred information fusion (adapted from [12]).

of a road or communications network. The focus has been to observe the physical situation via physical sensors. Increasingly, however, there is recognition and interest in monitoring the human landscape. In an extreme event such as environmental disaster, it is just as important to understand the make-up, mood, cultural factors, health and other factors that affect how humans would be affected by the disaster as well as how they would react. Similarly, in order to protect the critical infrastructures against criminal or terrorist threats, it is necessary to understand both the potential adversaries as well as the people affected by any adversarial action or threat.

The new human observer – The rapid growth of cell phone dissemination and continually improving cellular communications bandwidth provide the opportunity to create a dynamic observation resource allowing humans to act as 'soft' sensors. Information obtained by humans (via direct reports and information from open source information on the Internet) can be valuable and significantly augment data obtained from traditional sensors, such as unattended ground sensors, radar and sensors on-board airborne vehicles. While extensive techniques exist to combine data from traditional sensors, only limited work has been done on combining human and non-human sensors. Clearly, humans do not act as traditional sensors and their accuracy, biases and levels of observation are quite different than traditional sensors. However, humans can provide valuable inferences and observations not available from standard sensors, such as inferring identity, intent and interactions with other people. Llinas, Nagi, Hall and Lavery [25] describe a new research programme focused on the fusion of hard and soft information. Hall and Jordan cite a number of challenges in processing human source information, including (1) tasking, how to effectively task *ad hoc* observers; (2) knowledge elicitation, how to solicit information from observers without unduly biasing them; (3) how to translate human language observations (e.g., 'I see a man near the car') into quantitative values; (4) how to determine the reliability of the human observer; and (5) how to address the truthfulness of an observation and many others.

The human as hybrid analyst – A second new role of humans in information fusion involves humans acting in a cooperative way with automated computing processes. This may entail human visual and aural pattern recognition and semantic reasoning to augment the automated processing performed by a computer. We imagine a human/computer team working together to understand an evolving situation or threat. Pinker [26] notes that humans have the ability to recognize and reason with language, and the ability to recognize patterns and reason using a kind of visual physics. It is easy, for example, for a human to identify containers or objects in a room that could hold a liquid – despite the fact that these may include glasses, cups, pots, pans, a sink or a bottle. This would be challenging to automate. The variety of possible containers and the concept of 'hold liquid' would be difficult to encode into a pattern recognition algorithm. Similarly, we can express contextual knowledge via sentences, descriptions or stories about an event, activity, groups of humans or collection of entities. Despite advances in automated reasoning via rules, frames, scripts, logical templates, Bayesian Belief Nets or other methods [27,28], it is challenging for a computer to match the semantic abilities of almost any human.

However, computers are excellent at numerical calculations such as computing physical motion of objects, fluid flow, statistical estimation and physics-based modelling. Computers can perform calculations and predictions that are not feasible for humans. Clearly, information fusion systems should combine the capabilities of humans and computers to create hybrid reasoning systems capable of performing better than either alone.

The human as collaborative analyst – Finally, we believe that humans can perform a major role in information fusion by dynamic, *ad hoc* collaboration among multiple people. Examples of worldwide distributed collaboration are described by Shirky [29] and Howe [30]. The term 'crowd-sourcing' has been used to describe the concept of using a group to provide information or address problems. Sawyer [31] describes the concept of collaboration over a period of time, concepts of 'group flow' such as group improvisation and customer innovations and concepts of group genius. As a faculty member teaching information science and technology, I observe that the 'digital native' students, who have grown up in the age of the Internet, cell phones and online social networks, commonly address assigned problems by contacting 'the hive mind' to see if others in their social network have addressed such a problem before or have pertinent information. Similarly, Palrey and Gasser [32] describe the generation of digital natives and the impact that has on commerce, education and social interaction. New information technologies such as groupware, visual world tools such as Second Life, social networking sites and others provide the opportunity for distributed collaboration for problem-solving. Such concepts can be used in addressing complex situation awareness problems.

5 Implications for infrastructure situation awareness

What are the implications for infrastructure situation awareness? On the one hand, there is a rapid explosion of sensors throughout the world. Hall and Jordan [12] provide an extensive table of information (see Chapter 8, Table 8.5 in reference [12]) about categories of data such as the physical terrain, geology and natural resources; hydrography; weather; natural vegetation; transportation; agriculture; energy; commerce; communications; population; economic conditions; and human landscape information. The table summarizes the data types and sources of data and provides references for collection resources. The proliferation of embedded sensors, web cameras, commercial satellite resources and local sensors are available to virtually any user. Scientific data-collection projects such as the NASA earth observatory [33] provide global coverage of the physical environment, while projects such as the Gallup World Poll collect information about the human landscape. In addition, it is relatively easy to establish surveillance systems of physical environments using web cameras. A recent iPhone application (the iCam App) allows anyone to easily set up cameras to monitor a home or area and send alerts and video information about potential intrusions.

On the other hand, the emergence of *ad hoc* human observers provides an opportunity to extend the monitoring of critical infrastructures to human reports. Numerous examples are available regarding the value of human observations of an emerging event or activity. Examples include the following:

- Twitter reports of crime and information from first responders are available via a special website [34].
- International reporting of events and activities is enabled by the Ushahidi crowd-source project [2].
- The United States Geological Survey (USGS) earthquake hazards programme [35] provides a source for reporting civilian observations of earthquake activity.
- The use of sanitation workers' reports on unusual activities or crime [36].
- Multiple projects involving the concept of a global neighbourhood watch encourage local citizens to report on crime, the environment, accidents and other problems.

The emerging theme is that enormous amounts of data from physical sensors and human observers are becoming available to monitor the components of critical infrastructures. A challenge will be to fuse the hard and soft data to support situation awareness and effective decision-making.

6 Summary

Information fusion techniques have made great progress, spurred in part by funding of research for military applications such as target tracking, target identification, situation awareness and threat assessment. Thus, numerous techniques exist to support functions such as signal and image processing, data association and correlation, pattern recognition, state estimation and, to a lesser extent, automated reasoning for situation awareness. Such techniques have focused primarily on the use of physical (hard) sensors to observe the physical environment. Recent trends in information fusion have made humans a more integrated part of fusion systems as observers (soft sensors), pattern recognizers and conduct of semantic-level reasoning, and finally as collaborative decision-makers. Moreover, the object of fusion processing has extended to the human landscape as well as the physical domain. This human-centric evolution of fusion systems has significant application for critical infrastructures situation awareness. The rapid development and dissemination of sensors such as video, cameras, acoustic sensors, LIDAR and other devices provide a means of monitoring physical components of critical infrastructures. In addition, rapid deployment of cell phones and worldwide communications provides the opportunity for a 'global neighbourhood watch' in which everyone becomes a potential observer to defeat threats to critical infrastructures. Thus, it will increasingly become useful and necessary to fuse information from both hard and soft sensors, providing enhanced awareness of the current state and situation of our critical infrastructures.

References

[1] Burke, J., Estrin, D., Hansen, M., Parker, A., Ramanathan, N., Reddy, S. & Srivastara, M.B., 'Participatory Sensing'. Proceedings of the Workshop on World-Sensor-Web (WSW'06): Mobile Device Centric Sensor Networks and Applications, pp. 117–134, 2006.

[2] Ushahidi website (http://www.ushahidi.com), accessed 17 November 2010.

[3] Hall, D.L. & McMullen, S.A.H., *Mathematical Techniques in Multisensor Data Fusion*. Artech House, Norwood, Massachusetts, USA, 2004.

[4] Liggins, M.E., Hall, D.L. & Llinas, J. (Eds), *Handbook of Multisensor Data Fusion: Theory and Practice*, 2nd edition. CRC Press, Boca Raton, Florida, USA, 2008.

[5] Waltz, E. & Llinas, J., *Multisensor Data Fusion*. Artech House, Norwood, Massachusetts, USA, 2000.

[6] Bowman, C.L. & Steinberg, A.N., 'Systems Engineering Approach for Implementing Data Fusion Systems', Chapter 22 in M.E. Liggins, D.L. Hall and J. Llinas (Eds), *Handbook of Multisensor Data Fusion: Theory and Practice*, 2nd edition. CRC Press, Boca Raton, Florida, USA, pp. 561–596, 2008.

[7] Antony, R., *Principles of Data Fusion Automation*. Artech House, Norwood, Massachusetts, USA, 1995.

[8] McMullen, S.A.H., Sherry, R.R. & Miglani, S., 'Survey of COTS Software for Multisensor Data Fusion', Chapter 26 in M.E. Liggins, D.L. Hall and J. Llinas (Eds), *Handbook of Multisensor Data Fusion: Theory and Practice*, 2nd edition. CRC Press, Boca Raton, Florida, USA, pp. 677–689, 2008.

[9] Hall, D.L., Hellar, D.B., McNeese, M. & Llinas, J., 'Assessing the JDL Model: a Survey and Analysis of Decision and Cognitive Process Models and Comparison with the JDL Model'. Proceedings of the National Symposium on Sensor Data Fusion, June 2006.

[10] Kessler, O., Askin, K., Beck, N., Lynch, J., White, F., Buede, D., Hall, D. & Llinas, J., *Functional Description of the Data Fusion Process*. Report prepared for the Office of Naval Technology Data Fusion Development Strategy, Naval Air Development Center, Warminster, PA, November 1991.

[11] Steinberg, A.N., Bowman, C.L. & White, F.E., 'Revisions to the JDL Model'. Joint HATO/IRIS Conference Proceedings, Quebec, October 1998, and in Sensor Fusion, Architectures, Algorithms and Applications, Proceedings of the SPIE, Vol. 3719, 1999.

[12] Hall, D. and Jordan, J., *Human-Centered Information Fusion*. Artech House, Norwood, Massachusetts, USA, 2010.

[13] Jia Li and James Z. Wang, 'Real-Time Computerized Annotation of Pictures', *IEEE Transactions on Pattern Analysis and Machine Intelligence*, 30(6), 985–1002, 2008.

[14] Ristic, B., Arulampalam, S. & Gordan, N., *Beyond the Kalman Filter: Particle Filters for Tracking Applications*. Artech House, Norwood, Massachusetts, USA, 2004.

[15] Uhlmann, J.K., 'Algorithms for Multiple-Target Tracking', *American Scientist*, 80(2); 128–141, 1992.

[16] Bar-Shalom, Y. (Ed.), *Multi-Target-Multisensor Tracking: Advanced Applications*, Vol. II, Artech House, Norwood, Massachusetts, USA, 1992.

[17] Goodman, I.R., Mahler, R.P. & Nguyen, H.T., *Mathematics of Data Fusion*. Kluwer Academic Publishers, New York, USA, 1997.

[18] Bishop, C., *Pattern Recognition and Machine Learning*. Springer, New York, USA, 2007.

[19] Fan, X., Sun, S. & Yen, J. 'On Shared Situation Awareness for Supporting Human Decision-Making Teams'. AAAI Spring Symposium on AI Technologies for Homeland Security, Stanford University, pp. 17–24, 21–23 March 2005.

[20] Das, S., *High-Level Data Fusion*. Artech House, New York, USA, 2008.

[21] Salerno, J., Hinman, M. & Boulware, D., 'Building a Framework for Situation Awareness'. Proceedings of the Seventh International Conference on Information Fusion, Stockholm, July 2004.

[22] Fan, X., Sun, B., Sun, S. McNeese, M., Yen, J., Jones, R. Hanratty, T. & Allender, L., 'RPD-Enabled Agents Teaming with Humans for Multi-Context Decision Making'. Proceedings of the Fifth International Joint Conference on Autonomous Agents and Multiagent Systems (AAMAS'06), Japan, 8–12 May 2006.

[23] Gross, G., Nagi, R. & Samboos, K., 'Soft Information, Dirty Graphs and Uncertainty Representation/Processing for Situation Understanding'. Proceedings of the 13th International Conference on Information Fusion, Edinburgh, UK, July 2010.

[24] Mullen, T., Avasarala, V. & Hall, D., 'Customer-Driven Sensor Management', *IEEE Intelligent Systems*, special issue on Self-Management through Self-Organization in Information Systems, 21(2), 41–49, March/April 2006.

[25] Llinas, J., Nagi, R., Hall, D. & Lavery, J., 'A Multi-Disciplinary University Research Initiative in Hard and Soft Information Fusion: Overview, Research Strategies and Initial Results'. Proceedings of the 13th International Conference on Information Fusion, Edinburgh, UK, July 2010.

[26] Pinker, S., *How the Mind Works*. Norton, New York, USA, 1999.

[27] Russell, S. & Norrig, P., *Artificial Intelligence: A Modern Approach*, 3rd edition. Perwig, New York, USA, 2009.

[28] De Mantaras, R.L., *Approximate Reasoning Models*. John Wiley and Sons, New York, USA, 1990.

[29] Shirky, C., *Cognitive Surplus: Creativity and Generosity in a Connected Age.* Penguin Press, New York, USA, 2010.

[30] Howe, J., *Crowd Sourcing: Why the Power of the Crowd Is Driving the Future of Business.* Three Rivers Press, New York, USA, 2009.

[31] Sawyer, K., *Group Genius: The Creative Power of Collaboration.* Basic Books, New York, USA, 2007.

[32] Palrey, J. & Gasser, U., *Born Digital: Understanding the First Generation of Digital Natives.* John Wiley and Sons, New York, USA, 2008.

[33] NASA Earth Observatory website (http://earthobservatory.nasa.gov/), accessed 17 November 2010.

[34] Website (http://blog.crime.reports.com/tag/twitter/), accessed 7 November 2010.

[35] US Geological Survey website (http://earthquake.usgs.gov/earthquake/dyfi/), accessed 17 November 2010.

[36] 'Garbage Workers Help Keep City Safe'. *Jacksonville News*, 23 September 2009. Available at http://www.news4jax.com/news/21093406/detail.html, accessed 16 August 2011.

Simulation-based learning in the physical security industry

Brian Hennessey
Director Advanced Programs, Adacel Systems Inc., Orlando, FL, USA

Abstract

The term 'simulate' essential means to replicate the essential features of a task or situation. Simulations can be used for a number of purposes such as training and decision-making. Although widely used in the aviation and defence industries, the use of simulation technologies in the physical security industry is in a relatively embryonic stage of development and utilization. This chapter discusses the use of simulation technologies within the physical security industry. Some of the traditional learning theories that support the use of simulation in a training environment will also be covered.

Keywords: Physical Security, Simulation, Training

1 Introduction

The term 'physical security' refers to measures designed to prevent unauthorized access to personnel, equipment, installations and information, and to safeguard them against espionage, sabotage, terrorism, damage and criminal activity. Physical protection systems are designed for prevention and to provide the means to counter threats when preventive measures are ignored or bypassed.

The nature of physical security industry is such that there is very little real-time feedback on both the operator and the overall physical protection system's performance. The very nature of the industry is such that control room operators are rarely challenged on a day-to-day basis. They are expected to maintain high levels of detection performance day after day, month after month. In most cases the effectiveness of individuals, systems and procedures will only be known when an actual crisis occurs.

2 Simulation overview

The classical definition of the term 'simulation' is the imitation of some real thing, state of affairs or process. Simulation is used in many different and diverse domains, to replicate the operation and behaviour of actual systems and procedures in a safe environment. Other contexts include simulation of technology for performance optimization, safety engineering, testing, training and education. Simulation can be used to show the eventual effects of alternative conditions and courses of action.

3   Security simulation

The use of simulation is well established in areas such as Pilot and Air Traffic Control training and in research and development. Simulations are generally not widely used in the physical security industry, although their use is increasingly gaining acceptance.

In order to prepare for their anticipated future widespread adoption within the Homeland Security domain, the National Institute of Standards and Technology (NIST) has sought to categorize the major areas in which simulation activities will likely occur, along with the types of behaviours, phenomena, processes, effects and so on that are to be simulated.

The NIST research has identified several main components which are likely to be simulated [1]. These include simulating the following components:

- Social behaviour – this involves modelling individual and collective behaviours, movements and social interactions between people. Examples would include pedestrian behaviour in crowds, vehicular traffic and epidemics.
- Physical phenomenon – this includes fires, hurricanes, earthquakes or the simulation of airborne dispersal of chemical and biological agents.
- Economics – this involves modelling the economic impact of an incident.
- Organizations – this involves modelling the policies and procedures; activities and operations; decision processes, communications and control mechanisms; and information flows for various organizations and their members.
- Infrastructure – this involves modelling the propagating effects of an incident on interconnected, related or nearby infrastructure elements, the impact of incidents on system elements.
- Other system – equipment and tool simulators – This involves modelling the operation and performance of various systems, equipment and tools.

4   Security simulation domains

These components defined in the NIST research apply to two primary high-level domains in which simulation is used.

4.1   Computation simulators

Computational-type simulations use mathematical and probabilistic models to determine a likely outcome. These types of simulators are usually run by inputting raw data and running the simulation offline and then analysing the data output. In the physical security industry these simulators have been used for vulnerability assessment, planning, risk analysis and systems engineering purposes. There is a growing trend to utilize these for decision support purposes, often in a real-time environment. For example, decision-makers could use the real-time outputs of an atmospheric chemical dispersal simulation model to coordinate evacuation routes.

Monte Carlo simulation

The Monte Carlo method is often used in determining the outcomes in computational simulators. The term 'Monte Carlo method' was coined in the late 1940s in reference to games of chance, a popular attraction in Monte Carlo, Monaco. A Monte Carlo simulation is used to determine the probability of an occurrence by running multiple trial runs using random variables. The simulation is run over and over, thousands or even tens of thousands of times. Each time it is run it will use a different set of random values, each based upon the number of uncertainties in what's being calculated. The simulation will then produce probability distributions of possible outcomes.

In the physical security industry Monte Carlo simulations are used in areas such as facility vulnerability assessment. The simulation will factor in many things such as guard capabilities and patrol paths, intruder equipment and capabilities as well as the composition of the terrain. The simulation will run multiple mock attacks on the facility using different strategies such as fastest paths, least firepower paths and paths with the least likelihood of detection. The end result will produce statistics on the perceived effectiveness of the facility's security system.

Running this type of computation simulation can provide valuable statistical data to validate the composition and placement of a facility's security infrastructure, along with developing patrol routes and other operational procedures.

Organization wishing to run these computational simulations for vulnerability assessments or facility planning should understand that the outcome of these simulations should be treated as an early step in the overall process – not the final step. The outcome of these simulations should always be validated prior to being implemented. This validation can be via a human in the loop–type simulation exercise or some other mechanism.

A computational simulation is only as good as the mathematical models used. Human performance has proved to be inherently difficult to model – there are simply too many dimensions to consider. The statistical models used by a computational simulation can have difficulty in adequately factoring in such things as operator efficiency, safety, health, motivation and so on.

Many Air Service Providers have had similar experiences in using computational simulators to assist in modelling airspace. These tools seek to create optimized routes and traffic flows. However, these fast-time simulation studies will usually conclude with a human in the loop exercises using real Air Traffic Controllers. An experienced controller can often quickly determine aspects of a proposed change which are difficult to model computationally, such as safety and risk.

4.2   Interactive simulation

Interactive simulators are often referred to as 'human in the loop' simulations. These are physical simulations in which humans are an integral part of the system being simulated. Examples would include Air Traffic Control and flight simulators. These types of simulators are used primarily for operator training but can sometimes be quite effective in roles more traditionally undertaken by computational simulators.

Overview of an interactive security simulator

The Vulnerability Assessment Simulation and Training tool is an interactive security simulator designed to assist in training control room operators. Student control room operators sit at a typical control room console and interact with the simulator in the same manner they would their operational equipment.

The students are put through scenarios featuring day-to-day operations, along with mock attacks on the facility. Students must assess alarms and respond accordingly, such as dispatching and coordinating response forces. The simulator can also log user's inputs and measure response latency. Scenarios can be created which require student control room operators to

- conduct simulated day-to-day facility operations, including access control;
- deal with device and equipment failures such as cameras – both legitimate and as part of a coordinated attack;
- respond to alarm messages, including false and nuisance alarms mixed with real alarms;
- deal with system failures and maintenance issues;
- respond to mock attacks on the facility that require the operator to coordinate and dispatch response forces.

Background operations can include ground vehicles, patrol boats, unmanned aerial vehicles and foot patrols. Simulated attacks on the facility can be via the same entity types. Communications and radio dispatch is simulated using a network radio simulator. Students in the simulator sit behind a console which is typical of an operational command and control centre. Alarm assessment is a simulation of an alarm management system, while the video management is a simulation of a media control system, complete with pan tilt and zoom camera controls and video record and replay.

An Instructor Operator Station enables the instructor to load, run and control the scenarios. During scenario operation the instructor will typically role-play the response force commanders, outside agencies and so on. When the student uses the radio communications simulator to direct response forces the instructor

Figure 1: Physical security simulator student position.

will respond accordingly and direct the response forces as instructed by the student.

The simulator uses a photo realistic 3-D virtual recreation of either an actual facility where the student will eventually be deployed or a generic facility which contains common representative physical protection system infrastructure. This virtual environment enables scenario designers to define and place security assets, such as cameras, sensors, access control gates, turnstiles and so on (Figure 1).

5   Simulation in a training environment

A common mistake in the development and use of interactive simulators in a training environment is misunderstanding the difference between emulation and simulation. Generally speaking a simulator seeks to duplicate the behaviour of something, whereas an emulator seeks to duplicate the inner workings.

A good example of this in the physical security industry is in simulating sensors and other detection assets. For example, a passive infrared sensor may have a detection range of 100 yards. The simulator does not need to know how the sensor achieves this performance. It just needs to know what the detection range is. Emulating the actual sensor would require modelling the interaction of the inner workings to determine how the sensor has achieved this performance. This can be very useful for high-end modelling of sensor affects to say different environmental conditions but can be overkill for a general training environment.

5.1 Systematic approach to training for simulation

There is a common misunderstanding that by simply simulating the operational workplace and placing an operator in that environment the requisite training will magically be transferred to the user. More often than not simulators are employed with complete disregard to established practices in training theory [2].

Some training transfer will likely occur when a simulator is used in this manner. However, this is not an effective use. In order to get the maximum training benefit from a simulator there must first be a clear understanding of what underlying skills need to be taught.

Without knowing what these skills are it can be very easy to introduce a student into a negative training environment. This is where they actual regress in skill level. This can occur in a variety of instances, such as when they are allowed to use certain functions and procedures that do not exist in the real system. Students will become dependent upon these functions, and their absence will affect their operation in the real systems.

There is also the old adage 'garbage in garbage out'. If the students are taught poor training habits, extended practice in the simulator is only going to make them better at being bad.

The Systematic Approach to Training (SAT) process is a job and tasks analysis process designed to determine the content of simulator training and to ensure that performance-based standards are developed and maintained. The SAT process is typically broken down into five stages [3]. The first four phases occur sequentially in that the output of one phase provides the input for the next phase.

The phases of SAT process are as follows:

- Analysis
- Design
- Development
- Implementation
- Assessment.

Analysis

The Analysis Phase seeks to identify the overall organizational needs and then to identify the training requirements needed in order to fulfil those needs. For a facility looking to incorporate simulation into its training curriculum the first step is to characterize the facility [4]. The characterization will include information on operations, procedures and infrastructure. For example,

- What level of disruption to normal activities is acceptable?
- What are the consequences of a security breach?

- What are the facility's threat escalation procedures? What level of escalation does an event have to achieve before they need to contact their supervisor or an outside agency?
- What level of autonomy does the operator have?
- What is the response time for police, Emergency Medical Services?

This characterization of a facility's security requirements is the first step in the Analysis Phase. This will greatly assist in the next step to determine the specific knowledge, skills and attitudes/behaviours required for an operator to perform these tasks. This is called a Training Needs Analysis.

Training Needs Analysis   A Training Needs Analysis is a formal process of identifying the specific cognitive skills required in order to perform a task or series of tasks. In the physical security industry there has been very little formal research in this area. The exact requisite skills and corresponding level of proficiency required for effective control room operators remain largely unknown.

While there is a lack of formalized research in the physical security industry, there has been a great deal of research into control room operators in the power industry. The use of simulators for control room operator training is well established in this industry. It's reasonable to assume that control operators in these two industries share many common skill requirements.

One of the key skills identified for critical decision-making in the power industry is Situation Awareness (SA). Lack of SA has been found to be a key cause of several power blackouts around the world, including the 14 August 2003 blackout in the United States and the 4 November 2006 blackout in the Continental European Electricity Grid [5].

A common framework for defining SA is described as a user's perception of elements in the environment within a volume of time and space, the comprehension of their meaning and the projection of their status in the near future [6]. This model breaks SA into three levels.

- Level 1 – perception, the most basic level of SA, essentially means that a person is aware of multiple situational elements such as the actions, location and appearance of people, objects and events.
- Level 2 – comprehension entails a person understanding and interpreting what they are seeing, how everything fits together as a whole and what it means in terms of one's mission and goals.
- Level 3 – projection, the highest level of SA, involves anticipation of the likely evolution of the situation and the possible future states and events.

SA Example   Most physical protection systems include one or more surveillance cameras. The feeds from the cameras are displayed on monitors at the operator's control station. In order to provide a broad range of coverage, cameras are located at different locations and often provide surveillance of the same general area but from different viewpoints. For example, some point north, while some point south.

When multiple objects are being monitored and tracked it's essential to maintain SA and to be able to generate a mental picture of the location of all entities in three-dimensional space. Maintaining SA while monitoring these camera feeds requires that operators are able to discriminate objects' relative position to one another as they move at varying angles from the user's position, For example, if vehicles are moving towards or away from a fixed location, their left and right become opposite. The three levels of SA in this example can be described as follows:

- Level 1 SA would entail the operator simply observing an event on the video surveillance monitors.
- Level 2 SA would entail an alarm going off, the operator assessing the situation on the surveillance monitors and determining that it was an intruder and directing a response force to the location of the intrusion.
- Level 3 SA would be the ability of the operator to track a fast-moving target as it passes by multiple cameras, each viewing the situation from multiple perspectives and being able to anticipate the intruder's future location and calculate the correct speed and trajectory to determine where to send response forces.

Design phase
The Design Phase translates the skills and knowledge requirements identified in the Analysis Phase into specific learning objectives. These are broken down into specific instructional units along with corresponding assessment criteria. For simulation training this corresponds to scenarios designed to improve user's performance in specific areas.

Although some tasks may need to be learned as a single activity, certain activities can also be broken down into a sequence of individual part-tasks, which can be practised separately.

This approach to training is often referred to as part-task training. The training objectives for each part-task are established and specific scenarios are developed to reinforce student's performance in these areas. They must practise these sub-tasks until they can be performed to satisfactory standards. The sub-tasks are then combined so that the complete task can be performed to a satisfactory standard. This is often referred to as full-task training.

Performance measures   A user's performance will be measured against the tasks identified during the Training Needs Analysis. In order to measure the effectiveness of the human operators and their interaction with the simulation environment, quantitative metrics need to be defined to assess their performance.

As previously mentioned, in the physical security industry there has been very little formal research in user performance. As such there is a lack of standard metrics to measure their performance. Because of this, it's very difficult to determine or measure improvement. However, using the example of SA three basic metric can be used to measure a user's level of SA:

- Speed – speed could be measured by the time elapsed between when an alarm goes off, the student acknowledges the alarm, successfully determines its location and sends a response force to that location.
- Accuracy – accuracy could be measured as the ability to successfully track an intruder and send response forces to various locations when the intruder is moving through the facility.
- Subjective measure of SA – subjective measures of a user's current SA is often determined by pausing a running scenario and asking students to describe the current situation.

This then brings the question of what constitutes good performance against these measures? For example, in the example above one of the measures of SA is the time taken for a user to react to a situation such as an alarm message. What is considered to be a good time, 5 seconds, 10 seconds?

One common method used to establish baseline performance standards is to have an established expert run through training scenarios in the simulator. Their performance is then used as the baseline for which students will be measured. So if it takes the expert 10 seconds to respond, that would be considered the optimal time against which students would be measured.

Development
The Development Phase involves creating the specific exercises and scenarios defined during the Design Phase.

Implementation
The Implementation Phase involves the actual implementation and delivery of the training, including the scheduling of the training and instructors and so on.

Assessment
The Assessment Phase occurs on a continuous basis. It involves evaluating the training before, during and after it's been implemented; analysing the results; and comparing them to the overall learning objectives. Post-exercise assessment and debriefing of a student's performance is an important part of the assessment process. The instructor's debriefing can include discussions based on his or her observations and may require the trainees to rerun portions of the exercise.

6   Interactive simulators and simulation learning theory

Roger C. Schank is one of the world leading experts in artificial intelligence and cognitive psychology. Shank has conducted extensive studies on learning through simulation. According to Shank,

Learning by doing works because it strikes at the heart of the basic memory process that humans rely on. We learn how to do things and then learn how what we have learned is wrong or right. We learn when the rules apply and when they must be modified we learn all this by doing, by constantly having experiences and attempting to integrate those experiences into our existing memory structures [7].

Schank points out that given enough time, people are great on the job learners. However, the cost in time, novice mistakes and overall risk associated with on-the-job training can be unacceptable. In these instances it's beneficial to speed up the 'learning by doing' process. The use of simulations is an effective way of achieving this.

6.1 Learning retention

There are many statistics used in the simulation industry which propagate the benefits of simulation in learning retention. One of the more popular statistics is depicted in the so-called learning pyramid (Figure 2). This is sometimes referred to as the cone of experience.

The learning pyramid originates from the National Training Laboratories (NTL) for Applied Behavioural Science. The percentages represent the average 'retention rate' of information following teaching or activities by the methods shown. The numbers on the top and bottom of the pyramid suggest that while the

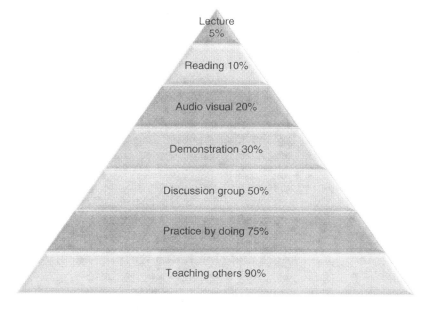

Figure 2: The learning pyramid.

retention rate from a lecture is only 5% users who practise by doing (simulation) have a 75% retention rate.

These numbers would appear to make a compelling case for simulation; however, NTL has not been able to substantiate them as the original research from the early 1960s has been lost [8]. Therefore these numbers are indicative only and should not be interpreted literally – though NTL still believes them to be correct. The widespread use and general acceptance of the learning pyramid has to a certain extent stymied additional research on the subject. As such there is little additional research that compares the retention rate of learning by doing verses other forms of instruction.

7   Security simulation and vulnerability assessment

A vulnerability assessment is an examination of the interrelationships between assets, threats, vulnerabilities and countermeasures. This process identifies which assets face the highest probability of attack and which threats pose the greatest risk. There has been a great deal of research into new technologies for assessing vulnerabilities of critical infrastructure and in developing technologies to assist in detecting and assessing threats. However, in conducting vulnerability assessments very little regard is generally given to the performance of the human operator. An example model used to assess the vulnerability of a facility is shown in Figure 3.

The problem with this type of formula is that the probability of assessment (Pa) number is usually input as 100%. This assumption assumes that once a threat is detected, the human operator will always assess, prioritize and act in a flawless manner. In real life this is very rarely the case [9].

The overall skill level of a control room operator can therefore be difficult to assess unless they are operating in an environment in which they must perform all aspects of their job on a continuous basis – including facility intrusions.

Human in the loop exercises running a virtual attack on a facility in a simulated environment is an excellent mechanism to assist in facility vulnerability assessment exercises. The vulnerability assessment model can then use an actual PA number generated from user's performance in the simulator.

8   Historical adoption curve of use of simulators

Other industries have paved the way in the adoption of simulation for multiple purposes, such as training, planning and decision support. Simulation is currently an accepted means to replicate an operation environment for the purposes of training, planning, decision, support and so on. However, some industries have adopted the use of simulators more readily than others. Why are they used more in some industries than others? In particular why are they not more commonly used in the physical security industry? There are multiple answers to this question. Different industries historically have different adoption rates for new technology. The physical security industry is no different.

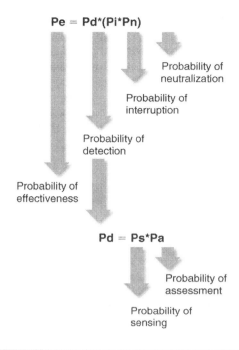

$$Pe = Pd*(Pi*Pn)$$

Probability of
neutralization

Probability of
interruption

Probability of
detection

Probability of
effectiveness

$$Pd = Ps*Pa$$

Probability of
assessment

Probability of
sensing

Pe	Probability of effectiveness	The probability that the physical protection system is effective. This will ultimately be reflected as a number derived from the rest of the equation
Pd	Probability of detection	The probability that the intruder has been detected. This is determined by multiplying Ps*Pa
Ps	Probability of sensing	This is used in calculating the probability of detection. It is the probability that a sensor detects the intrusion
Pa	Probability of an assessment	This is used in calculating the probability of detection. It is the probability that the control room operator correctly assesses the situation and reacts accordingly
Pi	Probability of interruption	The probability that the response force gets to the scene in time to neutralize the threat
Pn	Probability of neutralization	The probability that the response force successfully neutralizes the threat

Figure 3: Vulnerability assessment.

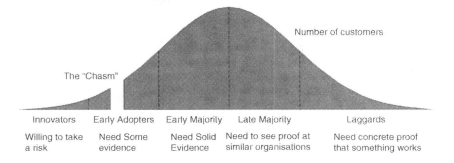

Figure 4: Moore's Technology Adoption Curve.

Geoffrey Moore has developed a model for the adoption of new technology within an industry (Figure 4). Moore's Technology Adoption Curve shows how technology is typically adopted by different end users across an industry [10]. Organizations on the left side of the curve are interested in the potential of the new technology and are willing to take a risk. Often their need is such that even if the technology only delivers a small improvement over their current practices, they can justify using it. Organizations on the right side of the curve are very conservative and will wait for 'solid proof' that the idea works in practice. Moore observed that the greatest difficulty in the adoption of new technology occurs in what he termed the 'chasm'. Chasm defines the bridge between the early adopters of technology who purchase it because of its potential and those who purchase because of real evidence of the technology benefits.

The uptake of simulation for training in the physical security industry is currently at the chasm stage. There are early adopters currently successfully training control room operators using simulators; however, the vast majority of security personnel are currently trained using a combination of books, slide presentations and on-the-job training. For many applications the expense of purchasing and running a simulator can be difficult to justify – at least until more solid proof is available.

9 Conclusion

The security industry is unique in that the immediate consequences of both excellent and poor systems, procedures training and personnel can be identical – nothing happens. Whether nothing happening is the result of luck or good systems usually is only uncovered after an incident has occurred. A physical protection system includes three main components, hardware, software and the biological component of these systems – the human operators. As more rigorous training standards are adopted and more concrete evidence is derived from the adoption and use of security simulators, they are likely to enjoy the same level of de facto adoption as they have enjoyed in other industries.

References

[1] C.R. McLean, S. Jain and Y. Tina Lee, Homeland Security Simulation Domain – A Needs Analysis Overview, National Institute of Standards and Technology (NIST), 2008. http://www.mel.nist.gov/div826/msid/sima/simconf/pubs.htm.
[2] E. Salas, K.A. Wilson, A. Priest and J.W. Guthrie, Design, Delivery, and Evaluation of Training Systems. Published Online: 28 FEB 2006, DOI: 10.1002/0470048204. ch18.
[3] U.S. Department of Energy, Training and Accreditation Program Standard Guidelines, DOE-STD-1077-94, 1994. http://hss.energy.gov/nuclearsafety/techstds/docs/standard/std1077.pdf.
[4] Mary Lynn Garcia, The Design and Evaluation of Physical Protection Systems, Sandia National Laboratories, 2001. http://www.amazon.com/Design-Evaluation-Physical-Protection-Systems/dp/0750673672.
[5] G. Andersson, P. Donalek, R. Farmer, N. Hatziargyriou, I. Kamwa, P. Kundur, N. Martins, J. Paserba and P. Pourbeik, Causes of the 2003 Major Grid Blackouts in North America and Europe, and Recommended Means to Improve System Dynamic Performance, 2005. http://www.giaelec.org.ve/fglongatt/files/files_SP2/pwrs_05_blackout.pdf.
[6] Dr M. Endsley, Theoretical Framework of SA, 1995.
[7] R. Schank, Designing World-Class E-Learning, 2001. http://books.google.com/books/about/Designing_world_class_e_learning.html?id=1PnxaM8gxa8C.
[8] Dr W. Thalheimer, People Remember 10%, 20% . . . Oh Really? 2006. http://www.willatworklearning.com/2006/05/people_remember.html.
[9] B. Hennessey, B. Norman and R.B. Wesson, Security Simulation for Vulnerability Assessment, 2007. http://ieeexplore.ieee.org/xpl/freeabs_all.jsp?arnumber=4350253.
[10] G.A. Moore, Crossing the Chasm: Marketing and Selling High-Tech Products to Mainstream Customers, 1999. http://www.amazon.com/Crossing-Chasm-Marketing-High-Tech-Mainstream/dp/0066620023.

Frameworks and tools for emergency response and crisis management

William B. Samuels, Farhad Dolatshahi, James R. Villanueva & Christopher Ziemniak
Science Applications International Corporation, McLean, VA

Abstract

A geographic information system (GIS) based framework has been developed that integrates natural and technological disaster models with critical infrastructure and population databases to assess the consequences of hazard events. The Consequences Assessment Tool Set (CATS) assesses the consequences of technological disasters on population, resources, and infrastructure. Hazards accounted for in CATS range from industrial accidents, terrorism, to acts of war. Developed under the guidance of the U.S. Defense Threat Reduction Agency (DTRA), CATS provides significant assistance in emergency managers' training, exercises, contingency planning, logistical planning, and calculating requirements for humanitarian aid. CATS emphasizes the calculation and analysis of consequences, not merely the display of hazard distributions. It contains models for converting spatial and temporal distributions into probabilities of casualties. These probabilities can be created for diverse exposure scenarios, including time-varying protective measures. CATS also identifies and locates resources required for an effective, sustained response and recommends the most effective roadblock distribution and routing to prevent unauthorized access to the affected area.

Keywords: Hazard Prediction, Consequence Assessment, Population, Infrastructure.

1 Introduction

The coupling of hazard prediction models with geographic information systems (GISs) is an important component in emergency response and crisis management. For example, in the aftermath of the September 11, 2001 attack on the World Trade Center, New York City was running a GIS for their emergency management needs. In addition, there were several other GIS operations around the City supporting the rescuers, local, state, and federal governments [1]. Crisis prediction disaster management is a concept that has gained appreciable momentum in recent years. The havoc wreaked by natural disasters such as earthquakes, hurricanes, and floods and the chilling consequences of chemical and biological weapons have starkly illustrated the inadequacy of pre- and post-disaster government planning and action.

In response to the need to predict damage and analyze consequences from natural and technological disasters, the US Defense Threat Reduction Agency (DTRA) and the US Federal Emergency Management Agency (FEMA) have funded the development of a GIS-based modeling and simulation tool known as the Consequences Assessment Tool Set (CATS). CATS employs a suite of hazard, casualty, and damage estimation modules to estimate and analyze effects due to natural phenomena, such as hurricanes and earthquakes, technological disasters, such as terrorist incidents, involving weapons of mass destruction, and industrial accidents [2].

2 CATS

The purpose of the CATS software is to provide the necessary tools to the incident and consequence managers and the first responders for analyzing and assessing the impact of potential disasters from natural and technological sources. The analysis includes the damage to the environment, the risk to the well-being of the exposed population, and allocation of the necessary resources in real time to mitigate the consequences. CATS is a GIS-based toolset that provides a generalized capability to estimate the extents of technological hazard areas. It also provides assessments of the hazard consequences to the population at risk and enables the incident and consequence managers and first responders to take steps and allocate resources for the mitigation of the hazard-related effects.

A sister program, the Incident Command Tool for Drinking Water (ICWater), has also been developed in conjunction with CATS, which generates downstream and upstream traces of the release of chemical, biological, and radiological (CBR) materials in rivers using the RiverSpill model [3]. ICWater calculates the downstream concentration using the dispersion equation to create the downstream trace and calculates the upstream trace using network navigation. Contaminant runoff is incorporated into the downstream calculation based on deposition from an atmospheric dispersion model or user input.

2.1 CATS architecture

The architectural framework in CATS relies on the Environmental Systems Research Institute (ESRI). GIS and various interface modules have been created to enable the seamless and transparent communication of the software components with the common GIS map background and with the databases (see Figure 1). The collection of these models, their specialized interfaces, and various assets allocation and report generation software comprise the toolsets in CATS. CATS can operate either as an extension to the ESRI ArcGIS desktop or as a stand-alone code using the ESRI ArcEngine runtime libraries.

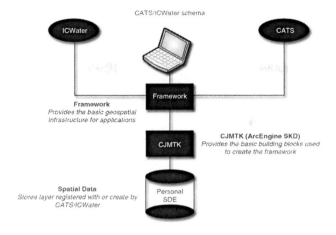

Figure 1: CATS and ICWater high-level architecture.

Using the hazard footprints described previously in conjunction with the population and the infrastructure databases, CATS can perform consequence assessment of population/infrastructure at risk, provide roadblocks to block streets and roads leading to hazard areas to enforce containment, and provide escape routes to avoid hazard areas. CATS uses extensive geodatabases to help visualize the dispersion of these hazards into the environment and predict the effects on the exposed and at-risk population. These databases include such libraries as LandScan population data [4], critical infrastructure datasets contained in the Homeland Security Infrastructure Program (HSIP Gold and HSIP Freedom) [5], and US and world base maps (see Figure 2).

The National Geospatial-Intelligence Agency (NGA) Office of Americas Domestic Preparedness Branch provides HSIP Gold, a common operational dataset, and serves the federal community in direct support of the Homeland Defense/ Homeland Security (HD/HLS) and Emergency Preparedness, Response & Recovery (EPR&R) missions. HSIP Freedom is a subset of the HSIP Gold dataset that has been identified as license free and distributable to state, local, and tribal HD/HLS and EPR&R mission areas. This dataset allows for nationwide, foundation-level infrastructure information access and assists decision-makers with the following: analyze threat (natural or man-made), modeling for emergencies, protection of borders, and expedite the response and recovery missions.

HSIP Gold is a disc that contains a common set of geospatial infrastructure data for use in homeland security missions. Acceptable federal uses of HSIP Gold within these mission areas include the following:

- Homeland security and homeland defense analysis, planning, and operations
- Critical infrastructure programs (national and defense)

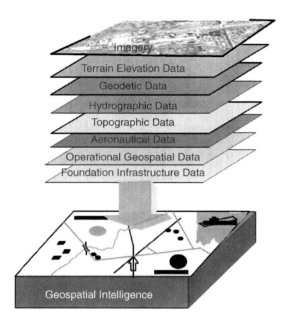

Figure 2: Example database categories in CATS.

- Infrastructure mapping, assessments, analysis, and modeling
- National response framework emergency support functions
- Fusion of foreign threat, domestic threat, infrastructure, and information
- Crisis, consequence, and disaster management
- Intelligence/threat analysis
- Antiterrorism/force protection (AT/FP)
- Defense support to civil authorities (DSCA)
- Man-made and natural hazard modeling and effects analysis
- Government facilities management
- Emergency planning, response, and recovery
- Training and exercise support related to the above mission areas

2.2   Model descriptions

Over the years, various versions of CATS have incorporated tools that generate the hazard footprints (see Figure 3) from technical disasters (CBR) to natural events (hurricane, earthquake, and storm surge). In its current form, CATS includes a High Explosive (HE) model [6], the Emergency Response Guidebook (ERG2008) phenomenology to predict keep-out zones from hazardous chemical [7], and the ALOHA (Areal Locations of Hazardous Atmospheres) model [8], a program that estimates threat zones associated with hazardous chemical releases. In addition, numerous tools are provided for simulating a

Figure 3: CATS in operational use.

disaster area of various geometrical shapes. CATS can also import hazard plume data in the form of shapefiles generated by such DTRA codes [9] as the Hazard Prediction and Analysis Capability (HPAC) and the Joint Effects Model (JEM). These footprints are generally from the release of CBR materials. For natural hazards such as hurricanes, earthquakes, and floods, CATS imports hazard footprints from FEMA's Hazards US (HAZUS) model [10].

ERG2008
ERG2008 was developed jointly by the US Department of Transportation, Transport Canada, and the Secretariat of Communications and Transportation of Mexico (SCT) for use by firefighters, police, and other emergency services personnel who may be the first to arrive at the scene of a transportation incident involving a hazardous material [7]. It is primarily a guide to aid first responders in (1) quickly identifying the specific or generic classification of the material(s) involved in the incident and (2) protecting themselves and the general public during this initial response phase of the incident. The ERG is updated every 3 to 4 years to accommodate new products and technology. The next version is scheduled for 2012.

The ERG2008 model was developed using the Table of Initial Isolation and Protective Action Distances. This table specifies the containment areas for the initial isolation and protective action distance, and incidents involving fires. CATS also includes a wind uncertainty circle, which uses the downwind distance as the radius. Plumes produced in the ERG2008 model correspond to 30 minutes after the spill occurs.

HE model
The HE model computes the distance to a blast overpressure level based on the explosion of a known quantity of material. The explosive material is assumed

similar in behavior to TNT. The explosive material in the calculation is unshielded, has no casing material, and assumes unhindered propagation across a flat plane. ANFO and C4 explosives used within the model have a set of TNT equivalency factors. Different sets of overpressure levels exist for the damage to personnel, damage to materials, and personnel safety distances.

Several publications and Web sites were reviewed to arrive at a set of blast effects relevant to the CATS HE [6] model. The first step was to select an established relationship between the peak overpressure and the distance from a reference base explosion of TNT in the open, that is, no protective shelter or posture. This data is available graphically from early measurements on the subject and have been reproduced in several references. This data is reproduced below for a baseline explosion of 1,000 pounds of TNT depicting pressure in pounds per square inches (psi) as a function of the ground range in feet.

ALOHA plume model

The plume model estimates threat zones associated with hazardous chemical releases, including toxic gas clouds, fires, and explosions. A threat zone is an area where a hazard (such as toxicity, flammability, thermal radiation, or damaging overpressure) has exceeded a user-specified Level of Concern (LOC). Key features include the following:

- generates a variety of scenario-specific output, including threat zone plots, threat at specific locations, and source strength graphs;
- calculates the rate of release for chemicals escaping from tanks, puddles (on both land and water), and gas pipelines and predicts how that release rate changes over time;
- models many release scenarios: toxic gas clouds, BLEVEs (Boiling Liquid Expanding Vapor Explosions), jet fires, vapor cloud explosions, and pool fires;
- evaluates different types of hazard (depending on the release scenario): toxicity, flammability, thermal radiation, and overpressure.

ALOHA is a modeling application released by the Environmental Protection Agency (EPA), National Oceanographic and Atmospheric Administration (NOAA), and the National Safety Council (NSC). It is designed for use in response to chemical accidents. As such, it can predict rates at which chemical vapors escape into the atmosphere from broken gas pipes, leaking tanks, and evaporating puddles. Finally, it predicts how the resulting hazardous gas cloud may disperse in the atmosphere. The ALOHA database contains information on approximately 900 common hazardous chemicals [8].

2.3   Consequence assessment

Consequence assessment is designed to examine the impact of an area of interest layer (hazard footprint) on an assessment layer (infrastructure or population). The outcome of a consequence analysis on an asset may be the raw numbers,

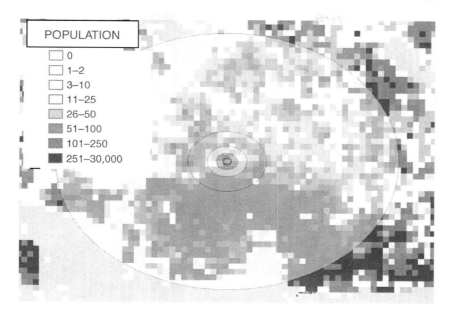

Figure 4: Example overlay of CATS HE model output and LandScan.

at-risk results, or the number affected. The results of such an analysis may be further refined by categorizing the results using a grouping layer (i.e., county boundaries, zip codes, etc.). Specific examples of consequence analysis may be given as effects of an explosion on buildings, fires in wooded areas, or chemical agent releases on a population.

Population at risk
Population at risk can be calculated by intersecting a CATS hazard footprint with a population database such as LandScan or US Census Bureau data (tracts, block groups, or blocks). The LandScan data provides a gridded population layer (1-km resolution worldwide and 100-m resolution in the United States). This database also provides both daytime and nighttime population data for the United States. Figure 4 shows an example of a consequence assessment report for population at risk using LandScan data and the HE hazard footprint.

Infrastructure at risk
Infrastructure at risk can be calculated by intersecting a CATS hazard footprint with an infrastructure layer from the HSIP Gold database or a user-supplied database. The HSIP Gold database contains over 300 layers representing 17 critical infrastructure and key resource sectors. Figure 5 shows an example consequence assessment map for a critical infrastructure layer (hospitals) and the ALOHA atmospheric plume footprint. The example plume is for a chlorine release from a rail car.

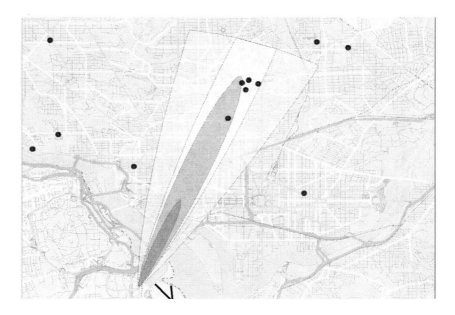

Figure 5: Example consequence assessment showing hospitals within an atmospheric plume footprint (ALOHA model).

Setting up roadblocks

The roadblocks model available from the CATS assessment menu determines all the intersections closest to the perimeter of an Area-of-Interest or Area-of-Interest buffer zone (polyline layers). Where there are no intersections (a single route), the roadblock occurs at the start of the road segment. CATS provides a capability for buffering hazard areas and creating a set of roadblocks to prevent road access to the buffered hazard zone. The roadblocks assignment may not necessarily be the most optimized due to errors in the underlying data, lack of resources to implement all the roadblocks, or perhaps errors in processing. In such cases, the analyst may need to manually intervene and make adjustments to the set of roadblocks to achieve the safety-zone objectives. To facilitate the user intervention and allow for the optimization of roadblocks, a roadblock editor tool was created. Using this tool, the user can generate a set of roadblocks and then add or remove individual roadblocks to accomplish the manual optimization. Figure 6 shows an example of a CATS roadblock report.

Vehicle routing

The CATS route tracing tools rely on underlying road datasets that are in a format suitable for point-to-point analysis. The road segments are defined by polylines and their end points and are collectively referred to as "edges" and "vertices." In the process of creating a CATS Road Network (CRN) dataset, various attributes of each edge and its vertices are collected and made

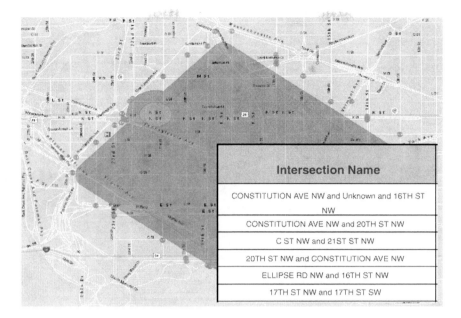

Intersection Name
CONSTITUTION AVE NW and Unknown and 16TH ST NW
CONSTITUTION AVE NW and 20TH ST NW
C ST NW and 21ST ST NW
20TH ST NW and CONSTITUTION AVE NW
ELLIPSE RD NW and 16TH ST NW
17TH ST NW and 17TH ST SW

Figure 6: Example roadblock report based on a 100-m buffer around the hazard footprint from ERG2008.

available during the routing exercise. These attributes include such information as the road type, directionality, cost of travel, and so on.

In the example shown in Figure 7, the detailed ESRI StreetMap North America street layer is converted into a CATS CRN file. The first step in building a network is determining the "cost" value. The cost parameter refers to the "value" field associated with a polyline feature. For instance, the cost used in this example will be based on the Feature Classification Code (FCC) field of detailed streets. The FCC values are contained in the street metadata as shown in Table 1.

The next task is to determine the directionality of the streets (one way vs. two way). This classification is often made with no value for bidirection, 0 for to-from streets and 1 for from-to streets. In this Streetmap example, bidirectional streets have no value while mono-directions use the TF and FT designations to indicate to-from and from-to, respectively. The route solver uses a CATS Network file registered with CATS and a start and end point to create a shortest path route. This route can also include a hazard footprint that must be avoided.

3   Summary and conclusions

CATS is a consequence management tool package that integrates hazard prediction, hazard containment, consequence assessment, and routing using critical

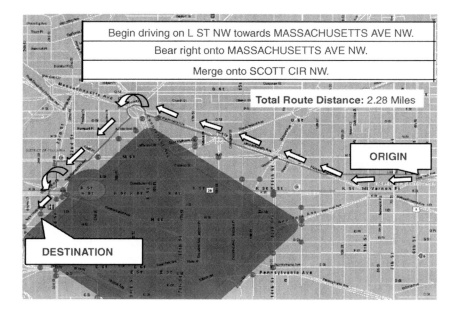

Figure 7: Example routing report avoiding the ERG2008 hazard footprint.

Table 1: Street attributes used to determine least cost path.

Code	Description	Speed (MPH)
A10–A18	Highway/freeway (high speed)	65
A20–A28	Highway with accessing roads	55
A30–A38	Major roads	45
A40–A48	Local roads	35

population and infrastructure data. CATS has been used operationally to assess damage from disasters such as hurricanes, the Northridge and Kobe earthquakes, and the Midwest floods [11,12]. In addition, CATS was deployed for the 2002 Winter Olympics in Salt Lake City, UT [13]. Using the overlay of the hazard footprint superimposed on the GIS streetmap data, a user can quickly establish areas potentially at risk, assess affected population and infrastructure, facilitate initial resource deployment, and assess needs and locate resources for a sustained response or mitigation strategy. It consists of the following capabilities to perform modeling and simulation for emergency management:

Models:

- High Explosive
- ERG2008—Initial isolation protective action distances
- ALOHA plume model

Net tools:

- Place and address finding
- Best and regional weather

Assessment tools:

- Consequence assessment
- Roadblocks
- Roadblock editing
- Network builder
- Routing

Interoperability

- Joint effects model
- Hazard prediction and assessment capability
- Hazards US multi-hazard

References

[1] Langhelm, R., The role of GIS in response to WTC—supporting the first 30 days. Proceedings, 2002 ESRI Users Conference, San Diego, CA, 2002. proceedings.esri .com/library/userconf/proc02/pap1348/p1348.htm.

[2] Swiatek, J.A. & Kaul, D.C., Crisis prediction disaster management, *Science and Technology Trends II*, SAIC, McLean, VA, pp. 1–13,1999.

[3] Samuels, W.B., Amstutz, D.E., Bahadur, R., & Pickus, J., RiverSpill: A National Application for Drinking Water Protection, *Journal of Hydraulic Engineering*, Vol. 132, No. 4, pp. 393–403, 2006.

[4] LandScan, www.ornl.gov/sci/landscan/.

[5] HSIP Gold, www.nsgic.org/hottopics/HIFLD_Regional_Concept.ppt.

[6] SAIC, High Energy Explosives—The CATS HE Model, *SAIC Technical Report – Defense Threat Reduction Agency Contract No. DTRA01-03-D-0017, Delivery Order # 42*, pp. 1–11, March, 2009.

[7] ERG2008, www.phmsa.dot.gov/hazmat/library/erg.

[8] ALOHA, www.epa.gov/oem/content/cameo/aloha.htm.

[9] HPAC, www.ofcm.gov/atd_dir/pdf/hpac.pdf.

[10] HAZUS, www.fema.gov/plan/prevent/hazus/.

[11] Kehlet, R., The use of the Consequences Assessment Tool Set, Proceedings, 1997 ESRI Users Conference, San Diego, CA, 1997. proceedings.esri.com/library/ userconf/proc97/proc97/to400/pap383/p383.htm.

[12] Kaul, D., Consequences Assessment Tool Set (CATS), Proceedings, 2000 ESRI Users Conference, San Diego, CA, 2000. http://proceedings.esri.com/library/ userconf/proc00/professional/papers/pap722/p722.htm.

[13] Davis, D., GIS and the Salt Lake 2002 Winter Olympics, GIS Vision 2002. www.gisvisionmag.com/vision.php?article=200204%2Fspecial.html.

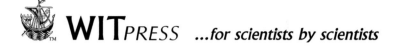

WITPRESS   *...for scientists by scientists*

Soft Computing in Water Resources Engineering
Artifical Neural Networks, Fuzzy Logic and Genetic Algorithms

G. TAYFUR, Izmir Institute of Technology, Turkey

Engineers have attempted to solve water resources engineering problems with the help of empirical, regression-based and numerical models. Empirical models are not universal, nor are regression-based models. The numerical models are, on the other hand, physics-based but require substantial data measurement and parameter estimation. Hence, there is a need to employ models that are robust, user-friendly, and practical and that do not have the shortcomings of the existing methods. Artificial intelligence methods meet this need.

Soft Computing in Water Resources Engineering introduces the basics of artificial neural networks (ANN), fuzzy logic (FL) and genetic algorithms (GA). It gives details on the feed forward back propagation algorithm and also introduces neuro-fuzzy modelling to readers. Artificial intelligence method applications covered in the book include predicting and forecasting floods, predicting suspended sediment, predicting event-based flow hydrographs and sedimentographs, locating seepage path in an earth-fill dam body, and the predicting dispersion coefficient in natural channels. The author also provides an analysis comparing the artificial intelligence models and contemporary non-artificial intelligence methods (empirical, numerical, regression, etc.).

The ANN, FL, and GA are fairly new methods in water resources engineering. The first publications appeared in the early 1990s and quite a few studies followed in the early 2000s. Although these methods are currently widely known in journal publications, they are still very new for many scientific readers and they are totally new for students, especially undergraduates. Numerical methods were first taught at the graduate level but are now taught at the undergraduate level. There are already a few graduate courses developed on AI methods in engineering and included in the graduate curriculum of some universities. It is expected that these courses, too, will soon be taught at the undergraduate levels.

ISBN: 978-1-84564-636-3   eISBN: 978-1-84564-637-0
Published 2012 / 288pp / £138.00

Co-evolutionary Algorithm & Multi-agent Systems

L. JIAO, J. LIU and *W. ZHONG, Xidian University, China*

The origins of evolutionary computation can be traced back to the late 1950s where it remained, almost unknown to the broader scientific community, for three decades until the 1980s, when it started to receive significant attention, as did the study of multi-agent systems (MAS). This volume focuses on systems in which many intelligent agents interact with each other. Today these systems are not simply a research topic but are also beginning to become an important subject of academic teaching and industrial and commercial application. *Co-Evolutionary Algorithm & Multi-Agent Systems* introduces the authors' recent work in these two new and important branches of artificial intelligence.

ISBN: 978-1-84564-638-7   eISBN: 978-1-84564-639-4
Forthcoming 2012 / apx 336pp / apx £145.00

Pervasive Systems and Ubiquitous Computing

A. GENCO and *S. SORCE, University of Palermo, Italy*

Pervasive systems are today's hardware/software solution to Mark Weiser's 1991 vision of Ubiquitous Computing, with the aim of enabling everyone to enjoy computer services by means of the surrounding environment. Mainly thanks to low-cost wireless communication technology and small portable personal devices, pervasive services can now be implemented easily. Advanced local or network applications can be joined everywhere simply by means of a mobile terminal like the ones we already carry (cellular, PDA, smartphone, etc). Pervasive systems aim to free people from conventional interaction with desktop and laptop computers and allow a new human-environment interaction to take place on the basis of wireless multimedia communication.

This book on pervasive systems discusses the fundamentals of pervasive systems theory as they are currently studied and developed in the most relevant research laboratories.

ISBN: 978-1-84564-482-6   eISBN: 978-1-84564-483-3
Published 2010 / 160pp / £75.00

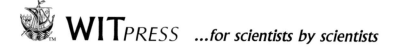

Data Mining X

Data Mining, Protection, Detection and other Security Technologies

Edited by: **A. ZANASI**, *TEMIS Italia, Italy;* **N.F.F. EBECKEN**, *COPPE/UFRJ, Brazil and* **C.A. BREBBIA**, *Wessex Institute of Technology, UK*

Since the end of the Cold War, the threat of large-scale wars has been substituted by new threats: terrorism, organised crime, trafficking, smuggling, proliferation of weapons of mass destruction. To react to them, a security strategy is necessary, but in order to be effective it requires several instruments, including technological tools. Consequently, research and development in the field of security is proving to be an ever-expanding field all over the world.

Data mining is seen more and more not only as a key technology in business, engineering and science but as one of the key elements of security. To stress that all these technologies must be seen as a way to improve not only the security of citizens but also their freedom, special attention is given to data protection research issues. This book contains papers presented at the tenth conference in a series. The conference reflected ways in which this technology plays an active role in linking economic development and environmental conservation planning. Of interest to researchers from academia and industry, as well as application developers from many areas, the papers in these proceedings are arranged into the following topics: Text Mining and Text Analytics; Data Mining Applications; Data Mining Methods.

WIT Transactions on Information and Communication Technologies, Vol 42
ISBN: 978-1-84564-184-9   eISBN: 978-1-84564-361-4
Published 2009 / 208pp / £79.00

WIT Press is a major publisher of engineering research. The company prides itself on producing books by leading researchers and scientists at the cutting edge of their specialities, thus enabling readers to remain at the forefront of scientific developments. Our list presently includes monographs, edited volumes, books on disk, and software in areas such as: Acoustics, Advanced Computing, Architecture and Structures, Biomedicine, Boundary Elements, Earthquake Engineering, Environmental Engineering, Fluid Mechanics, Fracture Mechanics, Heat Transfer, Marine and Offshore Engineering and Transport Engineering.

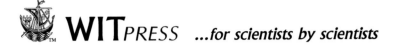

WITPRESS ...for scientists by scientists

Broadband Power-line Communication Systems

Theory and Applications

J. ANATORY, University of Dodoma, Tanzania and N. THEETHAYI, Bombardier Transportation, Sweden

Advances in information and communication technologies (ICT) have made it possible for broadband services to be used to bridge urban-rural areas efficiently and economically, using a readily available and largely distributed power line infrastructure. Power line networks can be used for multi-service data transmission, such as low-speed data that includes office and home automation, energy information systems, transportation systems, etc. and broadband services such as 'Last Mile' and 'Last Meter' high-speed internet access, Voice over Internet Protocol (VoIP), etc. Other applications include high speed data communications for indoor applications such as digital entertainment systems.

High capacity links in transmission systems could eliminate the need for fiber optic cables in telecommunication networks. Advances in this field led to the evolution of Broadband Power Line Communication (BPLC), which is essentially a blend of the other well known subjects, namely, classical transmission line (TL) theory, communication and networking theories. Based on these, this book covers both the theoretical and practical aspects of BPLC technology intended for graduate studies and industries dealing with PLC system design and power line network planning/segmentation.

The topics include classification of BPLC systems, models for analyses based on TL theory, estimation of channel capacity and performance and finally application of modulation, coding and media access control techniques for boosting the performance of BPLC systems. For the convenience of the readers, a couple of chapters are dedicated to the fundamental aspects of TL, communication and networking theories, acting as warm-up for the other chapters.

ISBN: 978-1-84564-416-1   eISBN: 978-1-84564-417-8
Published 2010 / 192pp / £75.00

WIT*Press*
Ashurst Lodge, Ashurst, Southampton,
SO40 7AA, UK.
Tel: 44 (0) 238 029 3223
Fax: 44 (0) 238 029 2853
E-Mail: witpress@witpress.com

CPSIA information can be obtained at www.ICGtesting.com
Printed in the USA
BVOW041623280312

286074BV00004B/3/P